Elementary School Counseling

Elementary School Counseling

An Expanding Role

V. Skip Holmgren
Sonoma State University

Allyn and Bacon
Boston • London • Toronto • Sydney • Tokyo • Singapore

Editor in Chief, Education: Nancy Forsyth
Series Editor: Ray Short
Editorial Assistant: Christine Shaw
Marketing Manager: Kathy Hunter
Cover Coordinator: Suzanne Harbison
Manufacturing Buyer: Aloka Rathnam
Editorial-Production Service: Electronic Publishing Services Inc.

Library of Congress Cataloging-in-Publication Data

Holmgren, V. Skip.
    Elementary school counseling : an expanding role / V. Skip Holmgren.—1st ed.
    p.   cm.
    Includes bibliographical references and index.
    ISBN 0–205–15719–X
    1. Counseling in elementary education—United States.
2. Elementary school counselors—United States. I. Title.
LB1027.5.H655   1995
372.14'0973—dc20   95–1608
                                          CIP

Printed in the United States of America

9 8 7 6 5 4 3 2 1   99 98 97 96 95 94

To all children, in particular to those who know me as "Grandma Skip"
Kara
Eric
Kacie
Karly Jo
Jackie and Joey
Kristi and David

v

Contents

PART II   Activities and Resources

PART IV   Appendices

Preface

Elementary school counseling has been a reality for nearly 50 years, with approximately 22,000 elementary school counselors in schools throughout the United States at the present time. Despite this apparent growth, there is confusion about the differences in expectations for school counselors across the country, particularly at the elementary school level. Only a few states require all school districts to provide guidance and counseling services in grades K–8. One of the reasons for this may be a lack of clarity regarding the role of the elementary school counselor. At the time of this writing, very few textbooks dedicated to the expanding role of the elementary school counselor have been published in the last 15 years.

As we move from the mid- to late 1990s and into the 2000s, it is necessary to keep pace with the current movement in elementary school counseling, including up-to-date research that addresses the elementary counselor's role with young children. This book is designed to be used in several ways: (a) as a textbook in elementary school counseling courses; (b) as a supplemental text in teacher education courses—this work will be helpful to broaden their perspectives of counseling in the elementary school; (c) as an aid to counselors in the field desiring to expand their knowledge of current practices and training, as well as future trends, in the area of elementary school counseling; and (d) as a resource for administrators needing information on elementary school counseling services. The first-draft writing was used in the author's graduate counseling course at Sonoma State University, California, titled "The Role of the Elementary School Counselor."

The book is organized into four parts. Part I identifies the role of the elementary school counselor in the context of the development of the elementary-age child in the school setting, with a brief but informative view of the characteristics of effective schools, including current trends. In addition to this, five theoretical approaches that lend themselves particularly well to the elementary school are presented, along with the consultant role of the counselor, the counselor's involvement in various problem areas usually found in the elementary school, and counseling culturally diverse students. Part II addresses the structured activities used by elementary school counselors—counseling with individual students, in small groups, with classroom guidance activities, and career guidance, with the resources available to aid in the understanding of the child. Part III looks at the expanding role of elementary school counseling services, including the professional responsibility of working with families, counseling program accountability and evaluation, the professional responsibilities of counselors and counselor educators, and recommendations for "getting there from here." Part IV contains extensive appendixes with all of the American School Counselor Association (ASCA) position papers applicable to the elementary school.

The book is, in reality, an outgrowth of 8 years as a secondary school teacher, and 25 years in the field of counseling in four different states as a counselor, state director of guidance services, guidance and counseling coordinator in a large city school district, director of counseling and psychological services in a county-wide school district, and counselor educator at three state universities. It would be difficult to spend this amount of time in the various school settings and not have some definite views as to what constitutes the role of a school counselor at all levels.

The more the author has become involved in various school district programs, the greater her awareness has been of the real need for elementary school counseling services. Elementary school teachers, administrators, and parents have increasingly expressed frustration over the problems of their students, ones for which they couldn't find answers. Problems that originate before the child starts school, or during their early school years, become full-blown by the time the youngsters reach junior high or high school if they are not addressed and resolved in the elementary school years. An elementary principal several years ago wrote to the author: "We may save a few bucks in the beginning (not having an elementary school counselor) but we pay for it tenfold by the time kids get to high school." The emphasis at the elementary level needs to be on developmental counseling—helping the child meet the normal developmental problems and developmental tasks of childhood. It is with this focus that the task of writing this textbook was undertaken.

I would like to acknowledge some of the many friends and colleagues that have been a source of encouragement on this journey. These include ones that encouraged me early on to complete my book and have it published, such as Dick Hackney, as ACES president, who connected me to Ray Short at Allyn & Bacon. Ray, as editor, has been a real source of positive feedback and encouragement; I can't imagine a better editor to work with! Others who encouraged me by offering suggestions or by reading parts of my manuscript in its early stages include Bob Cash, California State University, Long Beach; Mary Maples, University of Nevada, Reno; Ed Gerler, Jr., North Carolina State University; Wayne Maes, University of New Mexico; and Sandy Zimmermann, Sonoma State University adjunct professor and elementary school principal, Sonoma, CA. Particular thanks and appreciation go to Susan Zgliczynski, University of San Diego, for her invaluable input into the chapter on counseling culturally diverse students. In addition, the many helpful comments and suggestions from my reviewers, Reece Chaney, Indiana State University; Eileen R. Matthay, Southern Connecticut State University; and Kenneth Matener, Eastern Illinois University, are especially appreciated. Because of my personal style of creative writing, the task of getting this material into a readable form has been accomplished between my Macintosh computer and me. The contributions and ongoing help from Francine Sachs Cummings, faculty computer advisor at SSU, deserve my eternal thanks! My students provided rich material through sharing their experiences in their practicum and internship settings. I am grateful to the following former and current students for their permission to use their vignettes and exam responses to the vignettes in the introduction: Marilyn Boulanger, Cathy Hughes, Marylu Downing, Judith Brown, Letrice Patterson, and Marianne Waters.

Finally, to my best friend and husband, Dick Franzen, I give my love and appreciation for his constant encouragement, his support, his unending patience, and his faith in me to complete the journey!

V. Skip Holmgren
Sonoma State University

Part *I*

The Counselor and the Elementary School

Introduction

Concerns about the future of elementary school counseling have been voiced at state, regional, and national conventions in recent years. Elementary school counselors are still the "new kids on the block" and, as such, are often called upon to defend themselves and justify their services. A few years ago, I was observing a new elementary counselor in a fourth-grade classroom as she conducted a classroom guidance activity. I was sitting by the teacher's desk when the teacher began to quietly point out different children with problems: "He comes from a very physically abusive family"; "That one, that one, that one [until she had identified five] all have been sexually abused and have had the Child Protective Services involved"; "Her mother deserted the family three weeks ago and she has to care for three younger brothers"; "He has run away three times this year already." The teacher then identified which ones in the classroom were from single-parent homes, and two that were being raised by grandparents. By the time she finished, I realized she had identified almost every one of the 33 children as having some sort of limitation or concern from her perspective. Then she said, "Do you see why we so desperately need a full-time elementary school counselor?" The counselor I was observing was only there two days per week, making it virtually impossible to attend to the most needy children on an individual or small group basis, particularly since there were other classrooms in that school that were just as needy.

Is this an isolated classroom or school? Unfortunately, no; this type of classroom is becoming all too common across our country as we look at our elementary schools and note the widespread needs identified by parents, teachers, school staff, and principals.

Reading the titles of articles listed on the covers of three randomly selected issues of the *Elementary School Guidance and Counseling* journal, listed below, challenges our concepts regarding the preparation of elementary school counselors. How do we prepare our elementary school counselors to deal with these problems on a daily basis? Are we definitely preparing them for these challenging situations?

"Childhood sexual abuse prevention programs"

"Reporting suspected sexual abuse"

"Siblings' experiences of pediatric cancer"

"Children of substance abusers"

"Eating attitudes in girls"

"Dealing with religious differences"

"Sand play as elementary school strategy" (April 1994)

"Reducing parent resistance to consultation in the schools"

"Enhancing cultural adaptation through friendship training"

"Group counseling for preadolescent female victims of incest"

"Children's drawings and child sexual abuse"

"Substance abuse prevention in the schools" (December 1993)

"Children at war"

"When children's parents go to war"

"Understanding a child's problem behavior"

"Making young children aware of sexual abuse" (April 1992)

In addition to the journal articles noted above, some counseling vignettes portray the human drama that is played out on a daily basis in our elementary schools. In my year-long school internship class, students are required to submit weekly journals or logs detailing situations of concern at their internship sites. The following vignettes are all from actual journals submitted by students during the course of a school year:

"The principal called me at home one evening and asked me to come to his school the next day (where I spend one day per week). The teacher of the 3rd grade class had been injured in an automobile accident over the weekend. She was hospitalized in a town three hours away, her family was also injured in the accident and were hospitalized; there was very little information available about the teacher's condition or when she might be able to return to school. The children in the classroom were unruly, hard to control, had destroyed a piece of furniture the day before and had already had two substitute teachers in two days. Would I please come tomorrow and do something about the class!"

★

"Megan wouldn't say anything during our first session. She had been referred to me by her teacher. After hanging her head and barely speaking, I started probing for 'how are things at home?' She said that sometimes her dad got really mad at her and would kick her in the stomach and sometimes her step-mom would get very angry at her—in fact, had hit her in the nose and made it bleed. In general, Megan's appearance seems neglected with shoes that are much too large, and seedy-looking clothes."

"Mario is a little spitfire in the 1st grade. He wears a little tie, which is always askew, and no matter what kind of exercise we do, he is totally in motion. If he draws, it is pictures of him as a 'ghost buster' or of a car crash with Herbie goes to Monte Carlo. Mario was born addicted to drugs from a mother-addict. His mother lives somewhere on the streets in San Francisco, his grandparents have raised him from infancy, once he withdrew from the drugs. Now his grandmother, whom he knows as 'Mom' is hospitalized with a reoccurrence of cancer. His grandfather, in a phone conversation with me, says that her illness has been very hard on the family—he has a book from the American Cancer Society about death and cancer and will try to read it to Mario. Mario has been kept in the dark about his 'mother's' disease, but of course, intuits that something is seriously wrong with her."

"Janelle has 'home problems.' She is about 10 years old and appears rather nervous, chewing on her hair and biting her fingernails. As we talk, she volunteers that her mom has had lots of boyfriends and that she and her current boyfriend have loud fights which scare her. Her Dad lives out of state and she visited him at Easter break, but felt a little left out and sometimes blamed for the crying of a younger sibling born to her dad and his new woman. Nevertheless, she had a good visit, and although she doesn't wish to accept his offer for her to come live with them, she will spend the summer there. Janelle is amazingly forthright and can share her feelings quite easily in the small group of four which she attends. She has been somewhat anxious about the other kids breaking confidentiality but continues to share despite this fear."

✶

"A group of 5th grade boys were referred to me by the principal because of fighting on the playground. The principal met with the boys first; they identified the following problems:

1. *Mexicans against the Whites.*
2. *Unfair teams as far as skills go.*
3. *Cheating, tripping, changing rules, thinking you're better than the others.*
4. *Name calling, physical contact, fighting.*

My task: To find a solution to the problem!"

"Kent is an 11-year-old boy in the 5th grade at my school. He is a year older than his classmates due to the fact that he was retained at another school. He entered my school this past September and within two days he was demonstrating angry, acting-out behaviors. His records show that he has had a highly stressful life; his mother was reported to be using drugs and alcohol during her pregnancy and until she left the family when he was about two. Kent lived with his father for the next five years until the father entered a drug/alcohol rehabilitation program. Growing up in this setting Kent controlled to a large extent his own activities deciding whether he would go to school or not—he missed 7 weeks during kindergarten and 8 weeks during the first grade. Kent was close to his paternal grandparents who died when he was five or six; he then lived with his aunt while his father was in the rehab facility. After about two days in class he began demonstrating the following anti-social behaviors: fighting, swearing, being abusive with other children, talking back to anyone in authority, refusing to complete any assignments. On the fourth day of school the local police brought him in with two younger boys for truancy and for starting a fire under the overpass of the freeway.

As a counselor, I plan to focus on rebuilding trust and developing a solid relationship, knowing this will take a long time. I also plan to deal with his distrust of others which leaves him in such a fearful, insecure position."

"I have been working with the two youngest children in a family where the father was stabbed to death in a family feud. The mother is non-English speaking and was totally dependent on the father. The father worked on one of the big vineyards here in town and the family has lived on the same ranch for 17 years. The sudden death of the father six months ago was devastating to the family; the children have exhibited all of the expected symptoms such as stomach aches, crying, feelings hurt, etc. and have had more absences than usual since the tragedy occurred. I have been able to develop a close relationship with the 7 year old girl who is outgoing, loving, demonstrative and very easy to communicate with. On the other hand, I have had trouble forming a relationship with the 9 year old boy. He is closed, shows little affect and since the death of his father has been outwardly angry and defiant in many areas. Last week he was suspended from the school bus

*for throwing rocks at it. The teacher has noted that he is refusing to complete
work and is generally disinterested in doing much of anything."*

These counseling vignettes, from school counseling interns facing the reality of the societal changes that have affected our young people today, should cause all of us to be concerned. The environmental factors that children deal with when they are away from the
school setting has much to with the child's success or lack of success in school. We need
to be reminded of the real world of the children we work with and see on a daily basis. The
intent of this book is to help aspiring elementary school counselors, elementary school
teachers, and possibly some experienced counselors, deal with the reality of the role of the
elementary school counselor in today's society while providing some information, tools,
and skills to make their task more rewarding. Administrators, with or without the services
of an elementary school counselor, will be apprised of the variety of roles a counselor must
assume in order to respond to the needs of today's children.

There are many ways to respond to the concerns, problems, and referrals faced by an
elementary school counselor in a typical day. The seven vignettes were recently used by
the writer as a final exam in a course called "The Role of the Elementary School
Counselor." This is usually one of the first courses a prospective elementary school counselor takes in his or her master's program in school counseling. In order to gain an insight
into their progress, the examination asked them to respond to the following four questions
to help them devise a counseling plan using *two* of the previously described vignettes:

1. What additional information would you solicit? Why? How would you go about
   doing this?
2. What counseling format(s) would you use? Individual counseling? Small
   group counseling? Classroom work? Would you consult with the parent, teacher,
   principal?
3. What specific problems do you foresee at the outset? What could go wrong during your counseling intervention?
4. What do you envisage as the likeliest outcome for this case? Where would you
   go from there?

The students were given this exam in the final class of the semester with two and one-half
hours to complete their "solution" to the two cases they chose. Although the responses are
somewhat lengthy to cite here, it proved to be a valuable exercise, well worth the space to
relate three of the student's responses verbatim:

Situation 1: Third-Grade Class

*My first step in dealing with this situation would be to talk with the principal fur-
ther for any additional details as well as the current substitute teacher to ask
what exactly the children had been told regarding their teacher's accident.*

*I would then gather the correct information regarding the teacher's health status
and enter the classroom with information that I could offer in a concrete format.
For example: "Mrs. Smith was injured as you heard previously and will need to
recover in the hospital for an indefinite period of time—maybe up to 1–2 months."*

I would then talk with the group in a "Magic Circle" style asking each one of the students to talk about how they were feeling about the loss of their teacher. I would take enough time to hear each student's heartfelt message. I would acknowledge their fear, sadness and anger and how hard it must be for them as a classroom to not know exactly what happened to their teacher. Since 3rd graders are energetic, after this "Magic Circle" discussion we would take a recess.

Upon return from recess I would praise them for their shared offerings of concern, anger, anxiety and have ready at their desks a blank folded white card-like construction paper upon which they could send a message to their teacher or a drawing—whichever they preferred.

This developmental approach would be followed by a Reality Therapy discussion about "What are you as a classroom going to do about your behavior toward substitutes and school property?" I would approach this through group/social awareness and what strategies they as a group could come up with to improve their classroom behavior. All ideas would be considered and the entire class would vote for the top three ideas—written on the board for all to see. We would close the session with praise for their incredible work "as a group," and I would remind them that I would return the following day to follow-up on their ideas for improved classroom behavior.

The following day I would inquire if there were one or two students needing special individual help in dealing with this situation. This day's group activity would be to talk about how it felt to make their teacher a card, to be able to talk about their fears, and did their ideas work in helping to promote better classroom behavior for the substitute. I would also consult with the substitute teacher as to the effectiveness of my intervention and if, in fact, their behavior as a group had improved.

The circumstances here are that the teacher may die or she will get better. If the former occurs, I would use my "Stages" techniques regarding grief and loss and again acknowledge their anger, sadness, fears, and how sometimes when someone dies it reminds them of their own losses (a pet, grandma, etc.). If the teacher improves the class can continue to be praised for their efforts in sending cards, letters, and how well they have taken responsibility for their behavior in her absence. And praised for talking about their fear of death, too!

I would continually work with the school staff—principal and substitute teacher in getting a feel for how the class progresses. I would consult with any parents, also, of students that appeared to be struggling more with the loss than others. There would be follow-up weekly as their behavior improved and continued work (group activities) centered around their responsibility as a class and as individuals.

It would seem that there would be a great need for interventions, perhaps daily initially and then taper to weekly as the class processed the situation.

Situation 5: Group of Fifth-Grade Boys Fighting on Playground

I received a referral from the principal regarding a group of 5th grade boys' inappropriate behavior such as fighting, name calling, unfair team play, and possible racial issue of Mexicans against Whites. Because the referral directly stated "a large group of 5th grade boys" and named three specific boys as having the most influence, I decided to observe the 5th grade play area on Monday and Tuesday. And since I had met with the 5th grade class and completed the introduction of class meetings, I would be interested in the class's agenda for the next session.

There are a number of counseling formats to proceed with. For example, I would consider a classroom guidance activity of Reasoner's Building Self Esteem: Teacher's Guide and Classroom Materials, *on "Rules" at school, home, and community. We would discuss what if there were no rules and what if everyone made up their own rules. This would allow me to direct the session toward the school ground activities and team play.*

From my observations of the school ground activities during recess and lunch, I would be able to see what the students say about what they're doing and feeling during that time. The specific students who were named could be a part of a group that would allow them to share any issues that are interfering with their ability to interact in the classroom guidance or classroom meeting sessions.

If the problem is racial between the Whites and Mexicans, the teacher could be instrumental in incorporating ethnic awareness activities in the curriculum through cultural sharing, dressing, food, music, contributions of ethnics to other professions.

If the problems are isolated to only a few students that are in constant disciplinary infractions, then the parents must be a part of the remediation process. Because fighting is a suspendable offense, this consequence must be discussed within the small group sessions as a choice and not an alternative action.

Because the referral came from the principal, I would consult with him/her and the classroom teacher to update, get feedback, discuss the steps covered, and future plans.

I envision the likeliest outcome for this case as: in the classroom meetings the students could discuss and decide what would work, what rewards, and if there is still a problem during playtime. Students are empowered when they are the process of change and know that the meetings are designed to solve problems and not point out blame.

From this point, I would facilitate a conflict management team in grades 4, 5, and 6. This would allow individuals to choose to resolve conflicts before a larger group is involved.

Situation 4: Janelle

Janelle's situation, possibly referred to me by a teacher, is one of emotional stress and insecurity due to living in an unstable home environment. Although she seems to participate well in the group counseling sessions, I would want to see her individually in addition to her group work.

Drawing from Adlerian theory, Janelle is a child with social interest as she participates in group discussions and her teacher informs me that she plays well with other 4th graders. Because she has this need to belong, I will not remove her from the counseling group—that would only send a message that there is something "wrong" with her. Although she may distrust her peer's confidentiality, Janelle is very cooperative and shows an interest in group participation.

In my first individual meeting with Janelle, I discuss the group's confidentiality and her option to tell me certain things that are bothering her when we meet individually instead of worrying about the group. This may help her feel a sense of belonging in the group without threatening her peer's acceptance of her. Janelle is an anxious young girl, and for good reason. I will have to establish a sense of trust with her before she opens up and tells me the things she is withholding.

I need more information on her family position, so I check her cumulative record file and find that she is the youngest of two children that live with her mother. The information on her stepfamily is not available so I ask her. Janelle says she has a two-year old stepsister who lives with her dad and his fiance. This makes Janelle a psychological youngest child (with 8 years between her stepsister and herself). Although her mother gives her a lot of attention, the mother's boyfriend thinks she is a pampered brat and criticizes her often.

I also need more information on these "loud fights" between mom and her boyfriend. After trust is built in counseling, Janelle shares that her mother's boyfriend hits her mom sometimes. Janelle wonders if he will kill her mom. (No wonder she is anxious).

Plan of attack: 1) call Janelle's father about Janelle staying during the summer months. Ask for his help in my work with his daughter. Tell him Janelle is sensitive to the younger sibling (two-year old stepsister) due to having two "babies of the family" in one house. She may need extra encouragement and affection displayed during her summer stay. Expressing my enthusiasm in parenting classes, I'd recommend a class given locally on stepparenting to see if that may help her during this transition. 2) Ask mom for help. VERY CAREFULLY seek more information on abusive situation in such a way as to avoid her defensiveness. Refer mom to outside help or provide counseling myself based on Brief Family Therapy model. 3) Work with Janelle on self-esteem, protecting herself, general knowledge empowering her to know what to do if her mother is hurt, and work on dealing with family competition and possible resentment to younger sibling.

Problems that may arise: 1) Mother may be in denial to the problem and refuse counseling—worse, would stop Janelle's counseling sessions. 2) Mother seeks counseling, leaves boyfriend, and lives with Janelle and older child in a home for battered women. The home is out of the district and Janelle's meetings with me end. Or, Janelle remains at the school but is increasingly unhappy due to instability of living arrangements; she withdraws from peers. 3) I may place my own values and beliefs on Janelle (I have a strong dislike for batterers and abusers) thereby not seeing the case objectively. However, as a counselor I must "Respect the inherent rights and responsibilities" of parents (ASCA Ethical Standards). Should Janelle's parents be uncooperative, I will do my best to provide a safe atmosphere with encouragement and a sense of belonging for Janelle at school. I will maintain communication with her as a trusted adult, making sure she is not being abused or hurt (emotionally or physically) at home.

The likeliest outcome is for Janelle's dad and stepparent to provide support— Mom may take a while. In that case I would refer back up to the above "worst case" plan statement. If Janelle moves out of state, I would call her dad to follow-up and contact her new school counselor.

The three students' solutions to the previous vignettes are quite typical of the way new counselors would respond since they were not aware of the content of their exam prior to the class. The students received the situations in a manner very much like they would in an actual elementary school setting, thus their responses closely approximated a real-life counseling situation. It should be clear to the reader that there is more than one way to approach the various counseling situations as they arise in the course of a day, or week, for an elementary school counselor. The class had a variety of responses or "solutions" to the vignettes that they chose to write about; the three given above are intended to be examples of possible elementary counselor responses to the presented situations. There are no "right" or "wrong" answers, although when a particular theoretical approach is used as a basis for counseling, the counselor knows the direction to go and the strategies appropriate to use.

The text is divided into four parts:

Part I, The Counselor and the Elementary School, consists of seven chapters: the elementary school itself, including Educational Standards and Policy Making; the development of the elementary-age child—emotional, social, cognitive, and moral, with developmental age profiles; the role of the elementary school counselor, including ASCA's role statement; theoretical approaches to elementary school counseling, including Adlerian, behavioral, developmental, reality therapy, and self-concept theory; the counselor as consultant to parents, teachers, and principals; areas of concern, including attention deficit disorder, childhood depression, disruptive/impulsive/inattentive behavior, physical and sexual abuse, substance abuse, underachievers, gender bias, working with special education students, latchkey children, and transient students; and counseling culturally diverse students.

Part II, Activities and Resources, consists of two chapters: records and tests used in the elementary school, including reporting test results; and structured activities, which include small group activities, classroom guidance activities, and career awareness.

Part III, The Future of Elementary School Counseling, consists of three chapters: working with families in the school setting, including conducting parent education classes; program accountability and evaluation, including ethical standards and legal issues; and future directions for elementary school counseling programs, including proactive counselors, counselor education program requirements, establishing an effective advisory council, responding to guidance program challenges, and the counselor's responsibility to the profession.

Part IV, Appendixes, contains, in addition to ASCA's role statement and Ethical Standards for School Counselors, all of the position papers that have been referred to throughout the text.

The writer's goal has been to emphasize the areas and topics deemed most appropriate for an elementary school counselor to know and become aware of based on past and current experiences in the field as well as the directions elementary school counseling needs to take to be a viable part of our educational community.

Because many states do not require teaching experience for school counselors, it will be helpful for those not familiar with the background of the elementary school, and the educational standards and policy making behind the decisions made in the local schools and school districts, to gain some understanding of the processes involved. Also, the goals and objectives of the elementary school and the role of the teacher should be noted, including some implications for counseling and guidance. Chapter 1 is offered as a means to accomplish this. Readers familiar with the historical development of the elementary school and local, state, and national governance of the elementary school may want to move directly to Chapter 2, Development of the Elementary-Age Child.

$$Chapter\ \ 1$$

The Elementary School

Some Historical Background

The kind and quality of education for our young people are of current concern in America. Our elementary schools have long outgrown the "three R's." The importance of providing elementary students with the knowledge and skills necessary to be informed of the various problems in the world was stressed in an article in *The Elementary School Journal*. These problems include "poverty, pollution, hunger, nuclear conflict and human rights" (Evans, 1987, p. 545). Evans viewed "global education" in the elementary school as a way to accomplish this; global education would encompass a comprehensive, worldwide outlook. The *1991 Yearbook of the Association for Supervision and Curriculum Development* stated it this way: "To globalize American education is to expand opportunities to learn about the world beyond the borders of the United States, and to learn about American society's relationship to and place in the larger world system . . . it means helping American students to see things from the perspective of other peoples of the world" (Anderson, 1990b, p. 14). This is a significant change from the elementary school education that the majority of today's adults received or needed.

Education, and elementary education in particular, has been a major concern in this country since early colonial days. When Lambert (1963) traced the historical background of the elementary school, he noted that the Constitution of the United States, which was ratified in 1790, did not specifically mention education or its support. This is surprising considering that in 1642 Massachusetts passed legislation requiring children in that state to be educated, and in 1647 the Massachusetts legislature specifically required the teaching of reading and writing. Although the Constitution did not make provision for education, the "subsequent amendments and the Ordinance of 1785 did have a great effect on the public school system of education as it developed in the United States" (Lambert, 1963, p. 20). This ordinance, which set aside one section—640 acres—of public land for the support of public education, did much to enhance the further development of education. By the actual setting aside of land, the states were able to begin constructing schools without first having to obtain the land.

In spite of these beginnings, it was not until 1852 that a law was passed requiring compulsory school attendance, and not until 1918, when Mississippi adopted such a law, that it was accepted in all the states; once compulsory attendance laws required elementary-age children to attend school, education became available for all children (Lambert, 1963). With the passage in 1975 of Public Law 94-142 (1976), the Education for All Handicapped Children Act, the educational system in the United States truly became universal; this law required school districts to provide a free and appropriate education in the least restrictive environment for every child that is identified as handicapped. Now, almost 80 years after compulsory attendance was required in all states, the elementary school is still committed to universal education.

Although the intent of the curriculum of the early elementary schools was to foster reading, writing, and arithmetic, the "three R's," our present schools have not moved very far from this in the curriculum emphasis. Rodgers (1975) noted that as the number of hours available for instruction increased, a major portion of the instructional time in the elementary schools was still devoted to the three R's.

Looking at the role and function of the elementary school as it exists today, Rodgers (1975) identified three major functions:

1. It provides for the intellectual development of children.
2. It contributes to the socialization of children.
3. It fosters and develops self-awareness, self-understanding, and self-realization. (p. 114)

Educational Standards and Policy Making

In spite of the growing substantial involvement of the federal government, authority over matters of public education was given to the states. To see and understand how educational standards and policy making at the state level affect the local school districts it is necessary to look first at the categories of power and the responsibility for carrying out the operations of the schools.

Categories of Power

In the United States it is not necessary for the national government to operate or control the business of education—the forms of education that the states and localities generate for themselves will hopefully be adequate to serve the national interest. Jurisdiction is lodged in the governments of the states, most of which delegate the actual control to local agencies (Educational Policies Commission, 1967). There are three categories of power delegated to school districts that allow them to operate their schools to fit their particular needs within these parameters: (1) mandated powers, (2) permissive powers, and (3) prohibitive powers (Candoli, Hack, Ray, & Stollar, 1978). These are summarized below.

Mandated Powers   States frequently mandate that all school systems must do certain things—for example, state law may require that all school districts provide free transportation to students living a certain distance from their school. State departments of education have regulatory and supervisory power to oversee these mandates.

Permissive Powers   Because states vary in their needs in educational programs, they enact permissive legislation that allows a school system to offer a given program. For example, a school district may provide free transportation to all children in the district regardless of distance (without state subsidy), which goes beyond the state mandate.

Prohibitive Powers   The prohibitive powers element spells out what a school may not do, usually in no uncertain terms. Thus the state limits the action of the system to the extent of dictating what it must do and what it may do, and specifies what it may not do (Candoli et al., 1978, pp. 54–55).

Responsibility for Schools

As much as possible, the operational responsibility for schools should rest within the local districts. Local school systems have proved to be remarkably responsible and viable units of operational control. The tradition of local control of education has grown stronger over the years. "The most important exercise of local district authority is found in the local policies developed to carry out the state policies" (Candoli et al., 1978, p. 55). It is important for elementary school counselors to be knowledgeable about state and local education laws and policies that could impact their work with children and their families, particularly the local districts' response to state policies.

Many school districts look on outside governance with mixed feelings. Turnbull (1985) noted this, stating that "schools and districts carry out their school-improvement efforts in an environment crowded with governing bodies, special programs, mandates, and resource systems" (p. 337). Turnbull asserts that these outside systems of governance and support are highly important because they have the power to enhance or detract from local effectiveness.

All school districts are governed to some degree by external constraints as well as opportunities. As a former state Department of Education director of guidance services, the author had a firsthand view of the involvement of the federal and state agencies in the everyday workings of the local education agencies (LEAs). Members of the state Department of Education professional staff were charged with carrying out and enforcing mandates, both state and federal, and monitoring was an integral part of our visits to the LEAs. In addition to this, technical assistance was offered to the local districts to enable them to carry out their programs at the local level, which in turn contributed to their effectiveness. The latter provided opportunities for the districts to receive valuable input not always available at the local district level.

Purkey and Smith (1985), in response to reports criticizing education in the United States in recent years, looked at school effectiveness literature, suggesting "local strategies and policies to stimulate and facilitate local reform" (p. 353). They suggested a model for school improvement, summarized below, that integrates the characteristics of effective schools. The first nine can be implemented quickly, usually by administrative mandate:

1. *School-site management and democratic decision making.* The staff in each building is given responsibility and authority.
2. *Leadership.* Leadership can come from administrators, teachers, or integrated teams of both.
3. *Staff stability.* Staff stability is necessary for growth.
4. *Curriculum articulation and organization.* A planned curriculum emphasizing the study of basic skills is implemented.
5. *Staff development.* The expressed concerns of the staff are linked to the instructional and organizational needs of the school.
6. *Parental involvement and support.* Obtaining parental support is important for attendance, homework, and discipline policies.
7. *School recognition of academic success.* Recognition is a way of encouraging students to adopt similar norms and values.
8. *Maximizing learning time.* Class time is free from interruptions and disruptions.
9. *District support.* The support of the district is necessary for the improvement process.

The preceding characteristics set the stage for the four that follow:

10. *Collaborative planning and collegial relationships.* When teachers and administrators work together, attempts at change are more successful.
11. *Sense of community.* Schools build feelings of community that increase performance of students and staff.
12. *Clear goals and high expectations commonly shared.* Schools whose staff agree on their goals are more likely to be successful.
13. *Order and discipline.* Rules are established by mutual agreement and are consistently and fairly enforced. (Purkey & Smith, 1985, pp. 358–359)

The preceding model is considered a starting point for building school effectiveness. In addition to the suggested model, Purkey and Smith noted that the role of the board of education and district superintendent is to set the direction for the schools in a way that will blend both local and state interests. The board and superintendent would also determine the guidelines that would facilitate the school improvement process, specify the goals for the district's board based on input from school staff and parent and community groups, and would prescribe the timeline for the entire project. This puts the responsibility for the operation of the schools in the local districts, where it rightfully belongs.

Goals and Objectives of the Elementary School

The establishment of goals for elementary schools and classrooms, and the objectives designed to meet those goals, has been a major task of educators for a number of years. Whether the goals and objectives are established at the state Department of Education level, the district level, the school level, or a combination of these, the responsibility for carrying these out, in addition to establishing classroom goals and objectives, becomes the responsibility of the classroom teacher. The role of the elementary school teacher is discussed in the next section of this chapter.

Heathers (1967) raised a significant question a number of years ago: "Should the goals of elementary education be the same for all pupils?" (p. 192). Educators over the years have differed sharply on this matter. Responding to the question, Heathers made this statement: "Either we must allow pupils of different levels of maturity and ability to proceed at different rates through the elementary curriculum or we must provide them with different learning materials" (p. 193). It would appear that the answer to this question rests in local interpretation of the purpose of elementary school education. It would also seem that the input of teachers is critical to the establishment of meaningful goals and objectives for their school. In addition, elementary counselors trained in the understanding of developmental stages of the elementary-age child are able to make significant contributions to the important task of establishing goals and objectives.

Tyler (1971), in an earlier look at trends in the elementary school curriculum, noted that the basic functions of America's schools had not changed for a number of years. Two of the educational functions first emphasized when free public education was initially established were as follows: "For the individual child, education was to provide the opportunity to realize his potential and to become a constructive and happy person in the station of life which he would occupy because of his birth and ability" (Tyler, 1971, p. 5). We need to keep these basic functions in mind as we look at the current goals and objectives in the elementary schools where we are involved, either directly as counselors, teachers, or parents or indirectly as citizens concerned about schools in our communities.

Krathwohl (1971) viewed the task of specifying educational objectives to student behaviors a, a useful and powerful approach in the analysis of instructional process. He saw a renewed interest by teachers when they structured their courses in this way. He noted that when the educational process is viewed in terms of student behaviors, "'education' means changing the behavior of a student so that he is able, when encountering a particular problem or situation, to display a behavior which he did not previously exhibit. The task of the teacher is to help the student learn new or changed behaviors and determine when and where they are appropriate" (p. 45). Krathwohl believed that objectives become more detailed and operational when the teacher spells out the instructional goals in terms of desired skills and behaviors for which the students should strive. There has been a renewed interest in recent years of tying together student behaviors and educational objectives in the educational process.

Ames and Ames (1984) looked at goal structures and motivation in elementary school children. They studied how different goal/reward structures are influenced by the motivational processes of children. "The goal structure of a classroom may be described as competitive (students work against each other toward some goal or reward), cooperative (students work with each other for a common goal), or individualistic (students work toward independent goals)" (p. 39). They found that goal structure has a significant effect on the perception and evaluation by students of themselves and classmates. Ames and Ames also looked at goal structure and the teacher's perception and evaluation of students. Their findings indicated that teachers' evaluations of students are affected by the reward structure that is implemented. One of their conclusions is quite relevant to the examination of characteristics of goals and objectives in the elementary school setting: "it may be possible to alter the psychological meaning of failure merely by changing the structure of the learning environment" (p. 57). This appears to be an area that would merit further study in establishing goals for the elementary school.

In the process of establishing goals and objectives, Brandt and Tyler speak to the significance of goals in prioritizing learning. This helps "to prevent a common weakness in curriculum development: selection of goals that are obsolete or irrelevant, inappropriate for students' current level of development, not in keeping with sound scholarship, not in harmony with America's democratic philosophy, or for which the school cannot provide the necessary learning conditions" (cited in English, 1983, p. 47). The establishment of goals for a local school system should involve students, parents, and interested others to participate in the process. Brandt and Tyler do recognize that general goals are usually not controversial, but some specific ones might be and should not be subject to a majority vote. They differentiate between state goals and district goals: "State goals should furnish general guidance for the kinds and areas of learning for which schools are responsible in that state. The school district should furnish more detailed guidance by identifying goals that fall between the general aims listed by the state and those appropriate to the local school" (cited in English, 1983, p. 50).

Rodgers (1975) looked ahead to the elementary school in the year 2000 as he considered the goals of the elementary school. He saw the schools at that time reflecting what they will become in the future, noting that, "as we attempt to project the elementary school to the year 2000, we must not forget that the present conception of that school will dictate the nature and focus of that institution in the future. Many of the goals of the present elementary school will not change even though the means will be vastly different and the need for achievement of certain goals will be greater" (p. 377).

At the present time, goals and objectives formulated by the nation's governors and former President Bush are creating a national environment for our schools. As a part of this, school boards are urged to join in with community people to change the framework for strategic planning and thinking about education (Joint Study Group on National Education Goals, 1992). The establishment of appropriate goals, and the objectives designed to meet those goals, will continue to be a major task of educators, now and in the future. The Goals 2000 legislation, intended to provide structure for educational reform, provides the impetus to bring together many of the federal education programs.

The Role of the Teacher

The elementary school teacher plays the key role in the education of children. The elementary school child spends the major portion of the day under the direction and tutelage of one person, the teacher. The learning that goes on in that classroom is the responsibility, for the most part, of the teacher; the tone of the classroom is also set by the teacher. In research conducted to identify characteristics of effective classrooms, two important conclusions were identified: "One important finding is that students' classroom behavior is the most important direct link to student achievement. A second important finding is that teachers' behavior can affect students' behavior in ways that will lead to improved student learning" (Squires, Huitt, & Segars, 1983, p. 9). Teachers can and do have significant impact on the students' behavior and subsequent learning by planning and instructing in ways that insure student interest and involvement.

This raises two issues: (1) Just how much freedom do teachers have to run their class-rooms in the way they deem most appropriate? (2) How much input do teachers have in setting the educational standards and policies they are required to adhere to? As noted ear-lier, the policies, for the most part, come down from the state level through the district and local level and then to the classroom.

Before looking at the effects of these policies in the classroom, it is necessary to start at the state level. Darling-Hammond and Wise (1985) viewed the states as policy-making bodies in the educational structure. "State policies intended to improve education general-ly try either to set educational standards or to shape the educational process. Although states also seek to improve education through the allocation of funds, in recent years they have placed more emphasis on regulation setting standards in the form of tests to be passed or educational procedures to be followed" (p. 315). In order to enforce policies, those that write them must have a means to monitor them. Policies dictated at the state level must be enforceable at the district and local level and on into the classroom. "Educational policy-making at the state level is particularly problematic when it seeks to improve the quality of schooling by prescribing goals, processes, or outcomes related to the 'production' of teaching or learning" (Darling-Hammond & Wise, 1985, p. 316).

A variety of "solutions" to the real and perceived problems in the schools have been suggested in recent years; one of the recent trends is cooperative learning. Cooperative learning moves the emphasis away from a competitive structure in which only one student is called on for an answer, usually the high achievers. Kagan (1989/1990), in an article that discussed using a structural approach to cooperative learning, illustrated this through a 10-step cooperative structure called "Co-op Co-op" in which students in teams are each work-ing on one part of a class project. The involvement of all students tends to promote equal participation, resulting in positive learning experiences for all students. For schools and districts adopting cooperative learning, it can become an overwhelming task for a teacher to master yet another form of teaching, in spite of the positive results. The counselor, trained in working with groups, could assist teachers in this process.

Another educational emphasis in educational reform is outcomes-based education (OBE); this became a source of controversy in 1994, causing a stir among both educators and parents. Because the teacher seems to be the significant link in this process it is impor-tant to know how teachers perceive and react to policies and reforms such as these. O'Neil (1994), in the official newsletter of the Association for Supervision and Curriculum Development (ASCD), noted that "the debate surrounding OBE is complex, in part because there are no agreed-upon definitions of 'outcomes-based education' or 'out-comes'" (p. 4). Proponents of OBE view this as the only sensible direction for education to take; opponents view it as a weakening of what education is trying to accomplish by lowering standards to enable all students to achieve the objectives. It would appear to be fundamental to any discussion of outcomes-based education to apprise the general public of what is really meant by the term *outcomes-based education*. The confusion has caused many to take sides on the issue without really understanding the basic intent of this move-ment. The issue had become so controversial in 1994 that the Association for Supervision and Curriculum Development devoted their entire March 1994 journal, *Educational*

Leadership, to the challenge of outcomes-based education. Several of the articles were written by teachers—some enthusiastic and others concerned as to the anticipated difficulty of assessing the students' performance in a fair and accurate manner.

Teachers are seldom consulted by educational reformers before new programs are launched. Darling-Hammond and Wise (1985) believed that teacher performance standards set by policy makers as a way to improve teaching and learning in the classroom is not a promising situation: "attention must be paid to the collective impact of policies upon the role of classroom teachers—policies that in the aggregate may make teaching less attractive, thus lowering the quality of the teaching force, which, in turn, causes policymakers to regulate in an effort to improve education" (p. 335).

Teachers have been required to change instructional strategies many times over the years in response to the push by states to change academic emphases and boost school improvement. Sykes (1986) viewed the teacher at the heart of educational excellence. He noted that in all of the states improvement of teaching was considered the most critical for the achievement of educational mastery by business, education, and government leaders. He shared his concern regarding the emphasis on teaching with the fear that the teaching profession will not be able to attract enough capable persons in the coming decade. He reported the results of the second annual Metropolitan Life survey of teachers: "The most startling result is that over one-quarter of the teachers surveyed say they intend to leave teaching in the next five years. Most of these 500,000 teachers are veterans, not newcomers" (1986, p. 367). Sykes' recommendation was to develop the teaching profession by professionalism—replacing bureaucratic accountability with professional responsibility. The use of teachers themselves to set standards, with commitment from within the profession, should bring about the necessary improvements to the teaching profession. As controversial as this is, it may be the only way to bring about the needed changes in the education profession, attracting teachers who are truly able to hold themselves accountable. At the same time, it is vital to address how the schools have changed in their approach to education in recent years, causing teachers to become discouraged enough to want to leave their profession.

A recent newspaper article, "How We Fail Kids, Ourselves," identified the frustrations felt by many of today's teachers. The experienced junior high school teacher, resigning after 10 years as an English and French teacher in the local school district, spelled out her frustrations in a letter sent to the parents of her students explaining why she was quitting in the middle of the year: "At some point schools shifted emphasis from work and learning to 'fun' and 'creativity.' The result isn't pretty: Low expectations, rowdy, lazy students and a tolerance for bad behavior. How did things get so out of hand?" She told of her frustrations regarding the lack of respect for teachers from the students, citing some examples: "I have always received respect from my students in the classroom, but in the past year or so I have had a number of unpleasant experiences with students I don't know. Among these were having food thrown at my door and at my person, being called stupid, being physically harassed by two male students and, finally—the event that triggered my resignation—having my desk spat on" (Stephens, 1994, p. G6). Letters to the editor of the newspaper in the weeks following the appearance of her article expressed dismay over the loss of an outstanding teacher and "life model" for students in her school. All educators and policy makers need to take a closer look at what is not working in today's schools in order to keep teachers like this in the classroom.

Teachers have always been under pressure to effectively achieve the goals established by the school or school district. School districts often establish curriculum committees to write the goals of the elementary school curriculum; in other districts, it is the individual teacher who constructs the curriculum goals. Regardless of where the goals originate, it is the responsibility of the individual teacher to carry out the goals established for his or her school, often without the support needed to accomplish the tasks.

The challenge to the elementary teacher is of utmost importance. The role of the elementary teacher in helping children achieve the goals and objectives of our educational institutions is critical. In a much earlier view of the teacher's role in elementary education, Burdin and McAulay (1971) stated the following: "Curriculum development and teaching at the elementary level call for human engineering of great sophistication" (p. 450). It is clear that the teacher's role in educating the child in his or her classroom has not diminished in the intervening years and cannot be overlooked or underestimated as we continue to strive for effective schools.

Implications for Counseling and Guidance

This survey of the elementary school from its earliest beginnings until now underscores the significance of a developmental approach to elementary school counseling. To Blocher (1966), the principal theorist of developmental counseling, one of the central concerns of the elementary school is facilitating the students' mastery of developmental tasks appropriate to this age level. The elementary counselor is involved in a significant way in this process: "It is the role of the developmental counselor in the elementary school to help other workers understand the nature of these tasks and to help them organize school activities in a way that will best insure youngsters the opportunity to master them" (p. 201). This is as significant for today's elementary school as when Blocher wrote this.

One of the articles in the March 1994 *Educational Leadership* journal, referred to earlier in the chapter, discussed defining outcomes for guidance and counseling programs. It was encouraging to note that the Beaverton, Oregon, community, when faced with budget cuts, left only one support service intact—their newly restructured guidance and counseling program (Haack, 1994). The key to keeping this successful program was in the following statement: "Parents, teachers, administrators, mental health professionals, state and county agencies, and students had participated in the restructuring of the guidance and counseling program and endorsed its outcome-based model" (Haack, 1994, p. 33). The guidance and counseling program was designed to reach out to all students with a program that had clearly defined outcomes, enabling the counselors to assess the progress of the students. Another key to their success was the priority development of outcomes to support the academic success of the students with standards delineating observable behaviors. As a final task, they defined student benchmarks that "interpreted the standards into developmentally appropriate levels at grades 3, 5, 8, 10, and 12. All students are expected to achieve the benchmarks when they exit that particular grade level" (p. 34). A well-developed and thought-out guidance and counseling program with increased collaboration with teachers becomes a significant part of the entire school program. In this district, counselors are spending time team-teaching with classroom teachers, which in turn results in carry-over skills for the teachers. The result of this successful program is stated by Haack

(1994): "No longer an add-on frill, guidance and counseling is an essential element in the instructional program" (p. 35). This is an excellent, and encouraging, illustration of how effective learning is increased in a supportive atmosphere where a developmental guidance and counseling program is a crucial part of the entire school program.

Because of the increasing size and complexity of our schools, along with inadequate funding, classes are larger, and teachers often have little time for considering the individual needs of their students. In addition, there has been an emphasis on individual instruction. It is understandable that the teacher is hard-pressed to fulfill the demands without the added burden of considering the students' affective needs. A significant role of the counselor is to help the teacher deal with the students' affective needs; this is an area of expertise for the elementary school counselor. Elementary teachers more than ever are looking to the elementary counselor for help and involvement in this area.

Rodgers (1975), in justifying the elementary schools' role in influencing pupils' attitudes and values, looked to Dewey's classical work, *Democracy and Education.* He interpreted this as follows: "Careful examination of Dewey's comments suggests that education shaped by 'a particular social ideal' is an expression of the values of the society in question. Therefore, all education is concerned with teaching the young the values of the society. This is at least one justification for making the conscious influencing of pupils' attitudes and values a legitimate concern of the elementary school" (p. 232). The intervening years have not diminished this need to teach the young the values of the society in which they live. The elementary counselor can serve a unique role in this process by working with student attitudes and societal values in small groups and in the classroom setting.

Another area of involvement for the elementary school counselor is helping the primary age child become competent in the school setting. This involves helping the child fit in with his or her peers in developmentally appropriate ways. As Kegan (1982) noted: "Whatever other kinds of learning one might be told the primary grades are about, what they are most centrally learning about is learning to *go* to school, learning to live in a world of rules and roles where egocentric behavior is less and less tolerated" (p. 163). Elementary teachers are often overwhelmed with needy children who have not learned to respect rules or authority of any kind.

The motivational processes of students must be taken into account as we consider the elementary school child in the schools of the late 1990s and into the 21st century. Counselors are often confronted by frustrated parents and teachers with the following comment: "I just can't seem to motivate him (her)!" What is often not taken into account is how the child feels about himself or herself in the school setting, which in turn affects the child's desire to learn. Children are often grouped by abilities; in an attempt to "hide" the grouping, the group may be called the Bluebirds, or Robins, for example. It doesn't take long for the child to identify the Bluebirds as the "dummy" reading group, as a child in a Bluebird group once related to the author. All children need to feel cared for and valued as unique persons in order for the school to have the desired impact on their learning. Too often those in the school setting measure only their cognitive growth and ignore their affective needs. Counselors are particularly suited to conduct small group and classroom guidance activities that balance the emphasis between cognitive and affective learning. Thompson and Rudolph (1992), in classifying counseling theories, propose a three-dimensional model that shows the integrative relationship between behavior, feelings, and thinking. By including the behavioral category, equal emphasis is given to the affective, behavioral, and cognitive approaches to counseling; this, in turn, helps to identify appropriate counseling methods for our children.

Summary

The concern for the education of elementary school students has been a major consideration in America since early colonial days. For the most part, educational standards and policy making are left up to the states in spite of the substantial involvement on the part of the federal government. The responsibility for the operation of the schools is placed in the local school districts with many of the goals, and the objectives designed to achieve these goals, decided at the local school level. Within the structure of the elementary school the teacher plays the key role in the education that takes place. The challenge today for teachers to achieve the goals and objectives of their schools is significant. The elementary school counselor plays a critical role in helping teachers to help children master the developmental tasks appropriate to this age level. Developmental guidance, counselors working in the classroom with teachers on the developmental needs of students, can do much to enhance teacher awareness of developmental differences among students. This task of helping teachers and staff understand the developmental tasks appropriate to each age level will be addressed in Chapter 2 with a discussion of the emotional, social, cognitive, and moral development of the elementary-age child, and again in Chapter 5 in the discussion of the role of the counselor in consultation with teachers and staff.

Chapter *2*

Development of the Elementary-Age Child

This chapter focuses on the emotional, social, cognitive, and moral development of the elementary-age child. The elementary school counselor should know about these significant areas of development because they greatly affect the behaviors and achievement of the child in the school setting. Counselors and teachers typically receive training in child development with emphasis on what children are like at different ages rather than on looking at the child as a person with unique developmental needs, along with suggested activities geared to meet these needs. To attempt to bridge this gap, counselors need to look at a variety of views on the developmental needs of children as presented in this chapter. In order to expand this perspective, practical applications of the works of Piaget, Coopersmith, Havighurst, Kohlberg, and other leaders in the field will be presented in Chapter 4 in the section on developmental counseling.

Areas of Developmental Focus and Counseling Implications

Emotional Development

Few would disagree that emotions play a major role in the life of a child. The emotional ups and downs of the elementary-age child are all too familiar to those who live with and work with children in this age group. The emotional development of children has been a concern for a number of years; earlier professional publications indicate that educators and others concerned about this aspect of the child have shared their beliefs and views in research and writings. One educator, Coopersmith, noted that the importance of emotions in the learning process has been largely avoided by many educators. He believed that this avoidance was due to "long-term cultural reservations and uncertainties about the role of emotions in our lives and the conviction that emotions are out of place in our schools" (1975a, p. 1). He suggested that emotions are a valuable, largely unexplored domain in the education of children. Coopersmith was involved in a project funded by the Office of Child Development and the Office of Economic Opportunity to develop materials, guidelines, and principles for early childhood education programs. As a part of this, in addressing the role of emotions in education, he noted that "an unfortunate consequence of the taboos against emotional expression may be the current difficulties in motivation, involvement, and task orientation that are prevalent in our nation's classrooms" (1975a, p. 5). The author of this text, in checking the subject index of large number of counseling texts, could not find any references to emotions other than emotional disorders or emotionally disturbed children. This has been an area of concern in our schools for many years, but it is still largely unaddressed today.

We have, in the past, tended to view emotions as an indication of weakness. It is not uncommon for parents to say "Boys don't cry" when their sons cry and to say nothing when their daughters cry. Our culture has allowed girls to express their emotions, to be "sensitive," whereas we have expected boys to hold their emotions in check and be "strong" and masculine. When children fully express their emotions in a school setting, it is often regarded as a sign of immaturity. Many of the questionnaires that teachers, parents, and counselors are required to complete on "problem" children will have statements such as "cries easily," "has low frustration level," "seems immature," and so on. All of these are considered indicators of negative behaviors in the elementary school setting, behaviors that are undesirable.

It would seem to follow naturally that when children are taught to repress their emotions, much of their excitement, enthusiasm, and spontaneity will be lost in the process. Van Hoose, in an early look at the emotional development of elementary school children, noted that "the emotional reactions which a child experiences develop into habit patterns and as such become driving forces in behavior" (1968, p. 20). A similar view was expressed by Coopersmith: "To suppress emotions in the school is to deny a part of every child's humanity; to accept and utilize emotions is to utilize that humanity to increase realization of human capacities" (Coopersmith, 1975, p. 21).

Elkind looked at motivation and development of children in a program that he supervised using college students to tutor children. One of the findings that emerged in this process was that remedial work with children was not effective until an attachment, or emotional relationship, was established between the tutor and the child (Elkind, 1978). Another educator who earlier emphasized the relationship between emotions and learning in the elementary school was Faust. After spending 10 years in the elementary schools as a teacher, school psychologist, and coordinator of counseling services, he became a counselor-educator with an emphasis in the area of elementary education. These experiences made it clear to him that a developmental focus, working with all children in the school setting, was needed. In his book on the use of the counselor-consultant in the elementary school, he noted that "all learning, particularly learning of a nonreflexive type, seems to possess affect as an essential component" (Faust, 1968a, p. 240). He further stated that "emotions are to be considered here as possessing a significant relationship to intellectual functioning" (p. 241).

Breckenridge and Vincent, in an even earlier study of child development, found convincing evidence of the effects of emotional well-being on children. They noted "that the child's physical well-being affects and is affected by his emotional well-being, that his social development and his emotional development are closely related, and also that the child's ability to use his intelligence effectively is deeply influenced by the state of his emotional well-being" (Breckenridge & Vincent, 1960, p. 26). They also found that the child's adjustment to school is often an emotional strain, far more than most adults are aware. This is understandable, and it is a significant area to address. In assessing a child's readiness for school, factors usually considered are the mental, physical, social, and emotional development of the child. The author recalls observing from her district school office, over a period of six weeks, young children waiting with their parent(s) to be tested by one of the school psychologists for early entrance into kindergarten. A large number of these youngsters reverted to much younger behavior, such as sucking a thumb or fingers, climbing onto a parent's lap, and so on. The emotional strain was clearly evident in these children.

There is sufficient evidence for the elementary school to give strong consideration to the role of emotions in the education of children. Teachers need to be encouraged to address this aspect of child behavior and to accept that certain levels of emotions can be highly constructive in the classroom environment. "Teachers who accept children as they are recognize and respect affect as a legitimate concern of a school and a society that is involved in motivating and guiding the behavior of its youth" (Coopersmith, 1975a, p. 20). Keat (1990), in looking at multimodal counseling as an effective agent of change for children, noted that children can learn to expect others to put them down, "but they can also be given coping statements in which they learn to handle the situation so that it is not so upsetting or bothersome" (p. 256). This gives the child the power of control over his or her emotions. Multimodal counseling, originated by Arnold Lazarus, is tailored to the counselee by considering all aspects of his or her personality functions, such as behavior, affective, and cognitive. All of these functions, or modalities, are viewed in the counseling process. Children at this age can usually express emotions, but they have difficulty labeling them; helping them label emotions helps them handle these types of situations.

Implications for Counseling and Guidance   Elementary school counselors may be expected to know just what it is that makes children behave as they do. It is important that the counselor have an awareness of the range of emotional development from kindergarten, where the child is usually quite serious and shows little humor, to the sixth grade, where silliness and clowning around are common. Knowing what to expect in the development of the child at each grade level could assist in creating the kind of environment that children need in order to benefit fully from the elementary school experience.

Counselors concerned about the developmental processes of children will also extend their services to include teachers and parents in order to help them understand their roles in the emotional development of the child. In addition to offering the services to teachers and parents, the developmental counselor must also help the children understand their own behaviors in order for them to identify their feelings and be able to express themselves in acceptable ways. Classroom group guidance and counseling activities are an effective means to address this area. A major thrust of elementary school counselors should be affective education—working directly in the classroom setting with the teacher on activities and projects that emphasize the emotional development of the students. The focus should be helping each child develop his or her best potential. Co-leading these activities with the teacher helps to "normalize" the emotions that are expressed by the children.

Social Development

The school, by its very makeup, is a social situation. Within the school setting, the social development of elementary-age children varies widely. Children come to school representing a variety of family, neighborhood, and play groups. Some may argue that it is not the task of the school to socialize children, but it becomes an academic argument when the school has some unsocialized children in its midst. Many children are greatly affected by home factors such as divorce, abuse, parental fighting, and neglect, to name a few. Socialization of these children becomes the process by which the organization and purpose of the school are passed on to the students. Unfortunately, identifying whether or not a child's aggressive behavior is due to parental reinforcement or other factors is difficult. Conformity of behavior is expected in many elementary school classrooms; individual uniqueness is typically not valued.

Omizo, Omizo, and D'Andrea (1992) addressed children's psychosocial needs in connection with Erickson's tasks of middle childhood, stressing classroom guidance groups as especially appropriate for elementary-age children in their drive to master the environment. This emphasis on working with elementary children within the structure of the classroom is continually stressed in developmental counseling programs.

Tanner viewed "self direction in children as our overriding educational goal" (1978, p. 140). She further emphasized that "developing self direction in children means helping them to become responsible individuals who know how to act and how not to act and who care about the consequences of their actions for themselves and others" (p. 140). Tanner presented a developmental sequence of three stages in discipline, which are an extension of the foundational ideas of developmental psychology. These stages, summarized below, identify specific responsibilities for the student to master.

Stage I: Basic Disciplinary Stage

At this stage the child must be able to listen and follow directions; learn to share; be able to ask questions; and develop a sense of responsibility and consideration for others.

Stage II: Constructive Stage

At this stage, the children work cooperatively; participate in planning classroom projects; recognize other's rights; become self-directed; and acquire social responsibility.

Stage III: Generative Stage

At this stage, the children are self-directing and competent; able to uphold the concept of justice; and able to conceptualize problems—all to a greater degree than at the previous stage (Tanner, 1978, pp. 29–39).

It is obvious that the majority of children will need all of the elementary school years and beyond to pass through most of these stages. Social development is an orderly process in children, although they do not develop at the same rate.

Social growth is a never-ending task for a school child. The child is required to learn to "live" in a classroom and work in a group setting, because most of the tasks in school are done with others as part of a group experience or with others present in the classroom. The skills that children acquire for cooperation and collaboration as elementary students will equip them for a greater degree of happiness and success as adults. A child with few or no siblings will have a much more difficult time with this than a child from a larger family or extended peer group. For some of these children, the classroom becomes the first experience of working with others in a group.

Children who exhibit aggressiveness as part of their social behavior are often labeled as "troublesome" or "at risk." Most children are amenable to having this aggressiveness redirected into acceptable channels and not repressed. In our culture, particularly among boys, a certain amount of aggressive behavior seems to be a normal part of early social development and is accepted within reasonable limits. Group cooperation is important even as competitiveness is asserted. The elementary school is a vital setting for the child's early social development with peers. The interaction with peers becomes an important agent in the socialization process. Oden (1986) noted this importance: "Some children need to learn new social behaviors and also gain in their attention to and skill in evaluation of peer feedback and consequences of their behavior in various situations and relationships" (p. 247). The elementary school is an ideal setting for children to learn to live, play, and work effectively with others.

Implications for Counseling and Guidance   The role of the elementary school counselor in socialization is challenging and delicate. The developmental counselor has a basic commitment to individual growth and development, which in turn leads to group growth and development. The elementary school counselor needs to understand the various family, neighborhood, and play groups within which the children have developed. Most of the child's social development prior to starting school occurs in these groups. The elementary counselor also needs an awareness of minority-group/cross-cultural counseling in order to deal more effectively with all children in the school setting. Counseling culturally diverse students will be discussed in Chapter 7.

The development of social skills is a primary objective in the elementary classroom. The counselor and the teacher can collaborate and use small groups to teach social skills such as listening, making friends, and playing cooperatively; they should be provided feedback on their behavior in the group. An effective means of accomplishing these tasks is by using peer assistance and positive role models. The emphasis should always be on the positive rather than the negative if the child's social development is to be positive. There are a variety of ways the elementary school counselor can help children develop competent social skills in the classroom setting. Of particular importance to the counselor is knowledge of the social development of the child from kindergarten through sixth grade, from individual or solitary play in kindergarten (impatient for his or her turn; usually a poor group member) to the need for conformity as a sixth grader (with organized group activities and competitive teams as the norm). In the various available classroom guidance activities, much of this is taken into account; the suitability for each grade level is usually identified in the materials. The ways in which the elementary school counselor can be involved in this significant area of social development will be examined in Chapter 9 in an expanded discussion on structured activities in small groups and in the classroom.

Cognitive Development

Cognitive development is a continuous process, beginning at birth. In infants and young children, emotions are often closely tied to mental abilities; as children reach school age, their emotions are much less apt to interfere with their learning activities. Elkind (1978) noted that "the child must struggle with the same intellectual problems during each growth period but with progressively better mental equipment and with correspondingly better results" (p. 98). In other words, there is continuity in the child's cognitive development.

A major emphasis in the elementary school is cognitive learning; the focus has been and continues to be on academics. Our concern here is how we in the school setting can affect the cognitive development of elementary school children in positive ways. In order to help the elementary-age child achieve his or her greatest potential, it is necessary to look at motivation. We often hear a teacher or parent express frustration because he or she can't motivate the child to learn. Samples (1975) addressed the issue of motivation by reminding us that it is a *verb.* "I cannot motivate you (although I can move you to action), and you cannot motivate me (although you can arouse my motivation)" (p. 136). Counselors may need to remind parents and teachers of this.

Carlson viewed encouragement as the single most important factor in motivating students to learn (Carlson, 1980). In the encouragement process, we focus on the child's strengths, not weaknesses. Carlson noted that "as an educator changes or increases students' feelings of adequacy, he or she increases their ability to function fully" (p. 2). This in turn has an effect on building the child's self-concept. Teachers have a significant impact on the child's concept of self. Carlson referred to the many interactions a teacher has with an elementary school child during the course of a day, "bouncing" off the class in these many interactions. He saw the impact of this as follows:

> *Some teachers have a positive style of bouncing. "Good work." "That's fine, Betty; now explain it to the class so they can all understand." "Attaboy." "You are doing great!" This is a positive feedback that tells students they are worthwhile, they do count, they have value, they can make it.*
>
> *Other teachers, though, have negative bouncing styles. They are critical. They are sarcastic. They humiliate their students and degrade them in minor or important ways. Hundreds of times a day, thousands of times a week, millions and millions of times a year, they provide feedback to their students that implies they are not capable, they are not important, they cannot do it. Such is the stuff of which negative self-concepts are formed. (Carlson, 1980, p. 5)*

The author, in a recent observation of two practicum students in two different classrooms in the same elementary school, noted the extremes of teachers in an early grade. In one classroom, the students were required to sit quietly, without a sound, and were expected to raise their hands to be acknowledged during the classroom guidance activity. The teacher sat in the back of the room at her desk. In the other classroom, the teacher sat on the floor with the children, with various children crawling on and off her lap, all exuberantly responding to the classroom guidance activity. The difference was in the teacher's approach to children; it was not hard to imagine the difference in motivation and attitude of the students in the two classrooms.

It is important for the teacher, as well as the counselor, to be knowledgeable about motivation. A statement by Faust a number of years ago holds true today: "Many a child 'can' but 'doesn't,' and knowing the 'why' in a variety of possibilities makes the counselor and teacher of today a professional" (1968a, p. 15). This is still the goal today of professional counselors and teachers—to know the "why" and help children go beyond the place where they don't perform up to their capabilities.

Concern about motivation has always existed in classrooms, with the teacher providing the external "push" for the most part. A certain number of students are already motivated for a variety of reasons, but the vast majority are not motivated from within. It becomes the task of the teacher to create the type of classroom environment that encourages self-motivation in the students; this is a tremendous challenge for teachers. As Samples (1975) noted, "creating motivational environments is hard work primarily because it asks the teacher to give up postures that the abundance of training, experience, and instructional management in schools now reward" (p. 162). We can teach a child a new concept or a new behavior and allow him or her time to practice this new learning or behavior, but unless a child sees a "why," a reason to retain or internalize that new learning or behavior, no long-term gain will result.

It is encouraging to see an increased emphasis on developmentally appropriate teaching in today's schools. The Association for Supervision and Curriculum Development (ASCD) devoted the November 1993 issue of *Curriculum Update* to teaching young children using "developmentally appropriate practices" (Willis, 1993a). The newsletter addressed the best way to teach young children from preschool through the early grades, noting that the teaching must be age appropriate as well as developmentally appropriate. Active learning was stressed, with the teachers providing a lot of organized activity for the children. Working in groups with hands-on experiences and social interaction was emphasized (Willis, 1993b).

The following section will look at how the elementary school counselor can use Piaget's stages of cognitive development to help children gain competence in this significant area of development.

Implications for Counseling and Guidance   Counselor training programs should include a course on child and adolescent development in which child development specialists such as Piaget are studied in greater detail than what is covered in this text. The material here is intended to serve as a reminder for counselors and teachers of the significance of the work on child development carried out in the past and how it fits in to the elementary school of the present.

Elementary school counselors who familiarize themselves with Piaget's work on child development will have a greater understanding of the children they work with, according to Gowan, Coole, and McDonald (1967). Piaget believed that children pass through four stages of cognitive development, each built upon the previous one. Gowan, Coole, and McDonald stressed the importance of counselors' becoming familiar with Piaget's stages of cognitive development; this understanding of cognitive competence is a means for understanding children. They believe that this is central to mental health in the following ways:

1. At certain stages in the child's development, it is cognitive competence, rather than emotional development which is central.

2. Cognitive competence is the child's chief mainstay to reality, and hence the chief bulwark of his general emotional stability. Conversely, cognitive competence is the chief precursor of emotional stability.

3. Cognitive development on schedule is conducive to emotional health and a proper self-concept, and a lack of cognitive development on schedule is conducive to emotional disturbance and lack of a proper self-concept.

4. Cognitive development may be stimulated by proper and appropriate curriculum experiences directed toward the student's particular abilities and stage of concept development.

5. Cognitive competence can be enhanced by proper and appropriate guidance experiences that emphasize the development of realistic and optimistic self-concepts.

6. Guidance efforts to promote cognitive competence involve (a) sympathetic and supportive individual attention, (b) promotion by the counselor of a student's ability to make changes in his self-concepts through changes in his relationships, and (c) remedial retraining in basic skills. (Gowan, Coole, & McDonald, 1967, pp. 212-213)

If counseling is to be effective, the counselor must have an awareness of the child's level of cognitive development. The knowledge that each stage of cognitive development is built on the previous one helps the counselor and teacher identify where the child is in his or her development of cognitive competence. The counselor should pay particular attention to the guidance efforts suggested in item 6 above.

Thompson and Rudolph (1992) visualized "blocks" that children face in further development of their thought processes. By knowing the blocks that children are faced with, counseling activities can be appropriately geared to help the child benefit from the counseling activities. The blocks are as follows:

1. *Egocentrism block*—the inability to see another's point of view. For example, children believe that everyone thinks the same way and the same things they do. The egocentrism block prevents children from questioning their own thoughts and behaviors even in the face of conflicting evidence. The development of a sense of empathy in the child is made difficult by the egocentrism block.

2. *Centration block*—the inability to focus on more than one aspect of a problem. For example, a long line of five coins may be perceived to have more coins than a short line of six coins. Children are perception bound and cannot see the trees for the forest. The centration block makes problem solving in counseling more difficult; thus more detail and explanation by the counselor are necessary.

3. *Reversibility block*—the inability to work from front to back and then back to front in solving a problem. Children may have difficulty in working mathematics problems such as $17 - \underline{\quad} = 8$. The reversibility block is also characterized by being perception bound. Children often lose track of quantity when the shape of a substance is changed, believing, for example, that a clay ball flattened into a pancake contained more clay when it was in the form of a "taller" ball. Children generally do not understand the concept of irreversibility until after the age of 7;

consequently, children's reactions to loss and death may seem uncaring or inappropriate. Once again, any block to formal thinking would require a better "teaching" job by the counselor.

4. *Transformation block*—the inability to put events in the proper order or sequence. Children often have difficulty in seeing the relationship between events or understanding cause and effect. Children may find it hard to predict the consequences of their behavior and to evaluate the effect of their behavior on themselves and others. In addition, children faced with the transformation block have difficulty in seeing the gray areas in a given situation and view events as black and white or right or wrong regardless of the situation. (pp. 27–29)

The elementary school counselor must be knowledgeable about these significant blocks if the counseling experience is to result in successful growth experiences and learning.

Moral Development

Most textbooks on counseling do not address the moral development of children. With the current concerns of safety for our children, of violent, disruptive, and out-of-control behaviors exhibited by an increasingly larger proportion of school children, this stage in the development of the school-age child is far too significant to ignore. Many children come to school with an acceptable set of beliefs and values that make them a pleasure to have in the classroom. It is on the group of children who seemingly have no real idea as to the appropriateness or inappropriateness of their behavior, no governing set of values to guide or direct their actions and decisions, that we must focus our attention and concerns. It is not the school's task to change the values and beliefs the child comes to school with unless these very ideas, values, and beliefs regarding their relationship to others cause problems for them and others in the school setting.

With children's increased need for help in identifying the relationship between values and behaviors and their need for learning meaningful values, the author is concerned with the lack of emphasis in professional research and publications on ways to help these children. The author found only one recent article in the American Counseling Association (ACA) journals that addressed the role of moral development in counseling children and adolescents; the article addressed the role of moral development in deciding how to counsel and work with children (Parr & Ostrovsky, 1991). Another article, in 1994, addressed the field of moral judgment research from the early 1960s leading up to the Defining Issues Test (DIT), which is used to define moral judgment (Rest, 1994). The majority of writings on the moral development of children is from the 1970s and earlier.

Although the role of the school counselor was not discussed, the entire November 1993 issue of *Educational Leadership,* the journal of the Association for Supervision and Curriculum Development (ASCD), was devoted to "character education." The executive editor stressed involving parents: "School programs developed collaboratively with parents and community agencies can do their part to help young people develop compassion

Scattered excerpts on this and following pages are from *Counseling Children, Third edition,* by Charles L. Thompson and Linda B. Rudolph. Copyright 1992 Wadsworth, Inc. Reprinted by permission of Brooks/Cole Publishing Company, Pacific Grove, CA 93950.

and respect for others" (Brandt, 1993, p. 5). One of the articles stressing the need to return character education to the schools stated that "concern over the moral condition of American society is prompting a reevaluation of the school's role in teaching values" (Lickona, 1993, p. 6). Counselors and teachers concerned about the need for moral education in our schools can participate in the Character Education Partnership, Inc., a nonprofit, nonpartisan organization started in 1993, as reported in the journal. According to Berreth, it is "a broad coalition of educators, business people, faith community leaders, and others who seek to develop civic virtue and moral character in our youth" (cited in Lickona, 1993, p. 8). (Information on this partnership is available by contacting Diane Berreth, Deputy Executive Director, ASCD, at 1250 N. Pitt St., Alexandria, VA 22314-1453.) The entire journal should be required reading for all educators; counselors should be particularly interested in two of the articles: (1) giving at-risk students the opportunity to help others by substituting caring and feelings of worth for the cycle of failure they are used to (Curwin), and (2) focusing on learning through service to others as a means to motivate the unmotivated (Howard).

Kohlberg, long recognized for his contributions to the study of the development of moral reasoning, referred to the "cognitive-developmental approach" to moral education, recognizing John Dewey as the first to state this approach (1978). "The approach is called *cognitive* because it recognizes that moral education, like intellectual education, has its basis in stimulating the *active thinking* of the child about moral issues and decisions. It is called *developmental* because it sees the aims of moral education as movement through moral stages" (Kohlberg, 1978, p. 36). Dewey had a theoretical approach, whereas Piaget used actual interviews in his extensive work with children to arrive at his defined stages of intellectual development and moral reasoning. Kohlberg started to redefine and validate the Dewey and Piaget levels and stages in 1955. Both Kohlberg and Piaget concentrated their research on patterns of reasoning about moral decisions rather than on behavior. In the process of developing their theories of moral development, they clearly identify the stages that an individual goes through in achieving moral maturity. The concept of stages used by Kohlberg and Piaget imply the following characteristics:

1. Stages are "structured wholes," or organized systems of thought. Individuals are consistent in level of moral judgement.
2. Stages form an invariant sequence. Under all conditions except extreme trauma, movement is always forward, never backward. Individuals never skip stages; movement is always to the next stage up.
3. Stages are "hierarchical integrations." Thinking at a higher stage includes or comprehends within it lower stage thinking. There is a tendency to function at or prefer the highest stage available. (Kohlberg, 1978, p. 37)

The developmental theory of Piaget encompasses 40 years of research into the origin and development of cognitive structures and moral judgement in the early years of life. "Piaget's studies have indicated that the most serious obstacle to moral development in early childhood is the child's relationship of respect for and dependence on adults, because it results in a morality of submission to their rules" (Duska & Whelan, 1975, p. 39). This stage of morality is called moral realism. Rules to the child in this stage are rooted in adult authority and "obedience is synonymous with virtue" (Tanner, 1978, p. 23).

There is a gradual movement to advanced morality as the child grows older. Intent of the action begins to enter in as the child reaches middle childhood. Elkind (1978) observed a progressive shift in the elementary-age child's view from judging actions or deeds according to their seriousness to judging them by the intent behind the actions.

Havighurst, long known for his work on the developmental tasks of children, believed that a person's values and ideals fall into a hierarchy, with a scale of values emerging as the child becomes an adolescent. To the child, life is full of unforeseen conflicts of values; the individual is faced with the responsibility of choice because no moral rules have been made to cover such choices. Havighurst also believed that leaders among a group of children have tremendous moral influence on their agemates; because of this, schools should pay special attention to these leaders. "The student should be made to feel that his moral convictions are important to the teacher" (Havighurst, 1973, p. 73). This would seem to be a key area for the teacher and counselor: to identify the leaders and concentrate their efforts on training these children as peer helpers. Channeling the child's energies into a positive direction, by using his or her leadership abilities in this way, can't help but benefit all of the children involved.

In Piaget's view of the formulation of rules for home or classroom, it is more helpful for the child to participate in the formulation of rules than to have them pronounced by adults for his or her submissiveness. If the child understands the effects of his or her actions on the family or classroom, it will facilitate the development of cooperation and mutual respect (Duska & Whelan, 1975). They noted the benefits of this understanding: "As the child develops intellectually and socially, moral rules, referring to stealing, cheating, and lying, are understood in the context of community life and then become internalized principles" (1975, p. 40).

Kohlberg is undoubtedly the most significant psychologist in the field of moral development besides Piaget. Kohlberg's theories of moral development evolved over a period of 20 years. The stages of moral development are summarized below:

I. Preconventional level

The child at this level will respond to the labels of "good and bad, right or wrong." At the same time, they respond because of punishment, reward, or the power of the ones who make the rules.

The level is divided into the following two stages:

Stage 1: The punishment-and-obedience orientation.

Stage 2: The instrumental-relativist orientation.

II. Conventional level

The child at this level is less concerned with consequences and more concerned with fulfilling the expectations of family, peer group, or country. The child has a sense of loyalty to and identity with the group.

At this level, there are the following two stages:

Stage 3: The interpersonal concordance or "good boy–nice girl" orientation.

Stage 4: The "law and order" orientation.

III. Postconventional, autonomous, or principled level

The child at this level defines what moral values and principles are valid for him- or herself apart from the group or anyone in authority.

This level also has two stages:

Stage 5: The social-contract, legalistic orientation, generally with utilitarian overtones.

Stage 6: The universal-ethical-principle orientation (Kohlberg, 1978, pp. 50–51).

In examining the six stages of moral development, it is important for the counselor and teacher to be aware of a study that identified a difference in girls' stages of moral development. Gilligan, a colleague of Kohlberg at Harvard, spent a number of years studying people and the way they viewed morality, noting that women's development was different from men's development in identity and moral development. One of her studies, on rights and responsibilities, included children. In this study, with samples of males and females at various points across the life cycle, Gilligan compared the differences in response between a pair of 11-year-olds. The study was designed to look at different conceptions of morality from each of their perspectives. An interviewer presented one of Kohlberg's dilemmas to each child. Both children recognized "the need for agreement but see it as mediated in different ways—he impersonally through a system of logic and law, she personally through communication and relationship" (Gilligan, 1982, p. 29). Gilligan noted that when viewing the girls' responses in light of Kohlberg's definition of the stages of moral development, her moral judgments would be a full stage lower than the boy's. When the girl's responses were viewed from her world of relationships and awareness of connectedness of individuals, she shows sophistication in her understanding of choice. In another moral dilemma, in which the girl herself was involved in a dilemma of her own, she described an inner dialogue of voices, including her own, that she listens to when deciding what to do. Gilligan viewed this difference as one that should be noted in females across the life span. Knowledge of these stages of development, including the findings that identify the differences for girls in their stages of moral development, will help the elementary counselor and teacher select appropriate interventions to promote morality in children.

Implications for Counseling and Guidance   Elementary school students need to understand themselves and their society, they need to understand the relationships between values and behavior, and they need meaningful and valid values for themselves. Through interactions with others in a classroom setting, students discover that others also experience feelings of uncertainty, self-consciousness, and rejection. Through this, they are able to gain an understanding of themselves, which in turn leads to acceptance of themselves and others. Moral education will help them to gain moral reasoning—it will educate them to use the values they will have developed. As discussed in the previous section, there has been a paucity of research and writings on the effects of moral education in counseling children in the elementary schools. This is an extremely controversial area; a small but vocal group of parents in many communities have attacked some of the developmental guidance materials used to foster moral development, such as Pumsey and DUSO, both discussed in detail in Chapter 5. If we don't address the moral development of our children we are in danger of further eroding attitudes and actions of students in our schools, which in turn affects the quality of our present and future society.

The elementary school counselor is in a position to present moral issues and dilemmas to students, to help them think constructively about these problems. This in turn could suggest a higher level of moral judgment as these issues and dilemmas are discussed in the classroom setting. Moral development consists of changing one's way of reasoning rather than changing one's point of view on a particular issue. The aim, in moral education, should be to insure the optimal level for each individual. This can be done by first assessing the student's level of moral development. For the younger child, ages six to nine, Piaget's dilemmas can be used for this purpose. Pagliuso (1976) developed a workbook, *Understanding Stages of Moral Development,* which provides a scoring guide to Kohlberg's stages. Once the individual's stage is assessed, he or she can be confronted with dilemmas that cause the child to reason one stage higher.

Parr and Ostrovsky, in discussing counseling strategies used in moral development, stressed looking at the stages of moral development of the child as well as his or her personal characteristics. The child whose moral development has reached stage 2 of the pre-conventional level, for example, has a focus on interpersonal relationships. "The children by this time have come to emphasize peer relationships, and school counselors are often called upon to resolve conflicts that grow out of jealousy, transient alliances, broken promises, gossip, and competition for prizes and romantic pledges. Ideals such as fairness, loyalty, and justice are, at this point, beyond the child's grasp, so the counselor helps by appealing to the child's pragmatic sensibilities" (Parr & Ostrovsky, 1991, p. 16).

For the older elementary child, it would be appropriate for the elementary school counselor to set up groups with children in various stages of moral development. Moral dilemmas, available in a variety of literature, could become the basis for the group discussion. Teachers should always be included in these groups in order to insure that the classroom's climate is conducive to helping students determine their own attitudes, feelings, and behaviors. The teacher's task becomes one of encouraging students to identify values and value conflicts, which in turn leads them to behavior that furthers their goals.

A recent book, *Literature-Based Moral Education* (Lamme, Krogh, & Yachmetz, 1992), identifies how to combine high-quality fiction for children in discussions and class activities in order to teach cooperative social skills, values, and good judgment. It is an excellent resource for a counselor, as it discusses nine values important for a child's development: self-esteem; responsibility; sharing; truthfulness; solving conflicts peacefully; respecting and appreciating others; ecological values; diligence, perseverance, and patience; and unconditional love.

Implications for society in general should be considered as the place of moral education in our elementary schools is discussed. A retired school superintendent wrote a newspaper article titled "Teaching Values in Schools" (Parnay, 1994). In it he cited his concerns regarding "the moral breakdown that appears to permeate all segments of society," proposing that the teaching of values be carried out in the public schools with parent involvement. "The idea that a significant majority of parents cannot sit down with educators in virtually every public school in the country and work out a list of values to impart to children is absurd. There are basic values common to all social and ethnic groups, all creeds and colors" (Parnay, 1994, p. B5). He placed the burden of achieving this task on parents, noting that they will receive a surprising amount of support from within the education profession if they are determined to carry this out, demanding these changes. Counselors, who are very involved in the "values" controversy, are in a position to invite parents to observe demonstrations of how values are taught in an elementary classroom. Moral development in our children is an area that is too significant not to be addressed in a textbook on elementary school counseling.

Piaget summed this up as follows: "In a sense, child morality throws a light on adult morality. If we want to form men and women, nothing will fit us so well for the task as to study the laws that govern their formation" (Piaget, 1932, p. ix).

Developmental Tasks of Middle Childhood

Havighurst carried out extensive work on the tasks the individual must learn, which he called "the developmental tasks of life." They are "the things a person must learn if he is to be a reasonably happy and successful person" (Havighurst, 1973, p. 2). Although he originally wrote this in 1948 and made a substantial revision in 1971, these tasks are still appropriate today. The developmental tasks of middle childhood—the period from about 6 to 12 years of age—are summarized below:

1. Learning Physical Skills Necessary for Ordinary Games

Nature of the Task. To learn the physical skills that are necessary for the games and physical activities highly valued in childhood—such skills as throwing and catching, tumbling, swimming, and handling simple tools. (Havighurst, 1973, p. 19)

Educational Implications. Because the peer culture successfully teaches these skills to most children, the school needs to help the ones who have difficulty with the task.

2. Building Wholesome Attitudes toward Oneself as a Growing Organism

Nature of the Task. To develop habits of care of the body, of cleanliness and safety, consistent with a wholesome, realistic attitude which includes a sense of physical normality and adequacy, the ability to enjoy using the body, and a wholesome attitude toward sex. (p. 20)

Educational Implications. Success in this task leads to a well-balanced personality, with a reasonable degree of physical neatness and orderliness, and a set of attitudes about sex which permit sex to become a source of pleasure in later life without causing either guilt feelings on the one hand or complete servitude to the sex impulse on the other. (p. 21)

3. Learning to Get Along with Age-Mates

Nature of the Task. To learn the give-and-take of social life among peers. To learn to make friends and to get along with enemies. To develop a "social personality." (p. 22)

Educational Implications. School is the place where most children work out the task of learning to get along with age-mates. (p. 23)

4. Learning an Appropriate Masculine or Feminine Social Role

Nature of the Task. To learn to be a boy or a girl—to act out the role that is expected and rewarded. (p. 23)

Educational Implications. The school has little more than a remedial function in this task, which is to assist boys and girls who are having trouble with the task.

5. Developing Fundamental Skills in Reading, Writing, and Calculating

Nature of the Task. To learn to read, write, and calculate well enough to get along in American society. (p. 25)

Educational Implications. A large proportion of children come to the first grade "not ready" to learn to read. Many children have already learned to read before they enter the first grade. For perhaps half of the schoolchildren the process is interesting and rewarding.

6. Developing Concepts Necessary for Everyday Living

Nature of the Task. The task is to acquire a store of concepts sufficient for thinking effectively about ordinary occupational, civic, and social matters. (p. 27)

Educational Implications. In general, it may be urged that the school curriculum be as full of concrete experiences as possible in the early years, so as to help the child build concepts on a realistic basis; then more and more concept formation may be encouraged through reading in the later school years. (p. 28)

7. Developing Conscience, Morality, and a Sense of Values

Nature of the Task. To develop an inner moral control, respect for moral rules, and the beginning of a rational scale of values. (p. 29)

Educational Implications. The school affects the child's conscience and his morality: (a) through its teaching about morality, (b) through the teachers' punishments and rewards, (c) through the teachers' examples, (d) through the child's experiences in the peer group. (p. 31)

8. Achieving Personal Independence

Nature of the Task. To become an autonomous person, able to make plans and to act in the present and immediate future independently of one's parents and other adults. (p. 31)

Educational Implications. The school and the peer group are laboratories for the working-through of this task. Much of the success or failure of children on this task depends on the relationship between the teacher and the pupils. (p. 33)

9. Developing Attitudes Toward Social Groups and Institutions

Nature of the Task. To develop attitudes that are basically democratic. (p. 33)

Educational Implications. The school should work explicitly to inculcate certain basic democratic social attitudes which are generally agreed upon as desirable for all Americans. (p. 35)

The elementary school counseling program should focus on helping the child meet the normal developmental problems and developmental tasks of childhood. The following section addresses the developmental ages of elementary school children.

Developmental Age Profiles

In addition to the emotional, social, cognitive, and moral development of the elementary-age child, and Havighurst's developmental tasks, it is important to look at the developmental ages of the elementary school child, which may or may not coincide with his or her chronological age. Muro and Dinkmeyer called attention to the significant work done at the Gesell Institute of Child Behavior where profiles representing the developmental ages of children were established. These miniprofiles, generally representative of the age ranges of elementary school children, will give the readers an insight as to what might be expected from the child at these ages. It is to be emphasized that the ages represent the developmental ages of children, not necessarily their chronological ages.

The Five-Year-Old Child

They seldom attempt more than they can manage, they desire to be successful. The child is generally described as good, relating well to parents and teachers. They desire immediate attention and approval and, hopefully, affection. They can sit still and quietly, and tend to like school, particularly the girls. They like structure and routine, having a limited attention span. Their major activity is play; but they also like art including color, cut, draw, and paste activities. As the five-year-old approaches six, behavior is characterized by opposite extremes. They are much more restless than at the beginning of the year and tend to express frustrations more readily. The kindergarten child requires encouragement and a positive stance from those adults that work with this age.

The Six-Year-Old Child

The six-year-old child is the center of his or her own world, is extremely egocentric. They want to be the center of almost everything—first in line, "best," have the most crayons, etc. This is a dynamic age using all body parts, particularly the hands. They tire easily with poor habits and classroom problems more likely to occur in the afternoon. Many verbal sounds—clicking noises, tooth grinding, and throat clearing, and physical activity—swinging legs, incessant wiggling, mark the tensional outlets of this developmental age. The child may be brash, silly, argumentative, cry easily, and be boastful. They find sharing and taking turns difficult and especially find losing difficult. They may cheat, not tell the truth, and "collect" objects that don't belong to them. The concept of time is not meaning-

ful, they are here-and-now individuals. Fantasy is often real to this age child, sometimes as a way of achieving what real life hasn't provided. In working with the six-year-old child, praise and encouragement is very effective, criticism is ineffective and may be damaging. What may appear to be crisis situations to the adults in their lives, are in reality developmental concerns.

The Seven-Year-Old Child

The child who is developmentally seven becomes an active thinker, able to reason and arrive at conclusions. Their reflectiveness may lead to moodiness, sullenness, and self-criticism, frequently expressing a lack of self-confidence. They tend to internalize a lot and worry about school, their health, and their own or a parent's death. Seven's relationship with their teacher becomes more personal and may be extremely demanding of their attention. They are less distractible than the six-year-old and are able to concentrate more and complete tasks. Adults working with this age child can focus on affect because they are more in tune with their feelings. It is also good to keep in mind that the child still sees others as a primary source of problems.

The Eight-Year-Old Child

The relative calmness of seven is replaced by explosiveness in the child who is developmentally eight. They are energetic, highly dramatic, enthusiastic, inquisitive, and undertake more than they can perform. They are very physical, and are apt to run, jump, dance, whistle, climb on monkey bars, high fences, jump large mud puddles, and engage in rough-and-tumble activities. They are characterized by a "know-it-all" attitude and may be demanding of their parents and teachers. The teacher is still important but the group becomes increasingly important. They are able to assume responsibility for actions, still seek praise, and may be super critical of their own effort. Adults working with the eight-year-old need to be aware that they are ready for group counseling in the classroom or in the counselor's office, respond well to praise and encouragement, and find relationships with others important.

The Nine-Year-Old Child

The developmental age of nine can best be described as an age of general confusion. They are more placid and live more within the context of their own world. It is also an age of independence where the child increases the distance from parents and increasingly looks to the peer group. They work and play hard and love to test their own strength. Language now becomes a tool allowing them to express a wide range of emotions. They are able to think independently and critically. They are more interested in the community, life problems, cultures outside their own, maps, and geography. They have an increased sense of truthfulness and tend to lie only in minor matters. They prefer groups, are typically not self-confident, and are apt to compare themselves with group standards. They will rebel against authority, although they will still respond to adult demands. Adults working with these children will find group counseling works well. They also respond well to verbal counseling approaches, including clarification, tentative analysis, reflections, and even confrontation.

The Ten-Year-Old Child

Ten is apt to be obedient, generally good natured, fun to work with, shows a surprising scope of interest, and readily identifies with television characters. They are able to define time, get around alone, and run errands. They increasingly tend to tell the truth and are generally positive toward peers, school, and home. Tens accept themselves more, promoting greater acceptance of the behavior and attitudes of others. They are quite dependable, well adjusted, have a sense of humor, and are generally in a state of satisfactory equilibrium. They enjoy reading and talking more than writing, preferring an oral book report to a written one. Ten is the most delight for educators as they form good personal relationships with counselors and teachers. Adults working with this age need to be aware that they will participate actively in a group, in small group counseling, and in verbal one-on-one counseling. They tend to be more specific in naming their faults, they need counselor help to focus on what they do well.

The Eleven-Year-Old Child

Developmentally, this child shows more self-assertion, curiosity, and increased sociability. They are restive, they love to talk, and they wiggle a lot—this physical exuberance is sometimes equalled by the intensity of their emotions. They exhibit a wide range of emotions and are able to relate their feelings to adults. This is a social age and they fear being alone. They have a highly competitive spirit seeking to excel in the classroom, in sports, or in other activities. Their emotional mood swings reflect the developmental process. If an adult shows an interest, the child will respond with candor and relatively easy communication. Eleven likes group competition and has good peer interests. They will endlessly tease others and can be cruel to less fortunate peers. They can frustrate parents, teachers, and peers. Adults working with elevens need considerable patience as the child sometimes erupts so quickly and does not consider the impact of what they have done to others. They do enjoy group interaction and will usually function well in group settings. They also will respond well to contracts or plans worked out jointly with their counselor or teacher. (Muro & Dinkmeyer, 1977, pp. 38–54. Permission given by Wm. C. Brown Company, Publisher.)

Summary

A counseling and guidance program that emphasizes the developmental needs of students will assist teachers and parents in understanding and providing for these needs. The developmental viewpoint takes into consideration the emotional, social, cognitive, and moral development of each child. It also considers the developmental tasks of middle childhood and developmental ages of elementary school children. These areas greatly influence the personal development of the child; the developmental counselor will emphasize all of these areas to maximize the benefit to the child. The scope of this chapter does not allow for a complete discussion of child development; that is a course in itself. The elementary school counselor should become familiar with some of the major approaches to child development in order to gain an understanding of how the different developmental age levels can and do affect the children in the elementary school. The key to successful counseling at this age is flexibility: to meet the child at his or her developmental age and stage, and to help him or her develop the fullest potential for success at this most critical step of schooling. Accepting, caring for, and valuing the child are the greatest gifts we can give them.

Chapter **3**

$$\equiv\equiv\equiv\equiv\equiv\equiv$$

The Role of the Counselor

Why Counseling?

The Children's Defense Fund cites some frightening statistics concerning our children that move all who work with children to action:

- Every day, 2,989 American children see their parents divorced.
- Every 26 seconds, a child runs away from home.
- Every 47 seconds, a child is abused or neglected.
- Every seven minutes, a child is killed or injured by guns.
- Every 53 minutes, a child dies because of poverty.
- Every day, 100,000 children are homeless.
- Every school day, 135,000 children bring guns to school.
- Every eight seconds of the school day, a child drops out of school.
- Every day, six teenagers commit suicide. (Glosoff & Koprowicz, 1990, p. 3)

These statistics demand a response from those of us concerned with the welfare of our children in today's world.

In light of the above statistics about our children, it is disturbing to note a statement made by Van Hoose in the 1960s: "Recent research has concluded that potential school dropouts and potential delinquents can be identified during the elementary school years. Further, the evidence suggests that such problems could often be prevented through a broader program of school services and activities" (Van Hoose, 1968, p. 5). That statement has been echoed and re-echoed many times over the intervening years as those concerned about children have tried to counteract the deplorable statistics. The question is not the need for counseling in the schools or even the value of counseling; the confusion centers on the differences in expectations for school counselors across the country, particularly at the elementary level.

In the introduction to another 1968 book, Stone and Schertzer, in *Establishing Guidance Programs in Elementary Schools,* stated the following:

> *Few individuals, if any, question that elementary school guidance programs are needed. Demonstrably the need exists at several levels. Elementary school teachers and administrators increasingly demand a variety of specialized services to cope with pressing problems. Secondary school counselors bemoan the lack of earlier preventive efforts provided to minimize longstanding pupil problems. Parents are increasingly aware that the early school years are important to the later school and non-school development of their children. Various mental health authorities stress the contributions of early identification, prevention and treatment to good mental health. The elementary school becomes the natural focal point of these demands and expectations. (cited in Faust, 1968b, p. xi)*

The idea of elementary school counseling programs was not a new one at the time these two books were written. Elementary counseling was a reality in the 1950s, although little growth was noted until the late 1950s and mid-1960s. In 1954 a national study on pupil personnel services in the elementary schools indicated that there were 711 full-time and part-time counselors in elementary schools. By 1967 there were approximately 3,800 elementary counselors in schools throughout the United States (Van Hoose, 1968). The figure had jumped to 13,800 by 1983, and to approximately 21,340 by 1993 (American School Counselor Association, personal communication, April 1994).

Although the number of elementary school counselors is gradually increasing, elementary school counseling appears to need some significant advocates in order to be fully accepted as a viable part of the school program and not as just an ancillary service that can be eliminated when the budget in a school district undergoes serious cutbacks. In 1964 the National Defense Education Act (NDEA) was extended to include financial support to elementary school guidance and counseling programs (Van Hoose, 1968). This gave elementary counseling its first significant means to expand. In 1994, at the time of this writing, the Elementary School Counseling Demonstration Act (ESCDA) appears to be close to passing. If this act passes, it will "enhance the availability and quality of counseling services for elementary school children by providing grants to local education agencies to enable such agencies to establish effective and innovative counseling programs that can serve as national models" (ACA, 1994, p. 2). The monies provided in the bill would enable school districts to establish effective elementary school counseling programs, funded for up to three years. This would empower school districts in all states, particularly those where elementary counseling is not state mandated or state funded, to establish elementary school counseling programs, which in turn would provide evidence to help convince those who are not knowledgeable about the benefits of counseling at this level of exactly what can be accomplished. Historically speaking, it would be the biggest boost to elementary school guidance and counseling since its beginnings.

It is not the intent of this text to trace the history of the development of guidance and counseling in the elementary school; the intent is to establish the need for elementary school counseling programs, including the role description of the elementary school counselor. The remainder of the book, beyond this chapter, will be an expansion of this role as it relates to the established role and identified needs.

At the time of this writing only 12 states require all school districts to provide guidance and counseling services for all students in grades K–8, with 12 other states considering the requirement. One of the reasons so few states require elementary counseling may be the lack of clarity regarding the role of the elementary school counselor. Where the role and needs are clearly identified by the district, the mandating of counseling at the elementary level follows closely behind. An example of what happens when the need for elementary counseling is clearly defined was provided in the *Guidepost* of December 12, 1985. The article, "Dade County Mandates Elementary Counseling," identified the need for elementary school counselors, stressing the preventive aspects: "By hiring additional counselors at the elementary level, the county hopes to emphasize problem prevention" ("Dade County," 1985, p. 2). Dade County is the nation's fourth-largest school district and was the first of its size to require counselors in each elementary school. Each of their 176 elementary schools was assigned a full-time counselor to serve the county's students in grades K–6. Especially significant was the comment by Joyce Hickson, the supervisor of student services for the Dade County School District: "The impetus to hire the counselors really came from everywhere: from the building principals who knew the need, from parents who knew some of the children had counselors and theirs didn't, from students who might have had part-time counselors but didn't have one for their own school, from the professional organizations and from the division of student services" (p. 2). The Florida School Counselor Association President at that time, Betsy Folks, noted that the state's progressive attitude toward counseling also helped. Orange County, where she worked, had required elementary counseling for nine years, and the benefits of elementary counseling had been demonstrated. These programs focused on the developmental and preventive aspects of counseling; this is also the emphasis of this text.

The rationale for elementary school guidance and counseling programs was also supported by the Commission on Precollege Guidance and Counseling, appointed by the College Board, in their final report, *Keeping the Options Open: Recommendations.* Recommendation 4 stated the following: "Provide a program of guidance and counseling during the early and middle years of schooling, especially for students who traditionally have not been well-served by the schools" (College Entrance Examination Board, 1986, p. 16). The report discussed the need for children at an early age to receive help in building their self-esteem, developing their talents, and overcoming learning blocks. They noted that "a growing proportion of students are entering school with unmet physical and emotional needs that interfere with their ability to concentrate and learn" (p. 16). They also noted the limited or nonexistent counseling services at the elementary level. The six specific recommendations of activities for elementary school counselors fit in with the role descriptions delineated in the next sections that the American School Counselor Association and the State Guidance Consultants advocate.

It is important to establish a common ground in order to study the role of the elementary school counselor. The American School Counselor Association (ASCA) role statement for school counselors is an appropriate base for this; as such, it forms the base of the text. In the following chapters, the expanded role will be addressed.

ASCA Role Statement

The version of the American School Counselor Association role statement that specifically identifies an elementary counselor role was prepared in October 1980 by G. Dean Miller (the current statement is in Appendix A and Appendix D of this book). It incorporated and revised four role statements prepared separately in the 1970s: "The Unique Role of the Elementary School Counselor," approved in August 1977; "The Role of the Middle/Junior High School Counselor;" "The Role of the Secondary School Counselor," revised in 1976–77; and "The Role and Function of Postsecondary Counseling," May 1974. This role statement was approved by the 1980–81 ASCA Governing Board in January 1981.

The ASCA role statement for elementary school counselors stated the following functions:

- Provide in-service training to teachers to assist them with planning and implementing guidance interventions for young children (preschool to 3rd grade) in order to maximize developmental benefits (self-esteem, personal relationships, positive school attitude, sex-fair choices, and so forth) in the hope of preventing serious problems or minimizing the size of such problems, if and when they do occur.
- Provide consultations for teachers who need understanding and assistance with incorporating developmental concepts in teaching content as well as support for building a healthy classroom environment.
- Accommodate parents who need assistance with understanding normal child growth and development; improving family communication skills; or understanding their role in encouraging their children to learn.
- Cooperate with other school staff in the early identification, remediation, or referral of children with developmental deficiencies or handicaps.
- As children reach the upper elementary grades, effort is directed through the curriculum toward increasing student awareness of the relationship between school and work, especially the impact of educational choices on one's lifestyle and career development.

State guidance consultants in state departments of education are in a position to influence the directions of school counseling programs in their state. Because of this, their identification of important functions of elementary and middle school counselors will be considered, in addition to the ASCA role statement, in the following section.

State Guidance Consultants' Views

Miller (1986) surveyed guidance consultants throughout the United States in an attempt to identify what they saw as important functions of elementary and middle school counselors. A survey instrument, the "Counselor Function Form," was developed and used to identify these counselor functions.

The following list was identified by the state guidance consultants as the most important functions of elementary school counselors, in their order of importance:

- Consulting with teachers on student development needs and concerns
- Organizing and administering the school's guidance program
- Evaluating the effectiveness of the guidance program and its services
- Identifying students needing special assistance and making appropriate referrals
- Informing students, teachers, administrators, and parents about the school's guidance program
- Providing guidance activities for students in classrooms
- Consulting with students, parents, and school personnel for improving the school's educational climate
- Providing individual counseling to assist students in making personal and social decisions
- Keeping abreast of current professional developments by attending conferences and workshops. (Miller, 1986, pp. 166–167).

These functions mirror much of the ASCA role statement presented previously.

Elementary School Counselors

It is apparent from the above that the elementary counselor's role emphasizes working with the significant adults in the child's life—teachers, parents, and other school staff. It is clear that the elementary school counselor role expectation includes more than merely counseling. All of the five functions listed in the ASCA role statement mentioned the developmental processes of children. The significance of the counselor's role in maximizing opportunities for developmental task mastery is obvious; this can be accomplished by implementing guidance interventions. Hoyt expressed his concern that the term *guidance* was being dropped in favor of the term *counseling*. He stated that "it is essential that school counselors be viewed as educators by their colleagues in education—and this can best be done by emphasizing the guidance team approach" (Hoyt, 1993, p. 272). Working closely and collaboratively with teachers and other school staff is a significant role of the elementary school counselor, a role that assures the counselor of being viewed as an educator.

The author had the significance of this approach, working with all children in the classroom in a team approach with the teacher, illustrated in a very tangible way during the spring of 1993. The author was in a position to offer the superintendent of a small, two-school elementary district the services of six second-semester practicum students for an entire semester. The class and professor met weekly during the scheduled class time in one of the schools; the students each "adopted" a kindergarten and first-grade class, each spending a total of 2 to 4 hours per week in these rooms conducting classroom guidance activities. As a part of this, they met with a few of the children individually or in small groups, but the majority of their time was spent in the classrooms. The author solicited the assistance of one of her second-year intern students to help supervise the students, alternating between weekly observation and supervision sessions with the individual students. The services were enthusiastically received by the children, the teachers, the parents, the two principals, the superintendent, and the school board. This same superintendent and board dropped their counseling program three years previous to this. This is a low-income, high ethnic minority, gang-influenced area in a state that is undergoing severe financial difficulties; yet, at the end of the semester, this same superintendent and same board reinstated counseling, hiring a full-time counselor to serve the two schools. Three of the six practicum students decided to do their year-long, 600-hour supervised internship in these two schools. What made the difference? The superintendent said this: "We got rid of counseling because we couldn't justify a counselor serving 40 to 50 kids when we have 500 needy children." Emphasizing the classroom guidance team approach could have saved that counselor's job.

Professional Rationale

The training of the school counselor at all levels is grounded in the behavioral sciences. Along with this, the different stages of developmental growth of the students at each level becomes the focus of the school counselor in identifying the critical developmental tasks from childhood through adolescence to adulthood. Counselors become an integral part of the staff, functioning as developmental facilitators in student support-services teams that usually include school psychology, social work, and nursing. Humes and Hohenshil, in looking at the differences in role functions of elementary school counselors, school psychologists, and school social workers, noted that these specialists "must work together to see that pupils are served better" (1987, p. 44). Counselors can insure this by providing consultation and in-service programs for staff in the area of developmental psychology, in addition to providing parents with help in understanding child and adolescent development. This approach may include school psychologists and school social workers, as all strive to serve the students in their schools. At the same time, the student is the recipient of individual and small group counseling to complement the help given to the teachers and parents. Retraining, studying new approaches, and an active involvement in state and national professional organizations helps the counselor to continue to be informed and competently skilled throughout his or her professional career.

The Nature of the Helping Process

The developmental needs identified in the psychology of children, adolescents, and adults continues to be emphasized in the helping process. Elementary school counselors, by virtue of their training, are able to serve the developmental needs of all children. The personal development aspects most associated with life success become a focus for counselors in their work with the school program and with parents and the school staff. The cognitive developmental stages of psychological maturity are a major thrust of guidance and counseling interventions at the different educational levels. The important life success qualities include the development of competencies, ego maturity, reasoning, and so on. Structured developmental guidance experiences, conducted by the counselor in small groups and in the classroom setting, serve to promote the growth of these psychological aspects of human development. The school counselor, working closely with the classroom teacher, can insure the logical inclusion of these interventions in the curriculum and in the classroom. Chapters 4 and 9 will expand on the importance of and use of developmental guidance experiences in group and classroom settings.

Consultation with teachers and parents is a significant function of the school counselor at all levels in the helping process. The state guidance consultants identified consultation with teachers on student development needs as the most important function of the elementary school counselor. Consultation with teachers emphasizes communication skills; consultation with parents also emphasizes communication skills in the family, including the development of strategies for encouraging learning in their children. Consultation with teachers, parents, and principals will be covered in depth in Chapter 5.

The Developmental Approach

Havighurst (1973), an early pioneer in developmental tasks and education, first addressed the issue of developmental tasks in 1948 as a professor at the University of Chicago. He noted that the early elementary school counselors appeared to use the more traditional approach or framework similar to that used by high school counselors rather than a developmental approach. In the 1960s, as the focus turned from a problem-oriented, children-in-crisis approach to an approach dealing with all children, the developmental aspect of elementary counseling emerged. "The new elementary school counselor was first committed to building effective learning climates for children, all children, rather than 'curing' certain deviant students" (Faust, 1968b, p. 2). The need at the elementary level is for developmental counseling; helping the child meet the normal developmental problems and developmental tasks of childhood should be stressed. In a 1969 publication from the Minnesota Department of Education, Gum addressed the developmental needs of children. He strongly emphasized the developmental approach, stating that "it seems very illogical to have guidance services in the secondary but not at the elementary level, and the developmental approach would seem to be particularly appropriate to this beginning educational level" (Gum, 1969, p. 10).

An elementary school counseling program may be developmental, preventive, remedial, or a combination of these. In a sense, developmental and preventive approaches tend to overlap in the school setting. To differentiate between them, in order to focus on the developmental aspect of elementary counseling, we need to look at the widely accepted definition of the two words. To *develop* is to expand or realize the potentialities of someone; to *prevent* is to keep someone from doing something or to hinder or impede them. The developmental program is a more positive and growth-oriented approach to counseling than is the preventive program. A developmental counseling and guidance program emphasizes the developmental needs of students and is designed to assist teachers and parents in understanding and providing for these needs, which in turn expands or helps them realize their potential. The ASCA position statement on the "School Counselor and Developmental Guidance" (see the full statement in Appendix C) defines developmental guidance as "that component of all guidance efforts which fosters planned intervention within educational and other human development services programs at all points in the human life cycle. It vigorously stimulates and actively facilitates the total development of individuals in all areas—personal, social, emotional, career, moral-ethical, cognitive, aesthetic—and to promote the integration of the several components into an individual life-style" (American School Counselor Association, 1984).

Muro and Dinkmeyer indicated the positive aspects of developmental counseling: "Unlike some counseling theories, developmental counseling does not focus on psychopathology and remediation. It is a viable model for consideration by counselors working with large populations of school-aged children and adolescents" (1977, p. 63). Berry (1979), in an article addressing the need for a theoretical base for elementary school counseling, called attention to a "failure of elementary counseling and guidance to develop a theoretical base that relates guidance and counseling processes to the process of child development in the early childhood years" (p. 513). Myrick (1989) viewed developmental guidance as something for all students: "There is an organized curriculum that is sequential and flexible and that includes specific objectives related to personal and social development" (p. 15). Blocher (1980) noted that the developmental approach allows the counselor to draw upon a wide range of interventions, which expands the options available. Gibson, Mitchell, and Higgins (1983), in addressing elementary guidance and counseling programs, stated that "there is no universally accepted definition of elementary school guidance. However, there is considerable agreement that elementary school guidance programs should be developmentally oriented" (p. 183). Colwell noted that "elementary school counselors are a vehicle to help children get on with life. We are not providing crisis counseling, but developmental counseling. Children need developmental experts to help them grow throughout the different stages in their life" (cited in Schafer, 1990, p. 1).

Reynolds, in her position as the contact person for the Developmental School Counseling Professional Interest Network, outlined a model for developmental school counseling compiled from a number of implemented models, all based on the writings of Gysbers and Myrick. The foundational beliefs, listed below, form a basis of the developmental approach:

1. The School Counseling Program should meet the needs of all students.
2. The School Counseling Program should be balanced including preventive as well as responsive activities.
3. The School Counseling Program should be driven by a set of defined student outcomes which are based on universal and local student needs.
4. The School Counseling Program should include activities which are sequential in nature leading to defined student outcomes.
5. School Counselors should work collaboratively with other school and community personnel in implementing the Developmental School Counseling Program.
6. School Counseling efforts are most effective when spent in direct contact with students and coordination of those activities.
7. School Counselors and School Counseling Programs should be held accountable. (Reynolds, 1993, p. 12)

These beliefs should be an integral part of all elementary school counseling programs.

As ASCA president, Humphrey (1993) strongly stated her position: "We are obligated as stewards of the future of successive generations of American children, to demand and participate more in the creation and delivery of comprehensive developmental school counseling programs, which are integrated more into the school curriculum and educational programs. We are obligated to demonstrate leadership and proactive stances on these issues for they directly impact the future of our profession and those we work with and for in our professional and personal roles as school counselors" (p. 2).

For counselor education programs desiring accreditation by the Council for Accreditation of Counseling and Related Educational Programs (CACREP), all students in the program are required to have certain curricular experiences with demonstrated knowledge and skills in a number of areas. One of the areas under Program Development, Implementation, and Evaluation states that "studies in this area include design, implementation, and evaluation of a comprehensive, developmental school program" (Council for Accreditation of Counseling and Related Educational Programs, 1994, p. 76). The emphasis on developmental counseling is clearly spelled out.

It is interesting to note that over a period of nearly 50 years, the consensus of these various writers, including professional guidelines, still seems to prevail: that an elementary school counseling program should be developmental in nature, not remedial. With this emphasis, it is surprising that so many elementary school counselors are occupied full-time on a one-to-one basis with children who have problems in the school setting. Unclear role definition would seem to be part of the reason for this. In addition, some elementary teachers are not sure that they need help with any children other than those who are having problems of some sort. In a survey of elementary school principals in 38 school districts that examined their perceptions regarding elementary school counseling services, the results demonstrated that these elementary school principals seemed to have limited knowledge of the many functions that elementary counselors may perform (Fleming, Martin, & Martin, 1986).

In a more recent survey 536 California elementary school principals, randomly selected from all 58 counties in California, were sent surveys asking about their perception of the elementary school counselors' role (Holmgren, 1992). California, with approximately 12 percent of the school children in the United States, has relatively few elementary school counselors, which prompted the author to investigate this concern. A survey was designed based on the ASCA role statement and the nine functions listed by the state guidance consultants. A list of 10 statements was developed for the principals' response; in addition, the principals were asked to list other areas that they felt the elementary school counselor should be involved in. Principals perceived individual counseling, providing classroom guidance activities, and providing in-service training to teachers as the most important functions for the elementary school counselor. Principals wrote many comments on their surveys; one stated succinctly what many noted regarding the need for elementary school counselors: "We may save a few bucks in the beginning (not having an elementary school counselor) but we pay for it tenfold by the time the kids get to high school."

Another reason many programs do not stress the developmental approach to elementary school counseling may have to do with their training. In a 1986 publication of the Association for Counselor Education and Supervision (ACES), separate articles by two well-known and respected educators in the field of counselor preparation had conflicting emphases regarding counselor education/training. Patterson (1986) strongly stated that "counselor educators seem to have gone overboard on skill training" (p. 10). "Students who are to become professionals must have a theoretical foundation on which to base practice" (p. 11). Gazda (1986) began his article with this statement: "My belief is that the training/educating of counselors has over-emphasized teaching of theories at the expense of operationalizing the theory and the development of skills" (p. 30). Where there is lack of agreement on training, the professional journals and texts will reflect this, causing the reader to question if there is a "best" way.

Still another reason that elementary counseling programs seem to emphasize remediation rather than development is that, unfortunately, the remedial approach is well ingrained in the minds of administrators, teachers, and parents. A remedial counseling program locks the counselor into providing remedies, thus becoming a crisis counselor for a few rather than emphasizing positive growth experiences for all children. The developmental counseling program focuses on all children in the school, helping to build effective learning climates where all children will benefit. In order to carry this out effectively, it is important that the counselor know and understand the school's philosophy toward children and education. An elementary school counseling program, to be truly accepted and supported, must be an integral part of the school in philosophy and in practice. Riles, former superintendent of public instruction in California, in addressing approaches to providing guidance services in the schools, stated the following: "Address the predictable needs of children in programs that engage all of the school's personnel. Integrating the elements of guidance and counseling programs into the curriculum, the total education plan has to be excellent use of time and staff. And it is easy to see how quickly and directly the school atmosphere can be affected when the whole staff is participating" (Riles, 1982, p. 4).

The author emphasizes the ASCA's role statement for the elementary school counselor in the area of working with teachers in order to maximize developmental benefits such as self-esteem, personal relationships, and school attitudes. Elementary school counselors working with teachers in the classroom using developmental counseling and guidance experiences can have a positive impact on important developmental qualities of students, because the guidance program affecting the vast majority of children is that carried on by the classroom teacher. Developmental guidance experiences are designed to help students become more aware of their feelings and to practice expressing them; developmental guidance experiences emphasize positive growth experiences. A group of American School Counselor Association (ASCA) leaders, in a discussion of issues in elementary school counseling, succinctly stated that "the ASCA definition provides a foundation for the future of school counseling" (Bailey, Deery, Gehrke, Perry, & Whitledge, 1989, p. 12).

ASCA published a booklet in 1994, *Student Competencies: A Guide for School Counselors,* which was developed by the Ohio Coalition for the Future of School Counseling. The student competencies by grade level, K–12, are developmental goals in three areas: personal/social goals, educational goals, and career goals. The goals in each of the three areas are followed by competencies needed by the students to accomplish the goals; these provide an excellent basis to establish a developmental elementary counseling program. The booklet is available through the American School Counselor Association, 5999 Stevenson Avenue, Alexandria, VA 22304.

In addition to the above, ASCA developed an advocacy presentation packet for ASCA leaders to use in public presentations. The packet, School Counseling 2000, is intended to be used for presentations in school districts and other significant areas to enable counselors to connect school counseling programs to the educational reform movement. The six national education goals are identified and described; master copies enable the presenter to construct overhead transparencies for the presentation. The counselor's task in achieving the goals is delineated after each goal. The packet also includes "The Role of the School Counselor in Preparing Students for the Workforce," based on the June 1991 U.S. Department of Labor report, "What Work Requires of Schools." In this report, a comprehensive school counseling program is identified and described. The entire packet is available through the American School Counselor Association, same address as given for the booklet in the previous paragraph.

Professional Commitment of Elementary School Counselors

The school counselor is professionally committed to follow established principles and guidelines in counseling and guidance relationships. Confidentiality in the counseling relationship is of utmost importance to the effectiveness of the counseling relationship. The professional commitment of school counselors extends to students, parents, teachers, administrators, and others in the community.

The counselor's responsibility to the profession is also significant. It is the counselor's responsibility to insure good practice and continued growth in knowledge and skills for the benefit of students, parents, teachers, and the profession. Attending and becoming involved in in-service meetings, professional conferences, and workshops are ways of increasing professional competence. Using sound ethical practices for professional counselors as delineated in the *Ethical Standards* of the American Counseling Association (see Appendix B) is another responsibility of the school counselor; these standards will be discussed in Chapter 11.

A most important responsibility to the profession is to become an active member of the American School Counselor Association, a division of the American Counseling Association. It is a private, nonprofit organization dedicated to the growth and development of the counseling profession. In addition, membership and active participation in state and local (where they exist) associations enhance the personal and professional growth of the school counselor.

Summary

The impact of elementary school counseling as a means to address the frightening statistics cited at the beginning of this chapter should not be underestimated. The identification of many of the potential problem students can be accomplished at the elementary level where a developmental counseling program that addresses the needs of all students will help counteract many of these statistics. An elementary counseling program emphasizes problem prevention. A counseling program that follows the ASCA role statement for elementary school counselors can and will make a difference for these children.

Theoretical Approaches to Elementary School Counseling

Many strongly believe there is no single approach to counseling in the elementary school that is the "right" approach; there is a wide variety of appropriate theoretical approaches. An elementary school counselor's choice of the particular approach or approaches to use has much to do with the training of the counselor plus his or her subsequent practice and skill acquisition. What is important to consider, and what is usually stressed in counselor education programs, is the "fit" of the particular theory to the counselor's personality and style. The theory enables the counselor to know the direction to take and to anticipate with some degree of certainty the results of certain actions taken in the sessions.

There is a predictive quality present when a theory is used by the elementary school counselor. This is particularly significant for the counselor who conducts classroom guidance activities, because elementary school classrooms of today contain a diversified mixture of children and increasingly disruptive student behavior, which requires a knowledge base of effective classroom management on the part of the counselor. This knowledge base, built on proven theoretical approaches, allows the counselor more alternative strategies in working with elementary-age children. A counselor may use one theoretical approach in a classroom setting and another in a small group or individual session. The counselor may find that the approach that works with one child or a group of children may not work with another child or group of children, necessitating a working knowledge of a variety of theoretical approaches.

Five theoretical approaches that particularly lend themselves to the elementary school setting will be presented in this chapter: Adlerian counseling, behavioral counseling, developmental counseling, reality therapy, and self-concept theory. As the counselor implements the theory, it should be appropriate to both the setting and the counselor's personality characteristics and style. The elementary school counselor needs to know the alternatives available for use in the elementary school setting, selecting those he or she feels competent to use.

Adlerian Counseling

Alfred Adler was the founder of individual psychology, frequently referred to as Adlerian psychology. Adler was associated with Freud in the Vienna Psychoanalytic Society until 1911, when he developed his own approach, which became known as individual psychology. "The term Individual Psychology stems from Adler's stress on the uniqueness of the individual and the creation of his own 'Life Style,' as opposed to Freud's stress on general instincts or drives, common to all individuals, and the applicability of general symbolism" (Adler, K., in Adler, A., 1963, p. iv). Life style, to Adler, was completed in the child by four or five years of age, with new experiences interpreted from his or her point of life style view from then on. This style of life, unique to the individual, determines how the individual will think, act, and feel throughout his or her life. In Adler's approach the style of life, not the symptoms that the child exhibited, was to be treated.

Adler measured the mental health of the child by the social interest that the child is able to develop and make a part of his or her life style. These social feelings have their beginnings in earliest infancy and must be encouraged by those closest to the child in order to develop fully. Children with social interest, according to Adler, have a sense of belonging and are willing to cooperate and participate with others. Children who do not have enough social feelings will fear failure and suffer feelings of inadequacy, which leads to discouragement. Adler proposed early treatment of children, postulating that it was easier to change the life style when the child was young; based on this belief, he started his child guidance clinics in Vienna.

Adler contributed significantly to the understanding of problems associated with children in the establishment of the first child guidance clinic in Vienna, which was in connection with the Viennese school system. He realized the great need for child guidance, developing "the plan to teach the teachers, for through the school I could reach hundreds of children at once" (Ansbacher & Ansbacher, 1956, p. 392). By 1934 there were over 30 of these child guidance clinics, Adler had lectured to over 600 public school teachers and teachers-in-training on difficult children as well as normal children. These clinics had an unusual approach in that they were conducted in front of audiences of psychologists, teachers, and interested parents, with the children involved coming to realize that their problems were not private but of interest and concern to others, thus becoming a community problem. It was during this time, when Adler was working with these families in the child guidance clinics, that he introduced the term *inferiority feelings* and developed a supportive approach to work effectively with those so identified (Thompson & Rudolph, 1992).

To Adler, the family constellation, and consequent birth-order position, is a significant factor in the establishment of personality characteristics in children. There are exceptions to this rule, although generalizations of stereotypic behavior have been made that are widely used by Adlerians. Adler saw the psychological situation of each child influencing that child, the way the child perceives himself or herself. "It is not, of course, the child's number in the order of successive births which influences his character, but the situation into which he is born and the way in which he interprets it" (cited in Ansbacher & Ansbacher, 1956, p. 377). The effect of the birth order lacks sufficient research support; in spite of this, counselors using the family constellation in parent education groups, in teacher groups, and in classrooms believe there is a definite correlation of birth order and observed behaviors.

Unique Adlerian Contributions

Family Constellation   The following is a brief summary of the relativity of the birth-order position and its implications as Adler saw them (in Ansbacher & Ansbacher, 1956):

The Oldest Child.   The first-born child is generally given a good deal of attention and spoiling. It is a unique position, as he or she is an only child until "dethroned" upon the birth of a second child, a term Adler saw as exactly depicting the change in the situation. The oldest child often strives to protect and help others. At the same time, power and authority are important. Adler saw the oldest child comprising the greatest proportion of problem children.

The Second Child.   The second child is in a different position in that there is always an older child with which to share attention. The second child is usually trying to catch up with or surpass the first child. Sometimes second children place their goals so high that they will suffer for it for the rest of their lives. They often find different areas to compete in; if, for example, the oldest is a good student, the second one will find another area to become adept at, or will become defeated.

The Youngest Child.   The youngest child is the only one that can't be dethroned. To Adler, this child is always the baby and is probably the most pampered. In human history, there are countless stories of how the youngest child excelled the older brothers and sisters. A youngest child may also suffer from inferiority feelings because everyone in the family is older, stronger, and more experienced. Adler found that the second largest proportion of problem children came from among the youngest, because everyone spoiled them.

The Only Child.   The only child usually wants to be the center of attention all the time. Only children often feel that it is an injustice to challenge their position, and feel it is a right of theirs to have this attention. This child often has difficulties in later life when he or she is no longer the center of attention. Many times an only child is born into a timid environment with timid and pessimistic parents. It is usually more difficult for an only child to make friends with children in his or her age group.

Other Sibling Situations.   An only boy brought up among girls has a hard time in that he is raised in a feminine atmosphere with father usually gone most of the day. He feels that he must assert his difference and superiority, which will cause his development to be extreme. He typically will train to be either very weak or very strong. Similarly, an only girl among boys is apt to develop either very feminine or very masculine qualities; she may feel insecure and helpless in life. Children who come in the middle of a family of four or more children usually develop a more stable character, and the conflict between the children tends to be less fierce. In other words, the larger the family, usually the less conflict and strife among the children. In addition to these situations, one sibling in early childhood becoming a standout in some area often becomes the disadvantage to another (Ansbacher & Ansbacher, 1956, pp. 376–382).

It is the way the child experiences or perceives his or her world that becomes reality; it is how the child interprets what is happening, not what actually happens to the individual. Elementary school counselors and teachers might consider the birth-order position of children who are exhibiting behavior that is difficult to account for. A knowledge of the birth order, or family constellation, will help the counselor and teacher identify how the child perceives reality, which in turn may affect the child's relationships in the school as well as in the home.

Dreikurs, a student of Adler, is credited for establishing the Adlerian theoretical approach in the United States, in 1938 in Chicago. Here for the first time staff workers in the child guidance center heard about the goal of the misbehaving child. To Dreikurs every action of the child has a purpose; it is goal directed (Lowe, 1982). In 1947 the Individual Psychology Association in Chicago extended the child guidance movement into other areas of the city, resulting in several Community Child Guidance Centers. Dreikurs saw the purpose of these centers as providing practical training to help parents and teachers understand children: "Their main function is not to treat, but to instruct parents and children in new patterns of family relationships, leading to a better understanding and a more efficient resolution of problems and conflicts. The resulting corrective efforts on the part of parents and teachers, and the improvement of the child and of the family relationship in general is the result of a learning process" (Dreikurs, 1959, p. 17). These education centers treated both normal and problem children and created the framework for much of the Adlerian family counseling carried on today.

Goals of Misbehavior   Children, according to Dreikurs, are motivated by one or another of four goals when they misbehave and fail to cooperate. He saw these goals as not only able to explain the child's misbehavior but also recognizable by the child if the child is confronted with them in appropriate ways:

> *The child may try to get* attention, *to put others in his service, since he believes that otherwise he would be lost and worthless. Or he may attempt to prove his* power *in the belief that only if he can do what he wants and defy adult pressure can he be somebody. Or he may seek* revenge, *the only means by which he feels significant is to hurt others as he feels hurt by them. Or he may display actual or imagined* deficiencies *in order to be left alone: as long as nothing is demanded of him, his deficiency, stupidity or inability may not become obvious; this would mean utter worthlessness. (Dreikurs, Grunwald, & Pepper, 1971, p. 17)*

The four goals of misbehavior are observable in children up to age 10, which includes most of the elementary school period. Parents, teachers, and counselors need to be aware of these goals in order to help correct the child's mistaken belief that only in these ways can he or she be significant. Dreikurs proposed identifying the child's goal by asking four questions: (1) Are you looking for special attention? (Attention); (2) Are you trying to get your own way? (Power); (3) Are you trying to hurt others as they hurt you? (Revenge); and (4) Do you just want to be left alone? (Helplessness). The child will usually react in an observable way when his or her goal is identified by these questions. It is helpful to know the child's goal in order to understand the behavior and provide the necessary help for the child.

Wickers (1988) developed a "Misbehavior Reaction Checklist for Teachers" as a useful technique for determining the child's mistaken goal by recognizing the teacher's most frequent, immediate reaction. It uses a short checklist requiring only five minutes or so to complete. He has used this in conjunction with Manly's (1986) "Goal of Misbehavior Inventory" (changing the title to "Goals of Behavior") for the child to complete. With this he is able to note any differences in goals.

Natural and Logical Consequences   Natural and logical consequences constitute another significant aspect of the Adlerian approach. In this approach, "natural consequences" are viewed as the events that would occur naturally without a teacher or parent interfering in any way. An example of a natural consequence would be a child dawdling on the way to school and thus arriving late. The child is then faced with the consequences of being late for school. If the natural consequence is undesirable (for example, a child playing in the street and getting hit by a car), there is a need for logical consequences. "Logical consequences" are usually arranged by an adult so that the consequence is related in an understandable way to the misdeed. For example, a child leaving a bike outside at night so that the parent takes responsibility for it gives the parent the option of deciding what will be done with the bike as a logical consequence.

Dreikurs and Grey provide an excellent example of a logical consequence used in an elementary school situation:

> *A few weeks ago one of the boys in our classroom was constantly getting out of his seat, leaning on his desk, and doing his work from a half-standing position. I finally asked him whether he would rather stand or sit while doing his work. It made no difference to me which way he preferred. The boy stated that he would prefer standing. I explained to him he would then no longer need his seat and we could therefore take the chair out of the room, which we did, allowing the boy to stand up for the rest of the day. The following day, at the beginning of the period, I asked the boy whether he would like standing or sitting. This time he preferred sitting, and we no longer had any difficulty with him about his half-standing position. (Dreikurs & Grey, 1968, pp. 144–145)*

The child was not "put down" in this illustration. The child had a choice in his behavior and was allowed to act accordingly. A logical consequence is concerned with what the child needs to learn in order to function appropriately in the setting (the classroom, in this case). Punishment only reinforces that the adult is in control rather than holding the child responsible and accountable for his or her behavior.

Counseling Strategies

The relevance of the Adlerian approach to elementary school counseling is well demonstrated by Adler's child guidance clinics, where he emphasized working with the teachers. Teachers, and eventually counselors, adopted these preventive methods that Adler started in schools, using them in individual classes. Belkin (1975), in evaluating the application of different psychoanalytic principles to school counseling, noted that Adler's approach is particularly applicable to the school counseling setting. When using the Adlerian/Dreikursian approach in the elementary school, the counselor should understand the child's present goals and motivations in order to understand the child's behaviors. Only in understanding the child's goal can the behavior be placed in proper perspective.

In Adlerian counseling the individual is helped to see his or her life style, to understand the purposes of behavior and the ways of relating to others in order to change the behaviors that seem to work against his or her purposes. Adlerians emphasize the following points:

1. Man's every action has a purpose.
2. Social striving is primary, the individual seeks to be recognized as worthy among his peers and others; feelings of adequacy among others are vital to the individual.
3. Maladjustment is interpersonal; it is a lack of interaction with or concern for others. (Drum & Figler, 1973, p. 60)

As the counselor develops strategies for working with children, it is important to keep these points in mind.

Adler saw the classroom as a community where each member is accorded equal status and trained to enjoy cooperation. He believed that children, through the help and guidance of the teacher, can help each other in the classroom setting: "An educator's most important task, one might say his holy duty, is to see to it that no child is discouraged at school, and that a child who enters school already discouraged regains his self-confidence through his school and his teacher" (cited in Ansbacher & Ansbacher, 1956, p. 400). He viewed this task as fitting in well with the goals of an educator, noting that children can be educated only when they anticipate the future. Forty years later, this is an excellent goal for the elementary school counselor: to see that children are encouraged in the school setting. This is a goal to which all elementary counselors can subscribe.

Application of Adlerian Counseling Strategies   The author directed an ESEA Title IV-C project, termed the "Child Encouragement Project," carried out in several elementary schools in Albuquerque, New Mexico, from 1977 to 1980. The Child Encouragement Project (CEP) dealt with the philosophies and techniques of training behavior based on Adlerian psychology and further identified and carried out by Dreikurs, Dinkmeyer, McKay, and Christensen. The target population was the "discouraged child" as described by parents or teachers as being a nuisance, lazy, anxious, stubborn, angry, cruel, withdrawn, dumb, and/or hopeless. The project goal was the "encouraged child."

The encouraged child is one who demonstrates the following:

1. a respect for the rights of others
2. a tolerance for the misbehavior of others
3. an ability to work cooperatively with others
4. the courage to risk failure
5. a feeling of belonging to a group
6. a sense of personal value or worth
7. socially acceptable goals
8. the ability to adapt to changed situations
9. honesty
10. acceptance of responsibility for his/her own actions
11. an ability to share
12. some group oriented (we) goals rather than personal (me) goals exclusively. (Child Encouragement Project, 1977, Section C, p. 3)

An elementary school counselor was the project consultant for two elementary schools during the first year of the Child Encouragement Project. The project was expanded the second year to include three more elementary schools, with two more elementary counselors serving as project consultants for those schools. In the third year, a full-time project consultant was hired to train the project counselors as the CEP was expanded to include four more elementary schools. The elementary school counselors implemented training programs for students, teachers, and parents in the project schools using the Adlerian approach.

The Child Encouragement Project was designed to train teachers, parents, counselors, and administrators in skills and techniques necessary for facilitating "encouraged child" behavior. The program included identification of a child's purpose of misbehavior, the recognition and use of the child's strengths and assets, and procedures for utilizing the knowledge to effect change in the child's behavior at home and at school. The project also included training in skills and techniques for recognizing and affecting group dynamics and roles in the classroom and in family constellations. Emphasis was on teacher knowledge of the process of recognizing and overcoming "discouraged" behavior, parent knowledge of facilitating "encouraged" child behavior, and child knowledge of purposes of their own behavior. This three-pronged emphasis facilitated the recognition by the children of their mistaken goals, encouraging them to take control of their own behavior. It was fascinating to observe children in an elementary classroom able to identify their own behavior, as well as peer behavior, with comments such as "He is in a power struggle with you," or "She's just trying to get attention," and so on.

Parent Training in the Child Encouragement Project.   The parent groups in the Child Encouragement Project were trained using the Systematic Training for Effective Parenting (STEP) program designed by Dinkmeyer and McKay (1976, 1989), based on the Adlerian method of training parents. The project consultants found this to be a highly effective way to help parents deal with the frustrations caused by raising children in today's complicated world. Currently, many elementary school counselors across the country use the STEP program for conducting parent study groups in the elementary schools. It is a nine-session study group designed to help parents find more effective ways of dealing with their children. The areas covered in the nine sessions are as follows:

1. Understanding children's behavior and misbehavior
2. Understanding more about your child and about yourself as a parent
3. Encouragement: Building your child's confidence and feelings of worth
4. Communication: How to listen to your child
5. Communication: Exploring alternatives and expressing your ideas and feelings to children
6. Natural and logical consequences: A method of discipline that develops responsibility
7. Applying natural and logical consequences to other concerns
8. The family meeting
9. Developing confidence and using your potential

The Adlerian approach is particularly well suited to group and classroom settings, such as organizing classroom discussion groups. Counselors in the classroom setting, by the use of planned activities and exercises, help children learn to work together cooperatively, develop a sense of belonging to the group, and listen to each other. Many of the activities stress recognizing and using the child's strengths and assets rather than dwelling on negative behaviors. Dreikurs, Grunwald, and Pepper (1971) worked with teachers to implement class discussions in elementary schools. The group discussions provide an opportunity for participation for all of the children in an atmosphere of mutual understanding. The class as a group works on the same problem at the same time, helping the children realize that there may be a number of solutions to the same problem.

Class meetings can include a variety of activities that will take place in the classroom, in a discussion of how the classroom furniture should be arranged, where to go on a field trip, how to set up an environmental fair, and so on. Because the elementary school counselor finds classroom and group settings to be particularly advantageous in reaching all children, the Adlerian approach deserves an in-depth study by students of counseling.

Behavioral Counseling

Behavioral modification or counseling probably brings to mind some earlier classes in psychology and learning theory, where readers were first exposed to names such as Pavlov, Tolman, Thorndike, Watson, and Skinner. Later, in courses in counselor training, a name associated more with behavioral counseling than psychology or behavioral modification became familiar—John Krumboltz. Although behavioral counseling does not have a principal theorist, the works of Skinner and, later, Krumboltz have probably had the greatest influence on how teachers and counselors work with elementary-age students.

Behavioral counseling largely began through early efforts made by people such as Dollard and Miller and Pepinsky and Pepinsky to put existing counseling theories into a behavioral framework. In addition to their efforts, the Cubberly Conference at Stanford University in 1965, with Krumboltz playing a major role, gave behavioral counseling its momentum (Hansen, Stevic, & Warner, 1986).

For many years schools have expressed concern about behavior problems among their students. Disruptive classroom behavior greatly limits the benefits gained from the school experiences for the child or children involved. The question of how to help these children coupled with the behavioral approach to counseling fits in well with the elementary school counselor's role, because counselors deal with observable behavior and the results of that behavior. This section will look at the aspects of behavioral counseling that favor a behavioral model for elementary school counseling.

There are many viewpoints on just what constitutes behavioral counseling; we will look at several of these, from earlier views to more recent writings, ones that accept the view that most human behavior is learned. Thoreson (cited in Schertzer & Stone, 1980) characterized behavioral counseling with these five statements:

1. Most human behavior is learned and is therefore subject to change.
2. Specific changes in the individual's environment can assist in altering relevant behaviors; counseling procedures seek to bring about relevant changes in student behavior by altering the environment.
3. Social learning principles, such as those of reinforcement and social modeling, can be used to develop counseling procedures.

4. Counseling effectiveness and the outcome of counseling are assessed by changes in specific student behaviors outside the counseling interview.

5. Counseling procedures are not static, fixed, or predetermined, but can be specifically designed to assist the student in solving a particular problem. (p. 188)

With these statements in mind, the elementary counselor is able to see that the child's behavior, or misbehavior, can be changed and reshaped in a manner acceptable to those in the immediate environment. The elementary school counselor is in an excellent position to help students resolve the deviant behaviors that caused them to get into trouble initially, because most of the elementary school counselor referrals seem to center on inappropriate behavior on the part of the student.

Corey (1977) noted that behavioral counseling, or therapy, has some unique characteristics: "Behavior therapy, in contrast to most other therapy approaches, is characterized by (a) a focus on overt and specific behavior, (b) a precision and spelling out of treatment goals, (c) a formulation of specific treatment procedure appropriate to a particular problem, and (d) an objective assessment of the outcomes of therapy" (p. 119). Corey also stressed the central importance of goals in behavior therapy, with the client formulating the goals (Corey, 1991). Although elementary school counselors do not engage in "therapy" in the school setting, these are highly appropriate characteristics for use by elementary school counselors. The elementary school setting lends itself particularly well to behavioral interventions. Children who have learned inappropriate ways of handling their problems are helped to evaluate their own behaviors. When they are able to identify the undesirable behavior, the goal then is to teach them self-management through self-monitoring techniques followed by positive reinforcement. If the child is immediately rewarded, or reinforced, for appropriate behaviors, these behaviors will be apt to continue. It is important to involve the child in the entire process in order to gain the greatest benefit.

Hosford observed that there was a lot of misunderstanding regarding the behaviorists as counselors, noting that there is a feeling that they do not establish counseling relationships that are warm and personal. He contends that behavioral counseling goes beyond the "conditioning" process and, in a sense, beyond the traditional counseling approaches. His goal, in becoming a behaviorist, was to "seek more effective means of helping people achieve the desired changes in their lives—changes that would be observable not only to me, the counselor, but, more importantly, to the client and those around him" (Hosford, 1974, p. 297). Teachers experiencing problems in classroom management often look to the counselor for help and suggestions. Gerler supported this by stating that "elementary school counselors are in a good position to support and to help teachers manage classroom behavior" (1982, p. 20). Counselors able to step in and help students make desired behavior changes in the classroom and school setting do much to enhance the learning environment in the school.

Molnar and Lundquist (1989) addressed changing problem behavior in the classroom by causing the teacher to think differently about the problem. They noted a relationship between the behavior of the student and the behavior of the teacher and found that, by formulating a positive alternative interpretation of the behavior using the technique of reframing, they could identify successful results. Focusing on positive interpretations of behaviors may change the adult's perception of the problem behavior, thus changing the way he or she responds to it. We often assume that the child is the problem, and if we could change the child's behavior, all would be well. We need to look at the possibilities of influencing the teacher who may be reinforcing undesirable behavior in the child.

Krumboltz, an early behaviorist, believed that behavioral counseling goals should be stated in terms of objective behavioral changes. He had three criteria for judging counseling goals: (1) These goals should be different for each individual, (2) these goals should fit in with what the counselor values, and (3) the degree to which the goals are attained should be observable (cited in Shertzer & Stone, 1980). The idea that the behavioral changes, or goals, should be observable and be stated in terms of what the child could do to achieve and maintain these changes is a positive and growth-producing approach. It is with this thought in mind that the elementary counselor's involvement in behavioral management is viewed.

Because the child spends only part of the day in school, it is important that the elementary school counselor recognize the impact of events outside of school on the child's behavior in the school setting. Oftentimes the parents' cooperation is vital to a successful behavioral intervention. The ideal partnership includes the school and the parent working together with the elementary counselor coordinating the efforts.

Wielkiewicz (1986) used the term *behavior management,* rather than behavior therapy or behavior modification, to indicate the process of applying learning principles to correct problem behavior in children. Wielkiewicz, a school psychologist, believed that the child's home environment is equally involved with the school in that any behavioral problems observed in the school involve the entire system of the child. These systems need to balance if the problem is to be successfully resolved. In balancing these systems, it is important that the child's parents acknowledge that the problem exists and become actively involved in any remediation efforts.

Although it is highly desirable that the child's parent or parents acknowledge the problem and become actively involved, this does not mean that the problems are unresolvable without parent involvement. Some parents refuse to cooperate with the school in any area, feeling that it is the school's problem, not theirs. Working with these children to effect behavioral changes is a difficult process and, for a few of these children, may be unsuccessful without some parental involvement. Elementary school counselors spend a significant proportion of their time working with children referred by their teachers or principal where there is little or no parental involvement.

When children are able to identify the behaviors that are considered undesirable by the adults in their lives, they may or may not know what to do to change these behaviors. One way to help them accomplish this is to teach them self-contracting. Cormier, Cormier, and Hackney (1987) noted that it is the concreteness of self-contracts that make them so useful. They also found that self-contracts are more successful if a self-reward accompanies it. This would seem to be particularly true with elementary-age children, who are for the most part reward motivated.

Cunningham and Peters (1973) questioned whether the diminishing of rewards or reinforcers will have a negative effect on the conditioning brought about by the rewards. It is in long-term behavior change where the results of immediate rewards are seen. Gerler (1982) suggested activity privileges as classroom reinforcers, privileges such as extra recess time or being teacher's helper for the day. In this context of social reinforcement in the classroom, the concern regarding the diminishing of reinforcers or rewards should be lessened. The rewards used in a school setting need to be easily delivered and, at the same time, motivating for the child to the extent he or she will want to continue the desired behavior.

Unique Behavioral Contributions

Hierarchical Reward System   Christian (1983) suggested a hierarchical reward system to be used in the schools in behavior management, with the rewards ranging from the most concrete to the most abstract. He illustrated the reward hierarchy with some examples:

- Infantile physical contact: hugs, pats
- Food: milk, cookies, raisins
- Toys: marble, clay, doll
- School implements: ruler, note pad
- Privileges: free time, computer access
- Praise: certificate, attention of special adult
- Internal self-reinforcement: "I did well!" "My work is done!" (Christian, 1983, pp. 83–84)

Behavioral counseling provides the elementary school counselor with a variety of techniques to deal with the various behavior problems. Belkin (1975), in viewing the use of behavioral techniques, viewed them as mechanical, operational procedures with specific goals in mind. This removes the behavioral counseling approach from dependence on the counselor's personality, beliefs, and feelings. Belkin also noted the wide criticism that behavioral counseling has been subjected to because the human qualities of the counselor/client relationship are deemphasized: "Ironically, what has been generally cited as the greatest fault of behavioral counseling proves to be its greatest advantage in the school counseling situation, namely, that it deals directly with the symptom" (p. 286). To Belkin, behavioral counseling's emphasis on the symptom is a practical approach for the school counselor because most of the difficulties that the school counselor is confronted with are behavior problems.

Operant Conditioning   Operant conditioning is a method that trains the student via rewards and punishments. It is widely used in the schools, intentionally and unintentionally. Reinforcers, in operant conditioning, are the consequences that strengthen behavior. Positive reinforcers are rewards of some sort, such as tokens or free time. Negative reinforcers are punishments such as taking away rewards or loss of free time.

Contingency Contracting.   Contingency contracting, relating behavior to its consequences, is one of the behavioral counseling techniques used in operant conditioning. Thompson and Rudolph (1992) break contingency contracting down into six steps:

1. The counselor and the child identify the problem to be solved.
2. Data are collected to verify the baseline frequency rate for the occurrence of the undesired behavior.

3. The counselor and the child set goals that are mutually acceptable.
4. Specific counseling techniques and methods are selected for attaining the goals.
5. The counseling techniques are evaluated for observable and measurable change.
6. Step 4 is repeated if the selected counseling techniques are not effective. If the techniques do prove effective, a maintenance plan is developed for maintaining the new behavior changes. (p. 163)

Contingency contracting, which is a written agreement between the child and teacher or between the child and parent, may influence or cause changes in the teacher or parent as they deal with the child. Many times it is their actions that help reinforce the undesirable behavior in the child. It is important that the contract be fair and clearly understood by the child. The child should have some input into the terms of the contract and not have it dictated to him or her. Initially, contingency contracting is quite time-consuming, but this tapers off as the schedule of reinforcement becomes less frequent.

Modeling.   Another form of operant conditioning that can be used in the elementary school setting is modeling. The child may be exposed to desired behaviors through classroom guidance activities or through peer behaviors in small group sessions. The child is reinforced for imitating the model's behavior. The child is less aware of his or her own involvement with this form of operant conditioning. Modeling is also performed by the classroom teacher and the counselor in a classroom setting. It is important for these significant adults to model the appropriate behaviors for students.

Extinction.   In the use of extinction as an operant conditioner, undesirable behavior is ignored or not reinforced. Counselors, by virtue of their training, are familiar with the fact that the frequency of any behavior decreases if it is not reinforced. Because of this, when a teacher seeks help with a misbehaving student, the counselor will often advise, "Ignore it and see if she stops." Even though this method is successful, it is frustrating to a teacher to be told to ignore disruptive behavior on the part of a child.

Corey, in his view of behavioral counseling, took the process of extinction of unwanted behaviors beyond the school setting to the home and stressed the cooperation necessary between the home and the school. He felt it necessary for both the parents and the teacher to ignore the behavior as much as possible. While they are ignoring the child's attention-getting behavior, positive reinforcements can be applied to the acquisition of desired behavior (Corey, 1977). In attempting to extinguish the unwanted behaviors, it is important for the counselor, teacher, and parent to be aware that the undesirable behavior may initially increase as the child sees his or her misbehavior ignored. Persistence is necessary to make extinction a successful intervention in behavioral counseling.

Although there are other behavior management techniques available for use in the schools, the techniques discussed are some of the most commonly used in the elementary school. They are effective tools for influencing and changing behavior. Young children, especially, have behavior that is more manageable and easier to influence with behavior management techniques than older children, making this approach particularly suited for the elementary school and the elementary-age child. Elementary school counselors need to familiarize themselves with these techniques in order to effectively respond to teachers and parents requesting help with children with behavior problems.

Counseling Strategies

Counseling definitions applicable to behavioral counseling in the elementary schools haven't changed over the years since Krumboltz' definition in 1968: "Counseling consists of whatever ethical activities a counselor undertakes in an effort to help the child engage in those types of behavior which will lead to a resolution of the client's problems" (Krumboltz, 1968, p. 120). A definition of counseling by Shertzer and Stone (1980) that fits well within the framework of behavioral counseling and elementary school counseling states that "counseling is an interaction process that facilitates meaningful understanding of self and environment and results in the establishment and/or clarification of goals and values for future behavior" (p. 19). To Thompson and Rudolph (1992), there is a reeducation or process of relearning in behavioral counseling with the reinforcement of helpful behavior and an extinction of unhelpful behavior: "The counselor's role is, through reinforcement principles, to help children achieve the goals they have set for themselves" (p. 159). Behavioral counseling techniques have much to offer to elementary school counselors. A few of the techniques that have been used successfully in the elementary school setting will follow.

Case Examples   Hosford related an experience he had during one of his first years as an elementary school counselor a number of years ago. One of the students, Bobby, threw tantrums on the school playground whenever he didn't get his own way and would kick and scream. His teacher sought out the counselor to see how he could help her. Hosford observed Bobby on the playground when his teacher was on playground duty. When Bobby didn't get the ball or when someone took it from him, he refused to play and would cry or yell or kick other children. Whenever this happened, his teacher would go quickly to him and lovingly quiet down Bobby. What the teacher was doing was reinforcing the very behavior she was trying to get rid of. The teacher became the counselor's client, not Bobby; he suggested she ignore Bobby's behavior on the playground by busying herself with other children, asking him to wait when he came up to her crying or screaming. The teacher was to reward him with attention such as smiles, pats, or hugs when he played well. By changing the teacher's behavior, the counselor was able to change Bobby (Hosford, 1974, pp. 307–308).

Behavioral counseling is also effective with hyperactive children. Wielkiewicz (1986) noted that "hyperactivity is one of the most commonly identified behavioral problems of children, with estimates of the incidence ranging from about 3% to as high as 20%" (p. 103). The hyperactive child, usually a boy, annoys other students, runs around the classroom, fidgets, talks, and exhibits a variety of irrelevant behaviors. Teachers typically complain that this type of child does not pay attention or follow directions. Wielkiewicz makes a point of considering the age of the child and observing of the child's peers to see whether or not the child's behavior is that much different from the others. It is also important to note whether the behavior affects the child's academic success. A child diagnosed as hyperactive is often on medication such as Ritalin to control the hyperactivity. Whether or not the child is on medication, it is still feasible to use behavioral interventions whenever possible. Behavioral intervention may reduce or eliminate the need for medication, according to Wielkiewicz. Two of the strategies to use with a hyperactive child when one of the unwanted behaviors occurs is either a timeout or a response system with token rewards.

In using timeout, the child is typically placed in an area that prevents him or her from participating with the group or classroom. It should be an area that is not totally isolated, but the child should be removed from the activities in which the unwanted behaviors occurred. Token rewards are quite easy to use, because the activities need not be interrupted. The rewards need to be motivating for the child in order to increase the desired behaviors. Rewards can be anything the counselor or teacher identifies as effective for the particular child or group of children. A simple game, a book, snacks, and a segment of time to do what the child wants are all possible rewards. Tokens that the child can save and trade in for something of value are usually actual tokens, slips of paper, stars, and so on.

It is important for the elementary school counselor to help the teacher identify appropriate and inappropriate behaviors in order to reinforce the desired behavior. *CACTUS*, a publication from the Arizona State Department of Education, listed behaviors that are not compatible with desired behaviors:

1. Teasing
2. Unkind comments
3. Refusal to work
4. Calling the class a dumb class
5. Pestering neighbors
6. Talking without raising hand
7. Only partial completion of assignment
8. Chronic griping
9. Hitting classmates
10. Out-of-seat behavior (Arizona State Department of Education, 1976, p. 227)

CACTUS listed a number of social reinforcers as ways to increase desired behaviors over undesired behaviors. Here are a few of these:

Facial expressions: smiling, nodding, winking, looking interested

Verbal praise: "good job!", "I'm pleased with that!", "Thank you!"

Physical contact: touching, patting head or back, hugging

Proximity: sitting in a group, eating with the children

In addition to these, there are privilege reinforcers, which are easily used by the classroom teacher. Here are some of these:

Group: singing songs, going out to recess early

Individual: going first, getting to sit where you want

Tokens: marks on a blackboard, marbles in a jar, tickets (pp. 229–230)

An elementary school counselor can help teachers with these behavioral management techniques through in-service programs for teachers or working with individual teachers in their classrooms. It is important for the counselor to let the teachers know of his or her availability and expertise in the techniques of behavioral management.

It seems obvious that helping children to behave better in school is a major part of the elementary school counselor's task. Administrators, teachers, and parents all look for ways to affect the child's behavior whenever a problem of academic achievement or a behavior problem become obvious in the school. Behavioral counseling techniques should be a part of every elementary counselor's repertoire of counseling skills.

Developmental Counseling

Blocher (1966), the principal theorist of developmental counseling, viewed the developmental process as somewhat orderly and spoke to the developmental counseling function in this process: "One basic assumption of developmental counseling is that human personality unfolds in terms of largely healthy interaction between the growing organism and the culture or environment. From this point of view, development is seen as a reasonably ordered and patterned process of change, moving in directions that are typically desirable for both the individual and society" (p. 4). In a 1992 interview, Blocher noted the continuity of the ideas that led to his writing *Developmental Counseling* when he was a school counselor to the present time (Casey, 1992). It is interesting to note that Blocher's book, *Developmental Counseling,* was published approximately 30 years ago and yet many of our counselor education programs do not teach or emphasize a developmental counseling theory in the preparation and training of elementary school counselors. We as counselor educators have as our task to provide a variety of theoretical orientations for the prospective counselor to try out for "best fit"; in this process, the student develops a personal theory of counseling. Developmental counseling seems particularly appropriate in an educational setting, as it stresses growth and development rather than remediation. It is important to include developmental counseling as one of the approaches endorsed in the preparation and training of elementary school counselors. Our professional organization endorses this approach: "The American School Counselor Association recognizes and supports the implementation of comprehensive developmental counseling programs at all educational levels" (American School Counselor Association, 1990a, p. 10).

The American School Counselor Association (ASCA) earlier developed a position statement (see Appendix C), "The School Counselor and Developmental Guidance" (adopted 1978; reviewed and revised 1984), advocating developmental guidance as a dynamic and promising approach for the school counselor. The position statement defines developmental guidance as "that component of all guidance efforts which fosters planned intervention within educational and other human development services programs at all points in the human life cycle. It vigorously stimulates and actively facilitates the total development of individuals in all areas—personal, social, emotional, career, moral-ethical, cognitive, aesthetic—and to promote the integration of the several components into an individual lifestyle" (American School Counselor Association, 1984). The ASCA role statement for elementary school counselors (see Appendix A) emphasizes the developmental processes of children. The developmental counseling program focuses on all children in the school, helping to build effective learning climates where all children will benefit.

Within the developmental counseling framework, Blocher's five assumptions are summarized as follows:

1. Clients are not considered to be mentally ill, but are viewed as capable of choosing goals, making decisions, and assuming responsibility for their own behavior.
2. Developmental counseling is focused on the present and future and not on the past.
3. The counselor is essentially a teacher and partner of the client as they move toward mutually defined goals.
4. The counselor has values, feelings, and standards but does not impose them on the client.
5. The counselor focuses on changing behavior using a wide variety of techniques. The counselor is a helping person, a teacher, a consultant, and a confidant as these functions are seen as appropriate in meeting mutually defined goals. (Blocher, 1966, p. 11)

These assumptions all fit well within the framework of elementary school counseling and should be acceptable to an elementary school counselor desirous of implementing a developmental focus in their counseling program.

Dinkmeyer and Caldwell, as they addressed developmental counseling, made certain assumptions about the nature of the student. They stated these assumptions as the foundation of developmental counseling:

1. Behavior is dynamic, emerging, and in the process of becoming. It is important to recognize that rebellion, for example, may be an outgrowth of the need for independence and a sign of healthy development, not necessarily to be stifled. Thus, the developmental counselor is aware of where the individual is in his developmental process rather than looking at static traits.
2. The student is motivated by his desire for mastery and self-actualization. Counseling helps create awareness of how one is meeting the challenges of life.
3. Differences in behavior patterns are often due to differences in rates of development. Thus, an awareness of the individual's rate of development may clarify which problems are normal to development and which require special attention.
4. Behavior is purposive and takes on meaning when seen in terms of the goal and the specific social setting. Behavior thus reveals the individual's perception of his needs.
5. Psychological growth is continuous and patterned. As one focuses on the unity of the behavior the life style becomes more apparent. This suggests that the counselor should focus on the child's psychological movement and the basic beliefs that are revealed in this movement. For example, if the child believes he is not as much as others he will function in a way to obtain service.
6. Self awareness precedes self management. As the individual becomes aware of his alternatives and the opportunity to choose or decide, this increases self acceptance. As the individual comes to accept himself he is free to evaluate the expec-

tations placed upon him by parents, the school and peers. (1977, pp. 60–61). Permission given by Wm. C. Brown Company, Publishers.

These assumptions also fit well within the framework of an elementary school counseling program. Developmental counseling, with its emphasis on stages of development and normal developmental problems, lends itself to classroom guidance activities. There are many excellent programs for use in the classroom that emphasize child growth and development. These will be addressed in the next section, looking at counseling strategies used for developmental counseling.

Dinkmeyer has long been an advocate of developmental counseling from an Adlerian perspective in the elementary schools. He stressed this need a number of years ago: "With the greatly increased extension of counseling and guidance services to the elementary school level, counseling theorists have become aware of a greater need for a theory of developmental counseling with children" (1968, p. 105). The elementary school counselor plays a significant role in helping the child to belong, to develop successful social interactions, and to identify with others in the school setting. The counselor is involved with children, helping them to make choices and learn to become responsible for these choices. Developmental counseling in the elementary school setting is usually not crisis or problem oriented. Dinkmeyer noted that developmental counseling has as its focus the goal of helping the child to know, understand, and accept himself or herself. In this focus, the child learns to become responsible for his choices and actions and, in the process, learns self-understanding.

Blocher (1966) viewed maximizing human freedom as the primary goal of developmental counseling, with maximizing human effectiveness as a secondary goal. He also noted that developmental counseling focused on helping the child become aware of himself or herself and the ways in which behavior is influenced by the environment. It is the elementary counselor's task to encourage the teachers and parents to help children develop some goals and values that will encourage self-awareness and influence future behaviors.

The Human Development Program, often referred to as Magic Circle sessions, was developed by Bessell and Palomares. It uses a developmental profile for each child focusing on three main areas: "*awareness* (knowing what your thoughts, feelings, and actions really are), *mastery* (knowing what your abilities are and how to use them), and *social interaction* (knowing other people)" (Palomares & Ball, 1976, p. 1). At the end of the units, usually six weeks, the children are evaluated individually in order to ascertain each child's progress. In its broadest sense, the Human Development Program is a curriculum that has been designed to open and improve communication between the children and their teachers. Although this program has been available for a number of years, elementary school counselors and interns speak positively of its ease of use and effectiveness in a classroom setting. A summary of the scales used to analyze the child's development follows:

Awareness

1. Awareness of Self

   The aware child knows how he feels, what he thinks, and what he is doing. Although he is conscious of himself, he is not self-conscious, insecure, or embarrassed. This awareness does not produce anxiety. He accepts and can acknowledge how he really feels, thinks, and acts.

2. Sensitivity to Others

> The sensitive child is concerned about the well being of other people. He ascertains what others are feeling and adjusts his behavior in ways that are thoughtful and beneficial to them.

Mastery

1. Self Confidence

> The confident child is eager to try new things. Self-assured, realistic when coping with challenge. His acceptance of himself permits freedom of expression which is natural and uninhibited, without being dramatic or exhibitionistic.

2. Effectiveness

> The effective child copes appropriately. He is emotionally stable, and flexible enough to successfully implement his own desires to meet the external demands of his environment.

Social Interaction

1. Interpersonal Comprehension

> This trait assesses a child's understanding of how a person's behavior may cause approval or disapproval of that behavior in another person.

2. Tolerance

> The tolerant child recognizes and accepts individual differences. He accepts and gives full regard to others who have different feelings, thoughts, and reactions than his own. But he does not necessarily approve or yield to their influence. (Palomares & Ball, 1976, p. 48)

The developmental profile has five categories of scores, from zero to ten, by which to rate the child in each of the six areas. Through this means, developmental trends in the child are apparent. The next section will expand on the elementary school counselor's role in this and other programs.

Counseling Strategies

The 1984 ASCA position statement on developmental guidance defines the direction the school counselor should take: "Counseling should be habilitative as well as rehabilitative, proactive as well as reactive, preventive as well as remedial, skill-additive as well as problem-reductive, and characterized by outreach as well as availability. Developmental guidance is the summative terminology which connotes this emphasis" (American School Counselor Association, 1984). An elementary school counseling program using developmental counseling with this focus will emphasize the developmental needs of all students and will help parents, teachers, and other school staff understand and provide for these needs. The elementary counselor plays a major role in helping the school staff understand the developmental tasks as they plan and organize activities that will maximize the opportunity for mastery of these tasks by the students.

The ASCA position statement specifies certain questions that developmental guidance specialists must, at a minimum, be able to deal with effectively in discussing counselor competencies for developmental guidance intervention: What are the general characteristics, expectations, tasks, and behavior of individuals at this stage of development? What are this individual's characteristics, expectations, tasks, and behaviors? What can impede the process of development for this individual? What will facilitate the process of development for this individual?

It is obvious that the elementary school counselor will need to be knowledgeable about the personal and social development of the elementary-age child. There are many excellent books available to help the counselor gain this knowledge. For example, Part II ("The Child") in Elkind's book (1978) covers, in a highly readable way, the personal, social, and mental development of the child ages six through eleven. Elkind also included general behavior traits of each age period and the self-concept, social relations, and school orientation characteristics of each age group.

The ASCA position statement also states that because developmental guidance has been a fairly recent emphasis in the schools, "counselor educators may need to modify the counselor education curriculum in order to prepare counseling students as proficient developmental interventionists." Miller (1981), in discussing the benefits of developmental education, believed that the current guidance practice used by many counselors is inefficient and costly, "particularly if large amounts of counselor time are spent in remedial contacts with students" (p. 14). The implications for counselor educators should be obvious as developmental counseling in content and process is emphasized in the elementary schools.

One of the developmental programs used extensively by elementary counselors is Developing Understanding of Self and Others, usually referred to as DUSO (Dinkmeyer, 1973). DUSO uses a variety of puppet and role-playing activities with elementary school children. The puppet, Duso the Dolphin, is the main puppet used to narrate the recorded stories intended for use in small group and classroom settings. There are two levels to the DUSO program: DUSO 1 is used for children in grades K–2; DUSO 2 is used for children in grades 3–4. DUSO comes in a kit with a guide, story books, puppets, audiocassettes, activity cards, and activity sheets; it contains enough materials for an entire year. Children, through the use of these activities in the classroom with the counselor, learn to listen reflectively, express their feelings, and develop skills to deal with conflicts.

Another developmental program that is used extensively in the elementary school setting by elementary counselors is Toward Affective Development, referred to as TAD (Dupont, Gardner, & Brody, 1974). TAD is suggested for students in grades 3–6, as well as students with special needs. The TAD kit includes a manual, activity sheets to be duplicated, feeling wheels to help students identify their own emotions, career folders, discussion pictures, and audiocassettes. TAD has five sections comprising 191 sequenced lessons: Section 1—Reaching In and Reaching Out; Section 2—Your Feelings and Mine; Section 3—Working Together; Section 4—Me: Today and Tomorrow; and Section 5— Feeling, Thinking, and Doing.

The Magic Circle sessions from the Human Development Program, summarized in the previous section, are frequently used in the elementary schools; they provide a daily ongoing series of topics for discussion that covers an entire school year for each level, K–6.

In the preschool/kindergarten level, the circle sessions group seven to twelve children with their teacher in a small complete circle. In levels I–VI, the circle is gradually enlarged so that the entire class is seated in two circles, one inside the other. If the classroom group is large, it can be divided into three groups with one group on the inside and the other two groups forming one large circle on the outside. The outside group only listens and does not talk or interact in any way. Each session stresses listening to the one who is talking.

Elementary school counselors can be involved in this program in two different ways: They may lead the sessions themselves or provide in-service training for teachers interested in leading Magic Circles in their own classrooms. A summary of the first three levels of one area of the curriculum, "Awareness," may help prospective counselors understand their involvement in the program:

Level 1 (first grade)

The concept of ambivalence of feelings, thoughts, and behavior is introduced in a very personal way; children report their mixed reactions and listen to the mixed reactions of others. As the awareness theme progresses, the children are encouraged to tell how they distinguish between reality and fantasy.

Level 2 (second grade)

The children are provided with opportunities to tell stories that they are sure are true and to compare their true story with one that is make-believe. Finally, they are provided with opportunities in which they can develop their capacity for combining the best of reality and the best of fantasy.

Level 3 (third grade)

The children are presented with greater complexities in the area of describing their experiences. Just as important to these children as learning to describe their experiences is the appreciation they have of being encouraged to feel they are quite typical as they listen to what goes on in the minds of others. (Palomares & Ball, pp. 64–65)

Counselors, teachers, and students report positive experiences with the Human Development Program, Magic Circle, in the area of promoting emotional growth in elementary school children when used in a classroom setting.

There is a wide variety of materials and programs available to elementary school counselors that are appropriate for use in developmental counseling programs. The programs described in this section are just a few of the many available. The author has been actively involved in school counseling programs in four states and has found these programs to be universally used and acclaimed. It is up to the individual counselor to seek out, experiment with, and use the activities that are most comfortable for him or her. These have stood the test of time and are excellent training tools in counselor education programs for training elementary school counselors in the developmental counseling approach. As elementary counselors look for materials that aid in the mastery of developmental tasks, they will begin to compile their own favorite activities that address the important developmental needs of elementary-age children. Elementary counselor "idea-exchange" sessions at both state and national conventions are excellent sources for developmental guidance activities. A model to assist school counselors in implementing a developmental counseling and guidance program was created by a committee in Virginia consisting of two guidance supervisors and two counselor educators (Neukrug, Barr, Hoffman, & Kaplan, 1993). This model can be used as a starting point for a counseling and guidance program in the counselor's district or school.

Reality Therapy

William Glasser developed reality therapy during his residence in psychiatry at the University of California at Los Angeles when he saw the futility of classical psychoanalytic procedures with the clients that he was assigned. Glasser (1965) believes that people exhibit widely different behaviors to express their problems. Regardless of how one chooses to express a problem, everyone needing help or treatment has one basic inadequacy they suffer from, according to Glasser—he or she is unable to fulfill essential needs. Glasser views the needs to love and to be loved as basic needs. Equally important, he believes, is the need to feel worthwhile. It is in learning to fulfill these needs that we find meaning; if we don't learn to fulfill these needs, we will suffer all our lives. This need is continuous from infancy throughout our lives.

Glasser puts the burden of responsibility for actions needed to achieve these needs on the client. Reality therapy involves the "Three R's": reality, responsibility, and right-and-wrong. Glasser tends to view people with whom he works not as being sick but as not having learned to be responsible for their own behavior. His approach is to ask people who come to him to tell him their "plan," what it is they plan to do. This is a favorite reality therapy question, helping the person to realize that they need a plan, causing them to begin to do some constructive thinking rather than waiting for others to come to their rescue. The *what* instead of the *why* is stressed by Glasser. When the person is asked what he or she is doing rather than why he or she is doing something, the focus is changed from the implication that the reason for their behavior makes a difference to what is happening right now. Until the person becomes more responsible, he or she will not act differently even if the person knows the why of his or her behavior (Arbuckle, 1970). Reality therapy always focuses on the present because the person must gain responsibility right now. The past has contributed to what a person is now; but the past cannot be changed, only the present.

Glasser's reality therapy is included as an approach to be considered for elementary school counselors because of its practicality for use in our schools today. His approach to education, using reality therapy to create a successful learning climate, is both practicable and usable. A real advantage of reality therapy is its applicability in all elementary schools, from inner city to affluent suburb.

Glasser emphasizes the group approach because it encourages the development of reality, responsibility, and right-and-wrong much more rapidly than do conventional forms of individual treatment. He contends that individuals are free to meet their needs as long as they don't interfere with the rights of others to meet their needs. Elementary school counselors use groups for activities that emphasize growth and development; the group becomes a testing ground that provides feedback to the individual. One of the goals of the reality therapy group is to assist children in identifying values for themselves. Once the child identifies appropriate values, the counselor and the group help the child decide whether his or her behavior is effective to achieve what is valued. If it appears that the child accepts his or her behavior as ineffective, the group helps him or her develop a specific and realistic plan to meet the identified needs in more responsible ways.

Thompson and Rudolph (1992) note that the most significant difference between reality therapy and traditional therapy is reality therapy's emphasis on the teaching process rather than a healing process. In the counseling process, the child is taught how to solve his or her problems, becoming, in effect, their own counselors. This fits in with the elementary counselor's role of teaching children more effective ways to meet their needs. Glasser strongly emphasizes the importance of a child's achieving success in school. He believes that success in school, regardless of the child's background, gives him or her an excellent chance for success in life. Along with this, he believes that failure at any point during his or her educational career from elementary school through college will greatly reduce the child's chance of success in life (Glasser, 1969). This places a large burden of responsibility on the elementary school, the first school experience for children. An elementary school counselor can do much to help a child experience success in a significant part of his or her life, the school.

Glasser uses the term *identity* to describe what children require as a very basic need. The feeling of worthwhileness is significant for a successful identity. Much importance is placed on the school's role in helping the child achieve a success identity. As a part of this, Glasser suggests that all schools educate its students to assume social responsibility. It is because so many children fail to fulfill their needs at home that Glasser emphasizes the school's role in this process of achieving a successful identity and developing social responsibility. Elementary school teachers express a lot of frustration over the lack of motivation in children in their classrooms, resorting often to restrictions, threats, and punishment in an attempt to motivate their students. Glasser views this as the students' responsibility, noting that they need help from their teacher to achieve this; teacher and student involvement are integral parts of reality therapy. Students involved with teachers that are responsible and have a success identity will be in a better position to fulfill their own needs than without this modeling (Glasser, 1969).

As a part of the students' responsibility for fulfilling their own needs, they are also responsible for their own behavior. Glasser believes that children can make better choices and more responsible choices if they are strongly involved with someone who can: "In education, involvement may start with one person, be he teacher, counselor, or administrator, or it may start with groups of children or even with a whole class" (p. 19). Wubbolding (1988) notes that reality therapy begins with the establishment of a warm and caring relationship. The personal relationships between the child and teacher and the child and counselor are crucial. When there is authentic involvement by the teacher and counselor, and a feeling of trust on the part of the child, the child is more apt to choose the behaviors that will be positively reinforced. Involvement requires the most skill, because it requires an emotional involvement with uncritical acceptance and a willingness to have the values of the helper tested (McWhirter, McWhirter, McWhirter, & McWhirter, 1993). An elementary counselor is the ideal person to facilitate this involvement in the elementary school on an individual basis, in a group, and in classrooms. Elementary counselors are trained to become emotionally involved with children, to be personal, warm, and interested in the child and all aspects of the child's life.

Because reality therapy emphasizes the present and not the past, the counselor and the teacher do not address past failures. The only area of information regarding the past that is of interest to the counselor and the teacher is the successes the child has had. It is the knowledge of the child's successes, not failures, that can be used to help the child in the present. This approach is different from the usual approach used with children who fail. In other approaches, much time is spent trying to help the child analyze past failures in order to change the patterns of behavior. Dwelling on past failures is self-defeating for most children. The child who is failing will continue to fail if reminded of the failures. Glasser stresses helping them deal with and change their present behavior: "To help a presently failing child to succeed, we must get him to make a value judgement about what he is now doing that is contributing to his failure" (Glasser, 1969, p. 21). If the child believes that his or her behavior is all right, Glasser contends that no one can change the child at this point and the child must suffer the consequences of not changing the behavior. Each time the child fails, he or she should again be asked for a value judgement regarding the behavior until the child starts to doubt the behavior that is causing the failure. It is the responsibility of the child to decide whether or not this behavior is helping, not the counselor or teacher. If the counselor or teacher tells the child that he or she is doing wrong and that failure to change the behavior will result in punishment, the responsibility for behavior is taken away from the child. If the child accepts that the current behaviors are not effective or producing the desired results, the counselor can work with him or her to formulate alternatives, a positive plan of action. If the plan is kept simple with success built into it, the child is more apt to make a commitment to the plan.

Glasser views commitment as a necessary responsibility for children to learn: "This is the keystone of Reality Therapy, when a child makes a value judgement and a commitment to change his behavior, no excuse is acceptable for not following through" (1969, p. 23). Children need someone in the school setting who will not accept their excuses but will show true caring by expecting a commitment from them that they will do what they say they will do. As a part of this, the elementary school counselor can play a significant role in working with these children until they learn to fulfill commitments that they make. Again, it takes an authentic, caring involvement on the part of the counselor.

The Educator Training Center, created by Glasser, has a series of training programs that any elementary school can use to help eliminate failure. The program uses Schools Without Failure seminars for training teachers. The objectives of these seminars are to provide each school involved with an opportunity to learn the following:

1. How to develop a success-oriented philosophy
2. How to motivate students to personal involvement
3. How to develop respective communication with students through class meetings
4. How to help students develop responsible behavior
5. How to make curriculum relevant for today's students
6. How to remove failure from the curriculum
7. What exciting opportunities exist for teachers to improve their school
8. How to work effectively with other members of the staff
9. How to eliminate discipline as a major problem of the school
10. Effective techniques for involving parents and the community in the work of the school. (Glasser & Zunin, 1973, p. 291)

Programs through the Educator Training Center and through the Institute for Reality Therapy are offered throughout the country for school districts that are interested in in-service training for teachers and staff.

Counseling Strategies

Reality therapy has had many supporters as well as critics over the years. As educators became increasingly concerned about the lack of motivation in students, as well as the disruptive behaviors exhibited by many children, reality therapy appeared to have some of the answers they were looking for.

In his book *Schools Without Failure,* Glasser (1969) emphasized the counselor's role in the school. The counselor should help the teacher cope with classroom problems, both educational and disciplinary; it should be a cooperative effort between counselors and teachers. One way to involve both counselor and teacher is through the use of classroom meetings, used extensively in the school setting by Glasser. Glasser feels that the school counselor should take the main responsibility to introduce and start classroom meetings, particularly at the elementary level.

Classroom meetings, led by an elementary school counselor or teacher, are used as a way to get the students involved in relevant discussions. Classroom meetings often are difficult to get started when teachers are expected to run them, because teachers have had little experience with this type of format in the elementary school setting. Glasser (1969) noted that the counselor and the principal should introduce classroom meetings into a school. The elementary counselor could be the one that initiates and runs the initial classroom meetings until the teachers become more comfortable with this format and, more importantly, see that they truly do work. Glasser outlined three types of classroom meetings: social-problem-solving meeting, which is concerned with the social behavior of the students in school; open-ended meeting, which is concerned with subjects that are intellectually important; and educational-diagnostic meeting, which is concerned with the students' understanding of the curriculum. The classroom meetings concerned with social problem solving are excellent ones for the elementary school counselor to become involved with as a starting point for conducting these meetings. Wolfgang and Glickman give examples of real problems that affect all students, problems that are relevant to discussion in a classroom meeting:

- How the playground balls are to be distributed at recess
- What to do about missing items in the class
- How to cut down on asking the teacher questions when he or she is busy
- What to do about name calling among the students
- What to do about the length of time it takes to get the whole class settled before starting the next lesson
- What to do about graffiti and littering problems in the restrooms

In addition to these common problems, there are other problems specific to individual students that could also be a topic for problem solving meetings:

- A student who 'hogs' the playground equipment (balls, bats, frisbees, and the like)
- A student who physically pushes other students around
- A student who constantly distracts others from working (making loud noises, talking, and so forth)
- A student who takes items from others

- A student who plays cruel "tricks" on others (locks children into closets, writes on others' homework, and so on)
- A student who tries to be boss all the time, who is always telling others what to do but will not accept any criticism of self. (1986, pp. 119–120)

Glasser suggests several guidelines to be used in classroom meetings. These are summarized as follows:

All problems relative to the class as a group and to any individual in the class are eligible for discussion.

The discussion itself should always be directed toward solving the problem; the solution should never include punishment or fault finding.

Meetings should always be conducted with the teacher and all the students seated in a tight circle. (1969, pp. 128–132)

The length of the classroom meetings depends on the age and the experience of the class. Glasser found that primary-grade children have difficulty remaining attentive longer than 15 minutes. Fourth, fifth, and sixth graders can meet for 30 minutes or longer and still be interested. The meetings should be held at least once a week, preferably daily. Here are a few sample questions used in class meetings:

"If each of you could have a million dollars right now, a sum that would be ample for the rest of your life, would you continue to go to school?"

To those who say they wouldn't go to school, he asks,

"What would you do with your life?"

The more specific a question is, the more it will stimulate discussion:

"When you first came to school, how did you make a friend?"

"Have you ever moved to a new neighborhood? If so, how did the other children treat you?"

"What do you do when someone new moves into your neighborhood?"

Another series of questions that is apt to open a good discussion:

"Does the class have any explanation for the boy or girl who always wants to have the first turn?"

"What is wrong with the child who is a bully? Does anyone think that he might be lonely?"

Reversal questions are also good to stimulate the children's imaginations:

"If you woke up tomorrow as a girl instead of a boy, how would you behave?" (Glasser, 1969, pp. 165–177)

Belkin (1975) noted that many public school counselors have become followers of reality therapy since Glasser's first book was published in 1965, making a powerful impact on school counseling.

Another use of reality therapy in elementary schools was described in *The Guidance Clinic* (Nelson, 1978). A Reality Therapy Peer Counseling program was set up in two elementary schools; fifth- and sixth-grade teachers were solicited for students who were natural leaders to be trained as peer counselors. These students were interviewed to ascertain their interest and commitment in becoming peer counselors and were then trained in four sessions, summarized as follows:

Brainstorming: The first session was to teach step one of Reality Therapy—making friends. The students were asked to brainstorm on the important aspects of friendship and ways to create an atmosphere of friendship.

Second Session: In the second training session they were taught steps two through five of Reality Therapy as follows:

> Step Two: What Are You Doing?
> Step Three: Is It Helping?
> Step Four: Make a Plan to Do Better
> Step Five: Get a Commitment

Role Playing: The final two training sessions were spent role playing situations with the students. (pp. 9–10)

Counselees were referred by teachers who identified students to be seen and their problems. The peer counselors saw the students and were asked to write the solution they came up with in duplicate form so that one could be returned to the teacher who referred the student. Teachers were enthusiastic and supportive of the program and consequently referred many students. The steps used in reality therapy can be followed easily by elementary-age children when trained by elementary school counselors to become peer counselors.

In his book *Reality Therapy,* Glasser (1965) described several situations that involved teachers taking a one-semester course from him to learn the principles of reality therapy. Each week, during the last part of the class session, teachers would present cases of problem children in their classes. One particular case, involving a first-grade child, illustrates how reality therapy techniques can be effectively used in a classroom:

Recently we had a teacher present a first grade child who was wild, disorderly, and belligerent. The class suggested putting the necessary constant discipline on a personal level. She did so and reported poor results; in fact, the boy seemed to be worse. She was told to keep it up despite the poor results, not to remind him of past failures, and to start each day with the personal requests such as, 'I want you to stay in line,' or, 'It is important to me that you sit in your seat in class,' as if she were using them for the first time. Probably without the encouragement of

*the class she would have stopped. After about two months the six year old start-
ed to respond slowly and steadily. By mid semester he was no problem, and other
teachers who observed him in the playground remarked on his improved behavior. Although the consistent approach helped, it was the personal touch that
caused the change (pp. 199–200).*

An elementary school counselor, familiar with the techniques of reality therapy, would be
in a position to suggest these interventions for teachers and would be available to help the
teacher carry them out. The counselor should be familiar with reality therapy because it is
so applicable to the school setting. It is not necessary for a counselor to be specifically
trained in this approach other that studying Glasser's books and writings, but training sessions are given through the Educator Training Center in Los Angeles for those desiring
structured training.

Self-Concept Theory

Self-concept is how we feel about ourselves, who we are based on all the information we
have received from those around us. We are not born with a self-concept; we learn it. It is
the conditioning very early in life that develops the child's self-concept. A child with a
poor self-concept develops inadequate self-esteem. Self-esteem goes beyond self-concept,
how we picture ourselves, to the pride or lack of pride we have in ourselves. "Of all the
perceptions we experience in the course of living, none has more profound significance
than the perceptions we hold regarding our own personal existence—our view of who we
are and how we fit into the world" (Purkey & Schmidt, 1987, p. 31).

Coopersmith referred to the "self images" children form based on the way the significant people in their lives treat them. He noted the significance of this self-image in relation to self-esteem: "The positive or negative attitudes and values by which a person views
the self-image and the evaluations or judgments he or she makes about it form the person's
self-esteem" (1982a, p. 1). The child's self-esteem is formed in interactions at home with
parents, in interactions in school with teachers, and in interactions with peers both in and
out of school. Reasoner, a California school superintendent, well known as a speaker,
author, and consultant in building self-esteem in school children, defines self-esteem as
follows: "Self-esteem refers to the sense of self-respect, confidence, identity, and purpose
found in an individual" (1981, p. 1). These definitions of self-esteem fit well within the
self-concept theory.

Purkey and Schmidt (1987) identified some of the most recognized self-concept theorists to be Combs, A. Richards, F. Richards, Jourard, Rogers, Wiley, and Purkey. They
noted that these self-concept theorists agree that there is a generally stable quality to the
self-concept in individuals. Coopersmith (1981) demonstrated through research that the
self-esteem of a person remains constant for at least several years. Those involved in the
elementary school setting need to look at ways to change those children identified as having low self-esteem and, at the same time, strive to maintain those with high self-esteem.

Psychologists have been aware for a long time that an individual's behavior is strongly influenced by how that individual perceives himself or herself. Teachers are often heard
to exclaim, "If I only knew why Kristi or David acts like that!" Children act in ways that

seem appropriate to themselves. We need to go beyond the overt acts of behavior to look at the child's perception of self in our attempt to understand this behavior. Reasoner (1982a) believes that the child's sense of identity or self-concept is a key to his or her behavior. Children with a realistic sense of what they can accomplish are more apt to be successful than with unrealistic perceptions. He believes that a child who feels inadequate in the classroom is adopting some form of defensive behavior rather than trying. It is important to keep this in mind as we react to the children in our schools.

In looking at our personal view of who we are and how we fit in the world, our self-concept, five characteristics regarding the self are important to note: "It is (1) organized, (2) dynamic, (3) consistent, (4) modifiable, and (5) learned" (Purkey & Schmidt, 1987, p. 32). A brief summary of these characteristics will establish how important it is for elementary school counselors and teachers to be aware of them.

Self-concept is organized.

One of the findings in self-concept research was that perceived success and failure have a tendency to be generalized. For example, failure in an area that is important to the person lowers their self-evaluation in other, seemingly unrelated abilities. Conversely, success in a highly valued activity will tend to raise self-evaluation in other unrelated areas. Another aspect of self-concept is its uniqueness, no two people hold the same identical beliefs about themselves.

Self-concept is dynamic.

Self-concept is not the cause of a person's behavior, such as misbehavior. The person who misbehaves has learned to see himself or herself as a troublemaker. People tend to behave according to their perception of themselves. The person's perception needs to be reevaluated and reorganized. A counselor is in an excellent position to help a student with a negative self-image.

Self-concept is consistent.

Each person acts in accordance to the way he or she has learned to view himself or herself. A person accepts new experiences that are consistent with experiences already in the self-concept system. If the new experience is in opposition to what the person has already incorporated, the person will reject it. In other words, people seek support for their perceived self-identity and reject anything that threatens it. Counselors who understand this tendency toward consistency, are aware of the resistance to change.

Self-concept is modifiable.

This is optimistic news for the elementary school counselor and teacher. A counselor is in an excellent position to help students modify their self-perceptions. Knowing that motivation comes from within the person directs the counselor's process away from trying to motivate students to a cooperative relationship of mutual learning.

Self-concept is learned.

Children learn to see themselves as successes or failures as those around them repeatedly reinforce their self-concept in positive or negative ways. Children learn to behave the way they are treated. Since the self-concept is learned, the elementary school counselor should focus on activities that will build self-esteem. (Purkey & Schmidt, 1987, pp. 32–39)

There are many implications for the schools, and the education of our young people in general, in becoming involved in building self-esteem in our classrooms. Reasoner, author of *Building Self-Esteem: A Comprehensive School Program* (1982a), noted a growing concern throughout the country in what is happening in the schools: "Teachers, administrators, parents, and members of the community at large are concerned about the lack of student motivation, the decline in achievement scores in many schools, the accelerating rate of drug and alcohol abuse among students, and the rise in absenteeism" (p. 1). Reasoner noted that research studies indicate a lack of self-esteem as a key element to these problems.

Coopersmith, in identifying effective early education programs, found that many schools were seeking to raise the self-esteem of their children, and he became increasingly involved. In his early involvement with school programs, he became aware of four questions that seemed to keep people from getting involved with and committed to building self-esteem in the classroom: (1) "Why should the school get involved in the issue of building self-esteem?" (2) "Should schools that seek to build self-esteem do so at the cost of improving the child's skills and knowledge?" (3) "What makes you think the school can overcome the effects of the home?" and (4) "What's new about changing self-esteem—we've been doing it for years?" (1975b, pp. 95–96). Coopersmith noted that these questions need to be discussed and answered before schools will become seriously involved in programs designed to build self-esteem.

These four questions are answerable by those interested in carrying out self-esteem programs in the schools. There are many studies available that indicate students perform better when they feel good about themselves, when they have high self-esteem. Coopersmith, a number of years ago, made a strong stand for involving the schools in building self-esteem: "Since a child's attitudes about his abilities and expectations of success and failure are an integrated part of his school performance, it does not make much sense to treat these attitudes as something separate and unrelated to school" (1975b, p. 96). The previous statement is also a response to the second question, building self-esteem at the cost of improving the child's skills and knowledge. Self-esteem is an important and significant part of effective performance in the classroom. As stated earlier, when children feel good about themselves, they perform better. The nature of the relationship between the parents and the school should be positive and reflect a partnership between the home and the school. When this happens, the school is in a position to help the parents foster self-esteem and motivation in their children through parenting programs and other involvement. The elementary school counselor can do much to improve this area of communication via consultation with parents and parent education programs. Coopersmith responded to the last question with a look at the traditional school approach, noting that the competition for grades, fear of failure, and emphasis on verbal intelligence, to name a few, result in a system that more often produces feelings of failure than success. Unless we change the way we work with children in the school setting, we will continue to foster these negative feelings in many of our elementary school children.

Coopersmith's original research on self-esteem was published in 1967. He had long studied the kinds of conditions that lead children to see themselves favorably, finding three major conditions that seem to result in the child's development of self-esteem: "The first is *acceptance* of the child as he is, with his capacities, limitations, strengths, and weaknesses" (Coopersmith, 1975b, p. 103). The child needs full acceptance for his or her strengths to be viewed as well as his or her limitations. "The second major condition associated with feelings of self-esteem is a clearly defined set of *limits* that is spelled out early in a relationship with parents and teachers" (p. 104). The child needs limits to know what is and isn't acceptable on a consistent basis, both at home and at school. "The third condition for building self-esteem is revealed by *respectful treatment* for children who observe limits and play by the rules of the family and classroom" (p. 105). Coopersmith referred to this as a "bill of rights" for children, a bill of rights that recognizes differences in children. If children are accepted for themselves, given appropriate limits, and are treated respectfully, the conditions are set for an environment that produces high self-esteem.

The classroom teacher is an essential person in the development of happy, confident children, children motivated to achieve, according to Reasoner (1982a). He believes that any classroom can develop these children by recognizing their uniqueness, rights, and feelings, and by creating the classroom conditions essential to the development of these five characteristics:

1. A sense of security,
2. A sense of identity or self-concept,
3. A sense of belonging,
4. A sense of purpose, and
5. A sense of personal competence. (Reasoner, 1982a, p. 3)

Reasoner also emphasized the teacher's self-esteem, how teachers feel about themselves; teachers with high self-esteem are much more apt to create a classroom atmosphere that promotes self-esteem.

We can all remember the teachers who made us feel good about ourselves, who created an atmosphere where learning was enjoyable, where problems and issues were solved by class input, not by authoritarian methods. The teachers that demanded respect usually got the least respect. The warm, caring, humanistic teachers, who were not afraid to enjoy students, were highly respected. Although most of us were unaware of what it was, the latter group of teachers had high self-esteem and, in turn, were capable of fostering self-esteem in the youngsters in their classrooms.

We might ask, What can we do about the teachers with low self-esteem? The elementary school counselor is in a unique position to help teachers who lack self-esteem. This can be done directly through staff development sessions in the area of building self-esteem in the classroom. It can also be done by the counselor working directly with individual teachers on setting personal goals and providing feedback regarding these goals. Self-esteem can also be enhanced in teachers as they participate with their students in classroom activities designed to foster high self-esteem. Reasoner's *Building Self-Esteem* (1982a), with its teacher's guide, is an excellent model for accomplishing this task.

The recognition that all children need a positive self-concept has been the force behind one state's efforts to address the causes and cures of poor self-concept. California, through legislative mandate, created the California Task Force to Promote Self Esteem and Personal Social Responsibility, as an effort to reframe social problem solving in the state.

Their task was to compile research "regarding how healthy self-esteem is nurtured, harmed or reduced, and rehabilitated" (California State Department of Education, 1990, p. 1). Numerous studies were presented to the task force that identified a correlation between a healthy self-concept and positive educational outcomes. The two key recommendations that came out of the task force are as follows:

1. Every school district in California should adopt the promotion of self-esteem and personal and social responsibility as a clearly stated goal, integrate self-esteem in its total curriculum, and inform all persons of its policies and operations.
2. Course work in self-esteem should be required for credentials and as a part of ongoing in-service training for all educators. (p. 65)

After months of deliberation, the task force defined self-esteem as "appreciating my own worth and importance and having the character to be accountable for myself and act responsibly toward others" (p. 18). This definition is one to which all of us can subscribe. The extensive final report was dedicated to the memory of Virginia Satir, who served on the task force until her untimely death in 1988.

On the national level, Edwin Herr, in his keynote address at the ACA convention in Atlanta, urged counselors not to ignore self-esteem as "absolutely fundamental to feelings of dignity and self-worth" (McNamee, 1993). He went on to state that "a major counselor role is to help them acquire the personal skills to develop caring and productive relationships" (p. 13). The message is clear for all elementary school counselors.

The following section expands on the role of the elementary school counselor in this highly significant area of child development.

Counseling Strategies

In 1969 Reasoner, after becoming convinced that self-esteem had much to do with student behavior and achievement in school, conducted a survey of 3,000 parents and teachers. The results of the survey showed that both parents and teachers considered self-concept and motivation to be top-priority goals. Much effort, over a period of years, went into the development of ways to build these qualities in children. One of the consultants involved in this process was Coopersmith, who published a study, *The Antecedents of Self-Esteem,* in 1967. A training program was developed that addressed building the characteristics of self-esteem in children. The program has been refined over the years in several California school districts, resulting in *Building Self-Esteem: A Comprehensive School Program* (1982a), which includes guides for the administrator, teacher, and parent. The program describes the five essential characteristics, or components, considered essential for self-esteem and motivation. These desired characteristics and the roles that teachers perform in this process are summarized in Table 4–1.

The program materials contain suggestions for developing each characteristic of self-esteem, 122 activity worksheets that cover the five characteristics, and over 400 extension activities. The grade levels covered by this program are 1–8, with guidelines provided for grade-level use of the activities. Reasoner also suggests using these materials with students who have a low opinion of themselves because of learning disabilities or

TABLE 4–1   Essential Components for Self-Esteem and Motivation

Desired Outcome in Children	Adult Roles or Tasks
1. A sense of security	Set realistic limits. Enforce rules consistently. Develop self-respect and responsibility. Build trust.
2. A sense of identity or a self-concept	Provide feedback. Recognize children's strengths. Demonstrate love and acceptance. Aid students in assessing personal strengths and shortcomings.
3. A sense of belonging	Create a proper environment. Explore the responsibilities of group membership. Encourage acceptance and inclusion of others.
4. A sense of purpose	Convey expectations. Build confidence and faith. Aid students in setting goals.
5. A sense of personal competence	Aid students in making choices and decisions. Provide encouragement and support. Aid students in self-evaluation. Provide recognition and rewards. (Reasoner, 1982a, p. 7)

because of placement in special education programs. He also suggests the use of these activities as prescriptive solutions required for the individualized educational plan (IEP) required for each special education student. The elementary school counselor is usually involved with the planning and carrying out of the IEPs in the school setting. The author's students make extensive use of these activities—in their course on elementary school counseling, where they are required to conduct classroom guidance activities in local elementary schools, and in their supervised internships. They all enthusiastically endorse these activities.

All of the activities involved in the program developed by Reasoner and others are the kind that an elementary school counselor should be involved with in setting up a school program designed to build self-esteem in children. Many teachers would be hesitant to begin this type of classroom program without the help and encouragement of the elementary school counselor. Other teachers, especially ones with low self-esteem, would be unlikely to become involved in this process at all. It is in these classrooms, especially, that the elementary school counselor could have the greatest impact.

The classroom activities that promote self-esteem should be started no later than kindergarten to make the most productive use of the early school years. Thompson and Rudolph, in discussing poor self-concept in children, note that it is difficult to reverse a negative self-concept, although these children can be helped. Following are some of the ways these children can be helped:

1. Provide opportunities for success. Praise and reinforce the child's behavior whenever possible—for example: "You did a good job picking up the paper" (straightening the books, throwing the ball, and so on). Artificial and forced compliments are easily recognized by children and are ineffective.
2. Use strengths exercises with the children in a group situation. Give to each group member a list of the names of other group members. Each child should write a

positive adjective or statement beside each name. Have each child read his or her list aloud.

3. Discuss with the children what they would like to do or accomplish. Working with the children, set up realistic goals and a step-by-step program to guide the children toward achieving their goals. Continue this guidance until the children feel they can work toward their goals alone.

4. Allow children with poor self-concepts to help someone else; arrange peer teaching or tutoring. Doing something special for someone else helps the helper feel better about him- or herself.

5. Have the adult working with the children write out a list of each child's strengths to help the adult form a more positive conception of the children. Encourage the adult to capitalize on these strengths whenever possible to promote success in each child's life.

6. Ask the children to write down ten positive things about themselves—friendly, can play ball well, can repair a bicycle, can play the piano, and so on. Help the children find ways to use their positive attributes to increase positive feelings about themselves.

7. Supportive counseling with significant adults in the child's life will often help these adults understand the child and the inappropriate behaviors that often result from poor self-concepts. Instruction in effective parenting may be helpful.

8. Have the child list situations that he or she finds uncomfortable or difficult. Discuss ways of behaving in these situations and role play new behaviors. Encourage the child to try the new behaviors in realistic situations and report the results to you.

9. Use active listening. Teach the child problem-solving skill; being able to solve one's own problems builds confidence in self.

10. Involve the child in group activities at home and school. Encourage the child to join organizations such as the Scouts, church group, or a club in which he or she will feel accepted and achieve success. Adults should avoid encouraging participation in groups requiring skills that the child does not possess. Give responsibilities or tasks in school and in the home at which the child can feel success.

11. Use a contract with rewards for attempting new behaviors. Rehearse and practice the new behaviors in a safe atmosphere before they are tried in a real-life situation.

12. Help the child change thoughts of "I can't" to "I will try." Examine what would be the worst thing to happen if the child attempted the task. Encourage positive thinking. (Thompson & Rudolph, 1983, pp. 285–286)

In an article "The Elementary School Counselor as Consultant for Self-Concept Enhancement," Leonard and Gottsdanker-Willekens (1987) noted that for the past ten years,

---

(Scattered excerpts on this and following pages from *Counseling Children,* by Charles L. Thompson and Linda B. Rudolph. Copyright 1983 Wadsworth, Inc. Reprinted by permission of Brooks/Cole Publishing Company, Pacific Grove, CA 93950.)

elementary counselors and teachers have been encouraged to become involved in activities that will foster growth in self-concept. They suggest an in-service program in which the counselor, as consultant, can help teachers develop the self-concept of their students in the classroom setting. In-service presentations, coordinated by the counselor, can be used to help teachers identify and correct students' self-concept problems, to create learning environments for their students that are encouraging, and to incorporate affective action plans into their teaching. Their strategies include assessment of self-concept in students, a determination of the extent of low self-esteem, the decision or need for in-service, planning for intervention, setting goals, evaluation of the in-service, and the long-term impact on teachers and students. The elementary school counselor is an integral part of this process.

Gene Bedley, principal and former National Educator of the Year, related ten reasons to implement a civic values program in schools; within these he identified seven dynamic values that are critical for children to have if they are to lead value-driven lives: respect, compassion, cooperation, integrity, a positive mental attitude, perseverance, and initiative (Bedley, 1993, p. 22). Bedley also received the George Washington Honors Medal from the Freedom Foundation at Valley Forge for his comprehensive Values Curriculum program, *Values in Action!* This is a proven conflict prevention program with more than 15 years of research and implementation. It goes beyond conflict resolution to conflict prevention. This is an excellent program for an elementary counselor concerned with instilling these seven values in children.

Several additional programs and activities designed for counselor and teacher intervention in the classroom in the area of building self-esteem are very effective: *Self-Esteem: A Classroom Affair Volumes 1 and 2,* by Michele and Craig Borba (1978), contains a number of exercises and strategies for counselors and teachers. The Borbas have published over 30 books and articles for parents, teachers, and kids, many in the area of self-esteem. They regularly speak and conduct workshops for parents and teachers on ways to enhance self-esteem. The two other sources are books: *100 Ways to Enhance Self-Concept in the Classroom,* by Canfield and Wells (1976); and *101 Ways to Develop Student Self-Esteem and Responsibility, Vol. 1,* by Canfield and Siccone (1993). These books give excellent ideas for developing self-esteem in the classroom setting by teachers or counselors. Many elementary school counselors currently use these books as a basis for their classroom guidance activities geared to foster growth in self-esteem. Another program that has two parts is the Pumsey Self-Esteem Program: *Bright Beginnings,* grades K–1 (Anderson, 1990), and *Pumsey in Pursuit of Excellence,* grades 1–4 (Anderson, 1987).

These programs are a few of the many that have emerged to address the critical area of enhancing the child's self-concept by focusing on the development of self-esteem. Because we are not born with a self-concept, the elementary counselor's role is of critical importance in the appropriate development of a positive self-concept for all children in the school.

Summary

The author acknowledges that there are other theoretical approaches that would fit into elementary school counseling programs. The five approaches discussed in this chapter lend themselves particularly well to the elementary school, and all are a good "fit" with the American School Counselor Association role description for an elementary school counseling program. As stated earlier in the chapter, the counselor may use several of the theoretical approaches depending upon the classroom, the group, or the individual child. In addition to these approaches, Chapter 9 discusses brief strategic interventions with individual children, and Chapter 10 discusses six different theoretical approaches to family counseling, all appropriate for working with families in the school setting.

Chapter 5

Counselor as Consultant: A Key Role

The Consultation Process

When we think of the word *consultation,* we probably think of the coming together of two or more persons to discuss and make plans regarding an issue or problem of common concern. When we think of consultation in the elementary school setting, we might think of the elementary school counselor working with a teacher on a matter involving a student who is having problems of some sort that affect the child's functioning in that classroom setting. This chapter will expand this definition of consultation to consider the elementary school counselor's role in consultation with parents, administrators, and specialized school staff. The ASCA role statement, discussed in Chapter 3, emphasizes the elementary school counselor's role in consultation with parents and teachers.

This area of emphasis is so accepted as a professional service in the elementary schools that the entire February 1992 issue of *Elementary School Guidance and Counseling* was devoted to consultation. One of the articles (Dougherty, 1992) cited examples of various ways that elementary school counselors can consult:

- Assisting a teacher in developing a plan to manage a disruptive student.
- Conducting a parent group on effective parenting.
- Performing in-service training for school personnel in the area of self-esteem.
- Advocating in the school for the rights of children with special needs.
- Assisting a school administrator in developing a "Just Say No to Drugs" program.
- Providing input to an individualized education program (IEP) team regarding placement opportunities for a child. (p. 163)

When the counselor spends time with the significant adults in the child's life, the preventive and developmental aspects of interventions are stressed, rather than just crisis solutions to urgent problems. The teamwork involved when the counselor, teacher, and parent meet to make decisions regarding a student who has been referred to the counselor capitalizes on the special knowledge and skills each brings to the meeting. The counselor, teacher, parent, and child all benefit from this type of consultation. The efficacy of the elementary school counselor's spending a large proportion of his or her time as a consultant should be obvious. Elementary school counselors have been involved in consultation for many years as one of the three-C's approach that has been advocated: counseling, consultation, and coordination.

It is important that counselor preparation programs include training in the area of consultation. An increasing number of counselor training programs will be preparing counselors for this significant task in an organized way as they seek accreditation from the Council for Accreditation of Counseling and Related Educational Programs (CACREP). One of the CACREP standards requires consultation training and experiences for students in the program: Standard 3, Helping Relationships, specifies studies that "provide an understanding of philosophic bases of . . . consultation theories and their applications" (1988, p. 26). The training may occur in a single course or as an integral dimension of several courses. Under the CACREP Specialty Standards for School Counselors, two of the defined functions are concerned with consultation: B.2.c., "provides consultation to teachers with special emphasis on helping students with developmental needs, behavioral assessment and classroom management," and B.2.d., "consults with parents regarding the child's academic and social adjustment" (1988, p. 39).

In addition to the significance of the training, it is equally important for the prospective new elementary school counselor to find a school that views consultation as a significant role of the counselor and has teachers who want and need the kind of help a counselor consultant is able to give. Although consulting has always taken place in schools when a teacher, parent, or principal asks for help or suggestions regarding a particular child, a school that values consultation will be open to the counselor's identifying his or her role in formalized consulting relationships.

Myrick (1977), in an early monograph, described consultation in three different ways: (1) crisis-consultation, with the counselor consultant in a "hurry up and fix it up" situation; (2) preventive-consultation, when a teacher, for example, sees that a student or a group of students is headed toward some difficulties and seeks help; and (3) developmental-consultation, where the counselor consultant is concerned with classroom and school learning climates and focuses on positive ways to facilitate behavioral growth and learning. Nearly 30 years ago Van Hoose (1968) identified the elementary school counselor's role as a key member of the team that provides for more adequate growth of the student in the school setting. He viewed elementary counseling and guidance as a team effort, with the consultive role of the counselor an integral part of this team approach. It is significant that consultation continues to remain such an important part of the elementary counselor's role.

Child study teams made up of the principal, teacher, school nurse, school psychologist, and counselor are formed in many elementary schools. The counselor often becomes the case manager that pulls together the information, including that gathered in consultation with the parents, to present to the child study team as it seeks solutions to problems affecting children in the school; each person involved has an input into this process. Many elementary schools also involve the counselor in a consultive role in developing an individualized educational plan (IEP), which Public Law 94-142 mandates for each special-needs child as a part of requiring appropriate education for all children with disabilities. The elementary school counselor is in a position to make recommendations in the affective and social areas of need identified in these children. The IEP often spells out a counseling need or requirement, so it is essential that the counselor be involved in the development of the IEP in the role of consultant.

Conoley and Conoley (1982) discussed the personal qualities of a consultant necessary for facilitating the building of good relationships that will result in problem resolution. They suggest that "the personal qualities necessary for good consultation include: friendly, egalitarian, open, good with groups, non-threatening expertise, awareness of and sympathy toward the situations of the consultees, supportive, flexible, efficient, and good follow-up or follow-through skills" (p. 15). They view these skills as describing a process expert rather than a content expert. It is important for the elementary school counselor to be aware of the necessity of maintaining the various attending skills learned in his or her counselor education courses in order to increase consulting effectiveness.

Dinkmeyer and Carlson suggested a number of counselor competencies as consultant skills that characterize an effective consultant. These are summarized as follows:

1. He must be empathic and be able to understand how others feel and experience their world.
2. He must be able to relate to children and adults in a purposeful manner.
3. He must be sensitive to human needs.
4. He must be aware of psychological dynamics, motivations, and purpose of human behavior.
5. He must be perceptive of group dynamics and its significance for the educational establishment.
6. He must be capable of establishing relationships which are characterized by mutual trust and mutual respect.
7. He must be personally free from anxiety to the extent that he is capable of taking a risk on an important issue. He must be able to take a stand on significant issues that affect human development.
8. Perhaps the most important of all, assuming he is able to establish the necessary and sufficient conditions for a helping relationship, the consultant should be creative, spontaneous, and imaginative.
9. He should be capable of inspiring leadership at a number of levels from educational administrators to parents and to teachers. (Cited in George & Cristiani, 1986, pp. 237–238)

Counseling and consulting use essentially the same skills and techniques, and both have the goal of helping children to help themselves, according to Thompson and Rudolph (1992). They noted the major difference to be that those particularly concerned with the child are directly involved, not the child. It is essential for the counselor to realize that information, rather than advice, is provided in the consultation. A further benefit is that more children are reached by the use of consultation when the adults in the child's life are helped to relate in ways that effectively help the child.

For the graduate student in counseling, and for established elementary school counselors who are uncertain as how to make the best use of consultation, it is important to consider a systematic process. Myrick, in his monograph on consultation, suggested seven steps for a systematic approach to consultation. They are summarized as follows:

Step 1: Identify the Problem. The problem or concern needs to be identified as the first step in the consultation process. The consultant needs to be a listener.

Step 2: Clarify the Consultee's Situation. The consultant should be a selective listener and encourage the consultee to talk about feelings, what's been done to this point, what is expected, and any positive attitudes and behaviors already present in the situation.

Step 3: Identify the Goal or Desired Outcomes. Goals can be general or specific and need to be arrived at and agreed upon together as a part of the consultation process. It is usually best for the consultant to avoid giving advice and early interpretations of behavior. Reflecting the feelings of the teacher and clarifying ideas will usually encourage the teacher to present all aspects of the problem.

Step 4: Observe and Record Relevant Behaviors. Base line data is observed and collected in order to assess progress. This, in turn, highlights the problem areas that need to be addressed.

Step 5: Develop a Plan. A mutually agreed-upon course of action is developed by the consultant and consultee. Possible strategies are looked at and decided upon together before they are carried out by the consultee.

Step 6: Initiate the Plan. It is helpful to develop a time schedule which should provide a target date when the plan will start and a follow-up date when the consultant and consultee will meet again.

Step 7: Follow-up. It is important for the consultee to have the opportunity to talk about the process and the results. It is supportive and encouraging for the consultee to work through the problems that have emerged. Follow-up activities also can confirm whether or not the plan is working or needs changes in order to be successful. (Myrick, 1977, pp. 33–56)

The first six consultation stages can be accomplished in a single session if the consultant is skilled at building a helping relationship that is characterized by confidence and trust. The consultation session needs to be paced so that each stage is given adequate attention.

The elementary counselor needs to keep in mind that there will be resistance on the part of some teachers and administrators. This may be due to lack of awareness on their part as to what consultation is, how it is carried out, and what their role is (Dougherty, Dougherty, & Purcell, 1991). To deal effectively with this, and to help the consultees have positive expectations, the counselor should include the following components:

1. Maintaining objectivity
2. Getting appropriate support for consultation within the school
3. Making the counselor's role as a consultant explicit
4. Being aware of the organizational dynamics and the ways in which persons relate

5. Using social influence

6. Emphasizing the peer nature of the relationship. (Dougherty, Dougherty, & Purcell, 1991, p. 181)

When these factors are kept in mind, resistance can be kept to a minimum.

Another way to address resistance in consultation with parents is a system "designed to 'hook' specific parents into a more active involvement in their child's education" (Downing & Downing, 1991, p. 296). This approach evolved from the Downings' experiences in providing parent education in the same community for 17 years. The classroom teacher becomes the critical professional in this approach, but the school counselor "is a vital consultant, associate, and back-up referral person" (p. 297). Specific observation forms are included in the article, including some ideas about why kids do what they do. This is an excellent illustration of a counselor, teacher, and parent all working together, particularly in the face of resistance.

Consultation with teachers and parents is a truly critical part of the elementary school counselor's role and function. As mentioned previously, the counselor also serves in the consultant role with administrators and other school staff. The emphasis in the next three sections of this chapter will be on the consultant role of the elementary school counselor with teachers, parents, and administrators. The theoretical approaches discussed in the previous chapter are applicable to consultation.

Consultation with Teachers

A major task of the elementary school counselor as consultant will be consulting with teachers. Dougherty's statement regarding consultation is echoed throughout the current literature: "School counselors at all levels in public education, including elementary school, are increasingly being called upon to provide consultation" (1992, p. 163). George & Cristiani (1986), addressing consultation with teachers, stress a collaborative role: "The counselor who assumes the position of expert will eventually run out of solutions to problems and will create more problems as teachers find the 'expert' advice ineffective" (p. 245). The collaborative effort utilizes the resources of both persons involved, the counselor and the teacher, and neither is expected to have all the answers.

Consultation typically is one of the major roles of the elementary school counselor. The term *consultant* implies asking advice or seeking information from someone. The "someone" is presumed to be knowledgeable and is usually considered an "expert." For this reason the elementary school counselor should emphasize the collaborative aspect of consulting when consulting with teachers. The teacher has the greatest access to the child, seeing him or her on a daily basis, usually for the major part of the school day. Consulting with a teacher in a collaborative way reduces the possibility of the teacher's feeling that the counselor has "all the answers." Hansen, Himes, and Meier (1990) noted that the counselor needs to be concerned about objectivity based on his or her proximity to the situation. If it appears as though objectivity could become a problem, they suggest enlisting the assistance of some supervision in order to maintain the needed objectivity.

Counseling and consultation are similar in many ways. The major difference is in the type of relationship. In counseling, the counselor and counselee work together to try to

TABLE 5–1   Counseling and Consultation

Counseling	Consultation
1. Establish rapport by listening and communicating understanding and respect.	1. Establish rapport by listening and communicating understanding and respect.
2. Identify the problem. "What are you doing?"	2. Identify the problem. "What do you see as Jenny's main problem?"
3. Identify consequences. "How does this help (or hurt) you in reaching your goal of _____?"	3. Identify consequences. "What happens when Jenny does this?"
4. Evaluate past solutions. "What have you tried to solve this?"	4. Evaluate past solutions. "What have you (or Jenny) tried to solve this?"
5. List alternatives. "What could you be doing?"	5. List alternatives. "Can you think of other things that might help?"
6. Contract—make a plan. "Which alternative will you choose, and when will you do this?	6. Contract—make a plan. "Which alternative will you choose, and when will you do this?"
7. Follow up to evaluate results of plan.	7. Follow up to evaluate results of plan. (Thompson & Rudolph,1983, p. 238)

solve the problem or concern of the counselee; in consultation, the consultant and consultee are meeting together to try to work out the problems or concerns of another person—usually the student in the school setting. Thompson and Rudolph, in looking at the similarities between counseling and consultation, suggested that the two require the same skills (as illustrated in Table 5–1).

Combining counseling and consulting, direct service and indirect service, in many situations may result in multiplying the counselor's effectiveness (Dickenson & Bradshaw, 1992). The elementary counselor needs to be aware that both can be effective.

Because the developmental approach to elementary school counseling is a primary emphasis in this text, as noted in Chapters 3 and 4, consultation with teachers will also be viewed from a developmental perspective. Most elementary schools that employ counselors would have, at most, one counselor, and the large student-to-counselor ratio in most elementary schools makes it an almost impossible task for the counselor to be crisis oriented and at the same time be able to function from a developmental and preventive perspective. If the counselor's approach is crisis oriented, he or she will usually find an endless line of children needing help. Although the focus seems to be on crisis solutions to urgent problems in many of our elementary schools, counselors using consultation to resolve many of these problems will be investing themselves and their time more effectively.

Consultation, from a developmental orientation, emphasizes working with groups of teachers first and individual teachers second in order to affect the greatest number of children. It stands to reason that an hour spent with a group of teachers will have an impact on a larger number of students than an hour spent with one teacher. According to Myrick, group consultation with teachers is particularly effective in the following situations:

1. When the counselor wants a developmental emphasis in consultation and there is a desire to influence the learning climate of the school.

2. When there is a need to build a group where teachers can share their experiences and knowledge and learn from each other.

3. When the consultant's time is limited.

4. When members have a willingness to share and discuss problems, elaborate on solutions, and are interested in learning together. (Myrick, 1977, p. 59)

However, meeting with a teacher individually is more appropriate than meeting as a group with teachers in the following situations:

1. When confidentiality is essential to protect the consultee and others.

2. When there is a crisis situation that needs immediate attention.

3. When a group situation is threatening to the consultee.

4. When the consultee's problem suggests that personal counseling may also be needed as part of the process of change.

5. When there are factors present in a situation which prevent the group from becoming cohesive. (Myrick, 1977, pp. 58–59)

It is important that the counselor keep in mind the basic purposes of consultation with teachers. A major purpose should be to help the teacher identify the skills necessary in attending to problems in the classroom and in the school setting. Another purpose is to allow teachers to share their frustrations and concerns regarding students and experience acceptance and understanding on the part of the counselor-consultant. An additional purpose of consultation in the elementary school is to help teachers become more guidance and counseling oriented in their classroom setting.

Hansen, Himes, and Meier (1990) recognized the importance of developing mutual trust and cooperation in working with the teacher. They also noted the importance of developing clear communication with the teachers and other staff. This includes support for the teacher as he or she works with the children in the classroom: "The more substantial the support and encouragement received by the teacher from the consultant, the more capable the teacher becomes in offering the same to the children, modeling behavior learned from the consultant" (p. 83). This would appear to be a major goal in the elementary school counselor's consultant role.

Myrick and Moni (1972), in observing classroom interactions, found that many teachers respond infrequently to the feelings of students. They suggested a communication workshop for teachers that emphasizes the value of responding to their students' feelings and teaches them how to do this. The facilitative responses taught to the teachers in the communication workshop are basic to the elementary school counselor's training. This type of workshop could be part of an in-service or staff development program for teachers conducted by the counselor in a consultant role. The significance of the elementary school counselor's involvement in an in-service workshop is obvious. The counselors' value, impact, and visibility are increased by the use of developmental consultation ideas in an in-service workshop for teachers.

Gerler (1982) viewed helping teachers manage classroom behavior as an important role for elementary school counselors. Here are some of the sample topics that might be used in a counselor-led group:

1. Causes of behavior problems in the classroom
2. Home-school cooperation in modifying children's behavior problems
3. Teacher-counselor cooperation in solving behavior problems
4. Behavior problems that cannot be handled by school personnel
5. Preventing behavior problems. (Gerler, 1982, p. 22)

An elementary school counselor who would like to become involved in a consultant role with teachers and, at the same time, provide staff development or in-service programs for teachers using a structured program might consider running a Systematic Training for Effective Teaching (STET) group. The authors, Dinkmeyer, McKay, and Dinkmeyer (1980), based STET on a theory of human behavior that they had found effective for thousands of teachers. Human relationship skills and mutual encouragement principles are read, discussed, and practiced with their students. The program covers 14 different subject areas, from "Understanding More about Students and Yourself" to "Working with Parents." The author has noted an increased concern among both beginning and experienced teachers regarding effective teaching strategies and ways to effect positive discipline. The elementary school counselor that conducts a 14-week program, using STET as a guide, will find herself or himself well on the way to becoming a valued consultant to teachers.

Strein and French (1984), reporting the results of a survey to determine the skills, concepts, and attitudes needed by teachers to aid in the affective growth of their students, identified 30 essential skills for teachers. They noted that by providing individual teacher consultation and by in-service programs, the persons in the best position to give this help are the school counselors. They also viewed consultation with teachers as a rewarding activity for the school counselor.

Beginning teachers usually experience much anxiety regarding formal parent-teacher conferences, often resulting in requests for counselors to provide in-service training programs (Johns, 1992). Johns described a role-playing training session and follow-up required for teaching interns at California State University, San Bernadino. This role-playing activity can be used by elementary school counselors to lower the anxiety of first-year teachers in their school, as well as more experienced teachers that are uncomfortable conducting parent-teacher conferences. The article provided role descriptions of seven parent types with their child profiles for role-play activities. These role plays and their ensuing discussions could do much to alleviate this anxiety.

Another effective technique in consulting with teachers is the Brief Therapy model, as developed by the Brief Family Therapy Center in Milwaukee. This approach to problem solving is well suited to the school setting. The Brief Therapy model uses a consultation approach: "The focus of the consultation is to change the adult's interactions with the student in some fashion which will, in turn, result in change for the student" (Kral, 1988, p. 18). This approach stresses the need for the consultant to understand and accept the teacher's point of view about the problem and to be continually on the alert to identify whatever he or she is doing right. Kral stated that "even the most negative teacher can be complimented for caring enough to seek assistance with a problem student" (p. 19). Counselors without teaching experience need to be sensitive about recommending strategies that do not match the teacher's style. To be an effective change agent, the counselor must be a student of those he or she consults.

Meadows (1993) described a method to help the teachers in her district keep track of all the policies and procedures covering a broad range of crises as a way to enhance consultation with teachers. The counselors organized the policies and procedures into one notebook to give to teachers, administrators, and support staff in their school district. The topics covered in the handbook included a description of various behaviors to expect in a variety of situations, with legal implications and ways to handle appropriate referrals using community resources. The handbook enabled everyone in the district to gain a greater understanding of the counselor's role as a consultant and resource for a variety of school and mental health problems (Meadows, 1993).

Gumaer (1980) identified some basic hints that are related to the consulting functions:

1. Know your teachers. Each teacher lives with different psychological stress and anxiety. Take time to build relationships.
2. Discover teacher strengths and reinforce frequently.
3. Begin consulting relationships at the teacher's readiness level.
4. Never reject a teacher. No problem is too small. (p. 118)

A counselor who heeds these hints will go a long way in building successful consulting relationships with the teachers in his or her school.

Consultation with Parents

Parent consultation is a necessary and significant part of the elementary school counselor's role because of the tremendous impact the home environment has on the child. Today's parents continually express frustration in dealing with their children, often admitting a lack of knowledge of how to raise their children. Dreikurs, 20 years after establishing the Adlerian approach to counseling families in the United States, identified a lack of tradition in raising children as the reason for the predicament. Our generation of parents, according to Dreikurs, didn't have the age-old traditions that had existed for thousands of years; the traditional methods used in raising children today are obsolete: "Our children dare to do to us what we never dared to do to our parents. Adults have lost their power over children. Consequently they no longer can control them nor 'make' them behave or perform. Power from without has lost its effect" (Dreikurs, 1959, p. 19). Almost 40 years later parents are saying the same thing, with an increasing sense of helplessness in dealing with their children. For many years, parents depended on the reward-punishment process to control children; it is very seldom successful, as most children today don't fear punishment, especially with the attention given to child abuse and its ramifications.

Parents that try to run their home and children in an autocratic way find out very quickly that it just doesn't work. It is not unusual today to see a parent pleading with a child to behave, to eat, go to bed, straighten his or her room, do homework, and so on. Children seem to sense the power and control they have over their parents and use this to the fullest extent whenever they have been successful in getting their way. Muro and Dinkmeyer (1977) noted the struggle that parents go through trying to establish their own rights, in contrast to their children who well understand their rights but are not willing to accept the responsibilities that go along with these rights. They further highlighted the problem noting that for the most part, parents are not trained to use democratic methods in raising their children. Democratic methods stress mutual respect, equality, and the connection between rights and responsibilities. Most parents want their children to become successful and lead happy and productive lives; it is these parents that are more open to learning about their child's behaviors and the means to affect these behaviors in positive ways. It is in the home that the child's values, as well as the child's concept of self, begin to take form. Gerler (1982), in describing an elementary school counselor's parent group that focused on children's behavior, emphasized the importance of the counselor's role in parent consultation, helping parents teach children appropriate behaviors.

Sometimes parent consultation is counselor initiated and other times it may be parent initiated. Because many parents are experiencing similar problems, Mathias (1992) suggested developing handouts for parents that discuss major topics of concern or writing a column in the monthly school newsletter, which would provide the opportunity to reach all parents. Mathias described a variety of interventions that should be of interest to the elementary school counselor.

As noted previously, it is in the family that the child first develops a self-concept and along with this learns the behavior patterns that determine the effectiveness of social interactions. The child that has problems with social interactions is usually brought to the attention of the elementary school counselor. Administrators and teachers are often at a loss to help these children and look to the counselor for advice and intervention. The elementary school counselor's goal, in consulting with the parents, is to learn more about the child in order to facilitate appropriate behavior in the child. This should be a collaborative effort, using the resources of both the parent and counselor in order to have the most input in fostering positive interactions for the child.

A number of years ago, Van Hoose (1968) differentiated between consulting with parents and counseling parents; this still holds true today. The parent, coming to the elementary school counselor for help with his or her child, is seeking counseling. The parent sees the counselor as having the professional expertise to be of help. The parent is not as concerned with the *why* of the child's problem but is more often concerned about what can be done about it. When the counselor seeks out the parent, it is because of concern for the child, not because of the parent's need for personal help or counseling. This is consulting with parents. Van Hoose identified the major purposes of counselor-parent conferences as follows:

1. To provide parents with information that will enable them to better understand and help their child,
2. To interpret and clarify reasons for certain behaviors,
3. To secure information that will aid the counselor and the school to understand the child,
4. To identify unsound psychological practices and to help the parent reduce or eliminate such practices,
5. To help parents understand the child as a learner, and
6. To involve the parent in the school life of the child. (Van Hoose, 1968, p. 131)

The elementary counselor today needs to be more involved than ever before in counselor-parent conferences. Following these identified purposes of the conference should prove productive as the counselor shares with the parent his or her concerns regarding the child.

It is in the family unit that the child's emotional growth and intellectual growth are fostered and where values are formed; knowing this, the counselor needs to make the effort to develop a relationship with parents that allows successful interactions. At the same time, the counselor needs to be aware that even when he or she exhibits all the previously described personal qualities and competencies, not all parents will be responsive to the initiations of the school counselor as consultant. Hansen, Himes, and Meier (1990) noted that "this is frequently true because they have had few, if any, positive experiences with schools and school personnel" (p. 87). Most parents are not contacted by the school unless there is a problem; it is the rare school that contacts parents just to tell them how well their child is fitting into the school setting.

Gordon (1979), in looking at the effects of parents' involvement on the schooling of their children, noted the importance of school programs' having a positive view of the family. He referred to the success of programs involving parents that show a strong belief in the family itself and belief in the parents' ability to learn and to accept the help and information that is offered in order to assist their own family. Parents need help to know what they can do with their children in dealing with conflict and disruption as well as what they shouldn't do during these times. Parent education appears to be the key to helping parents learn how to deal effectively with their children. Parent education classes, conducted by the elementary school counselor, are an effective means to establish a consulting relationship with the parent or parents. Hansen, Himes, and Meier noted that "parents who know someone will respond positively to their inquiries and assist them in their questions will more than likely return to the school with a favorable attitude and will be able to consider a collaborative role with the school in the future" (1990, p. 88).

Muro and Dinkmeyer (1977) also believed that parent education is the best way to establish corrective efforts with parents. They believed that parents are more readily attracted to and are more willing to be involved with a program that addresses the normal needs of all parents rather than a program that addresses students with more serious or severe problems. Parent education programs with this emphasis are developmental and preventive rather than remedial. With a developmental approach, elementary school counselors will be the most effective in working with parents by using an educational approach that helps them understand how to communicate more effectively with their children and how to utilize encouragement and logical consequences to build a better self-concept, a sense of independence, and feelings of worth in their children. In parent education programs, normal child development and behaviors are studied; the intent is to involve the parent in positive ways in the school program. Setting up parent education and support programs will be examined in Chapter 10.

Other sources are available to help parents resolve parent/child problems. One source that has been very useful is *The Parent's Guide* (McCarney & Bauer, 1989). The book identifies 102 of today's most common behavior problems with children in the home and their solutions. A former elementary school counselor, now an elementary school principal, keeps the book close at hand; the pages with problem behaviors that are applicable in the school are well marked. She discusses these problems and possible solutions with parents when they come to school to address problems such as "Does not follow rules for behavior," "Does not complete homework," "Will not get up on time," "Talks back," "Is easily frustrated," "Is impulsive." There are as many as 50 possible solutions listed for some of the problems; this allows parents to choose the intervention that seems to work best for them and their children. The strategies are meant to be shared with parents by counselors and other professionals (S. Zimmermann, personal communication, February 14, 1994).

Reasoner (1982b) provided three suggestions for parents that eliminate the need for lectures or punishments:

1. *Use natural consequences.* The use of natural consequences can be an effective way to tie the punishment to the violation. For example, the consequence of creating a mess is having to clean it up. Natural consequences can be used in most situations and they help children understand that their behavior or misbehavior has particular consequences.
2. *Use "I" messages.* A clear, specific statement of what you want reduces or eliminates conflicts. The statement, "I need you to set the table now," is more effective than accusations such as "Why haven't you set the table yet?" or "You never set the table when you are supposed to."
3. *Set up routines.* When appropriate, routines reduce many conflicts and add to a sense of security. Children should know what is expected of them and should follow a set routine. Routines can be established for going to bed at night, doing schoolwork, completing chores, or getting ready for school. (pp. 4–5)

Thompson and Rudolph (1983) discussed contracting as a consulting technique to teach parents. The contracts are written agreements between the parent and child defining appropriate or desired behavior. The following is an example of how a contract between a parent and child might look:

Parent and Children Contract	*Points M T W T F S S*
1. Writes down school assignments	2
2. Completes homework before 6:00 PM	3
3. Receives an "A" paper	5
4. Receives a "B" paper	3
5. Picks up room and makes bed	3
6. Gets bath and to bed by 9:00 PM	3
7. Does weekly assigned household chores	5

Extra points may be earned by:

1. Running errands	3
2. Doing extra chores	3–5

Points earned can be cashed in for:

1. 10 points: Stay up hour later
2. 20 points: Special treat with friend
3. 20 points: Movie treat
4. 50 points: $2.00 spending money
5. Other rewards are negotiable. (Thompson & Rudolph, 1983, p. 244)

It is important to note that not all problem situations that come up in consultation sessions between an elementary school counselor and a parent may be resolvable. It may be appropriate for the counselor to refer the parent to outside sources, such as a psychologist, psychiatrist, family counseling center, and so on. Most elementary school counselors maintain a list of referrals to outside agencies in the community.

Consultation with Administrators

Depending upon the size of the school system, the elementary counselor could be in a position to report to more than one administrator. Most elementary schools have a full-time principal; some principals may serve more than one school, with a designated head-teacher in charge when the principal is at his or her other school(s). A larger school district might have a central office person designated as coordinator or director of guidance and counseling services. Some large districts have an administrator designated as coordinator of elementary counseling programs, in addition to the one designated as district director of guidance and counseling services. The author has served in several of these positions and is well aware of the confusion that might exist for the elementary counselor required to "report" to more than one person. The counselor in a consultant role with an administrator should use a systems approach, viewing the school as a part of a system that includes the school district as a whole. Chapter 10 elaborates on the systems approach in working with families; framing the consultation problem in terms of the system is an important perspective to remember, whether the system is the school or the family. Administrators are trained to view the impact of individual school problems on the school or the school district as a whole, not as an isolated individual incident; when the counselor thinks in terms of systems, he or she will approach the administrator from a different frame of reference.

The *Journal of Counseling and Development* devoted two entire issues to consultation: July/August 1993 and November/December 1993. One of the articles (West & Idol, 1993) discussed the counselor as a consultant in the collaborative school, noting the various organizational structures within the school where consultation is a vital role for the counselor. One of the identified roles, in a school-based management team, would include both the principal and the counselor. West and Idol focused on three roles in which the counselor may contribute his or her skills: "as a change agent or facilitator, team process facilitator, and team member" (p. 681). The skills possessed by the counselor become a valuable asset for the principal in a collaborative consultation role.

It is crucial for the elementary counselor to build a good working relationship with the principal; without this, the guidance and counseling program will suffer. The climate the school provides for the children and the teaching staff is significant to the development of the child. The climate of the school and the leadership of the principal in that school play significant roles in creating a positive environment that can affect the student's behavior and subsequent learning. The principal is one of the most important people in the school; the leadership provided by the principal determines whether or not maximum opportunities for developmental task mastery by the students in the school is promoted.

The counselor is in a key position to have an impact on the principal in the daily operation of the school. The elementary counselor is usually alone in his or her school, unlike secondary schools, which typically have more than one counselor; the principal is also alone, not having assistant principals as do the secondary schools. This could encourage collaborative teamwork if the counselor keeps the principal apprised of the various activities that make up the counseling program. Beginning counselors often think that the principal is too busy and has too many other issues to deal with and are hesitant to take the necessary time to talk to the principal. The importance of keeping the lines of communication open cannot be overstressed; principals do not like to be surprised about what is going on in their schools by finding out from other sources rather than from those working in the school. The counselor is in a unique, and sometimes conflicting, situation, representing the children, the teachers, the parents, and the principal. It is not an easy position to be in and requires delicate handling on the part of the counselor. In a school with open lines of communication, this task is not a difficult one; it is when the school is not open that the counselor may need to clearly define his or her role for all those that he or she serves.

Nugent (1990) suggested another role for the counselor in working with administrators, that of offering "information and guidelines about potential consequences of certain administrative actions upon the student body or the teaching staff" (p. 225). Again, this could be a complicated situation unless the counselor has established a good trusting relationship with his or her principal. If the counselor and the principal have established a good relationship this should be accomplished without any significant problems.

Parr identified some dilemmas that an elementary counselor might face, including demands from school principals, such as "This won't go beyond these walls: what are the teachers really saying. . .?" (Parr, 1991, p. 221). This places the counselor in a risky position: The principal might consider the counselor's refusal to respond as disloyalty. At the same time, it is imperative that the counselor maintain the trust of the teachers and not divulge any information. Here is another dilemma identified by Parr: "I just don't know what we would do without you—by the way, I couldn't find a substitute for Ms. Jones today" (p. 221). Asking a counselor to perform duties not related to his or her identified function as school counselor is inappropriate; performing unrelated duties can erode the real job role of the counselor, causing others to question their role. In order not to be caught in dilemmas like these, the counselor needs to identify and prioritize his or her task with the administration, the teachers, and the staff when first assigned to the school. The importance of an active and concerned Guidance and Counseling Advisory Council should be obvious. Chapter 12 discusses the organization of an effective advisory council, which would define the role of the elementary school counselor; this should, in turn, eliminate this type of problem situation.

Consulting with other administrators in the school district occurs when the district has central office personnel assigned to coordinate the guidance and counseling program throughout the district. Consultation like this might transpire when situations such as those described in the previous paragraph occur. A district coordinator usually sets up in-service and training programs for the counselors at each level on a regular basis. Meeting together with the other elementary counselors in a district with more than one counselor is an excellent way to brainstorm ideas and activities. Some of the most rewarding activities the author has been involved with have been in these kinds of situations; facilitating the coming together of elementary school counselors to share strategies and activities. Usually their enthusiasm at these sessions is infectious even when some of their concerns and problems seem overwhelming. They are able to provide solutions for many of each other's problems and dilemmas. This also creates the kind of atmosphere that encourages the counselors on an individual basis to seek out the counseling administrator for consultation needs.

Summary

The elementary school counselor is in a unique position to offer consultation to teachers, parents, and administrators for several reasons: The elementary school is usually small enough so that there is apt to be more interaction between the counselor and teachers, resulting in discussion of problems that children are experiencing; parents are more apt to seek help and be open for suggestions at this level than when their children are older; and, in a developmental approach to counseling, the focus is on meeting the child's needs rather than responding to crisis situations. It is imperative that counselor education programs make a commitment to address consultation with teachers, parents, and administrators as a significant part of the training of elementary school counselors.

Consultation as a school counselor role appears to be increasing, particularly as counselors are involved in a developmental approach to elementary school counseling. Counselor education programs will be required to teach consultation as more states see the importance of this vital role for school counselors. In 1989 California identified consultation as a critical role for school counselors; the Commission on Teacher Credentialing in California adopted a revision to the Professional Preparation Programs General Requirements for Pupil Personnel Services Credential, required of all newly credentialed California school counselors, K–12. The requirements provide that each candidate have a knowledge of consultation services to include the following:

- Individual and team consultation processes.
- Pupil-advocacy processes.
- Principles and practices of effective classroom management.
- Principles and procedures of effective school discipline.
- Methods of initiating consultive relationships with and between teachers, other staff, and parents. (Commission on Teacher Credentialing, 1989, p. 4)

The new standards resulted in increased dialogue between all counselor education programs in the state as they discussed how this standard would be addressed.

A research study of persons involved in master's level counselor programs, conducted by Brown, Spano, and Schulte (1988), demonstrated that students receive various amounts of preparation in consultation, with many probably not receiving proper preparation prior to graduating. This is a serious omission in a counselor training program considering the large number of students, teachers, and parents that can be reached with an effective school consultation model in place. The elementary school counselor that makes use of consultation as an important counselor intervention will be helping teachers, parents, and administrators fulfill their roles to a greater degree.

Chapter 6

Areas of Concern in the Elementary School

A typical elementary school counselor spends most of his or her day responding to problems involving children in their schools. Teachers, school administrators, and parents do not often seek the counselor's help for the minor day-to-day problems, the kind that can be expected to occur with most children; it is the chronic problems of children who don't seem to fit into the school setting, that are disruptive or demanding of "extra" attention, that finally cause a teacher, principal, or parent to seek the help of the counselor. Many of these children come from very unstable or dysfunctional families; more and more young children, because of low self-esteem, have a hard time establishing friendships and become easy targets for gang membership; it is not uncommon to find elementary-age children that are substance abusers, using and selling drugs; an increasing number of children are physically and sexually abused or are neglected; the issue of gender bias in our schools affects both girls and boys starting in the elementary school; children with learning disabilities and attention deficit disorder have special needs that are not always met in the elementary school setting; young children left alone for long periods of time, often referred to as latchkey kids, have their own special unmet needs; children that are angry or inattentive, or exhibit impulsive or bullying behavior, are more than teachers can handle in the elementary school classroom. These are the children that make up the group under consideration in this chapter—the areas that require response from the elementary counselor. These areas of concern for the elementary school counselor will be looked at in the context of the elementary school, how they affect the school and classroom, and the elementary school counselor's involvement in the resolution of these problems.

Attention Deficit Disorder

Identification of the Problem

Attention deficit disorder (ADD) appears to affect an increasing number of children; parents and teachers are attempting to find explanations for the behavior of these children. Robert Erk, an American Counseling Association counselor-educator in Tennessee with a son identified as ADD, has been actively studying and researching this disorder, producing a number of journal articles and workshop presentations. He noted that "many ADD children suffer countless hours of academic frustration, pay little attention to their behaviors, do not seem to grasp the seriousness of their problems, often display a guiltless demeanor, experience rejection by peers, are at the mercy of their impulsive actions, and suffer daily losses to their self-esteem" (Erk, 1995, p. 292). Many parents, suffering under the strain of raising a child who exhibits the symptoms commonly associated with attention deficit disorder, find parenting unrewarding and their marriage deteriorating. If there are older children in the family that are not presenting a problem, the parents are even more confused and wonder why this child should behave in such unacceptable ways. The possibility of the presence of attention deficit disorder (ADD) is usually not diagnosed until the child starts kindergarten or is placed in a preschool, where the behavior is too disruptive for the child to remain in that setting.

ADD may occur just this way or it may occur as attention deficit disorder with hyperactivity (ADHD). Both are disorders that involve a malfunctioning of neurotransmitters in the brain. Both of these, when unrecognized by the school, have resulted in untold harm to the children thus inflicted: "For many attention deficit children who are left unidentified, the cumulative effects of low self-esteem, chronic school failure, and inadequate social skills lead to adolescent antisocial behavior, alcohol and drug abuse, dropouts, and even suicide" (Bowley & Walther, 1992, p. 39). With this grim forecast for an ever-increasing number of children, identifying these children in the early elementary school years becomes even more critical.

The elementary school counselor needs to know the symptoms that must be present for a diagnosis of ADHD. The *Diagnostic and Statistical Manual of Mental Disorders, Third Edition* (DSM-III) lists the diagnostic criteria for ADHD as follows:

    A. *Inattention.* At least three of the following:

        1. Often fails to finish things he or she starts
        2. Often doesn't seem to listen
        3. Easily distracted
        4. Has difficulty concentrating on schoolwork or other tasks requiring sustained attention
        5. Has difficulty sticking to a play activity

    B. *Impulsivity.* At least three of the following:

        1. Often acts before thinking
        2. Shifts excessively from one task to another
        3. Has difficulty organizing work

    4. Needs a lot of supervision
    5. Frequently calls out in class
    6. Has difficulty awaiting turn in game or group situation

C. *Hyperactivity.* At least two of the following:

    1. Runs about or climbs on things excessively
    2. Has difficulty sitting still or fidgets excessively
    3. Has difficulty staying seated
    4. Moves about excessively during sleep
    5. Is always "on the go" or acts as if "driven by a motor"

D. Onset before the age of seven.
E. Duration of at least six months. (American Psychiatric Association, 1980, pp. 43–44)

This information should be considered when making a preliminary decision of whether or not to refer the child for further testing and evaluation. The *Diagnostic and Statistical Manual of Mental Disorders, Fourth Edition* (DSM-IV) further classifies the disorder into types based on defined criteria, such as attention-deficit/hyperactivity disorder, predominantly inattentive type (DSM-IV, 1994).

Hosie, in a 1992 *Guidepost* article, noted that the symptoms of ADD tend to dissipate after the child passes adolescence (cited in Backover, 1992). The intervening years, the formative years of child rearing and early schooling, are most affected by the disorder. Even when the disorder is properly diagnosed, a lot of frustration is in store for parents just trying to acquire an appropriate education for their child. Hosie and Erk (1993) view ADD as one of the most prevalent childhood disorders, affecting between five and ten percent of our schoolchildren. They discussed the impact on the child and the family, particularly because of the difficulty of diagnosis for children who do not exhibit severe symptoms. It is often the elimination of other possible causes of the problem behaviors, such as learning disabilities, that results in a diagnosis of ADD.

Counseling Strategies

The elementary school counselor is in a significant position in the early referral process for the ADD or ADHD child. The counselor needs to be knowledgeable about attention deficit disorders in order to effectively help the child, the teacher, and the parents. Although the counselor is not in a position to diagnose, he or she is able to do some initial screening and evaluation of the child through the school's student study team. A set of questionnaires that are quite simple to administer and score in the diagnostic process are the Conners' Teacher Rating Scale and the Conners' Parent Rating Scale (Conners, 1990), both one-page questionnaires to be filled out by the parent and the teacher (Conners, 1985). The norms break down the scoring into the following categories: hyperactivity, conduct disorder, emotionally overindulgent, anxiety/passivity, asocial, and daydream-attendance problem. These data, along with other information gathered from the parents regarding early behaviors, teacher's observations, and input from other members of the child study team, enable the counselor to refer the parents to outside sources if ADD or ADHD is suspected.

Because the parent has had the burden of the ADD or ADHD child from the onset of the symptoms, and has the child in the home during all of the nonschool hours, the most critical need would seem to be parent support and parent involvement in the treatment of the child. Erk, recognizing the needs of parents because of his ADD-diagnosed son, organized a parent support group for parents of ADD children in his area. He views the ADD-afflicted family as under much stress, needing the support of others to cope with all the frustrations surrounding parenting an ADD child (cited in Backover, 1992).

The Long Beach Unified School District in California developed a pilot project, funded through a California State Assembly Bill, called Project L.I.N.C.—Linking an Intervention Network for Children. It was developed and coordinated through the Office of Counseling Services and was coordinated in each project school by the counselor. The letter sent out to parents stated the following: "This group is for parents whose children are enrolled in the L.I.N.C. Project at Lowell, Harte, Lincoln or McKinley, and for interested parents in other Long Beach schools who have children experiencing academic or behavioral difficulties due to short attention span, inappropriate impulsiveness, or distractibility" (Fairbanks, 1988). One of the topics to be covered in the eight weekly sessions, listed in the letter to the parents, was "Specific management techniques to help parents increase cooperation and handle misbehavior of their children" (Fairbanks, 1988). The relief that parents must have felt knowing that others were experiencing these same problems and that help to address these problems was being offered cannot be measured.

The Virginia Department of Education made a series of recommendations to be used in training teachers in that state based on a task force report on attention deficit hyperactivity disorder in the schools (Bowley & Walther, 1992). One of the recommendations was to incorporate information on ADHD into all of the state's teacher training programs; another was to provide information on ADHD to all public school personnel in the state, including "development of programs/materials for education of all school personnel, physicians, and parents about ADHD. In addition to in-service training, pamphlets should be developed alerting teachers and parents to the presence and characteristics of the disorder" (Reeve, 1990, cited in Bowley & Walther, 1992, p. 42). Because Virginia is one of the states with mandated elementary school counseling services, conducting in-service training for teachers and other school staff would be an appropriate way for counselors to confront this growing concern in our schools.

Lavin (1991) stressed the need to provide both educational and psychosocial interventions to help alleviate ADHD children's academic, behavioral, and emotional difficulties. The counselor functioning in the role of coordinator and consultant, equipped with his or her knowledge of human development and learning, is in a position to help devise programs that will benefit the ADHD child (Lavin, 1991).

Erk viewed counselors as being in a unique position to be leaders in providing a multidisciplinary/multimodal treatment for children that have been identified as ADD. He encouraged counselors to take an active role, including coordinating an on-site multidisciplinary team, facilitating contact between ADD children and their peers, providing counseling programs for ADD children, and organizing and providing ADD workshops (Erk, 1995). Erk's article provides an excellent table of interventions identifying various categories of interventions in a multimodal treatment of attention deficit disorder.

By providing in-service to teachers and by providing group counseling in the schools for children who have been diagnosed with these disorders, elementary counselors will be providing an invaluable service that will be of help to the child, the school, and the family. Through parent education classes the counselor can offer help to the parents, which will in turn affect the siblings of the ADD child. Helping parents learn some of the behavior management skills necessary to work with their child, in addition to forming more realistic expectations of their child, can increase the child's potential success in the home and school environment. The elementary school counselor performs a key role in the successful treatment of children with ADD and ADHD in their school by being a supportive person in the child's life.

Childhood Depression

Identification of the Problem

Childhood depression is not often referred to in our professional counseling journals, although there appears to be an increase in teacher referrals noting that the child "seems depressed," according to elementary school counselors and counseling interns informally interviewed by the author in recent years. Hart viewed the significance of family breakdown and other societal fragmentation as having a great impact on children, thus causing depression in increasing numbers among our schoolchildren. She emphasized the significance of elementary counselors' knowledge of the problem: "The awareness of childhood depression may prove as important within the schools during this decade as awareness of child abuse has been in the past decade" (Hart, 1991, p. 277).

Ramsey (1994) noted that recent research findings have identified depression as a major mental health problem for children and adolescents. She also noted that researchers have found that "depression in school-age children manifests the same basic symptoms as depression in adults" (1994, p. 256). She voiced her concerns regarding the lack of specific interventions designed for treating these children: "Unfortunately, although student depression is being acknowledged, its identification and subsequent treatment remain a major problem because of the lack of referrals, parental denial, and insufficient symptom identification training" (Ramsey, 1994, p. 256).

Patros and Shamoo (1989) viewed depression as a reaction to many stress factors in the child's life, particularly if a series of stresses are experienced over a short period of time. They also viewed the possibility of a relationship between depression and suicidal behavior in children. The studies they examined suggested that a child may make an attempt to commit suicide, not intending to go through with it; at the same time they noted that the statistics on children from ages four to fourteen that take their own lives is not very reliable due, in part, to parents and authorities not wanting to believe it was suicide. It is important to intervene in the lives of children who appear sad and depressed in order to help those that may be thinking suicidal thoughts. "It is possible to distinguish between those children who are suicidal and those who are depressed but without suicidal ideations" (Patros & Shamoo, 1989, p. 23). These are the children that can be most affected by counseling if they are detected early and a school intervention plan is in effect.

In order to identify depression, we need to have an understandable definition of what it is and how it affects children. Several definitions have been provided in three different issues of *Elementary School Guidance and Counseling*. Lasko (1986) stated that "the child seems down, blue, or irritable and no longer takes interest or pleasure in usual activities" (p. 284); Downing (1988) added to this "the prolonged unhappiness or helplessness sometimes exhibited by children" (p. 232); and Hart (1991) noted that "depression can include feelings of hopelessness, guilt, separation anxiety, and, at the extreme, suicidal ideation and behavior" (p. 278). When these behaviors occur in clusters, or for an extended period of time, intervention strategies should be employed.

There are indications or signals typical of child depression that we should be aware of, according to Patros and Shamoo (1989). These include a lack of interest in activities that are usually pleasant; a change in appetite, either an increased appetite or a lack of interest in food; a change in sleep patterns, being restless and unable to sleep, or lethargic and lacking motivation from an excessive amount of sleep; a loss of energy in a formerly active child; inappropriately blaming himself or herself for everything that goes wrong; negative feelings of self-worth, feeling unloved and unwanted by everyone; feelings of sadness, hopelessness, and worry, causing the child to look and feel unhappy; inability to concentrate and focus attention on anything; and morbid thoughts, including excessive thoughts of death and/or suicide. Patros and Shamoo also viewed some possible "masked" depressive behaviors, behaviors usually not associated with depression: aggressive or negative behaviors, both in and out of the classroom; increased agitation, with difficulty completing tasks; increased psychosomatic complaints such as stomachaches, headaches, and just not feeling well; decreased academic performance, causing the child to function below grade level; and poor attention and concentration (pp. 81–89).

In addition to the signs listed above as indicators of depression in children, it is important to look at research concerning suicide among elementary school aged children because of the suicide risk of individuals exhibiting signs of depression. Nelson and Crawford (1990) sent a survey to all elementary school counselors in Kansas addressing suicide attempts and completions, suicide behaviors, and suicide prevention approaches. Part of the survey asked elementary school counselors to rank issues that they saw as causing the most concern among elementary school children. The following list is rank-ordered from most to least:

1. Parent divorce
2. Appearance/self-esteem
3. Peer pressure
4. Remarriage/reconstituted families
5. Academic failure
6. Student alcohol/drug abuse
7. Learning disabilities
8. Latchkey children
9. Suicidal behavior
10. Student illness/disability (Crawford, 1990, p. 125)

It is significant that many of these concerns mirror the symptoms and descriptors of childhood depression. Although all depressed children aren't suicidal, for many it could be a consideration not to be ignored.

Counseling Strategies

A number of studies over the years have addressed suicide among both children and adolescents. Stefanowski-Harding (1990), who researched characteristics and risk factors associated with the suicidal child, noted that the counselor should be aware of these, including the causes and signs of suicide. Children who are depressed typically show different signs of their depression than depressed adults. Children often hide the depression in a variety of ways, such as exhibiting acting-out behaviors, school phobia, or running away. She stressed the fact that counselors are usually at the forefront because they are the ones who handle referrals from teachers and parents.

The elementary counselor is in a position to help identify children suffering any of the symptoms attributed to depression through referral by the teacher. Prior to referring the child to other sources outside of the school, some preliminary assessment should take place.

A depressed child should be assessed to see if these feelings are apparent in all aspects of the child's life—at home, at school, and around peers. Often a child will display symptoms of depression when parents are separating or divorcing; at other times it may be the loss of a grandparent, a friend, or even a pet that causes the child's depression. If the child stays depressed, then the use of assessment measures such as Reynolds Child Depression Scale (Reynolds, 1989a) will help determine the severity of the depression. The Reynolds Child Depression Scale (RCDS) is a self-report measure; Reynolds believes that direct questioning of the child, rather than relying on teacher and parent observations, will better determine the child's experience and feelings. The scale may be used with children in grades 3 through 6, with a reading level of second grade. The RCDS takes about ten minutes to complete, is hand scorable, and can be administered individually or in small groups. An elementary counselor with graduate-level coursework in testing and knowledge of professional and ethical guidelines for test interpretation is a potential user of the RCDS.

Elementary teachers, in contact with the children in their classrooms on a daily basis, are in an excellent position to compare the children, noting if a child's behavior seems quite different from his or her peers. The cause of stress for some children could be in the classroom itself; some children do not handle stress of any kind very well, and if they feel pressure to be successful in the classroom as well as at home, depression could be triggered. A counselor in a classroom observing a child referred for depression should be aware of the possibility that the teacher is contributing to the stress of the child under observation. If this is noted, helping the teacher become aware of this could help change the action or behaviors that are leading to stress in the child. This is a very sensitive area, particularly because teachers are under a lot of stress themselves, with the myriads of pressures put on them by the various demands of children in their classrooms, by their administrators, by parents, and even by their own home situations. The value of elementary counselors building a successful consulting relationship with the teachers in his or her school will be apparent when situations such as these arise. It is much easier to help teachers see where their behaviors could be contributing to the stress of a child in their classrooms when a good working relationship has already been established. Lasko (1986) stressed the counselor's role as child advocate in the consulting relationship with teachers. This is done by helping teachers and other school staff become aware of the realities of childhood depression.

If several children that appear depressed or sad are referred to the elementary counselor, it may be appropriate to suggest to the principal that an in-service on recognizing some of the causes of childhood depression would be timely. Some of the topics that could be covered by the counselor in such an in-service program might include the assignment of homework that is beyond the child's ability to accomplish the task, ability grouping that causes the child to feel less than capable, and competition in groups that causes some children to feel belittled if they cannot compete. These are all school-related topics that teachers can easily relate to.

Hart (1991) views the counselor's role as "directly working with the child, indirectly assisting through professional development with teachers and other school staff, and acting as liaison with parents and community health workers" (p. 286). When the counselor is working directly with children, Downing noted, the child can be taught awareness of the depressive thoughts and feelings and can learn ways to avoid some of the problems that cause these feelings. "Children can change negative thoughts and feelings to positive ones by redirecting their thoughts to pleasant experiences and by using deliberate internal affirmations" (1988, p. 237). Other coping skills that can be taught to the child, according to Downing, include teaching the child to daydream and fantasize in positive ways; using a simple biofeedback system that causes them to have a measure of control over their bodies; and using affirmations, positive self-talk that helps them gain self-control (1988).

The school's child study team is the ideal place to start with a child who is suffering from depression. The counselor is often the case manager for this type of team and is the logical person to coordinate information-gathering from the parents, teacher, school staff, and the child. Often, if there has been a psychological referral either at this time or in the recent past, the school psychologist or diagnostician has run a battery of tests on the child under consideration by the team. He or she would be a valuable asset to have on the child study team.

School counselors are in a position to affect the depressed child through child study teams, through classroom observations and teacher in-service, through parent contacts, and through direct counseling with the child. A child with low self-esteem is often a depressed child, believing that he or she is "dumb," "not good" at anything, or is "not liked" by anyone. The use of classroom guidance activities in which building self-esteem is stressed is a positive way to affect a child that is acting sad or depressed. A child who gains a measure of self-esteem is a child who is better able to handle some of the many stressors that will come his or her way at home, among peers, and in school.

Disruptive, Impulsive, Inattentive, and Bullying Behaviors

Identification of the Problem

A complaint heard from a growing number of teachers today centers on the amount of time that they are forced to spend in "classroom management" rather than teaching because an increasing number of children in their classrooms are exhibiting disruptive and undisciplined behaviors. A large segment of our population is not aware of the existence of the problems that children are bringing to school, nor are they aware of the types of behavior these children are displaying on a daily basis that cause teachers to be so frustrated and discouraged that they sometimes wonder why they continue to teach. As disheartening as it sounds, the fact remains that this scenario is becoming all too common with the school-children of today.

Often children that display a lot of anger, have frequent fights, and show hostility and verbal aggressiveness come from homes where these kinds of acting-out behaviors are everyday occurrences; the child is simply exhibiting the behaviors modeled in his or her family. Sometimes, instead of striking out at others, children go to the opposite extreme, expecting to fail, which leads to a "giving up," where the child stops trying. Possibly too much has been expected of these children, and the resulting failure in one area becomes generalized to other areas, particularly in the school setting. These children may display inattentive behaviors, which in turn often results in their falling even farther behind. They may feel that they cannot accomplish the tasks expected by the teacher or their peers in the classroom, or in small groups. Wielkiewicz (1986) noted that an inattentive child will have many difficulties in school when their attention can't be directed toward such basic tasks as the various shapes of letters, for example.

Impulsive behavior is often associated with hyperactivity, but not all impulsive children come under the core description of hyperactivity. Children that are impulsive usually act without thinking, whether it is calling out the answer without raising their hands, grabbing something away from another child without asking, or just appearing to act without thinking. Impulsive behavior occurs when the child does not take the time needed to process all the elements of the tasks at hand, causing mistakes as he or she quickly completes the work (Wielkiewicz, 1986). Because boys are most often singled out for this type of behavior, it is important to consider whether this is "typical behavior" for a boy or girl or whether it handicaps him or her in any way. If the child still accomplishes most of the tasks, he or she may simply need help and direction in learning how to stay on task.

Another behavior to be considered in this section is one that has always been a part of school: bullying. Untold numbers of children have suffered at the hands of bullies for as long as schools have existed. At the 1991 American Counseling Association (ACA, formerly American Association for Counseling and Development) annual meeting in Reno, a presentation on "Bullying in Our Schools" revealed some startling statistics: 1 out of 10 students is regularly harassed, extorted, or attacked by bullies, and 25 percent of the students report that one of their most serious concerns is their fear of bullies (Garrison, Ivey, & Weinrach, 1991). They noted that bullying is more of an elementary school issue, with twice the percentage of bullying occurring in grades 2–6 as in grades 7–9. A study conducted by Perry, Kusel, and Perry (cited in Hoover & Hazler, 1991) identified 10 percent of elementary students as "extreme victims," and that both boys and girls were victims of bullies. Hoover and Hazler also noted that school professionals have a tendency to ignore or downplay the bullying, allowing some children to be scapegoats.

Counseling Strategies

Children with behavior problems demand a lot of attention from the teacher and are a continual distraction to their classmates; in the process, little learning takes place, which puts even greater stress on the teacher and students in the classroom. Problem-behavior children are often referred to the counselor to "fix." There are a variety of ways for counseling interventions to take place: individually, in small groups, and in the classroom. Depending upon the severity of the behaviors, most children will benefit with classroom guidance activities or small group activities that provide some success experiences for them.

Children who exhibit inattentive behaviors frequently develop learned helplessness and often fail to finish anything they start. They have difficulty concentrating on tasks for any length of time, believing that they do not have a lot of control over what happens to them. Attribution of causality to these children is outside themselves; "others," such as their teacher, their parents, classmates, or friends are to blame, which absolves them of any responsibility. Greer and Wethered (1987) asserted that the helplessness cycle can be broken by helping these children develop realistic attributions. As a part of this, the counselor and the teacher should provide success experiences that will help these children realize they can be successful and have a measure of control in their life.

Rathvon (1990) conducted a study that looked at the effects of encouragement on off-task behavior and the subsequent academic productivity with a group of six first-grade students. In this study, the teacher would provide encouragement to these children, individually, if they were engaging in off-task behaviors, delivering a minimum of five encouraging statements to each of them every morning. Although it was a limited study, the preliminary findings indicated positive effects on the classroom behaviors of these children. This study came about through the use of teacher consultation resulting in a "positive approach to classroom management involving minimal amounts of teacher and counselor time" (Rathvan, 1990, p. 197). A counselor that establishes consulting relationships with the teachers in his or her school is in a position to suggest that they attempt to duplicate this study.

Another study (Bowman & Myrick, 1987) looked at the effects of using a peer facilitator program on children with behavior problems. A group of fifth-grade students that were identified by counselors and teachers as leaders received peer facilitator training consisting of an orientation meeting, ten sessions on skills, and two review meetings. The peer facilitators at the completion of their training worked with targeted misbehaving second- and third-grade students individually, in addition to conducting sessions on friendship in their classrooms. The results of this extensive study indicated that the elementary school peer facilitators could effectively improve the classroom behaviors of younger children with behavior problems (Bowman & Myrick, 1987). Although this study was carried out in nine elementary schools in Gainesville, Florida, it could be replicated on a smaller scale in an individual school by a counselor with some knowledge or training in conducting peer facilitator programs.

Angry children are not often taught how to express angry feelings. When these feelings are not expressed, often out of fear of punishment, they will usually surface in other acting-out ways. Omizo, Hershberger, and Omizo (1988) discussed the difference in working with children that were sent to the counselor versus a preventive approach in which the behaviors are dealt with before they become problematic. They conducted a group counseling intervention with the intention of assisting children in coping with anger. Twenty-four children were selected, out of 47 nominated that behaved aggressively, to be involved in the project. The selected students participated in ten group counseling sessions that met weekly. The results indicated significantly decreased aggressive and angry behaviors in the children that were involved in the ten weekly counseling sessions. This proved to be an excellent means to teach children appropriate ways to handle situations that would create feelings of anger: "When counselors teach children self-discipline and appropriate responses to angry feelings, the frequency of anger-related problems will diminish" (Omizo et al., 1988, p. 241).

In order to introduce effective counseling strategies with bullies, the counselor and teacher should be aware that children who bully are basically unhappy children who need help in resolving the conflicts in their lives that bring about this unacceptable behavior. Allan, a counselor-educator and former school counselor, noted that counselors can help students that are involved in bullying and scapegoating by assisting them in confronting and dealing with the feelings that cause these behaviors (cited in Thiers, 1988). Allan also recommended classroom meetings geared toward helping all students understand the *why* of bullying. Hoover and Hazler (1991) envisioned the counselor in a consultant role in the school to teachers and parents in addition to providing a supportive role for the children that are the victims of bullying. They noted the significant role that the counselor plays in this, including addressing developmental factors in their work with teachers, parents, and children. "Strategies presented to these groups must focus on recognizing the problems, promoting confidence and assertiveness in passive children, and also encouraging children, particularly bullies, to participate in democratic activities, with issues being resolved by reason rather than force" (Hoover & Hazler, 1991, p. 217). Another approach to dealing with the issues of bullying was suggested by Mary Gehrke, elementary school counselor and former vice president of the Elementary Schools of the American School Counselor Association: "Clear and consistent consequences for those who bully are also important" (cited in Thiers, 1988, p. 11). She suggested "a school-wide program to deal with bullying, in which the whole school knows what the game plan is and what the consequences are" (p. 11). Gehrke's elementary school used a program called "Stop–Think–Practice" to help those children being bullied, giving them some control as a victim. Hoover and Hazler (1991), in looking at the victims of bullies, suggested teaching these children practical skills that will help them in interactions with bullies.

Oliver, Oaks, and Hoover (1994) looked at family themes and patterns in the families of children who bully, noting that bullying behavior in children at school may be a warning sign that there are problems in the family. They suggested two directions for the counseling process in addressing these problems in the families of bullies: "(a) increasing the closeness and togetherness of families; and (b) improving the structure, limits, and consistent, reliably-observed rules" (Oliver, Oaks, & Hoover, 1994, p. 200). They suggested brief family intervention with the families, not long-term family counseling. Chapters 9 and 10 both expand on brief solution-focused counseling with families in the school setting, a method of working with families within the parameters of the elementary school counseling role.

The counseling strategies suggested in the previous section are but a few that are available for the elementary school counselor to implement when confronted with disruptive, impulsive, inattentive, or bullying behaviors in children in his or her school. Teachers and parents, at a loss to know how to deal with these behaviors, are usually open to attending teacher in-service training or parent education groups to learn how to deal more effectively with these behaviors. The professional counseling journals and state, regional, and national conventions always include workshops that address some or all of these issues, providing further assistance to the elementary counselor on the lookout for new ideas or ways to address these problems in the school setting.

The February 1994 issue of *Elementary School Guidance and Counseling* was devoted to student behavior and how counselors can contribute to improving these behaviors in collaboration with teachers and parents. One article in the journal (Benshoff, Poidevant, & Cashwell, 1994) discussed school discipline problems and some of the packaged programs that address the management of student behavior, concluding that the school counselor is an excellent resource to address these problems. "School counselors—as counselors, consultants, and experts on developmental needs of students—are critical personnel in efforts to create effective school environments" (p. 168).

Physical and Sexual Abuse and Neglect

Identification of the Problem

What actually constitutes child abuse? In 1974 Congress enacted the National Child Abuse Prevention and Treatment Act (PL 93-247), which defined child abuse as "physical or mental injury, sexual abuse or exploitation, negligent treatment, or maltreatment of a child under the age of 18 or the age specified by the child protection law of the state in question, by a person who is responsible for the child's welfare, under circumstances which indicate that the child's health or welfare is harmed or threatened thereby." The National Committee for Prevention of Child Abuse (toll-free phone number: 800-835-2671) will send a catalog listing a variety of materials available to prevent child abuse in all its forms.

The federal definition of child maltreatment is included in the Child Abuse Prevention and Treatment Act, with sexual abuse and exploitation as a subcategory of child abuse and neglect. Sexual abuse is defined to include the following:

A. the employment, use, persuasion, inducement, enticement, or coercion of any child to engage in, or assist any other person to engage in, any sexually explicit conduct or simulation of such conduct for the purpose of producing a visual depiction of such conduct; or

B. the rape, molestation, prostitution, or other form of sexual exploitation of children, or incest with children. . . . In order for States to qualify for funds allocated by the Federal Government, they must have child protection systems that meet certain criteria, including a definition of child maltreatment specifying sexual abuse. (Faller, 1993, pp. 9–10)

Title 18, United States Code section 3509, includes three definitions that are essential knowledge for an elementary school counselor:

1. the term "child abuse" means the physical or mental injury, sexual abuse or exploitation, or negligent treatment of a child;

2. the term "physical injury" includes lacerations, fractured bones, burns, internal injuries, severe bruising or serious bodily harm;

3. the term "mental injury" means harm to a child's psychological or intellectual functioning which may be exhibited by severe anxiety, depression, withdrawal or outward aggressive behavior, or a combination of those behaviors, which may be demonstrated by a change in behavior, emotional response, or cognition. (National Center for Prosecution of Child Abuse, 1994)

This is without a doubt the most difficult area in which to work with elementary school children—children that have been physically or sexually abused or neglected.

Children have been subjected to various kinds of abuse throughout history. They have been beaten, burned, disfigured, even killed at the hands of people considered "responsible" for their safety. It is only in recent years, with so much attention focused on these acts, that the public has been made aware of the extent of child abuse and neglect. Newspaper articles such as the following cry out for our attention: "Center Offers Escape from a Life of Hell," complete with a picture of two young teenagers in an assessment and diagnostic program where they were being kept for 90 days. One of the girls, JoAnn, said she had been beaten and sexually abused by her father ever since she was a baby when her unwed 17-year-old mother would send her to be with her father alternate weeks. It was a life of horror: "The week I would be with my father, he would sexually abuse me the whole time and if I did something wrong he would beat me" (Esper, 1993, p. 11).

It is so terrible to imagine that we really don't want to believe this is really happening to our young children. We wonder why this behavior is tolerated, why children don't report this abuse. Hollander (1992) believes it is because of the child's limited access to adults outside the family as well as a limited facility with language when the child is young. Even when the child reaches school age he or she may be hesitant to report these behaviors for fear of parental reprisals. Sandberg, in discussing legal issues in child abuse, was concerned about adults not reporting an abuse case because of fear of reprisal against the child: "an abused child lives in a world of violence, threats, and coercion, so it is difficult for me to see that a reprisal would constitute something new and different" (cited in Sandberg, Crabbs, & Crabbs, 1988, p. 269). For some children, because of threats by the abuser, there is real fear of reprisal; for others, it may not hinder their reporting.

The April 1988 issue of *Elementary School Guidance and Counseling* was a special issue devoted to child abuse issues and interventions with the intent of providing practical information for the reader, particularly the elementary school counselor. The counselor is a significant person in the detection of child abuse due to teacher referrals or child self-referral contacts. The counselor is usually seen as a trusted person, one the child might confide in if questioned about unusual bruises or abrasions, acting-out behaviors, dirty or disheveled appearance, or frequent absences.

Gerler (1988) discussed some of the findings of child abuse research, noting that the nature of the abuse affected the child's perception of the abuse. For example, physically abused children will accept the blame for mild abuse but not for severe abuse, and the most negative abuse was verbal and sexual abuse. He also noted that there is little documentation regarding effective preventive child abuse programs. Even with the available research, it is almost impossible to determine the extent of child physical and sexual abuse in the United States, and the extent or success of programs designed to combat this abuse.

Some school districts emphasize the detection of neglect along with physical and sexual abuse. Children suffering from neglect usually appear undernourished, listless, or inappropriately dressed; are in need of dental or medical attention; or are unclean. Children that are neglected may also be physically or sexually abused, although neglect may occur without the abuse.

Counseling Strategies

Sexual abuse of children is probably the most serious indictment of our society of any we can make. It is far more common than the society is willing to accept. One statistic that is difficult to accept is that the offender is known in 8 out of 10 cases that are actually report- ed; the offender is usually an adult that is trusted by the child (ERIC, 1990). Moody (1994) noted the vulnerability of the elementary-age child, citing the mean age of the victims as 6.4 years. It is not hard to imagine how the child feels when betrayed by those who are trust- ed and expected to care for them. If the child summons up the courage to inform an adult, the child often is not believed. It is critical for an abused child to have someone at school he or she can trust and confide in; if the counselor has been able to visit all the classrooms conducting classroom guidance activities and has been visible on the playground at recess and at lunchtime, the child might feel that he or she could confide in the counselor.

There are many legal issues that govern the reporting of child abuse and neglect, but the most important mandate for the elementary school counselor to be aware of is that all states require the reporting of child abuse or neglect if the abuse or neglect results in phys- ical injury. The counselor should also be aware that they only need to have "reason to believe" or "reason to suspect" that the child is being subjected to abuse or neglect in order to report it. Failure to report the suspected child abuse, even if it occurred a number of years ago, could result in prosecution as a misdemeanor in most states. The elementary counselor needs to keep in mind that the primary intent of the law requiring reporting is to protect the child. The ASCA position statement, The School Counselor and Child Abuse/ Neglect Prevention (see Appendix E for the complete statement), reminds us that not only are school counselors mandated reporters, but it is a "moral and ethical responsibility of school counselors to help children and adults cope with abusive behavior, facilitate behav- ioral changes, and prepare for parenting styles and positive interpersonal relationships" (American School Counseling Association, 1985).

ERIC Digest has an excellent publication, "Child Sexual Abuse: What It Is and How to Prevent It," available through the ERIC Clearinghouse on Elementary and Early Childhood Education (phone: 217-333-1386). There are prevention measures in the digest that parents can use to safeguard their children, from ages 18 months to 18 years, against child abuse. Two age ranges cover elementary-age children: (1) 5–8 years, "Discuss safety away from home and the difference between 'good touch' and 'bad touch.' Encourage your child to talk about scary experiences," and (2) 8–12 years, "Stress personal safety. Start to discuss rules of sexual conduct that are accepted by the family" (ERIC, 1990, p. 23).

Remley and Fry (1988) addressed the conflicting roles for school counselors, noting that they become informants once they make the determination that a child may have been abused. Confidentiality and any claim to privileged communication is overridden by the legal requirements of reporting. Remley and Fry also stressed the importance of coun- selors' knowing the child abuse reporting statutes in their states, including the penalties inflicted on those who fail to report suspected child abuse. By not reporting, they become liable: "In addition to criminal penalties that could be imposed if counselors fail to report suspected child abuse, counselors could be held liable in civil suits as well" (Remley & Fry, 1988, p. 254). The counselor should know the school district's policy on reporting child abuse and neglect in addition to the state statute (Wilder, 1991). Some school or dis- trict policies may designate the principal as the primary reporter; if he or she is not avail- able, the suspected abuse must be reported by the counselor, teacher, nurse, or other dis- trict employee that has reason to suspect that abuse or neglect has taken place.

Another area that is not always clear to counselors, particularly where their state guidelines are also not clear, is past abuse reported by a child. "Counselors often must decide whether they should report abuse that (a) occurred in the past (sometimes years ago); (b) occurred in the past but poses no current danger to the child; or (c) was perpetrated on a person who is now an adult" (Remley & Fry, 1988, p. 254). Unless the state law is specific in these instances, the counselor should always make a report. Most states have strict penalties for counselors and other school personnel who fail to report suspected child abuse, regardless of when it occurred.

Elementary counselors in a school or school district that does not have an established policy already in place and in writing regarding the reporting of suspected child abuse or neglect should request that reporting procedures be established. These procedures should include clear-cut guidelines and appropriate referral forms that cover referral observation, documentation, and outcome, including confirmation of the report if a report is made. If a report is indicated, a separate child abuse report form should be completed that identifies the type of abuse (physical, sexual, or neglect) and the agency and individual to whom the incident has been reported, with the signature of the principal, counselor, teacher, nurse, or other school employee that completed the report. All school districts should have access to legal counsel that will review the district's policy prior to its implementation. This procedure, as a minimum, would protect the counselor and assure some form of protection for the child that is the suspected victim of abuse or neglect.

Elementary counselors are in an excellent position to establish prevention programs in their schools by virtue of their background and training. If a committee of school personnel is formed to develop a team approach to prevention, the counselor will be assured of the kind of support that will be needed to carry through a prevention program designed to meet the needs of that particular school. All students should be involved in a school prevention program to make them aware of their rights, including how and where to ask for help if they are being abused in any way. Classroom guidance presentations in every classroom are the most effective means of reaching all children in the school, with a follow-up procedure for individual children that seek out the counselor after such a presentation has taken place in his or her classroom.

Moody (1994) noted the increase in the number of treatment programs for survivors of abuse because of the lasting effects on the victims of abuse. He discussed various prevention programs, including printed materials in the area of curriculum; interventions that use drama, lectures, and discussions in classrooms; audiovisual materials; teacher training models; and parental workshops. He cautioned against programs that might make the child more fearful and distrustful, noting that these difficulties have their roots in the developmental level of the child.

In addition to prevention programs for children, the elementary counselor should provide in-service training for teachers and other school staff, using the help of a child protective services worker whenever possible. Teachers need to be trained to identify signs of possible abuse or neglect in children in their classroom and school. They are often the first ones in the school to become aware of physical or sexual abuse and may not be trained to deal with the suspected abuse. As a part of this in-service training for teachers and staff, Wilder (1991) suggested sharing information as a handout on physical and behavioral indicators available from the National Center on Child Abuse and Neglect (U.S. Government Printing Office). Wilder also listed a number of organizations with their addresses that will provide resources about abuse. Providing parent education groups and workshops for parents where effective parenting skills, including appropriate handling of discipline, can be discussed in a safe and supportive atmosphere is another significant area where an elementary counselor can provide service to the children and their families in his or her school.

There is always a concern in child abuse reporting that the situation is not as severe as was first suspected and that abuse may not have occurred. Howell-Nigrelli (1988) suggested a team approach, in which three or four members of the school community form a team to review suspected child abuse cases. She viewed this as a means to insure that if a report is to be filed, it is accurate and contains all the necessary information; at the same time, the team approach emphasizes the responsibility of society in cases of suspected child abuse (1988).

There are a number of resources available for counselors and teachers to help themselves and others become more knowledgeable about this problem area. Hollander (1992) lists a wide variety of materials such as videotapes, books, teaching aids, and early childhood curriculum helps that give techniques and information that is appropriate for various age levels.

Whatever means the elementary school counselor uses to help children that are abused and neglected, whether it is teacher in-service training, parent education or information workshops, coordinating a school support team, or working in a preventive mode with all children in the school, we need to keep in mind that the welfare of the child comes first; the child is not to be harmed or threatened. Children are our most valuable resource and they should be able to rely on those adults with whom they interact on a daily basis to help and protect them. This is stated well by David Sandberg, a practitioner of law relating to children's issues: "Neglect, psychological abuse, and even so-called minor physical abuse are all harmful to a child's development. Why should we as a society tolerate these forms of maltreatment? . . . I strongly believe that our nation's first priority should be the healthy maturing and development of our young people. Call it idealistic, call it naive, but I am convinced that this is the only policy which offers any long-range hope insofar as significantly reducing crime, delinquency, and many of society's other more costly ills" (Sandburg, Crabbs, & Crabbs, 1988, p. 274).

Substance Abuse

Identification of the Problem

A March 1993 Gallup poll survey of 400 parents of children aged 12 and under identified their key concerns with drugs as the top concern of 78 percent of the parents. The surveyed parents were more worried about drugs than they were about violence (Henry, 1993). Parents are well advised to be concerned about the use of alcohol and drugs among their school-age children, particularly if there is a problem drinker in the family. Statistics show this correlation, according to Schmidt (1991): "Estimates are that over 25 million children are raised in families with problem drinkers and the children of these parents are four times more likely to become alcoholics themselves" (p. 141). The discussion in this problem area of substance abuse in the elementary school will include children and their families, because the problem affects all of them when either the parents or the children abuse or misuse alcohol or drugs.

Elementary-age children are increasingly at risk of using and abusing drugs. "The percentage of students using drugs by the sixth grade has tripled over the last decade. One in six 13 year olds has used marijuana" (Bennett, cited in Bradley, 1988, p. 99); this is a startling statistic and one that should not be overlooked as we focus more and more on the elementary school to begin the attack on the use and abuse of alcohol and drugs. Many elementary-age children are experimenting with tobacco, which so often is a first step to the use of marijuana. The National Council on Alcohol statistics reveal that 100,000 ten- and eleven-year-olds reported getting drunk a minimum of once a week (McKay, Dinkmeyer, & Dinkmeyer, 1989).

Bradley (1988) noted that children that have had an overall negative experience in their elementary school years are more likely to become involved in drugs at a later time. Another factor that cannot be overlooked is the influence of movies and television on young viewers: "A 1987 *Weekly Reader* survey of fourth through sixth graders reported that television and movies had the greatest influence on them in portraying drug and alcohol usage as attractive" (McKay et al., 1989).

Children of alcoholics and drug users are usually quite hesitant to talk with anyone about the problems they are experiencing at home. Without knowing about the problem, the counselor and teacher are at a disadvantage in knowing what is happening to the child. It may be possible to identify a family alcohol- or drug-related problem by close observation of the child. Certain behaviors and characteristics in a child should be reason for concern, particularly when several of these are noticed consistently:

- Low self-esteem
- Antisocial behaviors
- Withdrawn and isolated
- Lack of trusting relationships
- Poor eating habits
- Signs of physical abuse
- Feelings of rejection
- Extreme self-criticism
- Overly responsible
- Passiveness
- Frequent school absences
- Poor school achievement
- Undone or incomplete homework assignments. (Schmidt, 1991, pp. 141–142)

The majority of secondary schools have some sort of a drug and alcohol abuse program in existence. The problem with many of these is that they occur too late to have a significant effect. Drug and alcohol abuse prevention ideally should start in the early grades of elementary school; the longer we wait beyond these informative years, the less impact these prevention programs will have. Like so many of the problem areas in the elementary school, the most vulnerable children are the children with the poorest self-concept or self-esteem. Programs aimed at building a child's self-esteem starting in kindergarten will have the greatest chance of affecting the child in his or her peer relationships and social effectiveness.

Counseling Strategies

There are a variety of strategies that an elementary school counselor can use to try to prevent young children from becoming involved in alcohol and drug use and abuse. Some of these strategies involve the use of commercial programs geared toward helping children develop the necessary skills to empower them to make wise choices. One of these is Drug Free, a Developing Understanding of Self and Others (DUSO) approach to preventing drug abuse (McKay et al., 1989). Drug Free 1 (K–4) and Drug Free 2 (4–6) focus on developing skills that help children ages five through twelve become resistant to using drugs. The activities help the students practice the skills they are learning to help them resist drugs. They promote self-esteem, develop understanding of appropriate and inappropriate drug use, develop decision-making and problem-solving skills, and help children gain insight into peer influences. Drug Free can be used alone or with the DUSO-1 or DUSO-2 programs; it can also be incorporated into existing school units or programs.

Another widely used program is Impact Training for the Elementary School, a program by the National Training Consultants (NTC). The goals for the Impact Training are as follows:

- To increase awareness of chemical dependency and its effect on the individual, the family, the school and the community
- To develop identification and intervention skills with high risk children
- To facilitate personal awareness of attitudes, feelings, and expectations as they relate to school programming
- To provide participants with the tools necessary to create an effective drug and alcohol prevention/intervention program in the elementary school setting (National Training Consultants, 1990)

In addition to these structured programs, many schools have developed their own programs to educate their children in the use and abuse of alcohol and drugs. Bradley (1988) noted that many of the materials and programs currently in use in a school's counseling and guidance program deal with the behaviors and feelings that appear to be associated with the potential use of drugs. She also stressed the fact that children's developmental stages, including the various stages represented by assorted children, should be taken into consideration in developing substance abuse programs.

Ostrower (1987) developed a curriculum and program for middle school children, grades 6–8, which can easily be adapted to the elementary school. The program, "What We Need to Know About Alcohol," focuses on alcohol and the various personal problems that become associated with alcoholism. The program has three objectives:

1. To provide correct information on the subject, so that students can begin to make informed and reasoned decisions about their own drinking
2. To offer an educational process that fosters the development of decision-making skills, so that students will be able to make responsible choices when confronted with situations involving alcohol
3. To develop a counseling and referral system to help specific youngsters cope with personal and family difficulties that occur and to enable them to admit that they or someone in their family is abusing alcohol (Ostrower, 1987, p. 210)

The program consists of eight 50-minute sessions that were designed to meet the preceding objectives. It is a voluntary program; the teachers agreed to have it included as part of their instruction. The counselor serves in a teaching role and presents the materials sequentially in the form of a course. Her emphasis included a decision-making component in addition to teaching facts about the use and abuse of alcohol. The description of the eight sessions indicates its adaptability to the upper elementary grades.

It is important to teach elementary-age children how to assert themselves when faced with peer pressure to get involved in drugs or alcohol. It is equally important to make sure they have correct information regarding substance abuse and not just the information obtained from their peers. Children who are in a safe environment will be more apt to share what they are being exposed to at home or among their peers and will be open to discussion in a classroom guidance session or individually with the counselor.

Underachievers

Identification of the Problem

One of the most frustrating experiences for teachers, whether first-year teachers or experienced, is having students in their classroom who are not working up to their potential. Sometimes this awareness of a child's true capabilities is reinforced when school-based standardized aptitude and achievement test scores are compared. At other times there may be some definite change in a child who initially did all the required work, completed assignments on time, and was actively involved in classroom activities. When a child gradually or abruptly changes to the extent that they no longer enter fully into the educational process, it is usually a signal that something is going on in the child's life that is causing him or her to give up, act out in class, or become apathetic about schoolwork.

Rimm (1986) referred to these children as suffering from "Underachievement Syndrome," noting that "millions of children who are very capable of learning—children with average, above average and even gifted abilities, including those from middle class homes where education is supposed to be valued—are simply not performing up to their capabilities" (Rimm, 1986, p. 1). Following are some of the characteristics that typify these children: disorganized, forget homework, lose assignments and misplace books, daydream, don't listen, look out the window or talk too much to other children, have poor or no study skills. Some are slow and perfectionistic; others work too fast and are careless. Some of these children are lonely and withdrawn; others are aggressive and bossy. They usually don't believe they can achieve goals if they work harder. Rimm hypothesized that all of these characteristics are learned, so the "cure" would be to involve new learning for parents and teachers. "They are competitive, internally pressured children who have not learned to cope with defeat" (Rimm, 1986, p. 4).

Teacher expectations and how they are communicated to children are often tied to children's performance in school. Smey-Richman (1989) found that teachers demand better performance from students that they have high expectations for; conversely, they accept poorer performance from low-expectation students. Because of this, these lower-expectation students have fewer opportunities to participate in classroom activities, which may discourage them from trying any harder. She noted that elementary-age children are more oriented to pleasing adults and more accepting of their authority, so teacher expectations seem to exert more influence on elementary school students than older students. If this is true, it would seem imperative that teachers and parents examine and revise their expectations, encouraging the lower-achieving students to perform beyond the level at which they currently are performing.

Gibbs (1990) addressed America's legacy to its children with some rather frightening statistics. In one national survey conducted in 1988, two-thirds of the teachers reported that a major learning problem for children, affecting their school achievement, was "poor health," yet only 20 percent of the children that are eligible for preschool medical and dental screening through programs such as Head Start actually receive these services. It has been shown that Head Start and other preschool programs improve the academic performance in the early elementary school grades; without this kind of help, a large percentage of our young children are placed in the at-risk category as they move into the elementary school. The term *at risk,* in the educational sense, often designates children who are not learning the appropriate grade-level skills necessary to compete favorably at the next grade, which in turn may eventually place them at risk of becoming school dropouts. Marian Wright Edelman, the Children's Defense Fund founder, forewarned us: "The inattention to children by our society poses a greater threat to our safety, harmony and productivity than any external enemy" (cited in Gibbs, 1990, p. 47).

The increasing number of school dropouts is a very real concern for our schools today. The problem of school dropouts is not just a secondary school concern; it is a K–12 concern. Children who haven't mastered the necessary skills in elementary school and are discouraged learners are the most susceptible to dropping out of junior high or high school. A large percentage of these children can be identified as early as kindergarten and first grade; many of these children are referred by their teachers to the counselor as "underachievers," not working up to their capabilities. Many times these children fall behind because of poor attendance due to lack of parental concern or enforcement of school attendance. The category of children we term at-risk are often from ethnic minority families or families that are economically disadvantaged and have not had positive experiences themselves in the school setting. Poverty has a high correlation with school failure and family stress; this results in increasing risk for these children. "The educational problems of poor youngsters often emerge at the very beginning of their school career. Many of these youngsters begin school developmentally unprepared to succeed in the classroom" (McWhirter, McWhirter, McWhirter, & McWhirter, 1993, p. 23).

Smith (1994) cited the New Jersey School Boards Association finding that the attitudes and performance of students in their schools improve when the parents are involved in the school environment. The study, reported by Smith, looked at six school-related behavior categories and whether or not they could be affected by the use of a behavior contract program; one of the behavior-related categories was lack of attention to classroom tasks. The program was able to report improvement of specific school-related behaviors when parents were actively involved.

The American Counseling Association (ACA) noted that all adults involved in education must respond to the challenge of providing all children with the proper education that will allow them to reach their greatest potential (Glosoff & Koprowicz, 1990). The publication "Children Reaching Potential" cites the various problems that become barriers for learning: family issues, such as "divorce, parental substance abuse, working parents, illiterate parents, incest, lack of attention, lack of positive reinforcement; Society/Peers: violence in media, gangs, drugs, poverty, threat of nuclear war, premarital sex, peer reinforcement of family-caused insecurities; School: high pupil/teacher ratios, pressure to excel at an early age, violence at school, lack of individual attention, lack of nonjudgmental child/adult relationship; Self-Concept: all the aspects of a child's life combine to create a self-concept. But to overcome a low self-concept developed before beginning school, a child needs an abundance of positive influences. By having a strong self-concept and by making positive decisions, a child can tackle the problems mentioned above and make progress" (Glosoff and Koprowicz, 1990, p. 3). A lot of these children who are not causing a problem in the classroom or in the school setting pass through the school system "unnoticed" unless they are obvious underachievers.

Counseling Strategies

Elementary school counselors are in a position to have an impact on this concern of teachers, parents, and administrators: how to help a child achieve up to his or her potential. What is necessary to carry out an effective elementary school guidance and counseling program is to have counselors in all elementary schools across the country with counselor/student ratios that are reasonable and workable. Des Moines, Iowa, provides an excellent role model for the rest of the country as to what constitutes a successful way to reach these children in our elementary schools. Business leaders in the community worked together to sponsor a program that they call "Smoother Sailing." They are providing the funding to furnish one counselor for every 250 elementary school students in each of the city schools (Gibbs, 1990). Des Moines residents believed in the program so strongly that they passed a $9.7 million property tax levy to fund this program, along with several others, for the next 10 years. (For how-to information, contact Charlene Wallace or Jan Kuhl, Smoother Sailing Coordinator, Guidance and Counseling Office, Des Moines Public Schools, 1800 Grand Ave., Des Moines, Iowa 50309, (515) 242-7717.)

With the ratio of counselors to students that Des Moines is supporting, a comprehensive program to prevent problems from occurring can become a reality. Where these problems are already in existence and children have already been identified as at-risk, early intervention can head off many of the problems while these children are still at a receptive age. The underachievers in our schools, children that are not achieving the potential they are capable of achieving, can be helped in an elementary school counseling program with a developmental emphasis.

One of the ways elementary school counselors can affect students that are underachievers or at risk is through the use of reinforcement. Most children need and will react in positive ways when reinforcement is genuine, not contrived. Nelson noted various reinforcers that are not difficult to carry out but take some time and effort: "acknowledge students" through eye contacts, smiles, or greetings; "be demonstrative" with a handshake or a verbal reinforcement acknowledging some accomplishment; "name a student of the week" in each class for improvement, effort, or achievement; "make telephone calls or send notes to parents" acknowledging efforts or improvement; "promote involvement" in various school organizations or as peer helpers or in other creative ways; and "offer computer time" as a reward for progress or effort (Nelson, 1991, p. 69). Nelson also noted the real need for reinforcement for at-risk children because their behaviors usually result in negative responses and the withholding of reinforcement. In addition to Nelson's ideas listed above, reinforcing strategies that work particularly well for such at-risk children include the following: "dig deeply for reinforcers" because these children have strong defenses and may not respond immediately; "write notes to students" so that they can selectively share these; "target children who are often in trouble" in order to intervene in their lives in positive ways; "turn deficits on their heads" by choosing to redirect one of their strengths, such as the leadership qualities of a gang leader, in positive ways; "explore alternative approaches" through first building positive relationships with these children and then helping them find alternative ways to accomplish their goals; and "help at-risk students get involved" by finding some tasks, such as peer helping or reading to younger children, to help them feel they can contribute in some way (Nelson, 1991, pp. 71–72). These are all excellent ways for a counselor to help children who need reinforcement; in addition, the counselor also models appropriate attitudes and behaviors toward these children for teachers and parents.

Group counseling for children identified as underachievers is another option for the elementary school counselor. Thompson (1987) investigated the use of a counseling program tailored to reach underachieving and high-risk students on the secondary school level. She used a comprehensive diagnostic and prescriptive team approach with intervention strategies, such as "skills training, internalized goal setting, reality perception, and personal responsibility," to reach identified underachievers in her school (p. 294). The counselor met with the identified students in weekly group sessions, concluding that "the study supports earlier findings that counseling seems to enhance academic performance and school attendance of underachieving, high risk students" (p. 294). Even though Thompson conducted this study with ninth-grade students, they all had a history of poor attendance, lack of interest in school, and low grades—some of the previously identified signs of elementary school underachievers. Using this format on the elementary school level fits in well with the conclusions of the National Conference of State Legislatures regarding elementary school counseling: "Early exposure to services such as comprehensive elementary school counseling programs can build an emotionally healthy foundation for children and result in improved academic achievement, reduced dropout rates, effective decision-making and problem-solving skills, and better self-concepts" (Glosoff & Koprowicz, 1990, p. 29).

Schmidt (1991) reviewed experimental studies that looked at the effectiveness of counselor interventions in working with low-achieving and underachieving students and arrived at the following conclusions:

1. Group procedures appear to be more effective than individual counseling with these students. In addition, groups that use structured, behaviorally-oriented sessions as opposed to unstructured, person-centered approaches tend to be more effective in improving student performance.
2. Longer treatment programs, those lasting more than eight weeks, are more effective than short-term interventions. This finding indicates that you should not expect a quick fix to student attitudes and behaviors related to school achievement.
3. Voluntary participation is essential to program effectiveness. When students agree to join a group, they are more likely to commit to change than if they are forced into a program.

4. Counseling in combination with study skills instruction is effective in helping students raise their school achievement.

5. Parent involvement is an additional factor related to improving student performance. Programs that include parent participation tend to show positive results. (pp. 147–148)

Underachieving students, although frustrating to their teachers and parents, often do not get the attention they need because these problems are not as distressing as some of the other problems that receive so much attention in our elementary schools today, such as physical and sexual abuse; disruptive, impulsive, and bullying behaviors; and substance abuse, to name some of the most pressing concerns. It is imperative that the elementary counselor provide appropriate interventions for the underachievers and at-risk children in order to help them achieve their greatest educational and individual potential.

Gender Bias in Our Schools

We would be remiss if the issue of gender bias was not included in a discussion of the elementary school, particularly because ASCA has approved a position statement, The School Counselor and Sex Equity (see Appendix F for the complete statement). In a 1992 report by the American Association of University Women (AAUW) Foundation, titled "How Schools Shortchange Girls," the common assumption that our public schools treat girls and boys equally was challenged. "Girls and boys enter school roughly equal in measured ability. Twelve years later, girls have fallen behind their male classmates in key areas such as higher-level mathematics and measures of self-esteem" (p. 1). The report expressed concern that Title IX of the 1972 Education Amendments did not resolve this issue as it was intended to do. We need to take a closer look at what is happening in our classrooms and in our elementary schools. We need to address and discuss the biases identified in the AAUW report to see just where this is occurring, because the report so succinctly points out that it is, in fact, occurring.

Three other areas addressed in the report need to be addressed. These came about in response to the question "What happens in the classroom?"

- Girls receive significantly less attention from classroom teachers than do boys.
- African American girls have fewer interactions with teachers than do white girls, despite evidence that they attempt to initiate interactions more frequently.
- Sexual harassment of girls by boys—from innuendos to actual assault–in our nation's schools is increasing. (p. 2)

We can't afford to ignore the facts: Our nation's schools do indeed favor boys and shortchange girls—the girls will be the women of tomorrow and we will have to live with what we have had a hand in creating if we don't step in as counselors and teachers to address this inequity. A major goal of our elementary schools should be to foster equity in education so that every girl and every boy has the possibility of achieving his or her potential.

Moore and Strickler (1980) questioned whether the counseling profession had made the same commitment to take action as other groups did that supported the Equal Rights

Amendment. They saw the 1970s as a period of awareness that sexism and sex-role stereo-typing were taking place among counseling professionals; to answer their question, they reviewed research on sex bias in the counseling profession. Their research revealed that many steps had been taken to encourage sex equity but, at the same time, noted a lack of counselor education programs giving priority to courses focusing on sex equity. They con-cluded that "until motivation to confront existing sexist practices is sufficiently heightened and change occurs so that sex equity becomes a reality, there can be no truly liberating counseling and guidance for either male or female" (Moore & Strickler, 1980, p. 87).

Wynne and Payne (1980) also addressed counseling and sex bias: "It is important for schools to keep abreast of social change and to integrate these changes into their curricu-lum and counseling program" (p. 7). They spent two years researching and compiling the necessary materials to develop and carry out a program of sex role and sex stereotype edu-cation. Their goal was to help students become aware of how biases are nurtured by fam-ilies, school, and the media so that they can begin to counteract these influences.

An article in *Guidepost* discussed a report that examined why more women were not studying and completing degrees in traditional male fields. In focusing on the academic climate that influences young women, the report coauthors found that "young women's experiences in elementary and high school are a major determinant of whether they pur-sue non-traditional interests" (Ehrart & Sandler, 1987, p. 16).

The *Guidepost* published two articles on the implications of the previously discussed AAUW study on gender inequity in schools (1992a, 1992b). In the first issue, the study noted that women make up 45 percent of the workforce, yet most hit the "glass ceiling," never reaching the top. Sharon Schuster, the president of AAUW at the time, stated that "it does not begin in the corporate executive suite. The 'glass ceiling' begins in kindergarten" (McGowan, 1992a, p. 8). The second article noted that many of the findings in the AAUW report are applicable to school counselors. School counselors should be aware of their interactional styles with girls versus boys in addition to having an awareness of potential problems for the girls and minorities they counsel.

A survey conducted in five Florida elementary schools in March 1993 found that the majority of boys surveyed "did not believe that girls were smart enough to become President of the United States" (Ruben, 1993, p. 6). Ruben viewed this as part of our cul-ture, resulting in shattered dreams for girls. These reports and articles should cause our ele-mentary schools to take a closer look at what we are doing to the girls, starting in kinder-garten—how we are truly "shortchanging" girls. Until we do this, both girls and boys will be shortchanged in their education. The elementary school counselor can play a significant role in this by introducing gender-free activities in the classroom, discussed in the next section. Another area is career exploration and career awareness, which will be discussed in Chapter 9.

Counseling Strategies

In the area of gender bias, counselors are in an excellent position to help teachers and par-ents understand the pressures, sometimes subtle, that are placed on girls to accomplish less than their capabilities would indicate. Counselors can provide interventions to encourage both boys and girls to look at various types of gender-nontraditional occupations. A study involving 82 third-grade boys and girls in a working-class neighborhood was carried out in which the children, in groups, interviewed two men and two women holding nontraditional jobs. At the end of the study the girls, in particular, showed measurable changes in sex stereotyping (Trice, 1991/92).

Wynne and Payne (1980) identified various strategies for sex role counseling in the secondary schools. They listed activities that teachers and counselors could use with each other in addition to activities suitable for use in classrooms or group counseling. Most of the activities can be modified for use in an elementary school. Another emphasis for change was reflected in the AAUW Report. The recommendations for change in the report include the following:

- Teachers, administrators, and counselors must be prepared and encouraged to bring gender equity and awareness to every aspect of schooling.
- The formal school curriculum must include the experiences of women and men from all walks of life.
- Testing and assessment must serve as stepping stones not stop signs. New tests and testing techniques must accurately reflect the abilities of both boys and girls. (American Association of University Women, 1992)

In addition to these recommendations, it is imperative that counselor educators model non-sexist attitudes and behavior in the training of potential counselors to insure that gender bias is not present in working with both boys and girls. It is only when all gender bias is removed from the training of school counselors, teachers, and administrators by discussions, activities, and modeling that we will accomplish this significant task.

Working with Special Education Students

Identification of the Problem

Public Law 94-142, the Education for All Handicapped Children Act, is the law that totally changed the way public schools provided for and educated children and youth with special needs. It was passed by the U.S. Congress and signed into law on November 29, 1975 (Ballard, Ramirez, & Zantal-Wiener, 1987). Anyone involved in education since PL 94-142 was passed is well aware of the need for school districts to comply with the language stated in the law that every child that is identified as physically or mentally impaired must be provided a free and appropriate public education in the least restrictive environment. Because federal funding is tied to compliance, school districts are closely monitored to insure that the intent of the law is followed. In addition, every child that is certified as eligible to receive these services must have an individualized education program (IEP) that contains the following components:

1. The child's present level of performance
2. An annual goal that includes short-term instructional objectives
3. Specific special and related services to be provided along with regular education participation
4. Date of initiation of services and expected duration of these services

5. Objective criteria and evaluation procedures to determine achievement of the instructional objectives. (PL 94-142)

The participants in the IEP planning meeting include the teacher, the parents, a school or district person that is able to provide or supervise the placement, and, if suitable, the child.

In addition to PL 94-142, Section 504 also needs to be considered as we look at children in need of special services. Section 504 "applies to all handicapped children ages 3 to 21 with respect to their public education both from the standpoint of the guarantee of an appropriate special education and from the standpoint of sheer regular program accessibility" (Ballard, Ramirez, & Zantal-Wiener, 1991, p. 2). Section 504 is part of the Rehabilitation Act of 1973, and it prohibits discrimination in all programs that receive financial assistance from the federal government (Anderson & Vohs, 1992–93). A major difference between the two laws is the federal funding that is provided to assist states to provide the necessary education for students eligible for special education under PL 94-142, now known as the Individuals with Disabilities Education Act (IDEA). Section 504 is less limiting than IDEA in its eligibility criteria, thus opening the door for services to children that have disabilities but do not meet the criteria for special education. Children that fit the disability definition under Section 504 are students with conditions such as "Attention Deficit Hyperactivity Disorder, Attention Deficit Disorder, and specific learning disabilities who were not found to be eligible for special education because they were not able to prove a discrepancy between achievement and intellectual ability as is required by IDEA" (Anderson & Vohs, 1992–93, p. 3). This is in addition to others with physical disabilities and students with certain health needs, essentially any person who has a physical or mental impairment that substantially limits their learning. The limiting aspect of Section 504 is the lack of federal funding to assist states in implementing these services. Section 504 applies not only to students but to teachers, administrators, and others in the educational setting that have a handicapping condition.

As a part of Section 504, a question has been raised as to the eligibility of children with AIDS (acquired immunodeficiency syndrome) and whether or not they are considered "handicapped" under the law. According to Fischer and Sorenson (1991), "it should be readily apparent that children with AIDS are 'handicapped' under Section 504, because they are regarded as having an impairment" (p. 116). Court cases (*Thomas v. Atascadero Unified School District* and *Martinez v. School Board*) have concluded that the child was "handicapped" under Section 504 and was "otherwise qualified to attend" school, thus making him or her eligible for school attendance (Fischer & Sorenson, 1991)

All states receive monies for carrying out the mandates and guidelines for IDEA and consequently have a composite of laws or education codes to regulate the services for children with disabilities; the intent of this section is to familiarize the reader with the basic laws that govern the inclusion of special education programs in the public schools. It is assumed that elementary school counselors have some coursework that covers the provision of services to children with special needs. In a basic course on counseling children with special needs the counselor-in-training would become knowledgeable about public school procedures specific to addressing the social, emotional, and behavioral areas that interfere with classroom learning; learn about the federal and state laws that govern the services for these children; and become knowledgeable about the categories of handicapping conditions, as well as counseling services for students with special needs and their families. Regardless of whether or not the counselor-in-training receives instruction in working with special-needs students, he or she should get a copy of the state's education codes or laws that govern the teaching and provision of other related services for these identified students.

Counseling Strategies

Maes (1978), in one of the earliest articles that addressed counseling for special education children after the passage of PL 94-142, noted that "the cornerstone of the counseling movement has been the recognition of individual differences, respect for the individual, and the belief that each individual has the right to conditions that will support the realization of full human potential. Nowhere within education has a clearer agreement on values and purposes been evidenced than that shared by special education and counseling regarding those beliefs" (p. 1). Elementary school counselors do provide appraisal, guidance, information, and counseling services; the development of an appropriate educational program that meets each student's needs is consistent with the counselor's treatment of each student as a unique, worthwhile individual. Counselors are involved with special education children in a variety of ways, from coordinating and monitoring the IEP in some school districts to the carrying out of counseling goals that supplement the instructional goals as indicated in the development of the individualized education program for the child.

School counseling services can successfully be provided for special-needs children in the following areas: learning handicapped, mentally retarded, hard of hearing or deaf, orthopedically impaired, speech and language impaired, seriously emotionally disturbed, visually handicapped, and seriously health impaired. The elementary counselor with little or no knowledge about children with special needs in his or her school should spend time with the special education teacher(s) to become more knowledgeable. A very rewarding partnership can be formed between the counselor and the special education staff as both attempt to meet the needs of these special children. ASCA's position statement, The School Counselor and the Education of the Handicapped Act (see Appendix G for the complete statement), identifies the reasonable functions as well as limits of the counselor's involvement in the implementation of PL 94-142.

Robinson and Mopsik (1992) developed an environmental-experimental model for counseling special education children. The section on developing the setting provides some excellent guidelines for elementary counselors working with these children:

- Counseling activities should be no longer than 20 to 30 minutes.
- Distractions in the environment should be kept to a minimum or eliminated.
- Tasks should be structured and followed consistently.
- Multisensory approaches including auditory, visual, tactile, and kinesthetic, should be used by counselors while presenting activities to the students. (Robinson & Mopsik, 1992, p. 75)

Many of the counseling programs developed for elementary school children to be used in the classroom and in small groups are suitable for use with special education students, especially those that help develop a child's self-esteem. Special education children are often lacking in self-esteem and are overheard making statements such as: "I'm stupid!" "I'm dumb!" "I can't learn anything." "I'm handicapped." Children who believe this about themselves often exhibit learned helplessness behaviors. Working with these children in small groups using some of the activities and materials identified in the section on self-esteem in Chapter 4 could affect these children in positive ways, building on their strengths and not focusing on their weaknesses.

Another area in which the elementary counselor can have a positive impact is with the parents of handicapped children. PL 94-142 assures parental involvement in the planning and decision-making aspects of the child's IEP. Simpson and Fiedler (1989) addressed parent participation in IEP conferences, focusing on ways to help parents or families become involved in the education of their handicapped children. They identified seven levels of potential parent involvement, summarized below, and suggested matching the entire family to the most appropriate level:

1. Attendance at IEP meetings and approval of teacher priorities for IEP goals.
2. Parents provide information to the educational staff regarding the child's level of functioning within the family.
3. Parents suggest specific goals that they would like in the educational program.
4. Parents and educational staff negotiate agreement on IEP goals when there is a difference of opinion.
5. Parents help to analyze and monitor day-to-day performance of goals.
6. There is joint programming of school and home goals and their implementation.
7. There is independent programming in the home or community of educational goals not being trained in school. (pp. 155–156)

If the school provides the proper training for the parents to enable them to participate in their child's education in meaningful ways, the children and families will benefit immeasurably.

An excellent place for an elementary counselor to become involved is in the screening and evaluation of exceptional students. Traditionally, counselors have taken the lead in appraising students in regular classrooms; they should also be involved in evaluating children referred for special education consideration. One way this can be accomplished is by intervening at the classroom level, providing assistance to the students and teachers in the regular classroom when problems first arise. Various intervention strategies can be implemented and their effectiveness evaluated before a child is formally referred for consideration for special education placement. This also insures that the child remains in the least restrictive environment, the classroom, during this process. This is a less restrictive means of gathering data about student performance than a traditional psychological evaluation. The elementary counselor plays a key role in this prereferral intervention system.

The most important attitude for an elementary counselor working with special education children is to view them as whole and not "damaged goods." The counselor that helps these children to see themselves as people with strengths and weaknesses, as not being "different," and as able to accomplish various tasks, will truly be fulfilling the role of a helping person—one who listens and understands.

Latchkey Children

Identification of the Problem

The term *latchkey children* has been around for a number of years, but it is only recently that we have heard the kinds of concern expressed for these children that should have been expressed all along. A latchkey child is a child that is left alone or with his or her siblings for a considerable length of time on a regular basis; the term is typically used for the children who let themselves into the house after school with their own key on a daily basis and are alone until the parent or parents come home from work. The age of these children usually encompasses the school ages of 5 to 13, with the sibling "in charge" under the age of 14. There are various estimates as to the number of children that come home after school to an empty house: 7.2 percent (Gray, 1987), 10 percent (Zinmeister, 1992); some experts estimate 25 percent (Gray, 1987), and a county survey in North Carolina identified 33 percent in one county (Seligson & Fink, 1988).

According to Frenza (1984), research on the effects of leaving these children alone and without supervision has not provided conclusive results. She did note, however, that interviews with latchkey children, their parents, and former latchkey children disclosed some common concerns and experiences: "For the children, there are unusually high levels of fear (of assault, noises, the dark, storms), and loneliness and boredom" (p. 146). In addition, the parents were concerned about the safety of their children and expressed some guilt feelings.

The potential for affecting the child's school performance should be considered, according to elementary school teachers and principals (Seligson & Fink, 1988). It stands to reason that children left alone will be less inclined to do their schoolwork, particularly if they have younger siblings to care for and supervise. Another area of concern with unsupervised children is the greater potential for substance abuse, according to a survey of 5,000 eighth-graders in Los Angeles and San Diego. The results of the survey showed that these children are "twice as likely to abuse alcohol, tobacco and marijuana"; that "the effects occur in two-parent households as well as single parent families"; and that "these trends hold up whether the family is affluent or poor" (Parman, 1989, p. 88). Stern, a Los Angeles–area pediatrician, sees substance abuse as a documented hazard: "There is no doubt in my mind . . . that latch-key children are at greater risk not only for substance abuse, but for emotional difficulties" (cited in Parman, 1989, p. 88).

Increasing violence on television in recent years has become a major concern for latchkey children, because television becomes the focus for most of the children left alone. The McWhirters noted that close to one-third of the children left alone have no way to reach either parent by phone, causing as many as one out of four to become so fearful that they keep a baseball bat by their side as they watch television (McWhirter, McWhirter, McWhirter, & McWhirter, 1993).

The impact of young children being left alone for periods of time on a regular basis seems to be a major concern of those who work with children in the school setting. At the same time, it is important for educators to accept the fact that working outside the home is a necessity for many families with young children, particularly single mothers, with adequate child care too cost-prohibitive or not available for many of these families. Because the numbers of unsupervised children seems to be on the increase, it is critical that educators continue to look for solutions to this problem.

Counseling Strategies

Gray (1987) noted the number of educational programs that are available to teach children how to care for themselves when alone. The programs are geared to helping the children develop the needed skills in addition to facilitating discussions within the family regarding the child's time alone. Where programs are available as resources to use in the school, it is an excellent use of an elementary school counselor's time to conduct some group counseling in skill building, as well as helping the children in the group feel free to express their fears and concerns with other children that are in the same situation.

Frenza (1984) suggested survival skill training, in which children are helped to cope with emergencies, as an intervention for counselors to use with children. She also suggested this as a part of a parent education program that could be offered in the school. In addition to the above, Frenza encouraged counselors to become actively involved in developing community and school system support for after-school care programs that go beyond just becoming "more school." These could include check-in programs and also could provide help for children in problem-solving and emergency assistance via telephone call-in lines.

An increasing number of child care programs have been put into place in recent years because of the widespread concern about latchkey children. An ERIC Digest by Seligson and Fink (1988) discussed various school-age child care (SACC) programs that are currently in existence. According to their research, the U.S. Army, considered the largest employer in the country, was in the planning stage to bring SACC to every army base, believing that no child under 12 should be without after-school supervision. The elementary counselor should be aware that school-age child care is provided by the following organizations:

- Elementary Schools: A National Association of Elementary School Principals survey showed that 22% of responding principals had some kind of before- or after-school care in their schools.
- YMCA: Approximately 50% of the 2200 YMCAs in the U.S. are involved in SACC.
- YWCA: About 29,000 children are served through its SACC programs.
- Boys Clubs of America: At least 18% of its 200 clubs now offer school-age child care on an enrollment basis.
- Camp Fire, Inc.: At least 17 of its 300 local councils operated before- or after-school care programs, mostly in public schools.
- Association for Retarded Citizens: A number of ARCs around the country offer daily after-school care for mentally disabled children.
- Private Schools: The National Association of Independent Schools reported that a steadily rising number of its members are offering extended hours. (Seligson & Fink, 1988, p. 97)

Although they did not have national figures on Catholic school participation in SACC, Seligson and Fink noted that a large number were in existence in addition to the organizations listed above; they also saw an increasing number of local parks and recreation departments offering after-school programs. The intent of the programs researched was not just to extend the child's school day or keep them safe, but to give the children considerable freedom to choose activities or become involved in groups or just read or do their homework.

Bundy and Boser (1987) used a group guidance approach to help fifth- and sixth-grade latchkey children develop skills enabling them to cope more effectively with their self-care situation. Their program was generated for use in a developmental guidance program, which fits in well with the developmental approach for elementary school counselors emphasized in this book. The program, Being in Charge, consisted of six 45-minute sessions, summarized as follows:

Session 1: Introduction. This consists of an overview of the program and a list of rules and responsibilities when home alone.

Session 2: Setting up a self-care arrangement. A model is presented showing them how to set up their own self-care with their parents.

Session 3: Personal safety when home alone. Children learn how to safely answer the phone and the door.

Session 4: Emergency and non-emergency situations. Children are helped to distinguish between these.

Session 5: Special problems of being in charge. The group brainstorms various ways to avoid boredom and loneliness.

Session 6: Other topics for being in charge. Children role-play ways to talk to their parents regarding their concerns and problems when home alone. (pp. 60–61)

The program was successfully field tested in an urban elementary school. This appears to be an exceptional program adaptable to any elementary school setting with minimal training on the part of the counselor in order to be successfully implemented. The elementary school counselor is in excellent position to help the children in his or her school work through the fears and anxieties of being at home alone.

Transient Students

Identification of the Problem

Many children grow up in families where a number of moves may be anticipated during the course of their school years, although not all children that move several times during their elementary school years suffer adverse effects. A survey of 274 fifth-graders in Florida identified 48 percent as having moved at least three times. Students that had relocated from other parts of the country because of a parental job promotion experienced less trauma than those that had moved from across town. Even when these families viewed the move positively, as with a promotion, the children may still view the move negatively because of leaving friends behind and having to fit into a new environment (Mason, 1986). Although moving can be traumatic for many students, families that provide a fairly stable home environment and encourage their children to express their feelings regarding the move are able, for the most part, to help their children adapt to the new school situation and all that it entails. These children are not the focus of this section—it is the child who experiences many moves during his or her elementary school career, referred to in the schools as a transient student, that we will address at this point.

When we refer to transient students we are referring to students who stay in a particular school for a short period of time, less than one school year, and are usually in several schools during the same academic year. The largest number of transient students are migrant students. For many generations, migrants have pursued seasonal work in the vast agricultural areas of the United States; in addition, there are also a large number of migratory fishermen. By the very nature of the work, following the crops from one season to the next, or the fishing activity in order to gain temporary or seasonal employment, the children of migrant workers are heavily penalized in our public school systems because they just don't fit into our September-to-June school year. Vast numbers of elementary-age children are uprooted each year as their parents move from one section of the country to another. Some states experience high rates of transiency because of their agricultural and fisheries base; California is one of these states. Because of the large number of migrant students involved in their public schools, the California State Department of Education published a handbook to address the needs of these children, "The School Counselor and the Migrant Student" (Strazicich, 1983). The introduction to the preface has this poignant statement by a former migrant: "I was a member of a migrant family from the time I was four years old until the day I went to college back in August of 1959, when I arose one morning in a camp in Hamilton, New York, went to a bean field, and picked 27 bushels of string beans by 2 o'clock. I returned to camp, took a bath in a number two tin tub in a room that was a converted chicken house, packed my bags, and drove to college" (Judson, cited in Strazicich, 1983, p. iv). A 1981 California Assembly Bill requiring a comprehensive program to meet the educational needs of migrant children provided the impetus for the collaboration necessary to produce the handbook intended to help counselors work with migrant children in all California public schools.

Lunon (1986) noted that poverty and deprivation are all too common with migratory children; in addition, these children become isolated from the community due to language and cultural differences, because the majority of these children are Hispanic. As a result of the many moves, it was virtually impossible to track migrant children and monitor their school records. Because of this, in 1969 the Migrant Student Record Transfer System (MSRTS) came into being in order to coordinate students' academic and health records. The MSRTS is a computerized information network that is available nationwide; it transfers the necessary information on the child until his or her formal records arrive at the new school (Lunon, 1986). The development of the MSRTS enabled the school to have both the educational and health histories of the migrant children enrolled in their school when the child enrolls rather than waiting weeks or months to obtain the much-needed school records.

Another area of concern with migrant children stems from research conducted from 1982 to 1985 by Eastern Stream Child Abuse Prevention and Education (ESCAPE), which identified migrant children as a high risk for mistreatment because of poverty, frequent moves, poor living conditions, and health problems (Wolverton, 1988). Wolverton provided extensive strategies and techniques to train teachers of migrant children in ways to recognize child abuse and to deal with this in the curriculum in their classrooms. The elementary school counselor, in partnership with the teachers, can implement many of the ideas and techniques recommended in the *ERIC Digest*. These will be discussed in the next section.

Counseling Strategies

Migrant students are particularly needy students because of having to adjust to frequent moves to new locations, new schools, new classmates, new teachers, and new curriculum. Many of these children suffer from low self-esteem because of their poorer living conditions, language deficiency, and often meager clothing. Strazicich identified a number of needs of migrant students that counselors should be aware of, summarized as follows:

- To compensate for inadequate living conditions
- To compensate for a frequently interrupted and itinerant education
- To be recognized for their potential and creativity
- To overcome health and nutritional defects which interfere with the educational process
- To know that others understand and appreciate the nature of their problem
- To find acceptance as individuals, as members of an occupational group, and as members of a particular subculture
- To identify with successful role models who are similar to themselves in background, culture, and language
- To be motivated to complete a high school education
- To receive personal, vocational, and family guidance
- To communicate
- To share common experiences
- To receive assistance from the community at large. (Strazicich, 1983, pp. 2–4)

All of these identified needs fit in with an elementary school counselor's role and should be carefully considered by counselors that have migrant students in their school.

As the elementary counselor considers the problem of child abuse and neglect with migrant children, Wolverton stressed bringing child abuse education into the classroom to discuss with all children in the room. She stated five major goals that can be accomplished by doing this. It can

- Provide support to the child who has suffered some form of maltreatment in order to lessen its devastating effects.
- Teach children prevention strategies that will help them wherever their migrant lifestyle takes them.
- Teach all children to accept those who have special problems.
- Improve self-concepts of all children in the class.
- Encourage the maltreated child to confide in an adult regarding the maltreatment. (Wolverton, 1988, p. 23)

In addition, Wolverton recommended bibliotherapy and self-concept activities for these children.

Frenza (1984) suggested that the counselor conduct guided sessions in small groups and in the classroom where children are helped to understand what kinds of problems and difficulties a child that moves often encounters. As a part of this, the other students are encouraged to give their ideas for helping these children adjust to a new school situation.

She also recommended an orientation program for new students and their families to help them become acquainted with the school.

Jennings, an instructor for the TI-IN Network (a Texas network that provides for distance education via the use of two-way radio, one-way video, and live-interactive education via satellite), discussed the innovative project started in the summer of 1992 that extended instruction during the summer months to elementary and secondary school migrant schoolchildren. She addressed the lack of instructional continuity as the greatest roadblock for migrant children receiving their education in the United States. A pilot program was started in Texas because their migrant families travel to more than 40 states to become immersed in seasonal farming and fishing. The Texas Education Agency, with the TI-IN Network, broadcasted live, interactive classes that tutored the migrant children in math, reading, and writing. The pilot program targeted Texas migrant students working in Montana sugar beet fields during the summer of 1992 (Jennings, 1993). Counseling was not specified as a part of the project, but because Texas has recently mandated elementary school counseling, this would appear to be a way for elementary school counselors to try to connect with the elementary-age children that may be involved in this project. In addition, the intent is to expand this program nationwide, which could be a focus for counselors interested in helping the migrant students in their schools.

Cranston-Gingras and Anderson (1990), in their journal article "Reducing the Migrant Student Dropout Rate: The Role of School Counselors," provided some excellent basic information for counselors, including a profile of migrant students, to help increase their awareness of the status of these students. Their suggestions for counselors included developing a parent and teacher advisory committee to bring migrant parents together in order to improve the education of the migrant student. It is understandable that these children would become easily discouraged in the school setting unless extra help and guidance are offered. This would also be an excellent place to provide some career education to help the children realize the greater potential of changing their lifestyle if they are able to complete high school and possibly beyond.

The ASCA position paper, The School Counselor and Migrant Students (see Appendix H), identifies the involvement of the counselor in this area. It is recognized that there are many demands on an elementary school counselor's time, and yet working with all children in the school should be the counselor's emphasis. A highly significant number of migrant children, estimated at approximately 400,000 students (Jennings, 1993), are distinctly disadvantaged in our public schools. An elementary school counselor willing to work with these children can't help but have a significant impact on them, their families, and their future. How effectively these migrant children cope with all the demands made on them can be greatly influenced by the help they receive in the schools they attend.

Summary

The October 8, 1993, issue of *USA Today* devoted almost a full page to letters from their readers called "A Report Card for Our Schools" (Jurensen, 1993). The readers graded the public schools A, B, C, D, or F. Very few of the letters addressed the kinds of issues and problems that our children bring to their elementary school classrooms. If the public had more of an awareness of some of the problems discussed in this chapter (attention deficit disorder, childhood depression, disruptive and impulsive behaviors, physical and sexual abuse, substance abuse, underachievers, special education children, latchkey children, and transient students), they might stop pointing their fingers at each other and start addressing the needs of children and how to make their education paramount. The children identified as at-risk need the help and concern of all adults involved in the school setting. The ASCA position statement, The School Counselor and Dropout Prevention/Student At-Risk (the complete statement is in Appendix I), defines the counselor's role in working with these children.

Many children are overburdened with the stresses of their home life coupled with peer pressures. They become angry and oftentimes resort to violence to "get even" with the system that they feel has let them down. Their very behaviors cause those that could help them to maintain a "safe" distance rather than reaching out to them. The majority of at-risk children have solid defenses coupled with a desperate need to belong, to get some positive reinforcement from some significant adults in their lives rather than the put-downs most have become accustomed to. An elementary school counselor can do much to effect some changes for these children through small group and classroom guidance activities for the children and in-service programs and consultation with the teachers.

Those of us involved in the education of our young people need to have some understanding of the problems that at-risk children face on a daily basis. Questions to address include the following: "What does it mean to live in a home filled with conflict and tension? What does it mean to go back to an empty house day after day? What does it mean to live with only one parent who is struggling to make ends meet? What does it mean to live in a neighborhood where violence is commonplace, alcoholism is rampant, unemployment is everywhere, and bad examples abound? What values are acquired? What anxieties are fostered? What happens to one's self-esteem? What does it mean to leave school at the end of the day and go home to a house without books, to parents who do not believe in learning as a way of solving human problems, to brothers or sisters who have already dropped out of school, to peers who are into drugs, to a local culture that supports skipping school, and to a noisy room filled with television, beer, and family brawl?" (Frymier, 1992, p. 74). These questions, from the Phi Delta Kappa Study of Students at Risk, *Growing Up Is Risky Business and Schools Are Not to Blame,* address problems that do not belong to the school alone but to the community at large. Frymier noted that the schools cannot solve these problems by themselves: "The problems will be solved only if society changes, and changes in ways that enhance children's lives instead of endangers them" (Frymier, 1992, p. v). There are frightening statistics in the two-volume report, statistics that should cause everyone concerned about the education of our young people to demand the necessary funds to mandate elementary school counseling for every child in our schools with counselors that are trained to work with all children in the school setting in a comprehensive developmental guidance and counseling program.

Hunsicker, a former teacher, identified some proven strategies that can be used to help at-risk children:

- Challenge them to think and act. Don't allow them to become helpless which reinforces a negative self-opinion.
- Connect new learning experiences with real-world interests and knowledge. Find ways to bring present day happenings in line with their academics.

- Teach thinking and problem-solving skills. This is an area most at-risk children are deficit in because of their home environment which is lacking in this area.
- Take time for class discussions. Identify at-risk student's special interests in order to draw them into the discussion; don't let a few bright students dominate.
- Help them learn to accept frustration and failure as a natural part of arriving at answers. Don't be quick to answer when they are slow in their responses. Get to know their primary care-givers in a positive rather than a punitive setting. Get in touch with the parent before the child is in trouble. (Hunsicker, 1993, p. 8)*

An elementary school counselor can be a caring person in the life of an at-risk child, helping teachers and other school staff address the needs of these children. Most of the activities suggested above can be carried out in a classroom or small group setting. Letting a child know that you believe in him or her, that you feel they are capable of achieving whatever tasks they are confronted with, becomes a priceless gift of hope and reassurance for that child. At-risk children desperately need someone who believes in them as they are, not what they could be.

---

*Reprinted by permission of Ranelda Mack Hunsicker.

Chapter 7

Counseling Culturally Diverse Students

Cross-cultural counseling, multiculturalism, and *multicultural counseling* are all terms that have been appearing in our professional journals in recent years. The *Elementary School Guidance and Counseling* journal devoted the April 1989 issue to cross-cultural counseling; The September/October 1991 *Journal of Counseling and Development* was a special issue on multiculturalism as a "fourth voice in counseling;" and the lead article in the first issue of *American Counselor,* the American Counseling Association (ACA) magazine, published in the winter of 1992, was on the challenge of multiculturalism. This is understandable; our nation exhibits a cultural diversity that has not been experienced before and one that promises to become even more diverse.

Sue refers to multiculturalism as the "road less traveled;" a road that "values cultural pluralism and acknowledges our nation as a cultural mosaic rather than a melting pot" (Sue, 1992, p. 8). To Sue, this approach causes us to lose our ethnocentric approach and become "more responsive to all groups, regardless of race, creed, color, national origin, sexual orientation, and gender" (p. 8). As a way to address this, he challenged counselors to develop an awareness of the biases and stereotypes that they bring to counseling; these biases can greatly affect our understanding of the worldview that minorities bring with them into counseling. He urged counselors to develop cultural flexibility, noting that it may be discriminatory to treat all clients equally, not taking into account the cultural dimensions of their clients.

Pedersen recommends a broad definition of culture, because "the narrow definition of culture has limited multiculturalism to what might more appropriately be called 'multi-ethnic' or 'multi-national' relationships between groups with a shared sociocultural heritage that includes similarities of religion, history, and common ancestry" (Pedersen, 1991b, p. 7). Pedersen noted that not all persons of the same culture share the same experiences, making it necessary for counselors to be able to deal with a variety of differences among the diverse cultural groups.

Educational Leadership, the journal of the Association for Supervision and Curriculum Development (ASCD), devoted its May 1994 issue to "educating for diversity." Janzen (1994) addressed the changing scene in American education—traditionally, the American educational system has practiced assimilation, believing that incorporating all groups into a single culture would meet the needs of individual students. The rival of this practice of assimilation is exactly its opposite—cultural pluralism. "The goal of cultural pluralism is that ethnic groups will remain intact and that their idiosyncratic ways of knowing and acting will be respected and continued" (Janzen, 1994, p. 9). This important dimension should be pursued in the educational system of today. As a part of this, Pedersen and Carey (1994) draw attention to the increasing evidence that children from oppressed minority groups continue to be placed in special education classes in greater numbers; at the same time, they are underrepresented in classes for the gifted and talented. Pedersen and Carey emphasize the need for American education to make some changes in the way it has been educating our young people: "This country's educators need (1) an explicit understanding of how assimilationist models of education damage students, (2) a sensitivity to how students' cultures interact with school institutions to effect self-concept, persistence, and achievement, and (3) knowledge and skills that will enable them to actualize their multicultural understandings" (Pedersen & Carey, 1994, p. vi).

Locke and Parker (1994) believe that school personnel must develop seven levels of awareness if they are to provide the type of education that effectively meets the needs of the culturally different students. These levels are identified and summarized below:

Self-awareness. It is necessary to have self-understanding of one's own thoughts and feelings regarding cultural beliefs and attitudes.

Awareness of one's own culture. An example given is one's name and its cultural significance.

Awareness of racism, sexism, and poverty. This can be viewed both in the context of personal prejudices as well as in the context of institutional prejudice, referring to the attitudes and beliefs that prevail in the educator's school system.

Awareness of individual differences. Educators must first become aware of individual differences before developing an awareness of cultural differences.

Awareness of other culture(s). The previous levels of awareness form the foundation for learning the dynamics of other cultures. School personnel need to be sensitive to verbal as well as nonverbal behaviors unique to a particular culture.

Awareness of diversity. The authors refer to a "salad bowl," rather than a melting pot, to describe the goal of all cultures retaining their unique cultural identity.

Skills/techniques. Educators need more than an awareness, they must have competent teaching skills in order to relate learning theory to the development of psychological-cultural factors. (Locke & Parker, 1994, pp. 44–48)

Locke and Parker also stress the necessity for schools to examine the values that are being taught and their impact on the culturally different student as well as the dominant-culture student: "It is time for our educational systems to become responsive to the values, ideas, beliefs, talents, hopes, dreams, and visions of all students, and especially children who are culturally different" (p. 40). They believe the commitment for change must come from the top down, starting with the school board and the superintendent.

Worzbyt and O'Rourke (1989) also addressed the need for multicultural education in our schools: "Multicultural education shows much promise for enhancing the working-living climate of the school; reducing tensions between and among ethnic, racial, religious, and national origin groups; and in establishing a positive direction for families, communities and the media in emulating and implementing multicultural programs which will permeate all dimensions of society" (p. 379). There is no doubt regarding the need for implementing multicultural education programs in our schools, considering the racial issues that continue to exist in our schools and in the larger society. The counselor's role in helping to create the kind of environment that fosters a cooperative atmosphere where all children are accepted is of great importance (Worzbyt & O'Rourke, 1989).

A suggestion for a redefinition of multicultural counseling comes from Speight, Myers, Cox, and Highlen (1991): The ability to work with another individual that is uniquely different from himself or herself is a basic counseling skill needed by all counselors, not just those working with culturally diverse students. They also emphasize the primary importance of self-awareness, not just an external focus on acquiring knowledge about the various culture groups. They suggest a change in counselor training programs to emphasize self-knowledge: "Counselors would explore their conceptual systems and subsequent worldviews. Unexamined, one's own sense of reality of worldview is frequently perceived as universal and just" (Speight, Myers, Cox, & Highlen, 1991, p. 32).

At the American Counseling Association (ACA) Convention in Minneapolis in 1994, the author attended a session that described an advanced course in multicultural counseling in the Kent State University counselor training program (Jackson & Hayes, 1994). The course, co-taught by an African American female professor and a white male graduate student completing his Ph.D., provided a practical approach wherein the awareness and knowledge learned in the introductory course were put into practice. Each week, one hour of the two-and-one-half-hour class was devoted to skill development and feedback. The experiential component was well defined, and the practicality of the midterm and final cross-cultural counseling sessions with four clients representing ethnic, religious, gender or sexual orientations, and disability insures that these counseling students have a greater degree of knowing "what to do" when involved in a multicultural counseling relationship.

Multicultural guidelines typically identify African Americans, Asian Americans, Hispanics, Native Americans, and "other" ethnic minorities as a focus for counselor and teacher education programs. The previous section identified a multicultural perspective, but a brief look at the four identified groups will highlight a few areas of which an elementary counselor should have some awareness. In a *Guidepost* article on Hispanic immigrants, Avasthi (1990) noted how heterogenous the Hispanic population is; it is actually composed of a highly diverse group of people. It was estimated that more than 10 million Hispanics will immigrate to the United States during the 1990s; these immigrants will arrive "from Mexico, Puerto Rico, Cuba, Central and South America" (Avasthi, 1990, p. 1). She noted that "Hispanics reside in every state, with more than half of the population located in California and Texas" (p. 1). The school dropout rate among Hispanic American children should be of particular concern to all who work with these children. They have the highest dropout rate of any single ethnic group, "losing hope in education during the middle school years" (Baruth & Manning, 1992, p. 114). Elementary counselors can and should address this need. John Aragon, president of New Mexico Highlands University at the time, in a forward to DeBlassie's book *Counseling with Mexican American Youth,* stressed the term *culturally different,* not *culturally deprived* or *culturally disadvantaged,* when working with clients culturally different from the counselor (DeBlassie, 1976). Although written a number of years ago, DeBlassie's book provides a challenge to the writings of today; he felt that accepting minority youth as unique and special human beings rather than as ethnic minorities is the most important factor in counseling these children. "Minority group children, therefore, can be worked with and helped by school personnel, regardless of the latter's ethnicity, as long as these children are perceived and accepted as human beings worthy of dignity and respect" (DeBlassie, 1976, p. 21). DeBlassie, a Mexican American, strongly stated his belief regarding counseling Mexican American children: "The literature is replete with the concept that Mexican American youth are different from other youth and therefore should be counseled differently. I feel obligated to go on record as being in complete disagreement with this concept" (p. 22). DeBlassie wrote in 1976, Avasthi in 1990—14 years apart. Avasthi discussed the heterogeneity of the Hispanic population with their *differing* needs. DeBlassie stressed the necessity to counsel Mexican American kids the same as other children. It is interesting to note these differences regarding working with Mexican Americans and the larger Hispanic population over the span of only 14 years between the writings of DeBlassie and Avasthi.

Rousseve looked at minority identity and personal empowerment from his "30 years of experience as a counselor and counselor educator of color," challenging students of color regarding their occupational ambitions with the following statement: "Beyond my sense of who I am from a racial/ethnic standpoint, *if* I choose to move toward the American occupational mainstream, then I must commit myself to the mastery of those skills and competencies that are aligned with security in *that* sector" (Rousseve, 1989, p. 85). He stressed his belief that racial and ethnic traits are only one element of a person's identity; that counselors working with minority children need to have an awareness of the subtlety of race and ethnicity, but what is most important is developing their potential so that they are motivated to take advantage of the opportunities available to them. At the same time, Rousseve acknowledged the emotional cost to those trying to achieve a balance between their capability to achieve and their allegiance to their racial/ethnic characteristics and attitudes. Locke (1989) challenged elementary school counselors to acquire new knowledge and skills in order to work effectively with culturally different children. He stated the necessity for African American children to develop positive self-esteem in order to be able to cope with difficulties they will encounter; this in turn will help them to become happier and more effective citizens.

Mitchum (1989) noted the special needs of Native American children in our public schools because of their small numbers. She also identified some barriers that arise in counseling these children: Some of the techniques used by elementary school counselors in small groups, such as increasing positive self-talk, is very uncomfortable because it goes against their culture and is considered ill-mannered. Native Americans stress cooperation within the group and contributions to the group, not individual accomplishments, which our schools so often emphasize. It is extremely important to become sensitive to the diversity of learning styles for Native Americans, according to Herring (1989). He noted the lack of expectation for academic success by many of their teachers; as a result, these children are not being challenged to achieve. Herring challenged the majority culture to incorporate teaching and counseling methods that would be relevant to the Native American children in their schools. Hammer and Turner (1990) noted that intervention of any kind is in contradiction to the Native American value of noninterference. Counselors need to be aware of how they work with these children so that their counseling interventions are not seen as interfering in the lives of the students.

There have been an increasing number of Southeast Asian children in our schools due to the high immigration incidence since 1975 combined with their above-average birth rate (Morrow, 1989). Some of the problems associated with these children center on the lack of parental involvement in schools; this is due to Southeast Asians' belief that all authority figures, including counselors and teachers, have the expertise to resolve any issues involving their children. It is important for school staff to have an awareness of these differences so that a lack of involvement by parents in the school will not be interpreted as a lack of concern. Morrow believes that it is possible for the parents to become involved in school activities when teachers and counselors take the time to try to understand their different value systems and family systems as a whole. The San Diego (California) City Schools Guidance Department has a Southeast Asian Guidance Team of bicultural aides that are able to deal with Vietnamese, Laotian, Chinese, Hmong, and Cambodian children in their native language, facilitating communication with parents and students who have limited skills in English. In addition to the language barriers of these children, there are cultural barriers as well. The guidance workers become role models for the Southeast Asian students, bridging the cultural gap between the American public schools and their own cultural heritage. The aides are under the supervision of a district counselor and primarily provide services in attendance, career planning, and home-school communication (Hinsvark, 1989–90). This model could be adapted to an elementary school with Southeast Asian students. Zgliczynski spoke of her concern with counselors' trying to address specific ethnic groups in the schools, noting that in the San Diego city school system there are 42 different Asian groups (personal communication, July 1994).

Another concern in our elementary schools involves children who need to learn English as a second language. This becomes a handicap for these children in the sense that they are required to spend so much time learning English that they fall behind their classmates in the curriculum instruction when all instruction is given in English. In a regular classroom these children slowly fall behind, which eventually puts them at risk of school failure, not because of their abilities but because of their language predicament. In addition to their academic problems, these English as a second language (ESL) children often have difficulty relating to their fellow students because of their language limitations. The author had the opportunity to observe a kindergarten classroom on several occasions during the past school year that was taught as a Spanish immersion class; almost all of the instruction was in Spanish. It was a joy to watch the eagerness of these children as they volunteered answers to questions and were animated and involved in their schooling. During the same week in the same school district, the author observed another kindergarten class, which had just a few Latino children, that was instructed in English, with a bilingual aide softly interpreting for these children. There was no sign of the joy of learning so prevalent in the other kindergarten class; these children obviously felt "lost" in this instructional atmosphere, seeking their own during recess and other play time. They obviously felt "different" from the majority children.

It would not be appropriate to end this section without addressing another minority group: biracial children. Interracial marriages and partnerships have greatly increased over the years to the point that their children have become a recognizable number in our schools. Herring (1992) addressed the lack of research regarding this population, pointing out that many biracial families resist being studied. He also noted the complication of the socialization process of these children based on the cultural differences of their parents. A major social and cultural issue in these families is the lack of transmission of the ethnic identity and, along with this, cultural heritage to the children. Herring also discussed the development of racial identity for these children, made more difficult by the need to integrate their racial or cultural identification. Attention is directed toward the counselor's involvement in helping the child address his or her confusion regarding ethnic identity.

It is not necessary to attempt to discuss all the various ethnic groups whose children make up our elementary schools; it is necessary, however, to address the importance of all elementary school counselors' taking courses in cross-cultural counseling in order to foster the idea of multiculturalism in our elementary schools. Pedersen (1991a) defined *multicultural* as a term that "implies a wide range of multiple groups without grading, comparing, or ranking them as better or worse than one another and without denying the very distinct and complementary or even contradictory perspectives that each group brings with it" (p. 4). This definition fits with a counseling perspective. Guild (1994) raised an interesting point: "Cultures do have distinctive learning style patterns, but the great variation among individuals within groups means that educators must use diverse teaching strategies with all students" (p. 16). This would also apply to strategies used by the elementary counselor in classroom guidance activities, as well as individual and small group counseling.

Counseling Strategies

For the elementary school counselor to assist students and teachers in the process of developing a foundation for multicultural understanding, he or she will find it helpful to develop a worldview as a basis for understanding the ways people are different from each other and learning to appreciate the differences. Considering the worldview of the teacher or student enables the counselor to approach the problems and concerns that are brought to counseling from a different perspective. Sodowsky and Johnson believe that viewing the situation from the counselor's worldview results in assumptions that may or may not be true. Moving to the client's worldview equalizes the relationship culturally. For example, "whether directive responses or listening responses are appropriate counseling skills will depend on the client's style of communication, which is derived from his or her view of relationships with others" (Sodowsky & Johnson, 1974, p. 71). By accepting this framework, the counselor accepts and affirms the student's values, which assures more successful interventions with culturally different students.

Banks espouses a "transformed" curriculum as an orientation to multicultural education, helping children to view reality in a different way. An example of this is "'the Westward Movement.' Westward to whom? It wasn't westward to the Lakota Sioux; for them it was their homeland, the center of the universe. And, of course, it wasn't west to the Mexicans, who considered it north, or for the Alaskans, for whom it was south, and so on. I think kids should talk about the many meanings of 'the west'—what it means to different people" (cited in Brandt, 1994, p. 28). In order for children to function effectively in both their ethnic community and in the mainstream world, Banks believes that the mainstream curriculum should be transformed to accept some of these differences. Students should be taught about their differences and their similarities. Banks recommends teaching civic action to students as an important goal of multicultural education; these action activities should be geared to the developmental level of the child: "Students in the primary grades can take action by refusing to laugh at ethnic jokes. Students in the early and middle grades can read about and make friends with people from other racial, ethnic, and cultural groups" (Banks, 1994, p. 8). An elementary counselor desiring to expand on this in classroom guidance activities might be interested in obtaining *The Kid's Guide to Social Action,* by B.A. Lewis (1991); the book describes a number of ways to use social action activities with children in the school setting.

Ivey and Ivey (1994) developed and co-led a Cultural Identity Group of fifth- and sixth-grade students with the goal of exploring race, ethnicity, and identity issues in the school where Mary Ivey is an elementary school counselor. Their pilot group of European American students met for seven sessions, summarized as follows:

Session 1. Who are we? Why are we here? What are our goals?

Session 2. Taking pride in one's ethnic/racial identity and the problem of oppression.

Session 3. Tolerance and self-esteem. To get along with others, you also need to respect yourself.

Session 4. Racism.

Session 5. Anti-Semitism and standing up for right.

Session 6. Sexual harassment—How can we get along?

Session 7. Concluding meeting and review of course concepts (Ivey & Ivey, 1994, pp. 3–4).

As part of the sessions, the students were assigned homework related to the activities. The homework assigned to the students for each session is designed to help the students see how they, as individuals, develop within their family and within their cultural system.

The racial identity theory was discussed by Helms (1994), who argues that it is useful to analyze the various racial dynamics that interfere in the educational setting. "Racial identity theory concerns a person's self-conception of herself or himself as a racial being, as well as one's beliefs, attitudes, and values vis-a-vis oneself relative to a racial group other than one's own" (Helms, 1994, p. 19). As a part of this, Helms viewed a person's concept of other groups to be either "reference group orientation (RGO)" or "affiliative identity" (p. 20). She cited as an example a person who is embarrassed to eat the foods that are traditional in his or her culture, always eating American food—in this area, the individual is abandoning his or her reference group. Helms makes the assumption that the children already identify with their racial group by the time they start elementary school; it is the family environment that determines this. Various groups of color have been studied using racial identity development, but most of the theory and research has been with

African Americans. Helms identified four stages of racial identity development, as developed with black identity theory, summarized below:

Preencounter

In this stage, Whites and the White culture are seen as superior. The children's reference group orientation will not change at this stage unless the educational environment includes the culture of various groups, not just Whites. This is also affected if the child is not exposed to a variety of people of color.

Encounter

There is confusion at this stage because the child begins to realize that he or she is not a member of the White group, with society's theme of superiority. The child becomes unpredictable at this stage: "On some days, he or she may be obviously trying to get attention in ways that call attention to her or his 'differentness'" (p. 23). If the child is disciplined because of behavior, the belief that his or her group is not valued by the school system is reinforced. Using classroom activities that cause all of the children to look at their own culture will help the entire class.

Immersion/Emersion

At this stage, Whites are defamed and the racial group is idealized. The child may be angry, depressed, or rebellious and may dress or behave in ways he or she thinks characterizes that race. These children can be guided into activities and/or assignments that affirm their group membership in positive ways.

Idealization

When the child reaches this stage, his or her own racial group is valued. The child with a positive racial identity is in a position to teach other students about his or her group and can be used as a role model. (Helms, 1994, pp. 22–24)

In addition to racial identity development, Helms also addressed white racial identity, proposing a six-stage model of progression, summarized below:

Contact

At this stage the child is not conscious of his or her own race and may have a naive curiosity about other groups. Classroom intervention by a counselor or teacher should provide simple but accurate information about racial or ethnic groups.

Disintegration

This stage is characterized by guilt and confusion and some anxiety when racial issues are discussed. The child at this stage should be helped to accept personal responsibility for racism.

Reintegration

At this stage the child adopts the attitude that everything White is superior, with an exaggeration of group differences. Children at this stage require interventions that reeducate them regarding the stereotypes of all racial groups, including White.

Pseudo-independence

The children at this stage are able to think about other's racial problems and generally feel positive about being White. This stage can be strengthened by providing activities that cause the children to think critically about racial issues.

Immersion/Emersion

The child at this stage often lacks White role models that have resolved their own racial identity issues. Interventions should include helping the child to recognize that as a White, he or she does have a culture of his or her own.

Autonomy

The person at this stage has a nonracist White identity, accepting that the White culture established his or her values and beliefs. (Helms, 1994, pp. 25–29)

It is valuable for the elementary school counselor to be aware of the stages of racial identity and to apply this awareness to the children he or she works with in the school setting. Depending on which stage the children are in, the counselor should identify activities that would help them learn some of the various differences, such as "What makes skin different colors?" and "Why are eyes slanted?"—these are the types of appropriate questions that require simple, honest answers for younger elementary-age children. When the elementary counselor conducts classroom guidance activities, with the teacher involved in planning and carrying out the activities, the opportunity is there to discuss these stages of racial identity development and white racial identity that the children are facing.

Atkinson and Juntunen (1994) express concern that as diversification increases, parental involvement will decrease, particularly if there are language barriers. They also noted other barriers, such as attitudes, beliefs, and customs, that may cause the parent to experience stress in the school setting; where limited finances require both parents to work, they may find it difficult to become involved in their child's education. The schools are usually in a position to draw upon community-based resources to help ethnically diverse students and their families. In addition to this help, Atkinson and Juntunen maintain the following: "We remain committed to the concept of parental involvement and we believe that schools must make every effort to include ethnic minority parents in educational activities" (1994, p. 108). They identify six responsibilities and functions for the school counselor/psychologist liaison in an ethnically diverse school:

Interpreting culture. The counselor should function in a position that interprets the culture of the school and the larger community to the student and his or her family as well as the ethnic minority culture of the family to the school or to the larger community.

Referral. This is seen as a primary function of the liaison role: to refer the students and parents to appropriate organizations and services in the ethnic and larger communities when needed or indicated. The counselor may be involved in this referral process to the extent of contacting the agency or referral source, arranging a meeting, and possibly even transportation.

Advocacy. Some parents are unable to advocate for their children for a variety of reasons; when this happens, the counselor should speak for the student and/or the family. An example given was the use of broadly based assessment techniques rather than standardized tests in order to evaluate the student's progress.

Program development. This ranges from finding interpreters within the community to translate at parent-teacher conferences to formal programs in the community such as a chapter of Big Brothers or Big Sisters.

Social modeling. The counselor can demonstrate an appreciation of diversity by promoting a social environment that is supportive of all students and parents.

Mediation. Where there is conflict between the cultural values of the ethnic community and the student/school/larger community, the counselor could serve in a mediation role. This could involve social activities that are in conflict with cultural values or forms of discipline that could be considered abuse by this country's standards. (Atkinson & Juntunen, 1994, pp. 109–117)

When an elementary counselor is in a school that has an ethnically diverse population, these functions become necessary to help ethnically diverse students and their families adjust to the school setting.

Another element to consider is career guidance in a multicultural setting. Herr and Niles (1994) addressed the emergence of a more culturally diverse workforce and the need for multicultural career guidance services. They stressed the importance of career guidance and career education starting in kindergarten: "Early intervention in the elementary school years is especially important, given the evidence that suggests that children begin the process of eliminating occupational options based on factors such as perceived gender appropriateness, socioeconomic status, and parental attitudes toward work during the primary grades" (1994, pp. 185—186). Along with the services for children, Herr and Niles identified the primary goal as working with the parents of culturally different students. The activities suggested in Chapter 9 in the section on career guidance in the elementary school should be viewed in the context of the elementary counselor's school population.

Elementary counselors should be interested in the research on multicultural education done by Ladson-Billings (1994); she noted that five areas in particular make a great difference in the education of children from a multicultural population:

- *Beliefs about students matter.* How the teachers view the students and their capability of achieving high quality academic work directly affects student achievement.
- *Content and materials matter.* The superficial celebration of heroes and holidays tends to trivialize multicultural education. Students will develop or strengthen existing stereotypes by the use of classroom materials that incorrectly portray diverse groups.
- *Instructional approaches matter.* The teacher may need to use cooperative learning or may use the language and understanding that the child brings to school to help them learn.
- *Educational settings matter.* There are still many segregated schools because a number of children attend neighborhood schools; others are resegregated within the school by tracking or ability groups.
- *Teacher education matters.* The lack of preservice preparation regarding cultural variations is very evident in our schools. Courses that deal with race, class, and

gender issues have a great impact on the potential teacher. (Ladson-Billings, 1994, pp. 23–25)

Each of these areas is highly significant for elementary counselors to be aware of. Most of these areas can be affected by the counselor through in-service training or education, particularly if the counselor has had at least one course in multicultural education.

Another area the elementary school counselor might find necessary to address is the issue of prejudice; this can be done by teaching children at an early age about the ways to accommodate the differences among people (Cano, 1994). Cano believes that because children are naturally curious about the obvious differences in people, these differences should be explained to our children in a clear and understandable way. If children are taught to have a positive identity, they will be less open to the effects of prejudice. Cano believes in a proactive stance: "Don't just wait for the issue or prejudice to arise. Discuss the stereotypical and negative images of African Americans, Asians, Latinos, women, and disabled that are portrayed in children's books and on television and the movies" (Cano, 1994, p. 9). Along with this is the need for each of the diverse culture groups, in addition to white people, to develop an understanding of each other, according to Cano.

The American School Counselor Association (ASCA) has a position statement on cross/multi-cultural counseling (see Appendix J for the complete statement), adopted in 1983, that defines cross/multi-cultural counseling as "the facilitation of human development through the understanding and appreciation of cultural diversities with respect to language, values, ethics, morals, and racial variables." We need to look closely at our counselor education programs as we train elementary school counselors to work in settings that are becoming so diverse and are feeling the impact of these population changes. Many states already have reached the point where the white students are outnumbered by racial and ethnic minority students, prompting those in education that are in the dominant culture to learn to value this diversity. Wittmer (1992) states this succinctly: "With the make-up of the student body changing so rapidly, school counselors, teachers and administrators realize that they are now required to learn new techniques and skills for understanding, motivating, teaching, and empowering each individual student regardless of race, gender, religion or creed" (p. 27).

We may need to help our counselor-in-training students to change their perspective of acquiring knowledge and skills to be able to work with a culturally diverse population, helping them first to recognize their need to understand their own internal beliefs and attitudes about counseling persons from other cultural groups (Kelly, 1990). In Kelly's graduate-level practicum class in multicultural counseling, one of the requirements is for each student to prepare and present a genogram of his or her own family of origin. As a part of this, the students focus on the cultural history of their own family in constructing the genogram. Kelly views this as a benefit for all students but particularly the Anglo students who have not known or shared in their family history after they have lived in the United States for several generations. Focusing on one's beliefs and attitudes that have persisted through the generations, plus the cultural heritage uncovered through the family of origin exercise, helps the potential counselor become more aware and appreciative of similarities and differences among the cultural groups (Kelly, 1990).

Locke (1989) identified five classroom guidance activities that can be used in K–6 classrooms by counselors or teachers. He recommended using appropriate experiences to help all culturally different students appreciate their differences. One of the activities, suitable for K–1, is the following:

Activity 1: Same or Different

Objective: To have each child recognize physical similarities and differences between children of similar or different racial groups.

Description: The counselor will discuss physical attributes of people in general. Children will look at themselves in mirrors and tell what they see. Children will look at neighboring children and take turns describing each other. Children will draw or paint pictures of themselves and a neighbor, paying attention to details already discussed. (Locke, 1989, p. 256)

All educators are in a position to end the at-risk practices that affect so many of our children and that appear to be so divisive. Robinson offers a number of recommendations to help counselors and teachers accomplish this as they work toward change:

- Recognize the preventive qualities of multiculturalism. This can be accomplished by providing an academic curriculum that is meaningful and culturally relevant.
- Teach children that racism is a threat to multiculturalism. Children can be encouraged to use reading as an activity which will help them learn about race bias.
- Teach children that sexism is a threat to multiculturalism. This can be done by exposing children to pursue careers that are nontraditional.
- Heighten your awareness of your attitudes about differences. This can be done by helping both Whites and non-Whites examine their attitudes, individually and in groups.
- Create multicultural learning environments. By displaying pictures in prominent places around the school of culturally and racially diverse groups, children will be given a strong message that these differences are acknowledged and valued.
- Create multicultural teams to more effectively serve students. This can be accomplished by establishing teams of caring adults as a support system for students. (Robinson, 1992, pp. 90–92)

At the national level, in 1991 the Professional Standards Committee of the Association for Multicultural Counseling and Development (AMCD), a division of the American Counseling Association, proposed 31 multicultural counseling competencies with the recommendation that ACA (formerly AACD) advocate their adoption to be used in accreditation criteria and in graduate counseling programs (Sue, Arredondo, & McDavis, 1992). They stressed emphasis on the development of multicultural standards, particularly in education and in counseling.

Summary

As the elementary school counselor approaches the difficult task of identifying the special needs of children who come from culturally diverse backgrounds, he or she must have special competencies to accomplish this task. The position statement on cross/multi-cultural counseling clearly spells out the competencies needed, including strategies to increase the awareness of school district personnel regarding culturally diverse populations. It is the elementary school counselor's task to see that the counseling program meets the special needs of all students. To be truly comprehensive, an elementary school counseling program should include activities that identify and value all cultural groups in the school.

Elementary counselors need to recognize that there is no way to learn everything about every culture in their school if they are in a multicultural school setting. Counselors will gain some basic knowledge to help them interpret student behavior by asking the youngsters questions and by listening to them. A Chicano male graduate student in one of the author's counseling classes said this: "Be persistent. Let us know you care—that you don't understand the experiences I've had but you want to know about me. No matter what I say to you, how I push you away, don't give up and go away—don't listen to me when I do this. Let me know you care" (J. Hernandez, personal communication, November 1994). Elementary counselors do care about and can make a difference for all of the students in their schools.

Part II

Activities and Resources

Chapter 8

Records, Tests, and Their Confidentiality

Cumulative Records

At the elementary school level, there is a strong sense of providing direct service to students and their parents, teachers, and school staff. The time-consuming record keeping and paperwork that secondary school counselors are often involved with is typically not a problem for the elementary school counselor. All students K–12 have records that follow them through school, usually referred to as their cumulative record. Prior to 1974, access to a student's cumulative records was limited, which allowed teachers to place potentially damaging or judgmental comments about children in their folders; this sometimes caused bias on the part of those reading these records. This practice ended, for the most part, when the Family Educational Rights and Privacy Act (PL 93-380), usually referred to as the Buckley Amendment, was established in 1974. As in the case of the previously discussed PL 94-142, certain provisions accompany an act when a school at any level accepts federal monies; in the case of the Buckley Amendment, the school must give parents or guardians access to their children's records. In addition, parents or guardians are allowed to challenge and correct any entries in their child's records that they feel are in error.

The type of information that is usually kept and maintained in the elementary child's cumulative record file is helpful in learning about the child's background, including who the child is living with; whether he or she has any siblings; whether the child has been retained in any grade; moves the child may have made before attending their current school; any possible problems that have been identified that might affect the child's achievement or potential development, such as attendance or serious illness; and any referrals for educational or psychological evaluation. Without this basic information, a counselor is handicapped in developing a helping relationship with a child that has been referred.

Sometimes teachers, particularly beginning teachers, are uncertain as to what should be placed in a child's cumulative record folder and may end up putting in very little or no helpful information because of this uncertainty. A summary of a child's coping skills will be invaluable for the next teacher. A number of years ago the author was involved in a project to compile a handbook on guidance and counseling for a large metropolitan school district. One of the sections on forms and records summarized an information sheet for a teacher to fill out to accompany the child's cumulative records. This is an excellent way for one teacher to pass on valuable information to another teacher.

Consider the child in light of the following:

1. What motivates him positively?
2. What classroom activities does he handle with least frustration—most?
3. When is the best time of day scholastically?
4. What needs for activity does he have?
5. What peer cooperation situations work best?
6. What effective communications methods exist between parents, child, and teacher?
7. What is the child's most effective mode of learning?

> Auditory—hearing
>
> Visual—sight
>
> Tactile—touch
>
> Kinetic—motion. (Albuquerque Public Schools, 1978, Section IV)

The following additional examples of statements that can be elaborated upon may also be helpful to the teacher:

Learns best when given only one instruction at a time

Operates best in a setting free from distractions

Works well in groups

Is good in sports

Enjoys art activities

Is very social in class

Contributes to class discussions

Gets attention by resorting to physical means

Accomplishes tasks when interest is frequently stimulated

Has shown improvements in controlling his temper

Has qualities of leadership in the area of _____. (Albuquerque Public Schools, 1978)

The records kept on children in the school setting are to help insure that the child receives an appropriate education and should be accurately maintained for this purpose. Only factual or documented information should be placed in the child's cumulative record.

A counselor desiring to make use of the profusion of information contained in a cumulative record folder might consider using a summary sheet to jot down the most significant information to keep in a locked file in the counselor's office. Schmidt (1991) suggests that, in addition to the child's name, address, and home phone, the following information would be useful for the counselor to keep on a summary sheet: family members, physical/medical notes, educational notes, previous schools, and a category called "other information." Most counselors keep confidential files concerning their sessions with individual children that are not kept in the cumulative folder in order to keep track of what they talked about, particular concerns, and anything of a confidential nature so that the child's privacy is respected. This is particularly important when the counselor is in a large school or in several schools, as often is the case for elementary counselors. It only takes a few minutes to glance over the notes from previous sessions; the child will then feel that the counselor remembers what was previously discussed.

There are clear conditions that govern the transfer of a child's school records if he or she transfers to another school. The school is required to "(1) notify the pupil's parents that the records have been transferred, (2) send the parents a copy of the transferred records if the parents so desire, and (3) provide the parents with an opportunity to challenge the content of the transferred data" (Salvia & Ysseldyke, 1991, p. 60).

The following section on tests used in the elementary school will include record keeping of tests, as well as reporting the test results to administrators, teachers, parents, and students, when appropriate, and various assessment instruments suitable for use in the elementary school in addition to the standardized achievement tests or aptitude tests that the school administers to its students in a regular testing program.

Use of Tests in the Elementary School

The first real national emphasis on program evaluation in our public schools, beyond that of teacher-generated tests and state- and locally mandated testing, came about when the U.S. Congress passed the Elementary and Secondary Education Act (ESEA) in 1965, which provided large sums of money to local educational systems. It was concern over the effectiveness of the nation's educational system that caused Congress to mandate the evaluation of whether or not the local educational agencies were using their federal grants appropriately (Popham, 1988). The continuation of funding beyond the current year level was tied to satisfactory evaluation of the project by the local education agency. The state legislators soon followed this lead, tying educational monies to evaluation requirements. Popham noted the confusion that exists regarding the terminology that many educators use as synonyms for the term *evaluation: measurement, grading, accountability, assessment,* and *appraisal.* Popham recognizes that there is no single best definition for most of these terms. For the purposes of the discussion of reporting test results at the elementary school level, we will use the term *evaluation.*

In many elementary schools, one of the tasks of the elementary counselor is the reporting of test results. To whatever extent the elementary school counselor is involved in testing in the school, he or she should not be responsible for the testing program itself; this is an administrative function not identified in ASCA's elementary school counselor role. This responsibility should be under the jurisdiction of the principal or a school district specialist.

It is important, though, that the counselor be knowledgeable about the various tests used in the elementary school as well as the interpretation of these test results. When we speak of tests used in the schools, we are usually referring to standardized tests, ones that have been constructed for, evaluated, and normed on an appropriate reference group. Standardized tests always adhere to a set of standard directions and conditions. These tests include achievement tests, aptitude tests, intelligence tests, interest tests, and personality measures. The use of nonstandardized tests will be discussed at the end of this section.

Tests are a resource for the principals, teachers, and counselors to use in conjunction with other pieces of information in assisting students. Drummond (1992) lists some of the possible goals that may be involved in a school testing program:

1. Identify the readiness of kindergarten and first grade students.
2. Determine whether or not students have mastered the basic and essential skills required by the school system.
3. Place individuals in educational programs.
4. Identify individuals with special needs.
5. Evaluate the curriculum and specific programs of study.
6. Help individuals make their educational and vocational decisions.
7. Assess the scholastic aptitude and cognitive skills of individual students.
8. Measure achievement in specific courses and subject areas. (Drummond, 1992, p. 332)

A school or district may utilize a variety of assessment instruments to evaluate its program, resulting in an assortment of test data.

In order for elementary school counselors to make appropriate use of the test data generated in their schools, they should become familiar with the terminology used to describe test results and communicate this to the principals, teachers, parents, and children, where appropriate. Because the counselor in his or her training learns test terminology applicable to tests and measurements used in the elementary school testing programs, this information is not included in this text, but the reader may need to review previously learned material. This includes the scales of measurement and scoring systems that give meaning to the scores achieved by the students individually and in a group, which could include their classroom, school, or school district as a whole.

Individual test results are commonly reported as grade-equivalent scores, meaning that the student's performance is compared with other students at whatever grade level the child is in that is being tested. What is sometimes confusing in viewing grade equivalence is that the average child at the beginning of the school year would score at the grade, that is, grade 3, plus 0 months, or 3.0. At the end of the school year a child scoring at 3.9 would show that the child had a raw score equivalent of an average third-grade student at the end of third grade. Because test scores are compared to a norming group, one-half the students typically would score above the median score and one-half the students would score below the median score. In the example, this means that at the beginning of the school year up to one-half of the children in an average class will score below the grade level, which actually means that half of them are below the median score, 3.0, not really behind as might first be suspected, whereas the other half will score above the median score of 3.0, not really above grade level as might be suspected. To further extend this discussion, a third-grade child scoring 6.0 in a reading test is not truly reading at the sixth-grade level; it is the score of a typical sixth-grade child on a third-grade reading test.

Another way that raw scores on tests are commonly reported is as percentile ranks, usually fairly straightforward and easy to understand by those involved in test taking and in interpretation of tests. In this type of derived scoring, a percentile rank of 75 indicates that the student scored higher than 75 percent of the students with whom he or she is being compared. The disadvantage of percentile ranking is the way the scores are distributed and emphasized, with an overemphasis of scores near the median and a greater distortion and underemphasis of the score differences at the extremes of the sample, the upper and lower ends. In addition, we need to be careful not to confuse percentile with percent correct; percentile ranking shows how an individual compares to the standardized sample with which the score is being compared. Percentile ranking continues to be the most commonly used method of reporting test results because of its relative ease of use and interpretation.

A significant term to remember is the *norm,* the standard of comparison for the individual or group taking the test. Test publishers provide a table of norms with the test interpretive data so that the individual or group will have a basis of comparison. The test manual also identifies the group on which the test was normed, including sample size, which makes a comparison easier. Sometimes school districts prefer to use local norms rather than national norms in order to provide more meaningful results, particularly if the normative group is quite different from the individual or group being compared, such as markedly different cultural or ethnic differences. It is extremely important to guard against any kind of cultural bias when making educational decisions about children in elementary schools. Another problem with the use of national norms is the test publishers' intention of providing tests that will serve the entire country, which does not take into account the curricular differences in elementary schools in different parts of the country.

Using criterion-referenced measurement is another way to interpret test scores. In this case, a criterion is established in a particular subject; the teacher's goal is to help the students master the subject. These tests measure whether or not specific performance standards were reached; they are measured against a particular criterion. In spelling, for example, criterion-referenced tests provide answers to specific questions: "Does Kara spell the word *dog* correctly?" An advantage of criterion-referenced tests is that the child is treated as an individual, where appropriate instructional goals or objectives can be established based on specific content.

Two concepts in the field of measurement that need to be understood as we seek to convey the meaning of tests to others are reliability and validity. When we test, we are interested in generalizing what we see today as the results of a particular test to another testing situation at a later time. To the extent that we can generalize from a particular set of observations, we can say that these observations are reliable. In other words, how consistently a test will measure what we seek to measure is its reliability. Validity simply means that the test measures what it purports to measure; it refers to the extent to which a test measures what the authors claim it measures, allowing us to make inferences from the test scores.

The standardized tests used in the elementary school setting are typically group tests and include the following:

1. Achievement tests—tests that are designed to measure the knowledge and/or skill a child has acquired, usually as a result of classroom instruction.

2. Aptitude tests—tests that measure the potential abilities of a child to perform in a given area.

Some of the most frequently used achievement tests in our elementary schools include the California Achievement Test (CAT) (California Test Bureau, 1978), the Comprehensive Test of Basic Skills (CTBS) (California Test Bureau, 1981), the Iowa Test of Basic Skills (ITBS) (Hieronymus, Lindquist, & Hoover, 1978), the Metropolitan Achievement Test (MAT) (Balow, Farr, Hogan, & Prescott, 1984), and the Wide Range Achievement Test—Revised (WRAT-R) (Jastak & Wilkinson, 1984). Two tests frequently used to predict scholastic success are the Otis-Lennon School Ability Test (Otis & Lennon, 1982), which is used to predict success in cognitive school-related areas and is considered an aptitude-type test, and the Coloured Progressive Matrices Test (Raven, Court, & Raven, 1983), a scholastic aptitude test for ages 5 to 11.

A number of textbooks that address the use of assessment instruments in the school setting are available for counselors desiring to expand their knowledge base regarding testing. One text that the author has found especially readable and easy to understand is published by the American Counseling Association (ACA): *Assessment in Counseling: A Guide to the Use of Psychological Assessment Procedures* (Hood & Johnson, 1991). An especially useful feature is a listing of publishers and distributors of all commonly used tests by counselors, including a list of the tests that they publish along with the test acronyms.

The previous discussion was concerned with group tests. Individual testing, for the most part, is in the realm of the school psychologist or psychometrist. Elementary schools that employ counselors will frequently have available the services of a school psychologist or psychometrist. Individual tests are usually given as part of a psychological assessment and evaluation whenever a student does not benefit from the regular classroom setting. The results of these tests are interpreted to the teacher and parents by the school psychologist or psychometrist, not the school counselor. At the same time, it is important for the school counselor to be familiar with the various tests used in a psychological referral assessment. Intelligence tests given in the school setting are very seldom groups tests, particularly because PL 94-142 mandates individual testing as part of the referral process for children under consideration for special education. The two most commonly used individual intelligence tests in the elementary school are the Kaufman Assessment Battery for Children (K-ABC) (Kaufman & Kaufman, 1983) and the two Wechsler Scales suitable for this age group: Wechsler Preschool and Primary Scale of Intelligence-Revised (WPPSI-R) (Wechsler, 1989), and Wechsler Intelligence Scale for Children-III (WISC-III) (Wechsler, 1991). Two additional tests that are frequently used are referred to as "nonverbal tests" because they are not dependent on the child's understanding English, having normal speech and hearing, and belonging to the dominant white culture. These tests are the Leiter International Performance Scale (LIPS) (Leiter, 1952) and the Test of Nonverbal Intelligence (TONI) (Brown, Sherbenu, & Dollar, 1982). These tests are used primarily to identify children with special needs and are typically given by a school psychologist or psychometrist.

Nonstandardized assessment tools at the elementary school level that counselors frequently use are rating scales and behavioral observations. When teachers, principals, or parents ask an elementary counselor for input on a child who is experiencing some problems, the counselor not only will visit with the child in his or her office and consult with the teacher and/or parent but will most likely observe the child in the classroom and on the playground. The behavior may be systematically observed over a period of time or, if time is a constraint, may be limited to one observation. Actually, observation techniques are the most natural type of assessment. Observations can be casual and unplanned or planned and directed, with a definite purpose, using checklists and rating scales to facilitate the process. When rating scales are used, often the child or others will be involved in assessing the occurrence of particular behaviors. A common weakness in observation is not really "seeing" what is taking place. The author, in her psychological and educational assessment class, always uses a popular question given in most driver's license examinations: the identification, by shape only, of the meaning of five common traffic signs. A surprisingly large number of students miss one or more of these, which becomes an important message regarding the lack of accuracy in the use of observation as a technique. Another potential pitfall in using observation is the tendency for the observer to "look for" poor behavior, the behavior that was identified beforehand by the principal, teacher, or parent. It is critical for the elementary counselor to keep in mind the limitations of observation as he or she uses this widely accepted technique.

Reporting Test Results

The elementary school counselor should be able to report and interpret test results to principals, teachers, and parents, as well as to the students, when appropriate. Children in the later elementary school years can benefit from knowing the results of the standardized tests they take during the school year. It has been the author's experience that children have some awareness of their abilities, usually feeling that they have less ability than what the tests reveal. In interpreting test results to children, it is important to keep all value judgments out of the discussion; at the same time, the students should be helped to identify their areas of strength and areas that are weaker and where they may need some help. A significant part of the interpretation of test results with children is making sure they understand what the test scores actually mean in terms of grade level, percentile rank, and norms.

It is equally significant for the parents to be informed of the test results of their children, and not just by receiving a copy of the results with a letter of explanation, as some districts are prone to do. Most parents are not knowledgeable about testing and need help in understanding the test results and their implications. An evening program at the school using an overhead projector with illustrations, and using actual profiles of test results at various levels without any names, will help parents understand the test results. If the parents each have a copy of their own child's profile in their hand during this time, as the counselor walks them through the profile as a group, they will feel more free to ask questions. By the evening's end, if any parents still have unanswered questions, the counselor should inform them of his or her availability to respond individually to them. The author has conducted this kind of session as a school counselor on several occasions for parent groups and has always had outstanding attendance and excellent feedback. Some typical questions asked by parents are "Does this test count very much?"; "Who sees the test scores?"; "What do you mean by standardized tests?"; "My child's grades are very different from the test results. What does this mean?" The elementary school counselor should be able to respond to the questions and concerns of parents.

Test interpretation for teachers can be done as an in-service program during the school year. Teachers often are hesitant to ask questions about the testing, thinking that they should already know the answers. The author has used an overhead projector with sample test profiles just as is done with the parents, telling the teachers that it is important for them to know exactly what the parents will be told about their children's test results so that if a parent contacts the teacher, the teacher will know what the parent has been told. This has proved to be a successful way of informing the teachers about the testing and the meaning of the results without making them feel that they have to admit a lack of knowledge about basic test and measurement concepts.

Test interpretation is an entirely different situation for the principal. Most principals are not as interested in individual results as they are in how their school compares on a local, state, or national basis. They are very interested in how the parents react to the test scores and are usually quite pleased to be involved in the parent night. This is an excellent way for an elementary school counselor to gain visibility in his or her school and community, in addition to broadening the principal's perception of the counselor's range of skills.

Interpreting test results is a significant part of the guidance program, enabling the counselor to assist the parent and the student in learning and understanding the child's strengths and weaknesses. It is important to use a report form that shows the scores in broad categories, such as high, above average, average, below average, and low, in order to include the variables that might affect the child's test score. Part of the discussion should include comparing the child's performance in class with his or her ability to perform. The child's strengths should be emphasized. It is also important to compare the scores with a comparable test taken previously, if possible, and not to weigh everything on the basis of a single test score, particularly if it is significantly different from the child's classroom performance.

Muro and Dinkmeyer emphasize using test results as an aid in decision making as well as to facilitate problem solving. They list certain steps that the counselor should follow in presenting the test results to the counselee:

1. Remember that a test is only one source of information, and it yields a sample of behavior at a given moment of time. Compare the data from the test with other non-test data and previous test data available on the student.
2. The test information is useful only if you can communicate the results clearly. The student on the elementary level will have difficulty grasping the meaning of T scores or even percentile ranks. Translate the results into non-quantitative language.
3. Don't over-interpret the data. Keep in mind the errors of measurement and the sample of behavior. Look at scores as they fall in the probability band, rather than just as absolutes. Look for data that will help you understand and explain puzzling aspects.
4. In synthesizing the results, try to piece the separate sets of information together to help understand the whole individual. (1977, pp. 200–201)

These four points should be kept in mind by the elementary school counselor and used in interpreting test results to administrators, teachers, parents, and students.

Additional Assessment Instruments Appropriate for Elementary School

There are some tests that an elementary school counselor may want to administer on an individual or classroom basis depending upon need or requests for help from a teacher or parent. Three tests that are helpful as screening instruments at the elementary level are the Peabody Individual Achievement Test—Revised (PIAT-R) (Markwardt, 1989), the Peabody Picture Vocabulary Test—Revised (PPVT-R) (Dunn & Dunn, 1981), and the Wide Range Achievement Test—Revised (WRAT-R) (Jastak & Wilkinson, 1984). These are individually administered achievement tests that do not require special training beyond a graduate-level tests and measurements course. The PPVT-R is a nonreading test, which is useful if the child is a poor reader or has a speech handicap.

For an initial assessment of a child referred to the counselor for the possibility of attention-deficit hyperactivity disorder, the Conners' Rating Scales are often used. Counselors use these scales for identifying hyperactivity as well as other types of behavior problems in children; the two scales are the Conners' Teacher Rating Scales and the Conners' Parent Rating Scales (Conners, 1990). The Teacher Feedback Form is used to provide feedback for the teacher regarding the results of his or her rating of the student. The form is used in the presentation and discussion by the counselor or school psychologist. Depending upon the results, school-based interventions are usually recommended; these might include individual counseling, classroom interventions, or working with the family. The Parent Feedback Form is used to provide feedback to the parents on the rating they completed in much the same way as is carried out with the teacher. The behavioral descriptions are given to the parents, not the scale names, as these labels are often alarming to parents. The tests are easily administered and quickly scored by the use of a self-scoring answer sheet, with an accompanying profile form using separate sides for boys and girls.

Two well-established self-concept scales are available for classroom administration or individual administration; these can be used when principals or teachers have concerns regarding children's perception of themselves, particularly because a child's self-concept is often related to achievement or lack of success in school. The Coopersmith Self-Esteem Inventories are available for grades K–6 (Coopersmith, 1981); the Piers-Harris Children's Self-Concept Scale has been standardized for use above the third grade (Piers & Harris, 1984). A less well-known, but excellent, measure is the Self-Perception Profile for Children Grades 3–8 (Harter, 1985). The instrument contains six separate subscales, such as Social Competence, Social Acceptance, and Global Self-Worth. The author has successfully used all three instruments in elementary school research on the effectiveness of counseling interventions with children.

A nationally standardized series of questionnaires that is useful for assessing children who have been referred for behavior problems is the Social Skills Rating System (SSRS), available as rating forms for teachers, parents, and students (Gresham & Elliott, 1990). The rating scales allow a counselor to evaluate a broad range of behaviors that affect teacher-student relationships and peer acceptance at the elementary school level.

An excellent instrument available to assess and measure depression in children is the Reynolds Child Depression Scale (RCDS), a self-report measure used with children in grades 3 through 6 (Reynolds, 1989). Children who have become socially withdrawn, have crying spells, seem tired much of the time, and seem unable to deal with classroom demands may be suffering from depression. The RCDS can be administered individually, in small groups, or in larger groups. The children are asked to respond to a 30-item questionnaire giving a response that best indicates their feelings for the past two weeks.

When a child communicates possible home problems, the counselor may need to asses the family environment. This can be accomplished by administering the Children's Version of the Family Environment Scales (CVFES) available for the elementary-age child (Moos & Moos, 1981). The child responds to 30 pictures representing ten scales, selecting the pictures that look most like his or her family. This area will be expanded upon in Chapter 10, with a discussion of the Family Environment Scales used in addressing problems and conflicts in the home that affect the elementary school child.

This is not meant to be an all-inclusive list of assessment devices available for use in the elementary school; it is a compilation of measures that have proved to be successful for elementary school counselors desiring to serve the needs of all of the students. The assessment instruments described above are appropriate for use by the elementary school counselor with at least one graduate-level course in testing.

Professional Use Standards

Prior to starting a testing program in a school, the elementary counselor should obtain the following three documents:

1. *The Code of Fair Testing Practices in Education.* This pamphlet was prepared by the Joint Committee on Testing Practices; it states the major obligations to test takers for those who administer tests in the school setting. The pamphlet is a cooperative effort by the American Educational Research Association, the American Psychological Association, and the National Council on Measurement in Education; sponsors that were added later include the American Counseling Association's Association for Measurement and Evaluation in Counseling and Development, and the American Speech-Language-Hearing Association. The code presents standards in the following areas that should be considered by those who develop and use tests:

   A. Developing/selecting tests
   B. Interpreting scores
   C. Striving for fairness
   D. Informing test takers

   The pamphlet is free and is not copyrighted material; a copy may be obtained by writing to the Joint Committee on Testing Practices, American Psychological Association, 750 First Avenue NE, Washington, D.C., 20002-4242.

2. *Responsibility of Users of Standardized Tests (RUST Statement Revised).* This document was developed in 1976 at the ACA (then APGA) Convention. It was published in the October 1978 *Guidepost;* the present statement is expanded from that review. It is organized into eight sections: Introduction, Test Decisions, Qualifications of Test Users, Test Selection, Test Administration, Test Scoring,

Test Interpretation, and Communicating Test Results (RUST Statement Revised). A free copy of the RUST statement may be obtained from ACA, 5900 Stevenson Avenue, Alexandria, VA 22304.

3. *Multicultural Assessment Standards: A Compilation for Counselors.* This pamphlet was published in March 1993 by the Association for Assessment in Counseling, a division of the ACA. These standards were developed in an attempt to address the many challenges faced by the increasing diversity of counselees in counseling settings. There are four assessment tasks to which the standards apply:

> Selection of assessment instruments: content considerations
> Selection of assessment instruments: Norming, reliability, and validity considerations
> Administration and scoring of assessment instruments
> Use/interpretation of assessment results

Thirty-four standards address the assessment tasks listed above. A copy of these standards may be obtained from Dr. Jane Swanson, AAC Standards, Department of Psychology, Southern Illinois University, Carbondale, IL 62901. At the time of this writing, the standards are $1.00 each for fewer than 20 copies.

Confidentiality in Student Records and Testing

An important issue for elementary school counselors to keep in mind is their responsibilities regarding student records and student tests and their interpretation. "Test data, along with other records of the counseling relationship, must be considered professional information and must not be revealed to others without the expressed consent of the client" (Hood & Johnson, 1991, p. 230). In the case of an elementary-age child, the parent must give consent for the test results to be released to an outside source. The American School Counselor Association's Ethical Standards for School Counselors contain a section related to the responsibilities of test users (see Appendix B for the complete statement). The elementary school counselor should become familiar with all these standards, and the following three standards in particular: Standard A.8, Responsibilities to Students: "Protects the confidentiality of students' records and releases personal data only according to prescribed laws and school policies. Student information maintained through electronic data storage methods is treated with the same care as traditional student records"; and A.12: "Adheres to relevant standards regarding selection, administration, and interpretation of assessment techniques. The counselor recognizes that computer-based testing programs require specific training in administration, scoring and interpretation which may differ from that required in more traditional assessments." In addition to the responsibilities to students, the counselor should be aware of Standard B.3, Responsibilities to Parents: "Provides parents with accurate, comprehensive and relevant information in an objective and caring manner, is appropriate and consistent with ethical responsibilities to the counselee" (American School Counselors Association, 1992, pp. 13–14). The confidentiality of student records and test results will be assured if the elementary counselor keeps these standards in mind in any discussions of the students in his or school, including the students' test results, with principals, teachers, parents, and students.

Summary

Elementary school counselors are not directly involved in record-keeping activities; however, they do need to be aware of the information that is usually kept and maintained in the child's cumulative record file. These files contain helpful information about the child's background, who the child is living with, whether or not he or she has any siblings, if there has been a grade retention, possible health concerns, and any referrals for educational or psychological evaluation.

The task of reporting test results to parents and teachers is an area of involvement for many elementary school counselors. Elementary school testing programs utilize a variety of standardized achievement tests, aptitude tests, intelligence tests, and personality measures. The elementary counselor should be able to report and interpret test results to principals, teachers, and parents, as well as to the students, when appropriate. Nonstandardized assessment utilizes behavioral observations and rating scales to provide additional input for a child experiencing problems. All counselors should obtain the following documents in order to be fully apprised of standards and issues in testing: *The Code of Fair Testing Practices in Education, Responsibility of Users of Standardized Tests (RUST Statement Revised),* and *Multicultural Assessment Standards: A Compilation for Counselors.*

The elementary school counselor should become familiar with all of the standards contained in the American School Counselor Association's Ethical Standards for School Counselors in order to insure that confidentiality in the student's records and testing is maintained. Most counselors keep confidential files concerning their sessions with individual children in order to keep track of their meetings, including confidential information that should not be kept in the child's cumulative record; these should be kept in a locked file in the counselor's office.

Chapter *9*

Structured Counseling and Guidance Activities

The elementary school counselor's role is often dictated by the principal in the counselor's school based on his or her perception of elementary school counseling. An elementary school principal related the following to the author in an evaluation of elementary school counseling in her school:

> *On a daily basis you are directly interacting with children, parents, teachers, administrators, specialized support services, and community agencies. In the elementary school setting a counselor participates more actively in true counseling experiences, as administrative responsibilities are not emphasized as is often the case in the secondary schools. A counselor has the freedom to set up a program which meets the needs of the school population and does not have to spend time scheduling classes, dealing with discipline, and serving as a quasi-administrator. . . . I feel you get more "bang for your buck" with classroom guidance activities where you affect 30 children and a teacher as opposed to one-on-one or even small group. An ideal program would have a balance of both classroom guidance and groups, with one-on-one for very special cases. . . . Overall an ideal elementary program should offer a happy balance of classroom guidance, small group counseling, staff in-service, and parent education. Individual support should be available but should not interrupt the ongoing established program as it could possibly fragment a counselor's time to the point at which one would be reactive as opposed to proactive. (M. Boulanger, personal communication, May 1992)*

The comments from this highly respected principal, with a wealth of experience, fits well with the author's emphasis in this text for elementary school counselors: to work primarily with students in classroom activities and small groups, with teachers and other school staff, and with parents, recognizing that it is also necessary to spend some time on individual counseling. The focus in this chapter will be on structured counseling and guidance activities conducted with individual students, with small groups, and in classrooms. Career guidance, carried out in the classroom setting, will also be addressed as a structured activity.

Counseling with Individual Students

Using Play Materials

An elementary-age child, particularly in the primary grades, is often uncomfortable in an individual counseling relationship without some kind of hands-on activity. Puppets, drawing materials, some type of clay, small toy people, and simple games can all be appropriate materials to help engage a young child in the counseling process. This is not to be confused with play therapy, which requires specific training under supervision and is very time intensive, a luxury not available to most elementary school counselors with large caseloads, often in more than one school. Play therapy in a clinical setting has proven very successful, particularly since Virginia Axline's work with children became so well known (Axline, 1947). Play therapy as an intervention with children was used prior to Axline, but her emphasis on nondirective play, plus her stirring book, *Dibbs: In Search of Self,* did much to bring attention to the use of play therapy in clinics and schools (Axline, 1964). Although play therapy is a successful intervention with young children, it will not be stressed in this text because of the reality of an elementary school counselor's counseling load. It is virtually impossible to devote the required time to the use of play therapy with individual children given the tremendous number of diverse demands on an elementary counselor's time, as indicated throughout this text.

Puppets are a familiar sight to elementary school children when their counselor makes use of material such as Dinkmeyer's *Developing Understanding of Self and Others I* (DUSO I), grades K–2, and *Developing Understanding of Self and Others II* (DUSO II), grades 3–4; and Anderson's *Bright Beginnings,* grades K–1, and *Pumsy in Pursuit of Excellence,* grades 1–4, in their classroom guidance activities. Having these puppets available in the counseling office will often bring a smile of recognition to the face of a child who feels hesitant being there. A turtle puppet in the hands of a counselor, who gradually peeks the turtle's head out from under the shell and says to the turtle, "It's OK to come out, Tommy Turtle, it's just Eric and me here," can also do much to draw a child out, particularly when the puppet is then handed to the child. One of the author's counseling interns bought a large dog puppet to use in her elementary internship site; she was bilingual and was hoping to get the children actively involved in some friendship skills in a Spanish immersion kindergarten class, so she asked the children to help her name the puppet. The children did, naming the puppet "Tigre," which gave them a sense of ownership. After that, every time she went into their classroom they immediately asked, "Maria, where's Tigre?" She found this to be an excellent way to reach these children, as the focus was on the puppet as an extension of her, and it helped them to talk more readily. When any of these children came in to see her individually, they would reach out for Tigre, establishing a more comfortable counseling relationship.

Having large sheets of inexpensive blank paper and a box of color crayons available on a small table in the counseling office will often put a child at ease, particularly if the counselor uses the same medium and starts to draw and talk at the same time. The child can be asked to draw his or her family, to draw a picture of a pet, or to draw a picture of what he or she likes to do the most, or the child can just be left to do whatever he or she wishes. The counselor should never ask, "What is that?" as this says it is not obvious to the counselor; instead, say, "Tell me about your picture, Kacie," and allow the child to talk about it no matter how hesitant he or she may sound. It sometimes takes a tremendous amount of patience on the part of a counselor to wait for a child's response.

The use of play material in an elementary school counseling session is accepting the child's expression of what he or she is feeling at the time. As was mentioned in the developmental age profiles discussed in Chapter 2, five-year-olds particularly like play and art; six-year-olds sometimes use fantasy to achieve what real life hasn't provided; and the child who is developmentally seven is more in touch with feelings and is better able to express affect. These primary-age children may relate to the counseling experience more readily by using one of the activities previously discussed. The emotional and social development age of the children at the elementary school level and their inability to express themselves verbally causes many counselors to use some sort of play material in order to communicate effectively with children who are difficult to reach. For elementary school counselors who are interested in the use of play in their counseling program and have the time and space to carry out these activities, there is the entire October 1993 *Elementary School Guidance and Counseling* journal, which is a special issue on counseling and children's play (American Counseling Association, 1993). The various articles describing the use of play in a school setting, including four theoretical orientations and their techniques used in play therapy, indicate the increasing interest in the use of this media.

Bibliocounseling

Bibliocounseling, often referred to as bibliotherapy, is frequently used by counselors in the elementary school setting. It involves the use of books on various topics designed to help a child learn about others experiencing similar problems or concerns, which then provides a basis for discussion with the child. Most children think that they are alone in their problems or concerns and are surprised to learn that others have gone through the same kind of situation or have had the same questions. When a counselor uses bibliocounseling, it is important to discuss the book that the child is reading, or has read, with the child. Discussing all aspects of the book, not just the content of the story, will help the child relate his or her feelings. Books used for bibliocounseling can be kept in the counselor's office, the teacher's classroom, the school library, or even the principal's office. The principal quoted at the beginning of this chapter also included a statement about this in her comments; she keeps a shelf of books in her office just for this purpose, handing them out to children she has identified as having a need or concern that can be resolved through this method: "Bibliocounseling has been most successful and of course serves a dual purpose, as reading is probably the most important academic focus in an elementary school. The teachers have picked up on the modeling and are using books as vehicles for the children to explore and express feelings and work out daily life problems. I have children coming in constantly wanting more 'sad' books, as they tell me it helps to read or hear about others who feel the same way that they do" (M. Boulanger, personal communication, May 1992).

To implement bibliocounseling in a school, an in-service program given by the elementary counselor describing the purpose of the reading, the kinds of books to be used, and the goals of the school in initiating this kind of program should insure a successful start. Teachers have a chance to ask questions, express their concerns, and share any previous experiences they might have had with bibliocounseling. Bibliocounseling can be carried out on an individual basis, in small groups, and in the classroom setting, with the counselor reading the book to the children in the younger grades, discussing their reactions as a class. This also becomes an introduction to the children as to what the purpose is behind the reading—helping them understand some of their concerns and the concerns expressed by others, and some of the family issues, such as divorce, moving, a death in the family, or the loss of a pet, described in the story.

An excellent source of inexpensive books to use in bibliocounseling is "Bibliotherapy for Children and Teens," a 65-page catalog listing paperback books in 59 different categories, including Abuse and Neglect, Adoption, Anger, Values, Weight Problems, and Wellness ("Bibliotherapy," 1994). The appropriate grade level and a brief description are listed for each book. For an elementary school counselor desiring to start a collection of appropriate books to use in bibliocounseling, the elementary school's Parent-Teacher Association is usually a good source of start-up monies for this valuable resource for the children in the school.

Brief Strategic Interventions with Individual Children

Some types of behavior cannot be addressed in small groups or in the classroom and, from the counselor's perspective, are not severe enough for outside referral; at the same time, children exhibiting these behaviors have their teachers, parents, and principals literally at the "end of their rope," wanting the counselor to "fix" the child. Children that exhibit problem behaviors in the classroom and in the school need help, and their teachers, principals, and parents are looking for answers. The elementary school counselor may wonder how to work effectively with these children when there are so many demands on his or her time. A constructive way to address these problems is by using the principles and techniques of solution-focused brief therapy (de Shazer, 1982, 1985, 1988), and brief strategic intervention (Amatea, 1989). These approaches are based on the model developed in the 1970s by Watzlawick, Weakland, and Fisch at the Mental Research Institute, usually referred to as MRI, in Palo Alto, California. Their book, *Change: Principles of Problem Formation and Problem Resolution* (1974), did much to further the idea of brief therapy as a quick and effective means to resolve the presenting problem. Amatea expanded the brief strategic approach to the school setting, "achieving remarkably successful results in the schools with students whose problems had not responded to simpler interventions" (Amatea, 1989, p. xii). The Brief Family Therapy Center was established by de Shazer in 1978 in Milwaukee as a research and training center where his own model of brief therapy began to evolve. In the mid-1980s, de Shazer and his associates became interested in "solutions" and how they work rather than the techniques of brief therapy (de Shazer et al., 1986).

The author has used the solution-focused brief therapy approach in teaching and training counseling interns and students in a graduate family counseling and parent education class. Two books and a manual that have proved very useful at the elementary school level are (1) *Brief Strategic Intervention for School Behavior Problems* (Amatea, 1989), (2) *Changing Problem Behavior in Schools* (Molnar & Lindquist, 1989), and (3) a manual that can be used as a primer to learn the basics: *Strategies That Work: Techniques for Solutions in the Schools* (Kral, 1988). Another book that does an excellent job of describing successful interventions with a solution-oriented approach, although it is geared to working with adolescents, is *Pathways to Change* (Selekman, 1993). These books are full of illustrations of this highly successful approach to working with individual students in a school setting within a reasonable time frame of up to five sessions of 30 minutes or less. There are many instances within a school setting where this model can be successfully applied. According to Kral (1992), "it can be viewed as a 'metamodel' that organizes the change agent's ideas about what needs to be done and then presents techniques or processes taken from other ways of intervening such as neuropsychology, cognitive behavior modification, learning styles research, Adlerian counseling, reality therapy, family systems therapy, and the like" (p. 338). An examination of the basics of solution-focused brief therapy will explain how the interventions can be used in an elementary school counseling program. Of particular importance when viewing this approach to counseling is the lack of emphasis on insight; the child does not need to understand the *why* of his or her behavior; elementary-age children are so often at a loss to explain why they have or haven't been doing something. Children rarely possess insight at this age. Chapter 10 will look at the use of solution-focused brief therapy with families of elementary school children; the focus in this chapter is on its use with individuals to resolve school-related behavior problems.

Techniques of Solution-Focused Brief Therapy

Client Roles.   The "client" may be the child, the teacher, or the parent; usually the child is not the one most concerned with the problem, although he or she is referred as needing help. Persons involved in this situation are classified in one of three categories: the visitor, the complainant, and the customer. The "visitor" is the one who has to be there, usually the child; the "complainant" will admit that there is a problem but isn't willing to take any action; and the "customer" is the real client, who comes in with a problem and wants a solution (de Shazer, 1988). Each person involved in the referral problem should be asked, "How is this a problem to you?" in order to find who is the real client. It isn't very productive to work with a child individually who doesn't see that a problem exists, or is not willing to do anything about it. The parents may be willing to admit that there is a problem but feel that it is the school's problem, particularly if they aren't having problems with the child at home because of indifference or more lax rules. The teacher may be the one most open to resolving the problem and may be willing to try something for a week or two; we now have our customer identified.

Reframing.   Reframing is a counseling technique that is easily used in a school setting. In reframing, the perceptions of the persons involved about another person or situation are addressed in a different way, or reframed. Kral (1992) cites an excellent example of a simple use of reframing: a sixth-grade boy, Marvin, was presented at a child study team because of increasing negative behaviors in the class that he was placed in for special education. He spent 57 percent of his day in a program for emotionally disturbed students and

the remainder of the school day in a regular sixth-grade class. In his special class he continually challenged the teacher, was negative toward other students, and disobeyed classroom rules; in his mainstream class, his level of behavior was tolerable. During the child study team meeting, the principal asked the staff, "If you were treated as a 'crazy kid,' wouldn't you act weird, too?" This comment changed the perceptions of the staff, who were considering placing Marvin in an alternative setting for emotionally disturbed children. As a result of this meeting, he was placed solely in a regular classroom. Although he continued to exhibit some negative behaviors, these were reduced enough to enable Marvin to pass sixth grade. The principal reframed Marvin's behavior as being expected and appropriate for the special education program where he was placed.

Reframing something negative as something that is positive often results in meaningful changes for the child and for the teacher or parent. Kral (1988) lists some common behavioral descriptors with their reframed phrases to show some of the possibilities: *Hyperactive* can be reframed to become *energetic, action-oriented; talkative* reframed to become *expressive, open to share; aggressive* reframed to become *unaware of his own strength; distractible* reframed to become *very alert, sensitive to surroundings* (p. 17). This helps a teacher or parent see the child in a different way. Reframing is one of the basic techniques used in solution-focused brief therapy.

"Do Something Different."   When a child, teacher, or parent seeks a counselor's help in resolving a problem, the counselor will typically ask what interventions have been tried. Often those seeking help will continue to use the same behaviors even though the behaviors aren't working for them. An appropriate task to assign could be the following: "Between now and the next time we get together I want you to observe and make note of what goes on (in your life, with this student, with your teacher, at home, in school, etc.) that you want to have continue to happen" (de Shazer, cited in Kral, 1988). This assignment causes the client seeking help to focus on the positive, things they want to have happen. This has been used effectively with children as young as second and third grade, as well as with teachers and parents (Kral, 1988).

Sometimes a simple intervention with the child, such as suggesting that if it isn't working to try something different, is all it takes to bring about a change. The following summarized case study, involving a fifth-grade girl, Betty, illustrates this strategy:

> *Betty was referred because she failed to complete her homework. Even though she got into trouble with her parents and teacher for not doing her homework, she couldn't get herself to finish it every night. She would always start her homework the same way: in the order the subjects came during the day with math first, reading next, etc. She also always started with the first problem in each assignment and went in order. If she didn't like what she was working on, she would quit and do something else. The counselor told her to assign a number to each subject in the order it came in during the day and then to toss a die every evening and do her homework in this random order. She was also to re-throw the die for each assignment to see what problem to start with, doing the rest of the problems in any order she wished. This intervention, as simple as it seemed, coupled with two more sessions with the counselor for encouragement and support, turned around a two-year pattern of homework not completed. (Kral, 1988, p. 27)*

"Miracle Questions."   To help define or set the goal for counseling or therapy, de Shazer developed his popular "miracle question." The client is asked: "Suppose you were to go home tonight, and while you were asleep, a miracle happened and this problem was solved. How will you know the miracle happened? What will be different?" (de Shazer, 1988, p. 5). Depending upon the response, follow-up questions can be asked to further elicit responses, which in turn can become the solutions. The child can be asked if there are any times when any pieces of this miracle happen, and, if so, what is different about those times, and so on. As a part of this, asking the child how he or she will know the problem is really solved helps the counselor and child know what needs to be done next. The questions used in counseling all focus on what will be happening, not what has already happened since: "An emphasis on why or in the past tends to focus the client on what is NOT working rather than directing him/her toward the positive—what is already working or what is realistically possible" (Kral, 1988, p. 9).

Exception-Finding Questions.   Nothing occurs all of the time even though children, teachers, and parents are prone to say *always* when describing a situation. While discussing a child's problem with her teacher, the counselor could ask a question: "Are there times when Karly Jo does pay attention in school?" Looking for exceptions to the situation usually surprises the client, since they think of these problems as always occurring: "Joey always teases me," or "I don't ever do it right." Finding out when the exceptions occur leads to one of the goals of intervention—increasing the occurrence of what is already happening that is working. One of the rules of solution-focused brief therapy is this: If it works, do more of it; if it doesn't work, don't do it again, do something else.

Using Solution-Focused Brief Therapy in an Elementary School

Not all problems that are referred to the elementary school counselor lend themselves to this approach. This kind of intervention should be used only when other simple, straightforward approaches have not worked or an outside referral does not seem appropriate (Amatea & Sherrard, 1991). The counselor must assess whether or not one of the three following conditions exists to decide if this approach is appropriate:

> *First, is the student in such emotional turmoil (e.g., as the result of a recent divorce) that he or she can neither hear nor act upon direct requests for changed behavior? If this is the case, counseling interventions that restore a sense of control, stability, and nurturance are more appropriate than brief strategic interventions. Second, is the student's life so characterized by chronic stressors (e.g., parental alcoholism) that it is impossible for him or her to act in a predictable way? If this is the case, long-term or family counseling may be more appropriate than brief strategic intervention. Third, are actual deficits in the student's learning abilities (e.g., dyslexia) causing educational underachievement or emotional difficulties? After ruling out these possibilities, brief strategic intervention could be considered. (Amatea & Sherrard, 1991, p. 342)*

The advantage of solution-focused/brief strategic interventions in the school setting is the possibility of quick problem resolution, which fits in well with the limited time an elementary school counselor can spend with individual children. Gerler (1992), in recommending various school counseling interventions, posed some questions that address the effectiveness of individual counseling: "How effective, for example, is a 15-minute counseling session, once per week, with a second grader who is a behavior problem in the classroom? Might the child be better served if the counselor met a few times with the child's teacher and parents and provided helpful suggestions for modifying the troublesome behavior?" (Gerler, 1992, p. 500). This fits in well with the solution-focused brief therapy model.

Another advantage is that it is not a complicated form of counseling intervention; the elementary school counselor should try some of the techniques discussed in this chapter and see what seems to work and what is initially comfortable. The books and manual discussed earlier in this section give an excellent overview of solution-focused brief therapy, with the techniques clearly spelled out and well illustrated. Kral (1992) views solution-focused brief therapy as uniquely suited to the school setting because it is not dependent upon the home for changing problematic behavior. The author particularly likes how Molnar and de Shazer (1987) view the solution focus approach: "It defines therapy as a process during which the therapist and the client *construct* something (a solution) rather than *fix* something (a dysfunction)" (p. 357). This should fit in well with an elementary counseling philosophy: to help children and the significant adults in their lives—teachers, administrators, and parents—find solutions for their problems and concerns, giving them the skills to generalize these solutions to other areas of their lives, not just "fixing" current behavior problems that are sure to recur.

Counseling with Small Groups

Group counseling in an elementary school is most helpful in situations dealing with problems such as social skills, making friends, anger control, drugs and alcohol use, and divorce. It is an important part of an overall elementary counseling program because some children are reluctant to open up in a classroom setting and may be in need of specific interventions. In a small group setting, children are able to learn from each other and learn to help one another. For an elementary counselor desiring to start groups in his or her school, group counseling may need to be "sold" to the school staff, starting with the principal, because it can be disruptive having several children leave the classroom at a time. If the school has an advisory council (discussed more fully in Chapter 11), then the way has been paved for small group counseling through the school's needs assessment process (Chapter 11). An advisory council that has teachers, parents, and students as its membership is an invaluable asset for the counselor in establishing appropriate goals for an elementary school's counseling program.

There are two kinds of groups that function well in an elementary school setting:

1. Counseling groups: groups that target specific needs; examples include divorce groups, anger management groups, friendship groups, alcohol and drug groups, and study skills groups.
2. Guidance groups: groups to help children gain insight into themselves and their peers, working on issues such as decision making, problem solving, self-concept, and enhancing social skills.

Organizing Small Groups

Some groups, such as anger management, study skills, or friendship groups, are formed through teacher referrals of individual children. When several children exhibiting the same kinds of problem behavior, or children identified as "loners," without any friends, are referred by teachers or the principal, for example, these children can be placed together into counseling groups. If the counselor has not conducted groups in his or her elementary school, it is extremely important to obtain the support of the teachers prior to putting groups into place; in addition, parental permission should be obtained for the children to become members of a group. The best way to gain teacher support is to ask to be on the agenda for the next teachers' meeting or in-service in order to share with the teachers the intent and specific purpose of the group. In response to possible objections from some teachers about the time out of class, it is important to stress the function of the group and the value of peer interaction as well as the efficacy of putting students together in compatible groups to enable the counselor to work with more children. Groups should be set up with a specific timetable, such as six weeks, with an evaluation at the end of that time to see whether the goals have been accomplished and whether the group should be reconvened at a later period of time. The length of time of each group may vary, but 20 to 30 minutes is about as long as elementary-age children can work productively in a group setting. The size of the group should be limited to six to eight children; more than this limits the amount of involvement for each child. Some groups meet weekly; others meet two times each week, depending on space, counselor availability, teacher willingness to let the children leave their class, and so on. Because most teachers follow a particular order of teaching, it is usually best to stagger the times the children leave a particular classroom so that they will not always miss the same activity in their classroom.

The availability of space does much to determine what the group meeting place will be like. The ideal spot is a corner of the counseling office around a small table or in a circle of chairs; some counselors use beanbags or floor pillows, with the children sitting in a circle on the floor. Whatever the surroundings or location, it is imperative that the privacy of the group is assured, with no interruptions allowed.

How does the group end? What is the termination process? These are questions that most beginning counselors ask. If the group was initially set up around a specific purpose, with specific goals in mind, then the issue has been decided. Teachers will expect the counselor to adhere to the schedule set up ahead of time; any variations of this schedule requires that the counselor discuss this with the teachers involved, outlining what is yet to be accomplished in the group and obtaining their permission. Most teachers are willing to go along with this kind of request if they have seen the positive results in children involved in a group. Requesting an extension for the group should be a fairly rare request so that the teachers and students accept small group counseling as a viable part of the elementary school counseling program.

Years ago Stanford (1980) wrote a monograph on "Improving Group Interaction with Skill-Building Activities" that the author has found invaluable for conducting all types of groups at all grade levels. Stanford does an excellent job of differentiating between effective and ineffective groups, pinpointing lack of skill development in the immature groups where the persons involved are not comfortable with each other and contribute very little, if at all. He identified the stages a group will most likely progress through if the leader helps the students master the skills needed to make the group effective and achieve maximum development. These stages lend themselves well to an elementary counseling program in which the counselor desires to lead groups and has not had much experience in organizing and leading groups. The various stages involved and the objectives of group development at each stage are as follows:

STAGE 1: ORIENTATION

Members need to:

1. learn what is going to happen in the group.
2. learn each other's names.
3. learn enough about other members to feel comfortable working with them.

STAGE 2: SKILL-BUILDING

Members need to:

4. learn to organize themselves without direct leader supervision.
5. learn to contribute when appropriate.
6. learn to encourage other members to contribute.
7. learn to listen to others.
8. learn to respond to others' contributions.
9. learn to cooperate rather than compete.
10. learn to make decisions through consensus.
11. learn to confront problems in group process.

STAGE 3: COPING WITH CONFLICT

Members need to:

12. learn to understand another person's point of view on an issue.
13. learn to communicate their own views or needs precisely.
14. learn to negotiate mutually satisfactory solutions to conflicts.

STAGE 4: PRODUCTIVITY

Members need to:

15. maintain skills developed previously.

STAGE 5: TERMINATION

Members need to:

16. learn to identify and express their feelings about the group's ending.
17. review the experience and tie up any loose ends. (Stanford, 1980, p. 6)

One of the keys stages in a group's development is the skill-building stage; it is the counselor's responsibility to spend the time necessary to train the members in the skills needed for group participation. This is not an easy task because children are used to the teacher being in charge of the classroom, directing their activities. If the counselor also directs all the activities of the group, the children will not develop the skills necessary to become productive group members. As in any group with a leader, the children will tend to direct the questions or comments to the counselor. A good way to handle this is to redirect the questions, asking, "Who would like to answer Jackie's question?" As the group starts to function, particularly the intermediate-age groups, the counselor should allow different students to assume leadership in the group discussions; this encourages participation from all of the children involved in the group.

Beginning group leaders tend to become discouraged when conflicts in the group arise. It is natural for conflicts to surface in small groups just as they do in the classroom, on the playground, and anywhere else children are involved with each other for a period of time. A group is an excellent place for children to learn the skills needed to resolve conflicts; this allows the group to become productive when the members have learned how to accept diverse opinions. Stanford identified seven steps to be used as a basic conflict reduction procedure:

Step 1: Use careful listening to determine how the other person sees the conflict.

Step 2: Describe how you see the conflict.

Step 3: Ask the other person to explain what he/she wants.

Step 4: Tell the other person what you want.

Step 5: Seek a solution.

Step 6: Agree on a solution.

Step 7: Make an agenda. (Stanford, 1980, p. 13)

Topics for Small Group Counseling

Children of Divorce   There have been a number of articles in professional publications discussing group counseling for children of divorce (Sonnenshein-Schneider & Baird, 1980; Tedder, Scherman, & Wantz, 1987; Corey & Corey, 1987; Burke & Van de Streek, 1989; Ciborowski, 1990). The divorce rate in the United States has grown to such proportions that it seems more uncommon today to find intact families with elementary-age children than to find children from divorced families. Even though this has become a common phenomenon, it is still traumatic for children, often resulting in depression, anxiety, anger, insecurity, withdrawal, guilt, loyalty conflicts, and often academic problems, resulting in lower achievement. A highly effective way to work with these children is by including them in a group of similar-age children who are also children of divorce. There are a variety of ways to involve these children in divorce groups; several will be discussed.

Group Play Therapy.   Ciborowski (1990) believes that group play therapy is an effective technique for children of divorce because play is a natural expression for them. It also allows the child to act out some of the feelings they have been harboring that they may have a hard time verbalizing, particularly in the younger grades. These children are also in a position to learn from other children in the group, which helps them to feel less alone in their reactions to their parent's divorce. He described the activities of a group of young elementary schoolchildren in an exercise where they were to use a drawing, some clay, or painting to tell how they felt when their mom and dad argued. After they all described their feelings the counselor brought out three hand puppets to represent the father, mother, and child. The children used the puppets to role-play how they thought the parents and child would act. This activity allowed all the children to express their feelings (Ciborowski, 1990).

Brainstorming in Divorce Groups.   Sonnenshein-Schneider and Baird (1980) noted the success of brainstorming as a counseling technique in an elementary school divorce group. They viewed this technique as a successful way to help children clarify and act on their feelings. Brainstorming is used when a group member expresses a problem or a concern that they need help with in order to resolve. The group brainstorms the possible solutions to the problem until it finds a potential answer to the dilemma. When the group arrives at an answer, it role-plays the response to help the child arrive at an appropriate solution to the problem. Sonnenshein-Schneider and Baird noted that the most difficult part of conducting groups for children of divorce is helping the children to set realistic expectations. They also noted that children will never like the fact of the divorce, although they can be helped to accept or tolerate it; they will usually fantasize about the parents getting back together again even if both have remarried and are happy. They went on to state that "it is important for the counselor to realize that this is not a sign of therapeutic failure, but rather it is the child's need to remember and maintain his roots—roots that serve to validate his or her very beginning" (Sonnenshein-Schneider & Baird, 1980, p. 91).

Banana Splits Groups.   Probably the most intriguing name for a group of children that meet together on a regular basis to share their pain and unhappiness is the group referred to as Banana Splits. Banana Splits is the name given to the children of divorce group by its founder, Liz McGonagle. In 1981 McGonagle started the program by counseling two girls in her elementary school in New York whose parents had been divorced. The groups are put together by age and grade, with the children entering the group on their own initiative and with parent permission. The Splits meet every two to three weeks to talk about the frustrations and worries in their changed family lives. One child's statement about the group confirmed the significance of a group like this: "'I didn't talk about the divorce to anybody,' said Mike, 'because I thought I was the only one it happened to . . . until I got with Splits. Now it seems like half the world is getting divorced'" (Hirshey, 1988, p. 85). McGonagle estimated that each child in the Splits groups received a total of eight to ten hours of group guidance each school year, and although she felt it was not enough, she saw tremendous changes in the children.

In the article by Hirshey, "What Children Wish Their Parents Knew," some immediate and long-term effects of divorce by age group are listed. For elementary schoolers (ages five to twelve), the effects are as follows:

Children 5 to 8 are the most open in showing their grief. They express fear of abandonment, feelings of rejection and a preoccupation with trying to get their parents back together. Children 9 to 12 are more apt to express intense anger at both parents. Health problems appear—frequent headaches and stomach aches. There is often a decline in school performance and in socializing with friends. (Hirshey, 1988, p. 86)

Information about the Banana Splits program can be obtained by sending a self-addressed, stamped, business-size envelope to Ballston Spa School System, Woods Road School, Ballston Spa, NY 12020.

Anger Management Groups   Students are often referred to the elementary school counselor because of their frequent outbursts of anger and/or explosive tempers. A very successful group for elementary school children was developed by Regina Peck, elementary school counselor in the San Diego school district. She conducts counseling groups with these children in six sessions covering the following areas:

I. Getting Acquainted—Building Trust
The children introduce themselves, learn the ground rules, work on relaxation

II. Feelings
The importance of feelings and what to do about them

III. Feelings
Discuss ways we mask/defend against uncomfortable feelings, acknowledge feelings

IV. Anger Awareness
Purpose of anger, identifying anger-provoking situations, identify anger in others

V. Anger Management
Coping strategies, role playing

VI. Anger Management
Relaxation, review of week, role-playing (Peck, 1992)

Peck's goal is to help children in the groups realize that anger is understood only in the context of where the anger occurred; when this context is identified, the children can be helped to react appropriately.

Friendship Groups   Students that appear very shy, appearing not to have any friends, and children new to the school are ideal candidates for a friendship group. Putting four to six of these children together in a small group activity, such as "Breaking Out," will help get the group started. In this activity the children and counselor form a tight circle, with one child left outside the circle, trying to get in. The group then discusses how it felt to be excluded from the group. The discussion can then be expanded to how it feels to be a loner or an outsider in a new situation. Teachers can easily spot these children and are strong supporters of these groups, readily referring children in need of friends to the counselor. The children often form lasting friendships with each other during the six to eight weeks the group meets.

Lunch Bunch   This is a group informally started by the counselor for children wanting to spend some time with the counselor but not having any particular concerns or problems. Forming a Lunch Bunch simply puts together a group that eats together with the elementary school counselor, bringing bag lunches and having informal discussions. These typically have a changing membership, depending upon arrangements made ahead of time with the counselor. Sometimes a need is identified in one of the groups, causing them to formalize the group around a particular topic.

Topics for Small Group Guidance

Guidance groups are formed for a different reason than counseling groups. Guidance groups are more "teaching" oriented and are intended to help children gain insight into themselves and their peers while they work on issues that have been identified by their teachers or parents. Some of the topics that are appropriate for guidance groups are as follows:

Decision making

Problem solving

Peer relationships

Self-concept

Communication skills

Social Skills

When a child is involved in a peer group with similar concerns or problems, he or she tends to feel less "singled out" and is often more willing to work through difficulties.

Talking Turns   An example of the type of group that could be formed along one of these topic lines is called Talking Turns, a group designed to give individuals an opportunity to discuss interpersonal peer conflicts and other school-related problems. The elementary school counselor requested ten minutes in each fourth-, fifth-, and sixth-grade classroom to explain the Talking Turns group. This group required self-referral, and the students were made aware that only school problems would be discussed, not personal problems. The counselor-referral slip listed the student's name, room, date, and the problem to be solved. It also listed what he or she has already done to try to solve the problem and why this didn't work. The problem was read by the counselor to the group without identifying who submitted the problem. Everyone in the group can offer suggestions for solution of the problem (Greenberg, 1992).

Group Guidance for Latchkey Children   Another instructional-type group was developed by Bundy and Boser to address the needs of children left alone for extended periods of time. The goal of these groups was to provide the skills to enable children to cope more effectively while in their self-care situation. The program, Being in Charge, consisted of six 45-minute sessions designed to help the children gain more control of their lives (this is summarized in Chapter 6). Each session was structured to contain four phases: (1) warmup—to set the frame of reference for the session; (2) review of homework—encourages children to talk to their parents about the sessions; (3) presentation of the skill—children role-play, brainstorm, and discuss activity; and (4) assignment of homework—children take home presented material to discuss with their parents (Bundy & Boser, 1987). Because so many children are left home alone for extended periods of time, programs like Being in Charge are increasingly vital to the welfare and needs of elementary school children.

Guidelines for Conducting Groups

There are several considerations the elementary school counselor should take into account when working with children in groups in his or her school. A major one is obtaining parental permission prior to starting the group. Many states require parental notification and permission for children to be involved in any type of individual or small group counseling, particularly children under the age of 12; the counselor should be well versed in the laws of the state regarding children. Even if this is not a legal requirement in the counselor's state, there is a certain degree of protection that will be assured if the parents have granted permission. The parents need to be aware of the purpose of the group and the counselor's expectations for the group; knowing this, few parents would object to their child being in a group, particularly if the counselor has sent a letter to all parents in the school outlining the counseling program, describing the kinds of activities that will be carried out in the classroom and small groups during the year, and inviting them to call if they have any questions or concerns.

Parent-Permission forms should state simply and concisely what the small group counseling sessions will consist of, how often they will meet, how long the sessions will last, and the support of the teachers allowing the children to leave their class for these groups. Either the counselor or the school principal should send these parent-permission forms to the parents. If the counselor sends the forms to the parent, it is a good idea to have a sentence or two from the principal stating his or her support; this can often get a hesitant parent to agree to their child's inclusion in a group.

It is also a good idea to present the counseling program at a school board meeting so that the board members know and understand exactly what will be happening. The author recalls a recent incident when an elementary counselor was hired for the first time in a two-elementary-school district. At one of the first school board meetings of the new school year, the counselor was asked about the counseling program. As she told them about the various activities carried out in classroom guidance and in small groups, she said how the children were taught to give "I" messages. A board member asked, "What's an 'I' message?" The counselor immediately replied, "I get nervous when I'm asked to speak to groups like this." The board members all enjoyed the response and proceeded to ask many more questions, resulting in their knowing much more about their new program, enabling them to respond to other parents or members of the community when asked about the counseling program.

Small group counseling is the most effective way of reaching a large number of students who have similar problems that are not resolvable in a classroom guidance situation. Most elementary school counselors are overburdened; some become overwhelmed when they attempt to provide guidance and counseling services for 500 to 1,000 children, depending on the number of schools assigned to them. Trying to work with individual children with a large caseload puts the counselor in a crisis-only situation. At the same time, some problems or concerns require more personal attention than classroom guidance allows; group counseling provides this opportunity for small groups of children. It is extremely important to the success of these groups to enlist the help and cooperation of the teachers in the counselor's school. If the elementary counselor has spent a considerable amount of time building a working partnership with teachers through consultation, offering to do classroom observations to help with acting-out children, spent time on the playground during recess and lunch, provided in-service topics of help and interest to teachers, actively attended Parent-Teacher Association (PTA) meetings, and established an advisory council, the teachers will not only understand the counseling program but will value it highly. Most teachers are aware of the children that need extra help and will be willing to allow the children to leave their classrooms for group counseling if they know the purpose of the group, exactly how long they will meet each time, and when the group will be terminated. Feedback provided to the teachers after the group has terminated helps insure the teacher's cooperation.

The American School Counselor Association (ASCA) has a position paper on the school counselor and group counseling (see Appendix K for the complete statement). The rationale for group counseling is clearly defined as an efficient and effective way to work with larger numbers of students. The parameters of the counselor's role is also identified as a way of using developmental guidance activities in an productive way. The position paper states that "it is an integral part of a comprehensive guidance and counseling program and should be included and supported by every educational institution."

Classroom Guidance

Importance of Classroom Guidance

Classroom guidance activities enable an elementary school counselor to reach virtually every student in the school where the counselor is located. Far more children have need of counseling services than are ever referred; the quiet child who is not bothering anyone, keeps to him or herself, and does not get into fights with other children may be far more in need of counseling services than the acting-out child who gets everyone's attention. When an elementary counselor goes into a classroom on a regular basis, conducting sessions on interpersonal skills, problem solving, decision making, self-esteem, and other topics appropriate to the particular classroom or age level, the child who is in need of help may learn to recognize that the counselor is someone he or she could to talk to. In addition, the teachers learn to see the children in their classrooms from a different perspective than they do in a teaching situation, which usually involves the enforcement of discipline.

Gerler posed some thought-provoking questions regarding the effectiveness of classroom guidance when an elementary counselor does classroom guidance with all students but goes to each classroom once a month or less, maybe spending only six sessions in a classroom in any year (Gerler, 1992). He suggested offering classroom guidance activities once each week for six to ten weeks in certain classrooms, in collaboration with the classroom teachers, who could continue the activities when the counselor is not there. It is an ideal situation when teachers make this kind of commitment; the problems arise when the teachers begin to have many other demands on their time and see these activities as less important. The author suggests that the elementary counselors reschedule themselves into these classrooms once a month after the initial six weeks of classroom activities have been carried out. This becomes a reinforcement for the teacher and encourages an ongoing working relationship between counselor and teacher. It is an ideal partnership, with the teacher more apt to refer individual children for particular problems that require the counselor's intervention; this may result in involving some children in small group activities, working with others on an individual basis, working with the family, or referral to an outside source for additional help.

Two studies that addressed the positive effects of classroom guidance will be helpful to an elementary school counselor who has a principal or teachers who are resistant to this approach. One of the studies discussed the use of classroom guidance to prevent school dropouts. Most elementary schools are not focused on preventing school dropouts; this is usually considered a secondary school problem. Ruben (1989), concerned with the growing number of school dropouts, identified several studies that tied together self-esteem and other psychological variables, noting that as early as third grade potential dropouts display recognizable characteristics. She believed that there was a great need for the Dade County, Florida, public schools elementary counselors to address this based on a school district study that showed a dropout rate of almost 30 percent of its eighth-grade students prior to graduation. Ruben volunteered her services to work with 37 fifth-grade students at a Miami Beach elementary school with the goal of training elementary school counselors to begin to use classroom guidance activities to address dropout prevention. Of the 37 students she worked with, 80 percent were of Hispanic origin and 19 percent of black origin, the group that had been identified as most likely to drop out of school. The program consisted of 50-minute sessions given twice a week for a five-week period. She used the Success in School program (Gerler & Anderson, 1986), reporting positive results. She recommended that "the program must be seen for what it is—a prevention program—and every effort should be made to encourage counselors to spend more time in the classroom modeling behavior for teachers that boost students' self-esteem" (Ruben, 1989, p. 28).

Another study that showed the effects of classroom guidance on student achievement was done by Lee (1993). Lee conducted an extensive study in the Long Beach Unified School District, California, in six elementary schools, involving 236 fourth-, fifth-, and sixth-grade students representing a variety of cultural, economic, and social environments. Her study was a replication of the Gerler and Anderson (1986) study carried out in North Carolina. The same ten-session classroom guidance unit, Succeeding in School, was used for this study but with a different focus than the Dade County School study. The lessons covered in the ten sessions were as follows:

Lesson   1—Models of Success

Lesson   2—Being Comfortable in School

Lesson   3—Being Responsible in School

Lesson   4—Listening in School

Lesson   5—Asking for Help in School

Lesson   6—Improving in School

Lesson   7—Cooperating with Peers in School

Lesson   8—Cooperation Between Teachers and Students

Lesson   9—The Bright Side of School

Lesson 10—The Bright Side of Me (Lee, 1993, pp. 165–166)

The six counselors involved in the study received three hours of in-service training prior to conducting the classroom guidance activities in the six schools. The results of the study indicated that the counselor-led classroom guidance lessons positively influenced the students' academic achievement in mathematics; in addition, the language and conduct scores and the behavior ratings were more favorable for the treatment group than for the control group.

These two studies were discussed in order to illustrate the many possibilities available to a creative elementary school counselor. Both studies utilized the same classroom guidance program, Success in School, employed in the Gerler and Anderson study in North Carolina in 1986, in order to look at two different aspects of a developmental counseling program: preventing school dropouts and increasing student achievement. The professional counseling journals are filled with many successful classroom guidance interventions that can be readily adapted to a variety of elementary school counseling programs such as one that was originally carried out in North Carolina and then replicated in Florida and California.

Classroom guidance fits in particularly well with the developmental approach to an elementary school counseling program; it involves counselors' working closely with teachers in order to maximize developmental benefits such as self-esteem, personal relationships, school attitudes, and sex-fair choices, all part of the ASCA role statement for elementary school counselors. Myrick (1993), long a proponent of developmental guidance and counseling, noted the high visibility of elementary counselors in the classrooms, playgrounds, and hallways rather than in their offices, reacting to crises. This higher visibility confirms the value of an elementary school guidance and counseling program that reaches all children in the school. A comprehensive assortment of materials are available to the elementary counselor desiring to help children address various age-appropriate developmental issues; these will be addressed and expanded upon in the next section.

Classroom Guidance Materials

One of the earliest structured programs of activities and material available to help elementary-age children understand their emotional and social behavior was Developing an Understanding of Self and Others (DUSO), dating back to 1970; many young adults today recall with fondness "Duso the Dolphin" from their elementary school days. DUSO has since expanded to reach preschool and early-primary-age children, DUSO-1(R), and DUSO-2(R) for third- and fourth-grade children, both available since 1982 (Dinkmeyer & Dinkmeyer, 1982). The two will be discussed separately with suggestions for their use.

DUSO-1(R)   DUSO-1(R) "encourages children to develop positive self-images, to become more aware of the relationship between themselves and other people, and to recognize their own needs and goals" (Dinkmeyer & Dinkmeyer, 1982, p. 7). This approach to learning uses a variety of techniques such as listening, discussion, and dramatic play to enable the children to concentrate on communication, feelings, and problem solving. There are five assumptions implicit in DUSO-1(R):

1. Children's social and emotional needs are related to their academic needs. Therefore the development of understanding of self and others is central to a complete educational process.
2. Learning is fostered by an environment that builds a child's positive self-concept and feelings of acceptance and belonging.

3. Children can learn to talk about their own feelings and the feelings of others.
4. Children can learn by talking with others about feelings, goals, and behavior.
5. Children can learn that feelings, goals, and behavior are dynamically related. (p. 7)

There are three units in DUSO-1(R): (1) developing understanding of self, (2) developing understanding of others, and (3) developing understanding of choices. These three units have a total of 41 goals that address 12 curricular areas. The curricular areas are art, careers, dramatic play, language, math, music, nutrition, physical education, relaxation, science, social studies, and story time. The revised DUSO-1 has a new split-page story book that provides an opportunity for the children to practice decision making: every story in the book has two possible endings. The children choose one ending, and then the alternative ending is presented, followed by a discussion of both endings. This is an excellent way to help young children make choices and learn of their consequences. An added bonus is that a career awareness activity is part of the curriculum activities for each of the 41 goals, helping to connect these activities with work situations.

The materials included in the kit are summarized below:

1. *The teacher's guide.* This includes an introduction, objectives, guidelines for presenting the program in the classroom, and explanations of the activities for each goal.
2. *Story books.* Theme-centered story books are the major part of the program. The stories are ideally set up in a lap easel, enabling the counselor to read the stories aloud or use the pictures if the recorded stories are used.
3. *Recordings.* Four audiocassettes include 36 recorded stories, 10 songs, and a recording for the guided fantasy activities. The song "Hey, Duso" is used to introduce and end the activities. "Aquatron Adventure" has a relaxation exercise for the guided fantasy activities.
4. *Guided fantasy activities.* There are 42 guided fantasy activities.
5. *Dramatic play activities.* There are 42 dramatic play activities with information about the purpose of the activities.
6. *Puppets.* Six puppets are used with the DUSO-1(R) activities. These are Duso the Dolphin, Sophie the Sea Otter, and four people puppets that include two children and two adults.
7. *Group discussion cards.* These list the five rules of group discussion and are usually displayed during the presentation.
8. *Blackline master activity sheets and letters to parents.* There are 48 activity sheets that can be reproduced, and three different letters to parents to be mailed out prior to beginning the three units.
9. *Chart of curriculum-related activities.* The chart illustrates which goals can be integrated into curricular areas. (pp. 21–22)

DUSO-2(R)   DUSO-2(R) "encourages students to develop positive self-images, to become more aware of the relationship between themselves and other people, and to recognize their own needs and goals" (Dinkmeyer & Dinkmeyer, 1982, p. 7). The five assumptions implicit in DUSO-2(R) are identical to those in DUSO-1(R). The activities encourage the children to seek to discover the ways that feelings, intellect, and behavior are interrelated. There are the same three units in DUSO-2(R), with a total of 42 goals addressing 11 curricular areas. These areas are somewhat different from those in DUSO-1(R): art, careers, dramatic play, language, math, music, nutrition, physical education, science, social studies, and independent reading. The materials listed in DUSO-1(R) are essentially the same, with the exception of the puppets; there is only one puppet, Duso the Dolphin, that is introduced in the introductory story and may be used throughout the program.

The rationale behind DUSO-2(R) is based on the significance of children understanding themselves as well as learning about their feelings. Children with positive feelings about themselves will be much more involved in their own learning process than children who have negative feelings about themselves and are poorly motivated. Because the classroom has much to do with how children view themselves, including self-understanding and social awareness activities will do much toward developing the whole child. The leader's manual states the following: "In this revised edition, the authors have indicated more clearly the relationship of the affective and behavior-oriented goals to the cognitive topics, skills, and concepts usually covered in the third and fourth grades" (p. 13).

Directions for Using DUSO-1(R) and DUSO-2(R)   The counselor should thoroughly understand group discussion procedures that accompany the presentation of the stories clearly explained in the leader's guide. The stories are either read to the children or are played on a cassette recorder, and the children are told that they will discuss the story after listening to it. The children usually sit on the floor in a semicircle so they can all see the puppets and the story illustrations. Unless the counselor elects to do otherwise, three levels of questions are used during the discussion: level 1 consists of questions that review the content of the story; level 2 questions focus on the feelings and behavior of the characters in the story; the third level of questions provides ways for the children to relate the message of the story to their own lives and experiences, discussing ways they could handle future situations that are similar.

DUSO-2(R) is intended for third- and fourth-grade children, but a counseling intern recently had an interesting experience with Duso the Dolphin involving older children. The intern was on her way to do a classroom guidance activity in a sixth-grade class and was running behind schedule after conducting a DUSO activity in a third-grade classroom. Not wanting to be late, she did not go back to her office to return Duso the Dolphin. This class of sixth-graders was one the intern had been having some problems with due to a particular group of boys in the class who were displaying a negative attitude toward whatever guidance activity she presented. The boys, with baggy pants slung low on their hips, baseball caps stuck firmly backward on their heads, and cynical know-it-all looks on their faces, were near the door when she walked in. One of the boys, spying Duso the Dolphin, immediately asked, with the first sign of excitement she had ever seen: "Are we going to get to do DUSO today?" Almost too stunned to reply, she asked, "Do you want to?" The immediate chorus of answers from the youngsters in this sixth-grade classroom was a resounding "Yes!" With a great deal of anxiety, she started to talk to them using Duso as her prop. The students for the first time responded to the intern with animation and became totally involved in the discussion; she never had a problem with this class again. Apparently Duso brought back some earlier memories to this group of students that caused them to drop their facade and become kids again.

DUSO activities are designed to be used on a regular basis in order to meet the affective goals in a developmental elementary school counseling program, yet very few elementary school counselors have the time to be able to do this. One way to insure a comprehensive affective education program would be to convince teachers to use these activities in their classrooms through workshops and an in-service training program designed to show teachers how the program builds cooperation, self-esteem, and mutual respect. The leader's guide suggests that the counselor serve a supporting and consultive role for the teachers if they are willing to carry out these activities in their own classrooms.

Another set of materials suitable for use in the elementary school is Bright Beginnings (Anderson, 1990) and Pumsy in Pursuit of Excellence (Anderson, 1987). These will be discussed separately with suggestions for their use.

Bright Beginnings   Anderson (1990) describes this program as "a skill-based program for building self-esteem in elementary school children in grades K–1. The program is based on cognitive restructuring and positive thinking skills" (p. ii). Bright Beginnings uses stories, story discussion, art, creative movement, poetry, puppetry, songs, sharing, and pantomime to present the various activities. Pumsy, a lovable dragon, is the main character in all the stories. Children relate quickly and easily to Pumsy and, as with Duso the Dolphin, usually beg to pet or hold her.

Bright Beginnings contains five related skill units, each subdivided into five sessions, totalling 25 sessions in the entire program. The units address the following concerns:

Unit 1: Pumsy Does Something Hard (feelings of capability)

Unit 2: The Rainbow Stones (knowing we are special)

Unit 3: Pumsy Meets the Sandbox Boss (anger control)

Unit 4: The Three-Legged Rabbit (coping with loss and significant changes)

Unit 5: Pumsy Meets Shadbelly Monster (coping with unfounded fears) (Anderson, 1990, p. 3)

The author recommends presenting three or more sessions per week in order to insure continuity and retention of the concepts. The sessions require 35 minutes or less; a small clock illustrates the amount of time allotted for each activity in order to keep the sessions within the time limits.

Six parent newsletters are included to initially inform parents of the program and to address the goals for each of the five units as they are presented. The Bright Beginnings newsletter is intended to accomplish several purposes:

1. It enhances communication with parents by informing them what their children are doing in the program.
2. It gets parents involved by inviting them (and providing them with specific suggestions) to help at home if they wish.
3. It models language and interactions with children that support parents' efforts to build self-esteem skills at home. (Anderson, 1990, p. 3)

Each of the units has a list of goals and objectives for that unit, indicating how each will be addressed. The individual sessions are complete with what is needed to conduct that session, suggested comments and questions, story time activities, story discussion, and a practice time in which the children pay particular attention to one thing.

Pumsy in Pursuit of Excellence   Pumsy "is a cognitive approach to teaching positive thinking skills and positive self-esteem skills to children at the elementary school age" (Anderson, 1987, p. 1). The concepts of the program and the materials used should be easily handled by second-, third-, and fourth-graders. Some of the basic concepts in Pumsy in Pursuit of Excellence are three distinct parts of her personality: "Sparkler Mind," "Clear Mind," and "Mud Mind." When the dragon called Pumsy is in her Sparkler Mind, it is like sparklers running and playing; when she is in her Clear Mind, she is peaceful and feels good about herself; when she is in her Mud Mind, nothing goes right for Pumsy, she doesn't like herself, and her mind is like a puddle of mud. The activities take Pumsy from an externally based self-esteem, waiting for something good to come along, to an internally based self-esteem where she learns how to feel good about herself all by herself. Pumsy has a partner in all of this, Friend, a boy who has positive-thinking skills and shares them with her; they unconditionally accept each other.

Pumsy contains eight related skill units, with each subdivided into three sessions, totaling 24. These address the difficulties that children may encounter as they work toward building a positive self-concept:

Unit/Chapter 1: Pumsy Decides

Unit/Chapter 2: "If Only Things Were Different . . ."

Unit/Chapter 3: "I Can't Stand It!"

Unit/Chapter 4: "I'm No Good!"

Unit/Chapter 5: "It's Not My Fault!"

Unit/Chapter 6: "Why Didn't It Work?"

Unit/Chapter 7: "But, What If I Say 'No'?"

Unit/Chapter 8: Pumsy Helps a Friend (Anderson, 1987, p. 2)

The sessions require 30 minutes to complete; the time allowances are indicated next to each activity by the use of a little clock.

The Pumsy songs in the Pumsy Songbook are familiar tunes and are thus easy to sing. In the second grade, the stories are usually read to the children. It is recommended that they read the stories independently by third grade. The author has found that it is easier to keep the class on task, talking about the same concepts, if the stories are read aloud to the children at all grades. Children love to have someone read to them! Each of the sessions is presented with an introduction, story book discussion, activity sheets, what is needed to carry out the activity, and field work, which consists of an assignment for the children to do prior to their next session. Children enjoy using the Pumsy puppet for the activities in Pumsy in Pursuit of Excellence, although the Pumsy puppet is not a part of this kit.

The leader's guide is extensive, with all the help needed to get started with the program. Included in the leader's guide are nine parent letters that should be sent out prior to the start of the program and for each of the units; the letters are to acquaint the parents with the goals and concepts that will be covered in that particular unit. In addition to the parent letters, there are overhead transparencies, posters, stickers, and Clear Mind certificates. These two programs, although much more recent than DUSO, have proven to be extremely popular with counselors, teachers, and children.

Toward Affective Development Another excellent program designed for the older elementary grades, grades three through six, is Toward Affective Development (TAD), published in 1974 (Dupont, Gardner, & Brody). TAD, designed to encourage affective and psychological development, is divided into five sections with 21 units and a total of 191 lessons. The authors stated that the major goals addressed by TAD are from child development theory and psychological education. The objectives of all the units and their lessons relate to these five program goals:

1. To extend students' openness of experience
2. To help students learn to recognize, label, and accept feelings and to understand the relationship between feelings and various interpersonal events
3. To help students develop skills of social collaboration through awareness of feelings and actions that weaken or strengthen group effort
4. To help students become more aware of their unique characteristics, aspirations, and interests and the adult careers open to them
5. To help students develop a thought process model which will help them choose behavior that is both personally satisfying and socially constructive (Dupont, Gardner, & Brody, 1974, p. vii–viii)

These five goals are the basis of the program; the program is organized to achieve these goals as illustrated below:

Section I: Reaching In and Reaching Out (51 lessons)

Unit 1. Developing Group Participation Skills

Unit 2. For Rainy Days and Fridays

Unit 3. Brainstorming, Discussing, and Evaluating Ideas

Unit 4. Developing Awareness Through Sensory Experience

Unit 5. Encouraging Openness and Creativity

Section II: Your Feelings and Mine (45 lessons)

Unit 6. Recognizing, Labeling, and Understanding Feelings

Unit 7. Posturing

Unit 8. Gesturing

Unit 9. Facial Expressions

Unit 10. Verbalizing Feelings

Unit 11. Role Playing

Section III: Working Together (37 lessons)

> Unit 12. Cooperating and Sharing
>
> Unit 13. The Individual and the Group
>
> Unit 14. Leading, Following, and Instructing Others
>
> Unit 15. Actions and Feelings That Weaken Social Collaboration
>
> Unit 16. Actions and Feelings That Strengthen Social Collaboration

Section IV: Me: Today and Tomorrow (39 lessons)

> Unit 17. Individual Differences—Level I
>
> Unit 18. Careers Open to Me—Level I
>
> Unit 19. Individual Differences—Level II
>
> Unit 20. Careers Open to Me—Level II

Section V: Feeling, Thinking, Doing (19 lessons)

> Unit 21. Choosing Behavior (Dupont, Gardner, & Brody, 1974, pp. viii–ix)

The TAD materials come in a specially designed carrying case and include the manual, which contains all of the lessons and an explanation of the program; a large red scarf used to encourage participation; forty-four $10'' \times 14''$ illustrations that show postures, hand gestures, and facial expressions; ninety-three $15'' \times 19''$ discussion pictures; a cassette with four recordings; two large posters; a deck of 36 shapes and objects cards; duplicating masters for student activity sheets; 40 feeling-wheels to help students identify and express their feelings; 80 blue and 80 red plastic chips used in lessons where students must work together in order to accomplish tasks; and two sets of 37 career folders, Level I for third and fourth grades and Level II for fifth and sixth grades.

Each of the lessons in TAD identifies the purpose of the lesson; the space requirement, such as a circle formation with desks pushed back; the approximate time required; materials needed; and the particular vocabulary used. The dialogue to be used with the lesson, questions for the counselor to ask, the expected outcome of the lesson, and the application of the lesson are all identified. Because there is so much material in the TAD program, it sometimes seems overwhelming for a counselor or intern to know how and where to start. The author for several years has required all of the students in her "Role of the Elementary School Counselor" class to become familiar with and demonstrate all of the various kits and programs discussed in this section in order to lessen the intimidation of learning it all at once, especially a program such as TAD, which has a total of 191 lessons and a wealth of materials in the kit.

Magic Circle: The Human Development Program   This program was developed by Bessell and Palomares using a developmental profile for each child that focuses on three main areas: awareness, mastery, and social interaction (Palomares & Bell, 1976). The topics for discussion in the Magic Circle program provide an ongoing series that covers the entire school year for grades K–6. (The program is described in detail in Chapter 4.)

Building Self-Esteem: A Comprehensive School Program   This program consists of a guide for the administrator, a guide for parents, and a guide for teachers. The teacher's guide, usually used by the elementary school counselor, contains suggestions for developing each characteristic of self-esteem, 122 activity worksheets that cover the five characteristics of self-esteem, and over 400 extension activities. The worksheets come in a loose-leaf binder, and permission is given to duplicate any of the worksheets for classroom use (Reasoner, 1982). (This program is also described in detail in Chapter 5.)

The ASSIST Program   ASSIST stands for Affective Skills Sequentially Introduced and Systematically Taught (Huggins, 1986). The ASSIST curriculum is grouped into the following manuals:

> Building Self Concept in the Classroom
>
> Teaching Cooperation Skills
>
> Teaching Friendship Skills
>
> Helping Kids Handle Anger
>
> Establishing a Positive Classroom Environment

"ASSIST incorporates concepts and procedures from social learning theory and behavioristic and humanistic psychology" (Huggins, 1986, p. iii). Each of the inexpensive manuals contains several hundred pages of activities to be used in a classroom setting. Each lesson has a variety of activities for both primary- and intermediate-level students. "These activities are designed to 1) involve students in the lesson concepts, 2) help them 'process' the ideas presented in the lessons, 3) provide opportunities for students to practice the personal/social skills related to lesson concepts, and 4) nudge students into higher levels of affective learning skills" (p. iv). The lessons covered in the Teaching Cooperation Skills manual provides an overview of one of these curriculum manuals:

> Lesson 1: Working with a Partner
>
> Lesson 2: Working in a Group
>
> Lesson 3: Learning How to Listen to Others
>
> Lesson 4: Encouraging Others to Share Their Ideas
>
> Lesson 5: Responding to Others in Group Discussion
>
> Lesson 6: Cooperative Problem-Solving Through Brainstorming
>
> Lesson 7: Cooperative Decision-Making Through Consensus
>
> Lesson 8: Dealing with Conflict in Cooperation Groups
>
> Lesson 9: Learning to Negotiate and Compromise
>
> Lesson 10: Working Cooperatively on a Long-Term Simulation Project
>
> Lesson 11: Using Cooperation Skills in Classroom Meetings and Discussions (pp. i–ii)

Each lesson provides an objective, a list of materials needed, and the presentation to be made. These lessons are simple for a beginning counselor to use; counselors, teachers, and elementary school students react positively to them. The ASSIST curriculum was developed with Title IV-C innovative education funds and was piloted in four school districts. The students displayed statistically significant gains in self-concept and social skills; as a result ASSIST has been validated, is designed cost effective, and is considered a Validated Washington State Innovative Education Program. Although not as well known as the previous classroom guidance programs, the ASSIST programs offer excellent, inexpensive materials for a variety of classroom guidance activities designed for the elementary school.

Grow with Guidance   The Grow with Guidance system is designed to help all children, not just a select group of children, through classroom guidance activities (Radd, 1987). The philosophy of the program states that "each child is entitled to learn about and experience activities in the areas of self, others, self control, values/decision making, cooperation, career awareness, behavior, and positive vision and self talk." The Grow With Guidance system views classroom guidance as not an "extra" but as important as other areas of the curriculum, considered as a visible curricular component. The program is designed to be used by either the classroom teacher or the school counselor and has activities for K–8.

STAGES   The STAGES project evolved from research and needs assessment in a California school district that indicated that 25 percent of the students in that district lived in single-parent homes, representing 60 to 80 percent of the discipline referral problems and enrollment in remedial reading and special education programs (Guidance Projects Office, 1987). The program was developed to help children accept and cope with change and loss such as the following:

- The loss of a relative or a pet
- Moving to a new area or changing schools
- Having brother or sister born or adopted
- Living away from home or being hospitalized
- Experiencing a parent's death, divorce, or remarriage (p. ii)

In the process of teaching children to cope with major life changes, lessons have been developed for use in the primary grades (one through three) and the intermediate grades (four through eight). The theoretical models used are from Marilyn Bates, David Kiersey, and Elizabeth Kubler-Ross. The lessons deal with change in the following areas:

- Denial
- Anger
- Bargaining
- Depression
- Acceptance
- Hope (p. iii)

The elementary school principal quoted in the beginning of this chapter also had comments about STAGES:

I have done the STAGES program for years and still find it meets the needs of most kids. Loss and separation are a part of every child's life, especially in this day and age with divorce so prevalent. During the last semester I started the program in a kindergarten class because of a SIDS death of a sibling. It turned out that out of 29 children, 3 had lost parents in accidents within the past year. The STAGES activities opened up an unbelievable amount of discussion among the children and seemed to really meet a need. (M. Boulanger, personal communication, May 1992)

This is another ESEA Title IV-C project available for use in the elementary school.

Conflict Resolution Conflict Resolution is a program used to teach children peaceful resolutions for the inevitable conflicts that arise in any school setting. Conflict Resolution Training addresses the issues that arise from disruption and violence in overcrowded schools, the tensions that are a natural part of multiethnic and multicultural student bodies, and discipline problems that seem to have escalated in recent years (Community Board Program, 1987). Conflict Resolution Training enables students to do the following:

- Learn new skills in communication conflict resolution
- Exercise responsibility for improving their school environment
- Build a stronger sense of peer cooperation and community at school
- Peacefully express and resolve their own conflicts without adult intervention
- Feel a sense of power and accomplishment at being able to peacefully resolve their own conflicts
- Express anger in constructive ways, so there is less likelihood of tension, hostility, and vandalism at school
- Develop the skills necessary to behave in a more disciplined way, thereby reducing the amount of time teachers must spend maintaining order in the classroom (Community Board Program, 1987, p. *i*)

The program described above provides a number of activities to be used in the classroom for grades three through eight. The activities are appropriate for conflict resolution work in elementary or K–8 schools. The activities provided in this program list the activity by name, the time involved, the objective of the activity, materials needed, the procedure to carry out the activity, and process questions to be used at the end of the presentation. This program provides training and services for schools training students in "communication, conciliation, critical thinking, and leadership skills" (p. A-1).

The Conflict Managers adhere to the following guidelines:

1. Talking to the Conflict Managers is the students' choice. If students decide to accept help from the Conflict Managers, they must agree to work hard to solve the problem.
2. Conflict Managers are helpers, not policemen. If there is physical fighting, Conflict Managers do not get involved.
3. The Conflict Managers' job is not to solve problems for other students, but to help other students think of ways to solve problems for themselves. (p. 81)

This has proven to be a successful program because children often would rather deal with other kids than teachers.

One elementary school counselor who put this program into place at two schools in the Los Angeles area presented lessons and activities in listening and communicating to fourth-, fifth-, and sixth-graders in their classrooms for a period of six weeks. At the end of this time, the students voted through a secret ballot for 12 of their peers who they thought were "good listeners and communicators, fair with others, willing to try new things, and are responsible" (Montoya, 1993, p. 1). The Conflict Managers chosen ranged from student council members to students with behavior problems. These students received a 15-hour training session in which they role-played disputes, critiqued each other, and learned the responsibilities of a Conflict Manager. After completing their training, the students monitored the school grounds in pairs at recess and at noon, looking for trouble. The Conflict Resolution program, piloted in San Francisco, is proving to be highly successful throughout the state of California, offering training through four-day Conflict Manager Institutes for grades K–12. An elementary school text provides over 70 activities that can be used to expose students to these concepts and skills. For information on this program, contact: The Community Board Program, Inc., 1540 Market St., Room 490, San Francisco, CA 94102, (415) 552-1250.

Another conflict resolution program is *Teaching the Skills of Conflict Resolution,* with activities and strategies for counselors and teachers (Cowan, Palomares, & Schilling, 1992). The book discusses the background and consequences of conflicts, with an overview of themes such as "Respecting Similarities and Differences," and includes a section on instructional strategies. There are a number of activities geared for grades K–8, using the Sharing Circle concept similar to the Magic Circle Program. Some of these are more suitable for small circles, particularly in the primary grades; others can be used in larger circles or in a classroom setting.

The use of Sharing Circles, in addition to the conflict resolution program, is provided in a book, *The Sharing Circle Handbook* (Palomares, Schuster, & Watkins, 1992), with topics for teaching self-awareness, communication, and social skills. The large number of activities in the book can be used in the classroom with the Sharing Circle separate from the rest of the class or with inner and outer circles.

A recent addition to classroom guidance materials is *Counselor in the Classroom* (Schwallie-Giddis, Cowan & Schilling, 1993). It is intended as a vehicle for instructional guidance to be used in the classroom in a systematic way. The emphasis is on becoming more visible in the classroom as partners with teachers, considered as vital contributors to the classroom experiences of the children, with the end result that "when counselors are perceived as vital to classroom and teacher success and, in turn, to the success of the school and district, counselor resources are likely to grow" (p. 9). The book has a number of counselor and teacher activities and a number of student experience sheets that may be reproduced for classroom use.

The various classroom guidance programs discussed in this section are not intended to constitute a complete list of available materials. The intent is to provide an overview of a range of materials suitable for use in classroom presentations from the older, more familiar ones to some of the newer, less familiar ones available for use in the elementary schools. The value of classroom guidance activities in the elementary school cannot be overemphasized. Gerler (1991) summed up the feeling of many of the proponents of a structured classroom guidance program with the following statement: "For years we in school counseling have labored under the perception that we provide ancillary services, that we are not central to the schools' academic mission. I am more convinced than ever that such perceptions will diminish as elementary and middle school counselors collaborate with teachers to implement classroom programs that improve childrens' attitudes toward learning, and promote a spirit of community within classrooms" (p. 242).

Career Guidance in the Elementary School

Career guidance should be an integral part of the structured counseling and guidance program in the elementary school. The American School Counselor Association (ASCA) role statement, "The School Counselor in Career Guidance: Expectations and Responsibilities," adopted in 1984, clearly spells out the high priority of career guidance for all students K–12 (see Appendix L for the complete role statement). It also clearly identifies the counselors' responsibility to see that this becomes a reality in their schools. Following are some of the statements that particularly affect elementary school counselors:

- Career guidance is developmental in nature (K-post-secondary) moving from self and career awareness—to career exploration—to career decision-making—to career planning—to implementation of decisions and plans. The entire developmental process can be repeated more than once during the life span.
- Career guidance recognizes and emphasizes education/work relationships at all levels of education.
- The School Counselor, as a Career Guidance professional, is the person to assume leadership in the implementation of career development outcomes. Furthermore, indirect services to parents, staff and the greater community, as they relate to the career development outcomes for students, are also the school counselor's responsibility. Indirect services include but are not limited to staff development, parent and school board presentation, and the establishment of strong supportive linkages with business, industry and labor.

The previous statements were part of the introductory section of the role statement. The statement also discussed career guidance as a five-phased approach in an education system, again emphasizing the role of the school counselor in the implementation of this program. Two additional statements particularly relate to elementary school counseling:

- Career Guidance calls for educational change beginning no later than kindergarten and extending through all of publicly supported education. Concepts must be delivered in an equitable manner to all students in order to bring a sense of meaningfulness and purposefulness to both the curriculum and the services of the educational system.
- Career Guidance concepts have been influenced by the school counselor for many years but must now be broadened to invite support from faculty, staff, administration, students, parents and the very diverse segments of the broader community.

Phase V had a statement that is especially significant, as it clearly defined the role of the school counselor in this process:

> *It should be noted that the role of the school counselor serving as a career guidance professional is one of coordinating and facilitating not the writing or implementing of the career infusion plan for the classroom teacher.*

This, then, is the premise on which this section is approached—with the elementary counselor as a coordinator and facilitator of career guidance in his or her elementary school. Career awareness should start in the elementary school in order to help young children begin to see the connection between their work at school and the broad world of work outside of school.

The focus throughout this text has been on the developmental approach to the counseling and guidance program in the elementary school; this is also emphasized in career guidance. Hoffman and McDaniels (1991) noted that the developmental approach to career guidance is consistent with the developmental philosophy of current contemporary counseling programs. They also noted ASCA's call to school counselors to assume leadership in the implementation of developmental career guidance programs. To meet elementary children's career development needs they recommended experiences that will help children accomplish the following career development tasks:

a. Develop self understanding and a realistic, positive self-concept
b. Acquire the knowledge, understanding, attitudes, and competencies to function effectively in their current life roles, such as son or daughter, family member, sibling, student, classmate, worker at home and school, friend, peer group member, team member in sports and games, and "leisurite"
c. Develop an awareness of the career development options available to them in school and the community. (Hoffman & McDaniels, 1991, p. 164)

These experiences, carried out in the classroom by the counselor and teacher working in a partnership, would help insure the successful implementation of career guidance at the elementary level. Hoffman also outlined the developmental elementary school curriculum for career guidance in the classroom that she developed for the Virginia Department of Education, to be used in grades K–5 in Virginia's public schools. The developmental tasks and needs of children at each of these grade levels are reflected in the content areas of the curriculum (Hoffman & McDaniels, 1991).

Elementary school counselors should know the basis for the emphasis on career education and career guidance in the elementary school and beyond. The National Occupational Information Coordinating Committee (NOICC) was established by Congress in 1976; its primary mission was to improve the communication and coordination among those that develop and use labor-market information. NOICC's mandate by Congress was as follows:

• To help states use occupational and labor-market information to design effective vocational education and employment and training programs, and
• To help states provide sound information about education, jobs, occupations and careers for individual career decision-making. (NOICC, 1990)

In order to accomplish the missions and mandates of Congress, NOICC works with a state network of State Occupational Information Coordinating Committees (SOICCs) to fund and provide technical support for occupational information programs at the state level. As NOICC represents the national producers and users of occupational information, SOICC represents the state producers and users of occupational information. The two major program areas in NOICC are (1) Occupational Information Systems and (2) Career Information Delivery. The Career Information Delivery includes three areas: (1) Career Information Delivery Systems (CIDS), (2) Improve Career Decision-Making (ICDM), and (3) National Career Development Guidelines. These last two areas, discussed below, should be of particular interest to elementary school counselors and teachers.

Improve Career Decision-Making (ICDM)   "ICDM is a training program designed to assist counselors and counselor-educators help their students and clients use occupational and labor-market information to make decisions about jobs and careers" (National Occupational Information Coordinating Committee, 1990). The two major thrusts of the ICDM program are the training of graduate program counseling students and the training of counselors in the field. In the states that are active in this endeavor, SOICCs organize workshops for counselors with training teams that include counselor educators, CIDS representatives, state employment services staff, and SOICC staff. The ICDM program for counselor-educators was designed to help them improve their understanding of the information and concepts of the labor market in order to incorporate this information into graduate counseling courses.

National Career Development Guidelines (NCDG)   "NCDG is a NOICC-sponsored project that identifies national guidelines which states and educational institutions can use to strengthen career guidance-counseling programs at all educational levels" (National Occupational Information Coordinating Committee, 1990). The guidelines form the basis for career guidance and counseling programs, which can be integrated into the entire educational program of the school. The guidelines are complete, containing specific competencies and indicators of performance for all educational levels from kindergarten through adult. The *Elementary Schools Local Handbook* (National Occupational Information Coordinating Committee, 1989) is an outstanding resource for the elementary counselor to plan, develop, and implement a career guidance and counseling program in his or her elementary school. The handbook also includes the competencies needed by the counselors charged with delivering these programs and the procedures necessary to implement the guidelines, including their evaluation. The career development competencies for the elementary level are as follows:

Self-Knowledge

> Knowledge of the importance of self-concept

> Skills to interact with others

> Awareness of the importance of growth and change

Educational and Occupational Exploration

> Awareness of the benefits of educational achievement

Awareness of the relationship between work and learning

Skills to understand and use career information

Awareness of the importance of personal responsibility and good work habits

Awareness of how work relates to the needs and functions of society

Career Planning

Understanding how to make decisions

Awareness of the interrelationship of life roles

Awareness of different occupations and changing male/female roles

Awareness of the career planning process (National Occupational Information Coordinating Committee, 1989, Appendix A)

Another career guidance and counseling program that is intended for the intermediate grades is Dream Catchers (Lindsay, 1993). The program was developed to address and fulfill Competencies IV-XII of the National Career Development Guidelines, "which relate to educational and occupational exploration and career planning" (p. 1). The program consists of a teacher's guide, a student activity booklet, and a book of 75 reproducible activity sheets.

The ASCA role statement for the school counselor in career guidance, discussed in the beginning of this section, stressed the inclusion of faculty, staff, administration, students, parents, and community participants in the carrying out of career guidance in the schools. To insure this, the elementary counselor should involve the counseling and guidance advisory council in establishing the desired goals, designing objectives to meet those goals, and forming a plan of action for carrying this out.

Parent Involvement in Career Guidance

Two studies looked at the influence of parents in the career decisions of their children, pointing out the value of involving the parents in this critical area. One study by Birk and Blimline (1984) surveyed 323 children enrolled in kindergarten, third, and fifth grades and 382 parents who had children enrolled in these three grades. Two of the questions on the parents' questionnaire asked them to (1) think of five jobs they would like their children to enter as an adult and rank order them, and (2) what their child wants to be when he or she grows up. Two of the questions asked of the children were (1) what they wanted to be when they grew up, and (2) if they couldn't be what they most wanted to be, what their next choice would be. The results of this study showed, among other things, that the parents were restrictive in their fantasies about their child's future occupational choices, and the children also showed a restrictive pattern of career options. The researchers believed that the biases and stereotypes of the parents are conveyed to their children, including "sex-appropriate" goals. Another interesting result of the survey was the response of many of the parents that "a survey about their children's career plans was ridiculous because the child was *only* in elementary school" (Birk & Blimline, 1984, p. 315). They recommended that counselors

---

The National Career Development Guidelines for the elementary school level may be ordered from the Oklahoma Department of Vocational and Technical Education, 1500 W. 7th Ave., Stillwater, OK 74074-4364, attention: Resale; phone (405)743-5197.

provide parents with career development seminars, community resources, and a parent support system because parents are the primary influence on career development.

Another study examined the career development of ten-year-olds to assess the relationship between their career awareness and interests, their perceptions of their family, and their family's feelings toward their own work. A larger study had included five-year-olds and 15-year-olds, although the subject of this report was the ten-year-olds. Although the sample size was small and somewhat homogeneous, the findings indicated that from the ages of five to ten the father's influence becomes less important and the mother's influence, particularly in the area of self-image, has increased. At the same time, by the time the child reaches ten, the family influence on professional goals appears to decline (Seligman, Weinstock, & Heflin, 1991). This would seem to indicate the significance of involving the parents starting in kindergarten in order to include them in this all-important aspect of their child's education.

Teacher and Staff Involvement in Career Guidance

One way to include the teachers and staff in an elementary school career guidance program would involve the establishment of a career development center in the school. McDaniels and Puryear (1991) described the Career Development Center (CDC) established at Virginia Tech to demonstrate to school counselors and administrators how a center like this could be developed at all school levels (McDaniels & Puryear, 1991). They viewed the CDC as a place where the counselor could provide in-service training on career guidance to teachers and administrators. They visualized the effective CDC of the 1990s and beyond to be multimedia in nature, with the media categorized into seven groupings:

One: Firsthand Observations

Learning about careers personally using $3'' \times 5''$ card files or computer lists of contacts with firsthand information, such as:

Shadowing experience
Role model contacts

Two: Action Pictures and Sounds

The use of videotapes

Videotape, commercially or locally produced
Television, film or tape from commercial or public broadcasting system programs

Three: Still Pictures and Sound

Slides, tapes, and transparencies—produced locally or purchased at reasonable cost

Slides alone or with an accompanying audiotape
Transparencies with script or audiotape

Four: Large Visual Displays

These visual displays need to be creative, current, and capture the person's attention quickly

Posters planned and created for various emphasis weeks, such as Vocational Education Week, National Career Guidance Week
Bulletin boards, changed weekly or bi-weekly

Five: Print Media

The standard core of most CDC's, with a wide variety of options

Books, paperback and hardcover
Comic books on career topics

Six: Automated and Semi-automated Systems

The resources available under this dimension are attractive, modern, timely, and usually expensive

Microcomputer, state career information delivery systems
Microfiche, state career information delivery system

Seven: Miscellaneous Career Sources

Various combinations of current technology as well as new technological developments need to be watched through professional journals and meetings

Games and puzzles
Simulation activities and hands-on kits (McDaniels & Puryear, 1991, pp. 328–329)

The CDC presented above is a model, an ideal to strive for; it is not necessary to have all of the seven groupings of media described above to start a career resource center at the elementary school level. Each elementary school desiring to set up a career development or career resource center should do this with the counseling and guidance advisory council paving the way by proposing this first to the PTA, in order to get its backing, and then presenting the plan to the school board in order to insure their support.

Many teachers are not aware of ways to infuse career information into the curriculum in their classrooms unless this has been a part of their teacher credential training program. It is imperative that teachers be responsible for the curriculum approach to career education in their classrooms, tying together the subject matter and the world of work. The ASCA's role statement stated this succinctly: "Faculty members must be able to make the same kinds of connections between the subject(s) taught and the world of work that the students will make between the subject(s) learned and the world of work" (see Appendix L). Career guidance should be an integral part of the curriculum, not a separate subject taught once a week or whenever it can be "fit in." A career development or career resource center established in the school could be an indispensable component of each classroom teacher's approach to career guidance. The interest of teachers will be aroused if they are involved with planning and setting up the career development center, a partnership that fulfills Phase II of the ASCA role statement for the school counselor in career guidance discussed at the beginning of this section: "The Counselor as a Career Guidance Professional, with the 'core committee' develops goals and objectives to form a skeleton around which sub-committees will add 'flesh' in the form of faculty/counselor developed lessons and activities" (see Appendix L, Phase II).

Herr and Cramer (1992) noted that career guidance plans and techniques identified in the elementary school will be of little use unless they are part of a systematically developed and planned process. They recommend that the elementary school counselor, in cooperation with the teachers, consider the following:

1. How to individualize those career guidance techniques that will be used
2. How to increase teacher, parent, and student knowledge of career development and the ways career guidance techniques facilitate it
3. How to coordinate career guidance activities
4. How to develop or acquire special materials
5. How to implement cooperation, planning, and evaluation (Herr & Cramer, 1992, p. 365)

A number of materials to address career guidance at the elementary school level have appeared over the last few years. Some of the programs described in the Classroom Guidance section have lessons that have career awareness as their focus. The Developing Understanding of Self and Others (DUSO) and Toward Affective Development (TAD) programs, bibliocounseling, and problem-solving groups are all appropriate for use in elementary school career guidance programs. An entire issue of *Elementary School Guidance and Counseling* (April 1980) was devoted to career development in the elementary school, providing many usable ideas for elementary counselors to consider as plans are put into place to establish a career guidance program or to expand an existing one.

Career guidance in the elementary school should consist of much more than an elementary counselor going into a classroom on a regular or infrequent basis with a variety of career guidance activities. The most beneficial programs continue to be those that use a core group or committee to develop the goals and objectives of the school's career guidance program, with everyone that has a vested interest taking part in this process—children, teachers, principals, parents, and community members. The elementary counselor, as the career guidance professional, assumes leadership in the implementation of career guidance outcomes through coordination and facilitation of the career guidance program.

Summary

Elementary school counselors are expected to provide a wide variety of services in their school, but often the demands for crisis counseling take much of their time. A counselor that truly desires to serve all the youngsters in his or her school will develop a strong program of structured counseling and guidance activities, activities that enable the counselor to provide a balance of classroom guidance and small group counseling, with individual counseling scheduled for smaller blocks of time so that the counselor is able to assume a proactive rather than a reactive role in the school. This also enables the counselor to provide in-service for teachers as needed or indicated by concerns in the school. An additional benefit of structuring activities in this way is the identification of the counseling program as central to the academic mission of the school. Another significant benefit of a structured program is a greater flexibility of time, allowing the counselor to work with the families of children identified as needing this additional help, including the provision of parent education. Chapter 10 discusses working with families in the school setting and the organization of parent education groups.

Part *III*

*The Future of Elementary
School Counseling*

$$Chapter \quad 10$$

Working with Families in the School Setting

Introduction

Elementary school counselors who are attempting to find solutions to the problems of children referred for services in the 1990s and beyond realize that effective intervention with the child's family is crucial to the successful resolution of a large number of these problems. At the same time, as schools promote and encourage greater parental involvement, it is oftentimes the parents, who are most frustrated by their child's behaviors and/or need the greatest amount of help in addressing these behaviors, that are the most reluctant to seek out the services of the elementary school counselor.

A newspaper editorial in a nearby city bore this eye-catching title: "Where Are Your Kids? We Blame TV. We Blame Schools. Maybe It's Time to Mention Parents" (Kyse, 1993). Another issue of the newspaper had an article by a Florida writer, titled "Parents are the real school dropouts." In this article the author described a kindergarten boy in an elementary school near where he worked who often walked around in his classroom "with a shell-shocked expression" (French, 1993, p. G1). He discovered that the boy came from a home filled with fighting and related the following: "Early one morning, after the stepfather shatters an ashtray against a wall, the child collects the shards and brings them to school. He clutches them to his chest, insisting to the teacher that he has to try to put everything back together" (p. G2). The Chief of Police in San Francisco stated on a recent television interview that "the core of juvenile delinquency is not the children, it is the parents themselves" (Ribera, 1993). An elementary principal stated to the author a few years ago, "The two worst problems in my elementary school are yelling and fighting. I used to think they learned the fighting in school but I now feel they bring this from home" (A. Huber, personal communication, 1991).

These are all strong indictments of parents, but, unfortunately, an increasing number of parents are so occupied with holding their own lives together that they have little time or energy left for their children. Their own problems are so overwhelming that they have abdicated their parental responsibilities, turning over the raising of their children to the schools, television, the neighborhood, or the streets. As we cast some of the blame for the actions of today's children on their parents, it is also important that the schools accept some of the responsibility for children failing to achieve to their potential. There are some teachers and principals that do not run classrooms or schools in a way that is conducive to the well-being of the children placed in their care. Although this has a definite impact on children, our focus in this chapter will be on helping parents fulfill their responsibilities.

Most parents do care what happens to their children but are finding defiance and even outright rebellion becoming more common in children, even young ones. It has been a long time since children accepted parent's judgments as absolute. Parents are ignored by their children in some cases and in other cases challenged to justify their actions or demands. Many parents want someone else, usually the school, to "fix" their child. Parents need to learn that they, not the school, are responsible for the emotional health of their children. It has become the school's task to consistently emphasize parental responsibility while at the same time offering help to these children and their families. Parents need help in developing parenting skills that will encourage the kind of conditions that promote learning and the development of a positive self-concept in their children.

Problems that arise in the classroom and on the school grounds may be the outward manifestation of problems affecting the family system. Children do not live and operate in a vacuum; only six to seven hours of a child's day is occupied by school. The child moves in and out of the family system to the school system and to their social system; when we look at children in the context of the systems they are involved in, we begin to understand why counseling the child individually is frequently not effective. Oftentimes when a parent is hurt or angry to the point of affecting everyone in the family, a child may take on the role of the problem bearer by misbehaving in order to help the parent. The child does not consciously make this decision but may feel he or she is somehow responsible for the parent's unhappiness or anger. This may then manifest itself by the child's acting out in the classroom or on the school grounds during lunch or recess. School counselors are often the most accessible person to both the school system and the family system when problems arise; by virtue of this unique position, in addition to their training and skills, an elementary counselor can be a significant force in facilitating solutions.

Some elementary school counselors do not believe that working with the families of the children in their school is a viable option for them, either because they do not have the training to work with families or they believe that they do not have the necessary time. It is the view of the author that the elementary counselor should spend a significant amount of his or her time working with the meaningful adults in the child's life, the teacher and the parents, in addition to spending time with the child in classroom guidance activities, small group work, and individually. It is usually easier to work with parents of elementary-age children because the parents are not as discouraged yet; it is when they have gone through these kinds of problems with older siblings that they are less apt to seek or accept the help of the counselor.

Working with the family in the school setting will be addressed in this chapter in several ways: (1) the systems perspective of working with families, (2) short-term family counseling with families where the child's problem is not severe enough to warrant a referral to an outside agency, using various approaches suitable for use in the elementary school, (3) parenting styles and viewpoints to consider in working with ethnic families, and (4) the use of various parent education programs.

Family Systems Perspective

Professionals involved in an elementary school setting are increasingly aware of the family's impact on creating or sustaining school-related problems. When one member of the family does something, all the actions and behaviors of the other family members are affected. This is often referred to as circular causality, meaning that the behaviors are a function of what is happening in the family and the family relationships and not something that can be definitely identified as the direct cause of the problem. Because of this, we look at the family as a whole to attempt to understand the actions of the individual member—in this case, the child.

There are certain characteristics of the family system that are typical of any other system, according to Thomas (1992): "(1) the family is dynamic and changing constantly; (2) the family regulates itself to maintain homeostasis (providing for routine functions like preparation of meals, cleaning of clothes, and the provision of shelter); (3) the family operates according to the principle of equifinality—regardless of the initial source of the problem, the same patterns are used in the family to maintain balance; (4) all family behavior, including symptoms, serve positive functions for the entire family system; (5) every member of the family plays a part in the working of the whole—a holistic approach; and (6) every action in the family influences a reaction or feedback, although it is not a causal relationship" (Thomas, 1992, p. 49). Viewing families in this context helps the elementary counselor see that each family member plays a role with behaviors that are predictable within the family system. When the family system is open, it is possible for the school counselor to work within the family structure to help bring about the changes necessary to insure the appropriate functioning of the child who is exhibiting problem behavior in the school.

It is important at this point to look at the relationship between family systems and school systems. Although the family exerts the greatest influence on the child, the school also significantly affects the children in the family. These influences are so great that when a crisis occurs in one system, the other system is usually impacted. The school, of course, sees the impact of the problem without any knowledge of the other systems involved. The home is more apt to see the results in two ways—in the home situation and in the school, because the problem exhibited in the school calls for their attention. Goldenberg and Goldenberg (1988) looked at the further breakdown of systems to include the classroom as a system, with the behaviors of one part of the subsystem impacting the overall functioning of the class. As an example, they refer to the clash of a slow-moving, deliberate teacher with an extremely energetic child resulting in a change in the classroom climate. When this becomes a problem for the entire class, the counselor may be involved in an intervention that calls for moving the overactive child into a different classroom with a teacher who is fast paced. This is a systems intervention on the part of the counselor that may take place without the counselor's viewing it in terms of a system intervention (Goldenberg & Goldenberg, 1988).

When the elementary counselor adopts a systems outlook in dealing with a child's behavior, he or she will look beyond the child to other persons in order to understand the child. "Understanding the child's behavior in systems terms, the school counselor may intervene effectively at a variety of levels—the child, the child-teacher relationship, the child-other-children-teacher relationship, the child-family interaction, the child-teacher-principal triad, and so on" (Goldenberg & Goldenberg, 1988, p. 28).

In a systems view, a child's negative behavior, such as acting out in the classroom or on the playground, serves some purpose for the child within that system. Fine (1992) noted the necessity of understanding the context of the behavior and the corresponding influences of others that are involved in the situation in any way. He views the counselor's task as one of helping parents and/or teachers alter their perceptions about the situation in order to approach it more effectively. "Within a systemic framework the notions of cause and effect are interactive and basically circular. What is cause and what is effect cannot be neatly partialed out because of a kind of continuous loop in which the child and his or her behavior interact with others and the setting" (Fine, 1992, p. 3). Knowing this enables the counselor to go beyond the *why* of the child's behavior to the underlying school and/or family system and the child's actions within that system. It is often the normal functioning of the family system that has broken down, causing the child to exhibit the negative behaviors.

The Goldenbergs illustrated the interactional effects of working with the child-teacher-family in a child's homework assignments, looking at whether or not the child completed them. In this situation, the contract, drawn up by the counselor, specifies the homework responsibilities and would be signed by the child, the teacher, and the parents when the assignments were completed successfully. All of them had to be involved in the planning and had to come to an agreement as to the way the plan would be carried out in order for it to be successful. This demonstrates the powerful effect of the family system on the performance of the child in the school setting (Goldenberg & Goldenberg, 1988). The elementary counselor that keeps the systems view in mind as he or she works with the child, the family, and the teacher will have a greater degree of success resolving a problem like this than just working with the child alone. Cooperation between the family and the school in a situation such as the homework assignment opens the door for further parental involvement if other problems arise in the school setting.

Not all school problems require the involvement of the family in order to arrive at a solution. Prior to contacting the family the counselor should meet with the child to get his or her view of the nature of the difficulty that the child is experiencing. It is when problems that do not seem to be school-caused persist in spite of the efforts of the counselor and the teacher that the elementary counselor should consider the family and the child's role in the family as solutions are sought. Often a counselor is hesitant to call the parents, not being sure how to approach them. A statement such as the following could be used: "There have been some problems in your son's classroom and we are all looking at ways to help Kerry. You know him better than anyone else and we need your input in order to help him. Would you be able to come during school hours or would it be better if we scheduled the meeting late in the day? I would like both you and your husband to come to the meeting." This approach does not put the parents on the spot, blaming them for their son's behavior; instead it views them as part of the solution to the problem. It is usually enlightening to observe the parents' interaction with each other in the meeting; this often is a clue to the child's behavior. If the child is included in the conference, observing the parental interactions with the child is another way to gain some possible insight into the problem behavior. It is very important for the counselor to be patient, comfortable, and at ease—this, in turn, helps put the parents at ease.

The approach used with the family by elementary school counselors depends upon their training as well as their comfort with the particular model. The Adlerian family counseling approach, behavioral management for families, Bowen's theory of family therapy, the family counseling and consultation model, Haley's problem-solving approach, and brief solution-focused counseling with families are all appropriate to use in the elementary school by counselors who have received some training in these models. The various approaches to working with families in an elementary school setting, discussed in the next section, are based on the concept of the family as a system in which each of the members influences the others in various ways.

Family Counseling Approaches

Adlerian Family Counseling

Alfred Adler, once a colleague of Freud, started Child Guidance Clinics in Europe in the 1920s and 1930s. His teachings were brought to the United States to Chicago in the late 1930s by Rudolf Dreikurs, a student and associate of Adler. To gain an understanding of the Adlerian approach to family counseling it is important to know the integral elements of Adler's philosophy:

1. The notion of equality of individuals in terms of human rights.
2. A declaration of the importance of respect in contrast to love.
3. The value of making contracts and forcing others to keep them by letting violators suffer the natural consequences of their behavior.
4. The issue of democratic establishment of responsibilities.
5. The point of firmness in dealing with others; being constant and consistent. (Corsini, 1959, p. 6)

Looking at this philosophy from the perspective of a family, it would be the ideal to have all families operate in this manner—everyone in the family holds equal status in the sense that there is a give and take in the family, with everyone doing their share; the mutual respect between the various family members, which fosters love between family members; allowing children to suffer the natural consequences of their behavior, something many parents find hard to do, which teaches them social responsibility; the responsibility of children to contribute to the welfare of the family by not expecting the parents to do for them what they are capable of doing for themselves; being firm and consistent in actions, particularly dealing with children in a consistent manner—unfortunately, a large number of families have not been able to achieve this level of functioning. The goal in Adlerian counseling is to help families achieve this through practical applications that helps them develop a family atmosphere in which everyone is valued and feels a sense of belonging.

The Community Child Guidance Centers, started originally by Rudolf Dreikurs in the Abraham Lincoln Center in Chicago in 1938, were formalized as a separate organization in 1948 (Dreikurs, 1959). The centers were designed to help parents and children by offering a practical training program for the parents in order to help them understand and deal with their children. "Their main function is not to treat, but to instruct parents and children in new patterns of family relationships, leading to a better understanding and a more efficient resolution of problems and conflicts" (Dreikurs, 1959, p. 17). Dreikurs' idea was to have these facilities and services available for both normal and abnormal children, which at that time was an entirely new way of treating children with problems.

It is interesting to note that Dreikurs made the same statement in 1959 that professionals dealing with children are heard to say today: "Parents today simply do not know what to do with them" (Dreikurs, 1959, p. 18). Dreikurs believed that it was necessary for parents to acquire practical knowledge regarding what they should and should not do with their children, particularly in conflict situations. He saw the Community Child Guidance Centers as parent education centers, offering parents an opportunity to learn about family conflicts and their solutions, because the centers opened the counseling sessions to observers as well as to families with problem children. The parents were required to attend at least two sessions as observers before they would be scheduled for counseling; with this type of format it is easy to see that the parents that were observing the sessions were learning some valuable lessons themselves by noting the interactions of the family and the responses of the counselors.

Some of the basic principles established by Dreikurs were intended as recommendations for the parents. These were not specific recommendations to be used with every child but were considered as general recommendations applicable to any child. These recommendations, summarized below, should be basic to all parent education groups:

1. *Encouragement.* Because most children are exposed to discouragement, deliberate encouragement is needed to counteract these. Encouragement implies faith in the child as he or she is now.

2. *Natural consequences.* These are needed because the parent does not have the power to control the child. Natural consequences requires training to understand and use appropriately and effectively without it assuming the role of punishment.

3. *Action instead of words.* Verbal corrective measures are almost completely ineffective; children soon become "mother-deaf." Words more often aggravate the situation and do not bring the desired results. Effective action can include natural consequences or physical removal from the scene, with explanations required only if the child really did not know what is now explained to him.

4. *Take time for training.* Teaching the child essential skills or habits requires definite instructions and training. A trained child does not require a lot of time for correction.

5. *Firmness without domination.* The child will respect the firm parent and rebel against the dominant one. For example, the child has the right not to eat if he does not feel like eating; at the same time, the parent has no obligation to cook special food when the child is hungry and no right to press the child when he is not.

6. *Efficacy of withdrawal.* Withdrawing from the scene when the child demands undue attention or tries to draw the parent into a power contest is not letting the

child "get by;" the child simply does not get the attention sought or win the power struggle.

7. *Understanding the child's goal.* Recognition of the child's unconscious scheme may prevent parents from falling into provocation; without recognizing the child's goal, no one can successfully counteract them.

8. *Withdrawing from provocation, not from the child.* The less attention the child gets when he disturbs, the more he needs while he is cooperative.

9. *Stimulating independence.* Never do for a child what he can do for himself! They become irresponsible only if we fail to let them take on responsibility.

10. *Minimize mistakes.* Emphasizing mistakes only discourages the child; the courage to be imperfect should be the right of every child.

11. *Noninterference in children's fighting.* In many cases the child fights to get the parent involved; children often get along better when allowed to resolve their own differences.

12. *Having fun together.* Playing together, working together, and sharing interesting experiences all fall in the category of "having fun;" these activities lead to close-ness in the family.

13. *Family council.* It is very difficult for families to establish and maintain a demo-cratic relationship where the children are accepted as equal members in the affairs of the family. This does not mean equal function; but it allows all members of the family to express themselves freely in all matters pertaining to the family as a whole. The child also accepts responsibility for what goes on in the family and shares in the contributions that all make. The family council should meet at a reg-ularly designated hour, once a week, with all members having one vote, depend-ing on the age level of the child. The family council becomes the "authority" with no individuals allowed to make decisions for the others. Children are usually more reasonable than parents expect them to be in this situation. (Dreikurs, 1959, pp. 23–29)

Keeping these principles in mind while working with a family using the Adlerian approach will facilitate the elementary counselor's interaction with the parents and child. Some of these principles can be modeled by the counselor as he or she interacts with the child in front of the parents.

An excerpt from an actual counseling session conducted by Dreikurs illustrates his method of addressing the problem with the parents. In response to the mother, Mrs. K., saying, "I don't want to let Larry go on this way," Dreikurs responded as follows:

> *You're absolutely right! You can change things if we help you. But by yourself you can't do it because you don't know what you're dealing with. You don't know your own role in the situation. Right? And it is very fortunate that you came with Larry when he is eight, and not when he is twelve or thirteen, because then it becomes increasingly difficult for him to change. The younger the child is, the easier it is to influence the child, if we can change the behavior of the parents. The older the child is, the less the parents are in a position to improve matters. At his age, we can be pretty sure, that if you catch on—if you begin to understand what is going on, and what you are doing—that you should be able to influence a different*

Larry. Is it clear? Do you go along with that, Mr. K? You are willing to see what's going on—to learn what you can do? (Dreikurs, 1959, p. 112)

It is obvious that Dreikurs fully expects the parents to be involved and for the problem to be resolved if the parents learn how to change their behavior with Larry.

There are certain techniques that are appropriate to use in Adlerian family counseling; the most important one is the initial interview, as this sets the tone for the counseling that will be done with the family. Lowe (1982) stressed interweaving the sequence with the process of encouragement, building on the parents' strengths. The following summarized sequence is used to diagnose the goal of the child, assess how the parents train the child, understand the family atmosphere, and develop recommendations:

1. Initial rapport (seeking to establish a working relationship with the family)
2. Family constellation (birth order of the family members and how each relates to the others)
3. Subjective situation (how the parents view the situation)
4. Objective situation (how the situation relates to Adlerian psychology)
5. Typical day (for purposes of determining the crisis periods in the day)
6. Children's interview (For purposes of validating tentative diagnoses of goals)
7. Teacher's and other's reports (a source of additional information in situations outside home)
8. Recommendation (homework for parents and significant others designed to encourage new ways of relating to each other) (Lowe, 1982, pp. 345–346)

Any subsequent interviews are follow-up sessions to explore how the parents have carried out the recommendations from the initial session and what they have learned; they do not focus on successes or failures.

In the early years of Adlerian family counseling in the United States, counseling sessions were conducted with the parents seen separately from the children; in more recent years, the entire family is seen together in counseling. During these sessions, the counselor makes use of several roles such as informing, teaching, and facilitating interactions among the family members. The Systematic Training for Effective Parenting (STEP) and the Active Parenting programs are based on the Adlerian approach to working with families. The elementary counselor interested in pursuing this approach with families should conduct a parent group using one of these programs in order to get a "feel" for this approach. These programs will be discussed in greater detail in the section on parent education.

Behavioral Management for Families

Behavioral family counseling or therapy can be traced primarily to social learning theory. This refers to learning that takes place in a social environment; this could be a family or some other system of significant others with whom they interact. Because people are born into a social system, they will all be exposed to a great variety of learning experiences throughout their lives. Children learn ways of behaving by having some of their actions supported and others punished—this, in turn, forms the child's personality. Social learning theory is a systematic means of looking at family interactions and generating interventions that are appropriate to help the family function in more satisfactory ways.

The applications of behavioral therapy to family therapy developed primarily after the late 1960s (Thomas, 1992). It became apparent that working with children by traditional methods left much to be desired in terms of effecting lasting change in behaviors at home and at school, particularly with children exhibiting aggressive, acting-out behaviors. One of the earlier, predominant groups that worked with families with child-management problems was the Oregon Social Learning Center, directed by Gerald Patterson and John Reid (Horne, 1982). They worked with families in the laboratory setting initially and then moved to the natural environment of the family, the home, where more realistic observations were obtained. The parents were offered instruction in effective child management techniques to help them with parent-child conflicts. Patterson and Reid also addressed in-school problem behaviors of children; teachers received instruction in the use of techniques based on social learning theory such as points and time-out. They reported the success of the changes in the child with little cost to the teacher and persistence of the changes through follow-up.

Most family counseling starts with a concern about one family member who has been identified as "the problem;" very often it is the child that has been labeled as disruptive, impulsive, a troublemaker, or some other tag by the teacher or the school. Social learning theory acknowledges that the family members behave in an interdependent manner where each member impacts, and is impacted by, the other members of the family. The family, by each member's use of cues and reinforcers with each other, influences the interactions of each other. Because of this, change for one member of the family, such as the child, will require change for all of the other family members. Horne (1982) stressed the need to address the family's interactional patterns by involving all members of the family in the treatment process.

It is important to recognize the role of positive and negative reinforcers as behavior determinants—these greatly impact every member of the family, particularly the child. When a child is young, the family may use encouragement to reinforce a particular behavior because it is "cute;" when the same behaviors are still exhibited at five or six, they are no longer cute but an aggravation. Negative reinforcement is another way to learn inappropriate behaviors. If a child in the checkout lane in the supermarket whines and cries for some candy or a toy on display in that area, the parent frequently gives in to avoid a scene. When this happens the child has been reinforced for the very behavior that the parent does not want him or her to exhibit. This type of behavior is very difficult to change once the child has learned it. This kind of learning occurs frequently in families and often carries over into the school setting.

Not all behavior problems arising in school need to involve the family. It is when a school problem concerning a child has been identified that is not resolvable by direct means that a team effort of the parents, the teacher, the counselor, and sometimes the principal is required to resolve the problem. By not attempting to understand or acknowledge the system of the child outside of the school, those attempting to work with the child are ignoring the many happenings affecting the child that are out of the control of the school. Wielkiewicz (1986) cited as an example of this a child with school phobia. A child that has severe school phobia usually becomes extremely resistant and distressed when it is time for school, exhibiting behaviors that may include crying, fighting, or physical illness. If the parent allows the child to stay home for several days, the child will usually build up such resistance that the parent can no longer cope with trying to send the child to school. The school has a different concern than the parents; their concern is attendance and its reinforcement. If the school simply states that the child must be in school, the parents may become antagonistic because they have been doing their best to get the child in school. A situation such as this requires both the school and the parents to cooperate with each other to devise a plan to get the child in school. By viewing the child's behavior within the system he or she comes from, it is possible to identify how the behavior relates to the system as a whole. "If the individual child's behavior is changed without a complementary change in the system, the system as a whole is likely to resist the change so that the original problem behavior will be likely to reappear, perhaps in a different form or in a sibling" (Wielkiewicz, 1986, p. 79).

One of the most difficult tasks in bringing about change in the family system is that often the child's behavior serves to reinforce or maintain some unhealthy functioning within the family. For example, if the child's acting out causes the parents to focus on the child rather than their own deteriorating relationship, it may be to their advantage to keep the child in the problem position. If the elementary counselor is meeting with a lot of resistance from the parents, including a lack of interest in getting involved with the school to help the child, it may be necessary to make a suitable referral for the family, because the school counselor's role does not include couple counseling. Family systems are extremely resistant to change, making the counselor's task more demanding.

Communicating with the child's family about a school problem is typically threatening to the parents. Schools very seldom call parents to tell them how well their child is doing; a call from school requesting an appointment with the parents usually signifies bad news, not good news. As a part of this, parents usually feel that the school is inferring that they are not doing a good job of parenting if their child is having problems in school. All of the skills the elementary school counselor learned in his or her training comes into play in communicating with parents, particularly listening skills. Reflective listening, giving feedback to the parents as to what the counselor hears them say, will do much to clarify what is being discussed as well as letting the parents know they are being heard. Reflecting the feelings that the parents are expressing will also help the parents know that the counselor is trying to perceive their world. It is important for the counselor to realize that the parents will probably be defensive and may verbally lash out at the teacher, the principal, the school, and the entire system. All of this may simply be a reflection of their own frustrations and feelings of inadequacy at not being able to cope with or control the child or the situation. Showing respect for them by listening to them will be much more effective than trying to defend the school system or teacher. Stressing the cooperative relationship of the school and the family joining forces in their attempt to help the child will be more apt to get the cooperation of the parents than by telling them what they need to do.

According to Nichols (1984), behavior therapists accept the parent's view that the child is the problem and not the family, and thus the emphasis is behavioral parent training, training the parents to work with the child. The first step is assessment of the behavior to be changed; this entails defining the behavior, observing its frequency, and noting the events that precede and follow the undesired behavior. Once the necessary information has been gathered from the parent conference, the child and parents agree on a contract specifying which behaviors will be changed and what the rewards and punishments will be. The contract needs to be specific so that there is no doubt as to what exactly needs to be accomplished. One of the most important thoughts to keep in mind when negotiating a contract is that the child must be involved. If the child is not willing to agree to the contract, it will not work. If the child has a choice of what the rewards will be, chances are he or she will increase the desired behaviors; when the parent or teacher makes the decision of what the reward will be, what they choose may not be an effective reinforcer. The parents should be the ones that monitor the behaviors at home, handing out rewards for accomplishment of specified behaviors as well as punishment where indicated. The last step would be to work on implementing the essential changes to insure the child's appropriate functioning in the school setting. Horne (1982) emphasized that the role of the teacher is to teach, not to discipline; the teacher's role is to define the problem behaviors and track them so that the parent can provide the consequence. The teacher is more apt to be involved if his or her role is one of cooperation, not just discipline.

Part of the elementary counselor's work with the parents involves helping them learn appropriate parenting skills when they have trouble controlling their children's problem behaviors. It is important to teach parents how to increase the behavior they want from their children; this is done by teaching them a variety of reinforcement methods. These are summarized below:

> *Attention.* This includes verbal and nonverbal responding, ways to demonstrate interest by talking and asking questions.
>
> *Social praise.* This is an extension of attention and includes ways of demonstrating approval, appreciation, and satisfaction.
>
> *Physical contact.* The contact many parents have with children is of a negative or punitive method, or is nonexistent. This method of reinforcing requires teaching parents affectionate physical contact.
>
> *Spending time.* This involves teaching parents the importance of setting aside time on a daily basis to have contact with their children, scheduling it in if necessary.
>
> *Access to activities.* This involves allowing children to do activities that are important to them, including special trips, movies, bowling, and other activities agreeable to parents and desired by the child. These activities may also be in the form of work around the house or yard or on a project.
>
> *Points and rewards.* This involves keeping a point or reward chart for the child and allowing some special activity or treat or privilege as a result of earning sufficient points. This is presented as a last choice: Parents don't like to keep point cards, and children often perceive them as punitive rather than rewarding ("How many points did I lose today?"). (Horne, 1982, pp. 378–379)

It is important to help parents realize that the goal is not just reducing or eliminating negative behaviors; the family should also work toward positive activities, which helps them all gain appreciation of the family unit and its rewards. Working directly with the parents in individual counseling sessions may require more time than the counselor can allow in his or her schedule, particularly if more than three or four sessions seem to be needed. In this case either of two options could be presented to the parents: (1) they could become involved in a training-type format for a group of parents that need to learn some management skills to help them manage their children's behavior, or (2) referral to the parent education program for the parents in the school, which are conducted on a regular basis by the elementary school counselor.

Bowen's Theory of Family Counseling

Murray Bowen, a psychiatrist originally associated with the Menninger Clinic for a number of years, initially worked with families of schizophrenic patients in a research project. He asked the families to move into the hospital setting with the patient, where he was able to observe their interactions as a family. It was his study of these families and their relationship patterns, combined with studying normal families and their relationship patterns, that became the foundation for his conceptualizations of the family system and how they could change to a more open system as they developed individually into stronger persons (Bowen, 1978).

Bowen is known for his use of the family of origin concept, in which the degree of unresolved emotional attachments to one's family of origin has a great deal to do with a person's current functioning. He had families construct a genogram in the process of looking at their family of origin, which enabled them to look back over several generations in order to help resolve issues arising in their current family. The basis for this was Bowen's way of looking at how well persons were able to differentiate, or separate, themselves from their family of origin. Bowen used the term *differentiation of self* to describe this most important goal of his family systems therapy. Constructing a three-generation genogram as well as writing a paper containing an extensive examination of their own family of origin is a popular assignment in the instruction of marriage and family counseling and parent education courses. The author has found that counseling students usually see this as one of the most valuable assignments in their entire program as they prepare themselves to work with children and their families.

It is important to look at one's own family of origin before working with anyone else's family. Bowen discovered this when he began to trace his own family of origin, after realizing that in six generations, a person is the product of 64 families of origin and would have much to learn from conducting a multigenerational family study. An emotional crisis in his own family provided a basis for Bowen to try out his newly completed theory with spectacular results. The outcome of this was the presentation of his own family experience at a national family conference in lieu of a formal academic paper. He then started to train new family therapists to use this method of going home to detriangulate from their own families of origin. Bowen stated that "no single development in almost twenty-five years in family research and family therapy has changed me and my approach to families as much as that one" (Bowen, 1978, p. xvi). We see triangulation often in families where the parents won't communicate directly with each other about emotional or controversial issues but will each talk to the child, thus triangling in a third person to avoid focusing on each other.

The goal in Bowen's therapy is to help each member of the family toward a better level of differentiation of self, with very little discussion of techniques. Bowen's lengthy book on family therapy does not deal with "techniques" to be used with families. He also did not insist that all members be present, because everyone who is a participant in the problem plays an equal part and needs to work on his or her own end of it (Singleton,

1982). If a child-focused problem was being addressed, Bowen focused his efforts on the most motivated parent, because he held the parents responsible for the children's problems. By holding this view, he believed that the parents will not be able to triangle him into being responsible for the child's problems.

Mullis and Berger (1981) provided examples of practical applications of Bowen's work in the school setting. Two of the ways suggested were parent conferences and classroom activities that encourage children to learn about their families, which in turn might influence the families to become involved in various school activities. Another area was staff development, with the counselor helping teachers learn more about themselves and their families through the use of Bowen's concepts; this knowledge could be applied to the teachers' classrooms.

Classroom activities, in which the counselor assists the teachers in the role of a consultant, would give the teacher a better understanding of the child's reality. As a part of the general academic curriculum, classroom guidance activities and classroom lessons could have as their focus the children learning about their own nuclear family as well as their family of origin. Assignments in language arts could include having the children write to grandparents and aunts and uncles about their memories of the student's parents during their growing-up days. Teaching children decision-making skills in the classroom environment could also help teach them to differentiate themselves in their own families rather than have others think for them. "Someone who knows a decision-making schema and who practices this schema, might be more capable of making decisions based on his or her own wishes and goals, and might be more likely to have a real self, rather than a pseudo-self" (Mullis & Berger, p. 200).

Family counseling using Bowen's theory does not accept that children and their problems are the cause of marital problems or discord; the children's problems only become evident when the parents project their anxieties onto the children (Nugent, 1990). Using this approach, the elementary school counselor interested in pursuing Bowen's methods of counseling with families would work with the family on tracing their family of origin and constructing a family genogram. Russell, in working with families in the school setting, has them draw a "floorplan," a three-generational family genogram, in order to get the family to identify where each of them is in the family, any special relationships that exist, any health problems, or other indicators of concern (Russell, 1993). These all lead to various ways of addressing the identified problems of the child that brought the family into the counselor's office. The assessment process carried out in constructing the genogram helps to identify the interventions that may be required, including home and school recommendations.

Bowen believed that the level of differentiation is established in childhood as a reflection of the parents' own level of differentiation. Triangles form, for example, as tensions build between the parents, who then argue over the child as a means of reducing their tension, resulting in the child's becoming the scapegoat. The child is then identified as the one with the problem, serving as a valuable escape for the parents. A child triangled into this kind of conflict has trouble in differentiation and is at the mercy of the family's emotional stresses (Worden, 1981). Bowen's approach to working with families is appropriate for use in the elementary school to the extent it was discussed here. The counselor meets with the parents only a few times with a week or two in between these sessions; it is not as time-consuming as many other methods that are currently being used to help children that have been referred to the elementary counselor. If the child is the scapegoat in the family, working with the child individually may never resolve the problem, just lessen the symptoms.

Family Counseling and Consultation Model

It is critical that elementary school counselors develop effective family-counselor interactions whether or not they become involved with family counseling in the school setting. Because so much emphasis in recent years has been placed on the significance of the family's interactional patterns on the behaviors of the child, the elementary counselor is in a position to intervene in the family when a child's behaviors are not under control. It is important for the counselor to acquire the skills necessary to establish a harmonious relationship with the parents, showing care and concern as he or she represents the school's interest in the child's education and welfare.

Strother and Jacobs (1986) view the counselor's role as being knowledgeable about family systems but acting as a consultant to the parents. The counselor gathers information about the child, meets with the parents to share this information, inquiring about the family dynamics in order to get a better picture of the situation. The parents are helped to explore some strategies for implementation at home. This is followed up by a phone call to see if they are experiencing any success in carrying out these tasks with the child. If they are having some degree of success, they may need one or two more consulting sessions with the counselor; if they are not experiencing any success, a referral to an outside agency is recommended.

Hinkle (1992) views consulting with parents about their child and assisting them in understanding child behavior as important family counselor competencies for the school counselor to learn. He also noted that parents need help in the reestablishment of their executive role in the family as primary decision makers. In addition, many parents need help in learning appropriate discipline for their children, including establishing realistic behavioral expectations. The consultation with parents role discussed in Chapter 5 fits with this discussion on counseling and consulting with families.

The school counselor is ideally the one to assess family system dynamics and classroom system dynamics when working with students with learning and behavioral difficulties, according to Nicoll (1992). He viewed the parent-teacher conference setting as the place for the counselor to conduct both classroom and family assessment, providing consultation for the parents. The counseling-consultation model is intended to be used by the counselor with the parents and designed to focus quickly on family interaction patterns that need attention. The model is summarized below:

Establishing the Tone. This is crucial to the success of the session. The parents, because they know the child the best, are invited as consultants to help the school staff learn how to meet the educational needs of this student more effectively. The school staff involved should not outnumber the parents by more than one so that the parents don't feel overpowered. The counselor should keep all communication honest, clear, and directly focused on the problem at hand.

Description of the School Problem. In order to focus on the referral problem, the teacher is asked to describe the specific difficulties he or she is having with the student in class. The teacher should not label or categorize the child but should describe the problem. The counselor seeks a clear description by asking questions such as "What did the child do? Then what did you do? How did the child respond? Then what did you do? How did you feel during this incident?" This shows the circular causality that happens as a result of the responses by the teacher, which reinforce or maintain the behavior.

Sibling Constellation and Parenting Style. The counselor at this point would address some questions to the parents such as "To help me get a better picture of your daughter, tell me a little more about her." The counselor asks about the name, age, and sex of any siblings, including whether they are natural, adopted, or stepchildren. Through the parents' brief description of each child the counselor gets a picture of the family's value system, when they use terms such as hard working-lazy, obedient-rebellious, shy-outgoing. The counselor will also ask questions to determine the parenting style; this can be done by having them describe a typical day in their home. This will reveal the parenting style (autocratic, permissive-indulgent, or authoritative-democratic) and also interactional patterns that may, in turn, show up in the classroom.

Description of the Home Problem. The counselor at this point discusses concerns or problems that the parents might be having at home with their child. This can be accomplished by asking the parents if they are having any problems similar to what the teacher has described having with their child. The counselor should also inquire how the parents have attempted to deal with this problem (or problems) in the past.

Reframe or Relabel the Problem. The counselor at this point shares his or her hypotheses regarding some possible family and classroom dynamic factors that could be involved in the presenting school problem. This is done to help the parents and teacher understand what functions the problematic behavior serves for the student, as well as what circular interaction patterns are now serving to maintain the problem. Reframing or relabeling the presenting problem is seen as the most important step in this process. The only way to help the parents and teacher recognize the need for a change in the intervention strategy is to alter their perceptions of the problem.

School Recommendation. By reframing or relabeling the presenting issue, the parents and the teacher can now recognize the need for alternative intervention approaches focused on changing adult-child interaction patterns rather than seeking to change the student. The counselor helps the teacher focus on one specific aspect of the problem for change. All recommendations should be clear and practical, stated in specific behavioral terms, with a clear description of the goal. Begin by suggesting interventions to increase positive behaviors; by doing this, the student and teacher are viewed as allies, not adversaries.

Home Recommendation. An intervention related to the school intervention should also be suggested to the parents. The parents and teacher should try to work on different aspects of the same problem. By doing this, the parents and the school are working together on a cooperative plan of action with well-defined boundaries, roles, and responsibilities. Keep this to one recommendation only.

Terminate Session and Schedule Follow-Up. The session ends by reviewing the insights gained and the specific recommendations that are to be carried out at school and at home. To clarify things, the counselor should write out both recommendations and give a copy to the parents and the teacher so that the expectations will be clear. The counselor should schedule a follow-up session to be held in one to two weeks; this usually assures compliance, because everyone recognizes that he or she will be accountable for implementing the recommendation by that time. (Nicoll, 1992, pp. 353–359)

This step-by-step family counseling-consultation model provides a format for the elementary school counselor to assess and provide interventions from a family systems perspective. Nicoll noted that the sessions typically require approximately 45 minutes.

Haley's Problem-Solving Model for Families

Jay Haley's problem-solving therapy approach focuses on solving the problems brought to counseling within the framework of the family. Haley emphasizes the social context of human problems, designing interventions in the client's social situation to help bring about change in the presenting symptoms (Haley, 1987). His approach to therapy can be summed up in this statement: "If therapy is to end properly, it must begin properly—by negotiating a solvable problem and discovering the social situation that makes the problem necessary" (Haley, 1987, p. 8). He also believes that it is a handicap to interview only one person; in the case of a child, the whole family must be involved from the start. Interviewing a man, woman, or child alone without seeing the rest of the family is forming a "coalition in the dark," according to Haley (p. 10). If the problem is a school problem, the counseling interview should be held at school with the parents, teacher, and child all present, because these persons make up the social group of the child.

Peeks (1992), in the article "Parent-Student-School: The Problem-Solving Triad," illustrated the use of Haley's model as a family-based intervention to solve chronic school problems. The model can be used by all school professionals with the recommendation that the parents be involved as soon as it is determined that the problem cannot be solved using traditional individual counseling interventions. The use of the problem-solving triad can best be portrayed by relating the case study given as an example in the article. Although the student was an eighth-grader, the methods can be used by an elementary school counselor. The student was refusing to turn in any of his homework in his English class and, as a result of this, was failing. The decision was made to contact his parents using the problem-solving model, summarized below:

Step 1. Contacting the Parents.   The mother was contacted at home during the early evening and was asked if this was a convenient time for her to talk. Ms. Smith acknowledged the parents care and concern for their son and told the mother "I need your help. . . ." The mother was asked if she and her husband had time to meet with Ms. Smith to discuss how they could work together to get their son, Anthony, to turn in his homework so he could pass English. This was a statement of the problem and the goal of the meeting.

Step 2. The Meeting.   Four chairs were arranged in a circle for the meeting. When Anthony and his parents arrived, Ms. Smith shook the parents' hands and sincerely expressed her appreciation for their coming to school. She spent a few minutes talking with the parents about their other children and their jobs. Mother was employed and Father had been unemployed since he injured his back and lost his construction job.

Step 3. The Problem Stage.   Ms. Smith told the parents that the reason she asked to meet with them was that their son was failing English because he was not handing in his assignments (a clear definition of the problem to be solved). Ms. Smith also focused on Anthony's positive characteristics and strengths and asked the parents to point out his positive qualities to him.

Ms. Smith had formed the hypothesis that Anthony's failure to do his work was a behavioral metaphor for Father's not working, which was causing stress between the parents. Anthony's failure to work had protectively diverted his parents' focus from Father's not working; this was the basis for her actions in the interview.

Ms. Smith had the parents talk to Anthony about why he had not been handing in his assignments and whether or not someone at school was picking on him or if he didn't like his new school. Ms. Smith asked Anthony about his worries in life, acknowledging that people of all ages have worries. Anthony hung his head but didn't respond. She also said that people his age often worried about grandparents, money, and divorce, asking him if he ever worried about any of those things while he was in school. Anthony covered his face, trying to push the tears back. Ms. Smith asked the parents to ask him what he worried about at school. After a few minutes of coaxing by his mother he admitted that he worried that there wouldn't be enough money to buy food and that his little sister, who had health problems, might become ill from not eating. The parents seemed shocked at his thoughts. Ms. Smith asked both parents to reassure Anthony that they were the adults in the family and would be responsible for providing food and money for the family and that he should not worry about it.

Step 4. Problem Resolution.   The parents agreed with Ms. Smith that Anthony was capable of doing the work required of him. The parents were then asked to ask Anthony his opinion about possible solutions to the problem. When Anthony just shrugged and did not answer, Ms. Smith asked the parents for permission to ask him to wait in an adjoining room while the adults talked.

Step 5. Action Stage.   Ms. Smith restated Anthony's strengths, commenting on his obvious sensitivity. She asked the parents for an agreement to work cooperatively, stating that children do well when they know the adults in their lives are in agreement. The parents agreed to do anything necessary to help him. Ms. Smith asked if they could talk in an open manner about Anthony's family concerns. She said she knew that even though the father was unemployed the parents could take care of their family. She said Anthony needed help and the father was in an ideal position to help him since he temporarily had unlimited time. The parents did not have any suggestions to help Anthony, so Ms. Smith proposed that every day he did not turn in his assignments Father would come to school the next day, attend English class with Anthony and supervise the day's homework. She focused on "reminders" from the father rather than this being viewed as punishment. Initially the parents looked shocked, but then the father had a smile on his face and said he thought it would work. The mother reluctantly agreed to try this plan for two weeks. Ms. Smith asked the mother to spend 30 minutes each day with him reassuring him of their concern and love. Anthony came back in the room and the father told him what would be taking place. They agreed to meet in two weeks if the plan did not work.

Step 6. Follow-Up.   Anthony missed one assignment the following week, so Ms. Smith called the father, who said he would be in school the next day. The next morning the father and Anthony were waiting for Ms. Smith when she arrived. Father could not attend the class because he had a job interview and hoped to start work immediately. He saw that Anthony handed in the missing assignment and the current one, assuring her he would supervise Anthony in doing a 20-minute household chore for the family during the evening for each assignment he did not hand in that day. From then on, Anthony handed in assignments. (Peeks, 1992, pp. 27-28)

The reason for involving the parents in the problem-solving process was to provide them with some indirect counseling services concerning the social conditions in their lives as well as gaining support and cooperation for Anthony's school problem. Two commonly used family problem-solving strategies are used with Haley's model: (1) inviting a parent to school to supervise, and (2) reminder chores. Although the case illustrated was carried out by the student's English teacher, this model could very successfully be used by an elementary school counselor for similar school-based problems that are not responding to the traditional individually-based interventions. Haley's problem-solving model is not difficult to implement for the counselor using Haley's book, *Problem-Solving Therapy.*

Brief Solution-Focused Counseling with Families

Steve de Shazer, director of the Brief Family Therapy Center, developed solution-focused brief therapy based on work done by Milton Erickson and Gregory Bateson plus his own work and association at the Mental Research Institute (de Shazer, 1982). Brief strategic interventions, discussed in Chapter 9, is ideally suited to the elementary school setting because it is a short-term approach to providing solutions to children's behavior problems exhibited in school. It exercises the strengths within the person to solve the problem. Kral believes that the concepts and the methods used in family therapy "can be applied in the context of the school in several ways: (1) to provide a framework within which to conceptualize problems and solutions, (2) to give an educator assistance in understanding and intervening with family-school issues, or (3) to offer a menu of techniques for intervention within the school" (Kral, 1992, p. 330).

From the systems perspective, a child's problems in school result from various interactive patterns in the systems where the child is involved. The school typically looks for the origination of the child's problems within the child, something that results in problems in the classroom or on the playground, a cause-and-effect relationship (Kral, 1992). One of the techniques used in solution-focused brief therapy, discussed in Chapter 9, was a "do something different" prescription. This technique is used when a pattern of response is used over and over again and has not worked; doing something different interrupts the pattern so that new behaviors can be tried. Kral illustrated this with a case study, summarized below:

Mr. and Mrs. B., their son, Jimmy (age 10), and daughter, Claire (age 6), came to the elementary school counselor after the mother expressed concern to the teacher regarding Jimmy's behavior at home. Jimmy was disrespectful, belligerent, and argumentative to his mother; the father was not concerned, because "boys will be boys." The counselor met with the family for six sessions with the goal of "teaching" the parents good parenting techniques. The school year ended without any resolution to the problem. Over the summer the elementary counselor learned about brief solution-focused therapy at a workshop. In the fall, the mother called, still concerned about Jimmy's behavior. The counselor told the mother about the therapy.

The therapist in the workshop said that Jimmy recognized his mother's position of having given up a potentially successful career to raise her children and was stifled in her current position as a parent. He discovered that when he misbehaved, his mother had some excitement in her life and was making new social contacts through involvement in a parent training class at her church and frequent trips to school about his behavior. The counselor said she didn't understand it, but somehow Jimmy thought he was being helpful to his mother by acting out. Mrs. B. said it didn't make sense to her at all.

Several weeks later Mrs. B. called back and told the counselor that she had thought a lot about it and every time Jimmy misbehaved she remembered it and couldn't stop herself from laughing. Jimmy had picked up on it and laughed, too. The problems between them had subsided considerably.

A month later Mr. B. called and said the idea of Jimmy "helping" his mom was the most ludicrous concept that he had ever heard. He was calling, however, because it seemed to have made a difference. The conflicts between Mrs. B. and Jimmy had diminished and there was a lot more peace in their home. He was so pleased that he and Mrs. B. wanted to take the counselor to lunch. (Kral, 1992, pp. 337–338)

When the mother "did something different" when Jimmy was acting up, laughing and not getting upset, Jimmy changed his response patterns. The counselor reframed Jimmy's behavior as "helpful" to his mother rather than belligerent, disrespectful, and argumentative. Although this was not a school-based behavior problem, the counselor, by making herself available to help the parents, opened the door for them to approach the school when and if a school problem with their child surfaced; in addition, this was excellent public relations for the elementary school counseling program.

Kral (1992) noted that parent conferences are another area where this model can be successfully used. In this model parents become part of the solution instead of being considered part of the problem. During a counseling session the parents are asked their thoughts about the problem while the counselor and teacher construct some idea of what would be helpful. Kral views this approach as different from the usual school conference, in which the parents are overwhelmed with all the problems their child is having in school. This typically puts the parents on the defensive, causing them to feel fairly hopeless about their child. In this model the parents are asked what kinds of things they have done with their child that works, placing them in the role of the "expert" as far as their child is concerned, where they have some valuable experience that can be shared. This does much to create a positive working relationship between the parents and the school.

Golden (1988) assesses the functioning of the family first to decide if the family dynamics lend themselves to brief interventions in the school. He developed the Quick Assessment of Family Functioning for use by school counselors and others who have brief contacts with families. The information can be drawn from the school records, the teacher, and an interview with the child and his or her family. Five criteria of family functioning are scored on a scale of one to five, with a mean of three as a cutoff score. A mean of one or two predicts a poor outcome for brief family interventions. The five criteria are summarized below:

Parental Resources. Are the parents capable of providing for the basic needs of the child? If the family has a history of extreme poverty or alcoholism, for example, they would have limited resources to bring to the complex task of managing childhood behavior problems.

Chronicity. A chronic behavioral problem indicates that the family needs more help than a school counselor is prepared to give. A response such as "His grades have gone downhill since October. That's when I lost my job," is a more favorable prognosis than She's always been a difficult child."

Communication Between Family Members. Can family members communicate well enough to solve problems?

Parental Authority. Are parents effective in asserting authority? When parents have surrendered authority to avoid conflict with a child, family therapy may be required to rebuild the hierarchy of parental authority.

Rapport with Professional Helpers. Can parents work with school professionals as part of a team effort to resolve a child's behavior problem? Central to the issue is dependability and follow-through: Does the family do its "homework?" (Golden, 1988, pp. 180–181)

The potential success of a family that is capable of consistently implementing an intervention plan is assured if the family is functional enough to make the counseling sessions productive. This is equally important for the elementary counselor and the family so that they will not be frustrated in their attempts to successfully implement a plan of action for a child who is misbehaving in school.

In the solution-focused model, the student's, teacher's, or parent's thoughts and actions are the center of attention. Feelings are not a focus, because feelings are more personal and usually require a longer period of time to be uncovered. To Kral (1988), the child is only one element of a triad that also includes the teacher and parent. When any of these individuals makes a significant change, the effect will be felt throughout the triad. The child-teacher and the child-parent relationships are the most crucial in this model, more so than the parent-teacher relationship. Recalling the visitor-complainant-customer positions discussed in Chapter 9, it is usually the most effective to work with the customer. The next one to focus on is the individual who has the most power or influence. When the customer/complainant/visitor comes to see the elementary counselor about a problem, the focus is entirely on the solution; what does the client want to have happen?

In Kral's view the interview is the most useful tool the counselor has; he suggested asking questions similar to the following in the interview:

"What brings you in today?" An open-ended invitation to talk, which does not assume anything, letting the client describe his or her situation in any way they desire.

"How can I be of help to you?" Helps to define the contract for intervention.

"Please describe the problem." During this part of the interview, concrete behavioral descriptions are necessary. "When Mike talks out in class, how do you respond?" "After you put your finger to your lips while looking at Mike, what does he do next?" These sequences are very useful in designing interventions.

"When don't you have this problem?" This initiates the search for exceptions, times when things are already working. When exceptions can be found, the course of your work is to increase their frequency.

"What is different at those times?"

"Who does what differently?"

"What will have to happen for that to happen more often?"

"How will you know when the problem is solved?" (Kral, 1988, p. 8)

The client is helping to provide the solution when these questions are posed. In addition, the counselor has built in the expectation that a solution will be found by asking in the last question how things will be *when* the problem is solved. The focus in this model is on what will be happening, not *why* things have happened. The solution-focused brief therapy model requires understanding the techniques and practicing them to find what works. The methods described can be used on a trial basis with parent interviews and parent conferences. Additional readings on the techniques and the model, using the references on solution-focused therapy cited in this section, will reinforce the ability of the elementary school counselor to use this very effective intervention with families. Workshops using this model have also been given at recent state, regional, and national counseling conventions.

Ethnicity and Family Counseling

Parenting styles and viewpoints vary widely among the various ethnic groups in the United States. In addition to this, the use of counseling to resolve problems has traditionally taken place with white, middle- to upper-class individuals, couples, or families. Because of the distinctive characteristics of the various groups, it is important for the elementary school counselor to have a working knowledge of any group he or she intends to counsel individually or as a family. There are significant differences in values, family structure, parental roles, and the way any kind of authority is viewed. A family's ethnicity should always be considered in any counseling intervention with families. At the same time it is important to avoid falling back on any ethnic stereotypes that the counselor may have learned.

McGoldrick, Pearce, and Giordano (1980) presented 19 specific American ethnic groups in their book, *Ethnicity and Family Therapy.* Each of the authors, in writing about the various ethnic groups, was asked to respond to the following questions, relating them to a family therapy context:

1. What do they define as a problem?
2. What do they see as a solution to their problems?
3. To whom do they usually turn for help?
4. How have they responded to immigration?
5. What are the typical family patterns of the group?
6. How do they handle life cycle transitions?
7. What may be the difficulties for a therapist of the same background or for a therapist of a different background? (McGoldrick, Pearce, and Giordano, 1982, p. *xv*)

It was not the intent of the authors to provide ethnic generalizations but to help the counselor maintain a sense of openness to a new experience of working with families that may come from a different ethnic background. This is an outstanding reference book for elementary counselors in ethnically diverse school settings, particularly because 19 specific American ethnic groups were discussed.

In addition to acquiring some knowledge about the different ethnic groups in the elementary counselor's school, it is also important to know whether the family immigrated recently or has been in the United States for a generation or more. Recent immigrants may not be knowledgeable about school counseling and may need to decide if it fits with their cultural needs and values. Elementary counselors trained in a CACREP-accredited program will have had coursework in cross-cultural counseling, including human development needs of a multicultural society. Many ethnic minorities prefer to discuss their educational and personal problems with friends, parents, or relatives rather than someone outside of their culture. This is a concern because of the lack of ethnic minority counselors in many of our elementary schools across the country.

Does all of this mean that a counselor that is not an ethnic minority in an elementary school that has a number of ethnic minority children cannot develop a successful counseling relationship with the students and their families? To answer this takes the reader back to basic counseling tenets: There is no conclusive evidence that a counselor must experience everything that his or her client does, whether the client is a student, a teacher, or a parent, in order to carry on a successful counseling relationship. If this were required, counseling as a profession would be doomed to failure because no two individuals can ever fully share the same life experiences. What is required for working with diverse populations in our schools is the same that is required for any counseling relationship—a respect for the other person and his or her values and a caring, concerned attitude on the part of the elementary school counselor. The reader might want to refer to Chapter 7 and the cultural identity model to see where the parent might be in the stages of racial identity development; if the parent is "stuck" in an early stage, the counselor needs be aware of this.

Summary

The word for the 1990s in education throughout the United States appears to be "restructuring;" it is difficult to attend any meeting in the public school sector and not hear this term, even at counselor meetings. Parents, businesspersons, and politicians are all demanding change and educational reform. This national concern with education appears to be school centered, ignoring the impact of the family on children's attitudes and behaviors. This type of thinking causes those at the decision-making level to try to fix the schools rather than help children and their families. The focus needs to be on the families and the help and support they need to be able to parent their children appropriately. We cannot leave the parents out of the loop as we endeavor to rescue their children and tend to their various needs. As a part of this, elementary school counseling is moving into the spotlight as many parents and educators are beginning to realize that a large number of today's children start elementary school with a multitude of problems that require services far beyond just educating the child. Marian Wright Edelman, founder and president of the national Children's Defense Fund and an advocacy voice for children since 1973, states so well the meaning of caring parents in a child's life in a May 1994 Mother's Day tribute: "I feel I am the luckiest child in the world to have had a mother and father who lived, rather than just preached, their faith and family values—who taught their children that being honest was more important than being honored, and that faith was a safer and more enduring harbor than fame" (Edelman, 1994, p. 4).

Peeks (1993) views family therapy as the revolution in school counseling, noting that the family systems philosophy can constitute the basis of meaningful relationships between the school and the parents. Parents are a significant part of the educational process: "Students learn at their fullest potential when the two most important influences in life, home and school, have a positive relationship based on cooperative interactions" (Peeks, 1993, p. 248).

Elementary counselors not trained in family counseling should consider some retraining to acquire this valuable and necessary competency. There are many workshops on family counseling available throughout the country as well as graduate courses in university counseling departments. The author recently offered a three-unit elective graduate course called "Parent Education: Working with Families in a School Setting;" the course was limited to 20 students, with all spaces taken and a waiting list prior to the first class. The class was almost evenly divided between students in the school counseling track and students in the marriage and family track. This was a clear indicator of the demand for help with families in the schools and in the communities surrounding the university. The demand created by the course has since caused the course to expand from a three-unit course to a four-unit course. One-half of the course covers family systems, family of origin, basic family counseling techniques, and solution-focused family counseling. The second half of the course focuses on parent education, with an experiential component requiring the students to conduct parent education classes in a school setting. The department now requires this course for students in the school counseling track.

The sources previously cited in each of the approaches to working with families provide excellent resources for the elementary counselor desiring to become better informed about family work in the schools. Reading these should provide the stimulus for pursuing one or more of the approaches to working with families. The following section on parent education is another way for an elementary counselor to begin to get involved with families in the school.

Parent Education

The term *parent education* may not be the appropriate term for the services that will be discussed. *Parent involvement* might be more appropriate and also more acceptable to parents desiring assistance as they seek to understand their children and learn the necessary skills relevant to today's demanding child rearing. It takes the elementary counselor out of the role of "expert" and places him or her into the combined roles of facilitator and supporter, as well as educator. The reader is encouraged to think in terms of parent involvement, although the term *parent education* will be used in the following section because the programs discussed use this term.

A variety of approaches to parent education have appeared over the years. Some of the most successful ones include: (1) the Adlerian psychology approach, developed by Rudolph Dreikurs, in which a group of parents meet to discuss and analyze the behavior of children, lending support to the parents as they attempt to be more effective. This was one of the earliest approaches to parent education, proving itself successful to the extent that parents felt supported and helped as they sought to increase their parenting skills; most of the programs currently in use are based on the Adlerian approach; (2) Thomas Gordon's Parent Effectiveness Training (PET), which emphasizes teaching parents how to listen to children and solve conflicts between the parent and child; (3) Systematic Training for Effective Parenting (STEP), a nine-week audio-or video-based study group that encourages the development of parenting skills to help identify effective and ineffective ways of responding to their children; (4) Active Parenting, a six-week video-based program that emphasizes the cooperative method of parenting; (5) Responsive Parenting, a group learning experience that teaches a positive and creative approach to child rearing in single sessions, and (6) the Next STEP, a six-session course used as a follow-up to the basic parenting course, STEP.

In addition to the above, there are two additional parent education programs that are designed for parenting in single-parent families and stepfamilies: (1) Strengthening Stepfamilies is a group study program designed to increase the knowledge, skills, and effectiveness of stepfamilies; and (2) New Beginnings, based on the parent education principles found in STEP, offers ideas and skills to single parents or stepfamily parents to help them cope with parenting issues. The programs listed above that are available as packaged kits will be reviewed so that the elementary counselor interested in conducting a parent education or parent involvement group will become familiar with their content.

Gordon's Parent Effectiveness Training (PET)

Thomas Gordon started the first PET class in 1962 in his own community in Pasadena, California, with 17 parents. Initially the groups attracted parents with problem relationships with their children; later the groups began to interest parents who wanted to learn the necessary skills to prevent problems with their children. The early groups were made up of middle-class parents who could afford to take the course. It wasn't until later, when federal monies were available in districts with low-income parents, that the Title I monies were used to finance the PET courses; this enabled all parents to benefit from this program. A significant difference between the PET courses and the other ones reviewed is the cost factor—the majority of the other programs reviewed in this section are conducted in the schools by counselors or interested teachers with no charge to the schools or the parents, other than the cost of handbooks.

Gordon's Effectiveness Training Associates (ETA) published training modules in 1971 to be used with Parent Effectiveness Training (PET), Teacher Effectiveness Training

(TET), and Leader Effectiveness Training (LET). These were a revision of the earlier lessons that were presented according to particular class sessions; the newer ones were divided by concepts and skills and were called modules: one for active listening, one for I-messages, and so on. The modules were an improvement on the original lessons, as their basis was the core ideas and skills common to all three; these were basic to the understanding of all of the courses. Starting in 1971–72, the parents taking the course used textbooks; prior to this time it was all in lecture format with role-playing and skill practice. Parents are taught how to effectively manage conflicts with their children. Some of the topics included in the training course are "How to Listen So Kids Will Talk to You: The Language of Acceptance," "How to Talk So Kids Will Listen to You," "Putting 'I-Messages' to Work," and "The 'No-Lose' Method for Resolving Conflicts."

The classes are structured to meet one night a week for eight successive weeks in groups of 15 to 30. The PET courses are usually conducted by authorized PET instructors, but an elementary counselor interested in using the methods can purchase the PET paperback book that explains the concepts and lessons taught in the course. Information on these classes can be obtained from Effectiveness Training Associates, Inc., 531 Stevens Ave., Solana Beach, CA 92075 (Gordon, 1975).

Systematic Training for Effective Parenting (STEP)

Don Dinkmeyer and Gary McKay are the authors of STEP, a practical parenting course consisting of nine sessions on effective communication skills. Dinkmeyer and McKay believe that many parents do not have the necessary skills to establish the kind of democratic environment where all family members are treated with equal respect. To respond to this need, parent study groups are formed using a format that helps parents increase their effectiveness in communication and encouragement. The objectives of the parent study groups are as follows:

1. To help parents understand a practical theory of human behavior and its implications for parent-child relationships
2. To help parents learn new procedures for establishing democratic relationships with their children
3. To help parents improve communication between themselves and their children so that all concerned feel they are being heard
4. To help parents develop skills of listening, resolving conflicts, and exploring alternatives with their children
5. To help parents learn how to use encouragement and logical consequences to modify their children's self-defeating motives and behaviors
6. To help parents learn how to conduct family meetings
7. To help parents become aware of their own self-defeating patterns and faulty convictions, which keep them from being effective parents who enjoy their children (Dinkmeyer & McKay, 1976, p. 14)

The suggestions for conducting STEP study groups include limiting the size of the group to 10 to 12 so that all members have a chance to participate in the discussions. Another important point to consider in setting up a group is to get a commitment from the parents to attend all nine sessions. The writer has been involved with STEP study groups for over 15 years and has found that this is an important point to emphasize. Typically the study groups meet once a week, with the sessions lasting one-and-a-half to two hours if the leader keeps the participants on task. All participants should have a parent's handbook in order to read the assignments and be prepared for group discussion. Having some kind of refreshments adds to the informality of the group; often members will take turns bringing cookies or some other kind of treat.

The session topics, one of which is covered each week, are as follows:

Session 1. Understanding Children's Behavior and Misbehavior

Session 2. Understanding How Children Use Emotions to Involve Parents and the "Good" Parent

Session 3. Encouragement

Session 4. Communication: Listening

Session 5. Communication: Exploring Alternatives and Expressing Your Ideas and Feelings to Children

Session 6. Developing Responsibility

Session 7. Decision Making for Parents

Session 8. The Family Meeting

Session 9. Developing Confidence and Using Your Potential (Dinkmeyer & McKay, 1976, pp. 3–4)

Every session in the leader's manual lists the necessary materials for that session, the objectives of the lesson, the procedures to follow, the reading assignment, the description and use of the chart for that session, the presentation of the audiotape or videotape, the exercise instructions and discussion, the problem situation and its discussion, summary points, activity of the week, and the reading assignment. The leader's manual is so explicit that an elementary counselor could easily use the STEP program without any further training. The study group leader skills, the guidelines for discussion leaders, and problems of group leadership are all thoroughly discussed in the manual. The second edition of STEP (1989) includes video vignettes in addition to the audio version. These programs are available through American Guidance Services (AGS), 4201 Woodland Road, PO Box 99, Circle Pines, MN 55014-1796.

Active Parenting

Active Parenting is a video-based program written by Michael Popkin, Edward Garcia, and Harry Woodward. It uses the democratic approach to parenting with the goal of improving the lives of children and their families. The authors use a video format because of the powerful learning involved in behavioral modeling. In addition, they view the video as a coleader, allowing the leader to be more relaxed and prepared. The video has full presentations of the content of each lesson, providing a negative example of how autocratic or permissive parenting fails to handle the situation followed by an alternative democratic skill. Each two-hour session has approximately 16 minutes of video scenes; these scenes depict three families, portrayed by professional actors, in a variety of family situations. The three families include a single-parent family and a minority family, with the children's ages ranging from 5 to 15.

The parent's handbook is the textbook for the program, with readings for each of the six sessions; it is considered user-friendly by the authors. The photographs in the text are from the videos so that the parents will associate the video scenes with the discussion of the lessons. In addition to the handbook, there is a parent's action guide, which contains review questions, guide sheets for completing the home activities, and group activity sheets. This is to increase the parents' participation. The Active Parenting Learning System uses the following format:

- Participants reads contents in Handbook
- Completes Action Guide Review Questions
- Leader reviews contents through class discussion
- Material modeled on video by "the players"
- Material experienced through class activity or video practice
- Skill applied at home with Action Guide support
- Feedback and encouragement given during class "show and tell"
- Participant applies skill regularly; Improves with use
  (Popkin et al., 1986, p. ix)

The section in the leader's manual on group leadership skills emphasizes that the leader's role is to facilitate the learning process and not to present information. The authors encourage the leader to modify the guide to adjust to his or her own style—to pick and choose, to omit what doesn't fit, and to improve the course as the leader sees appropriate.

The six session topics are as follows:

Session I: The Active Parent

Session II: Understanding Your Child

Session III: Instilling Courage

Session IV: Developing Responsibility

Session V: Winning Cooperation

Session VI: The Democratic Family in Action

Each session has a suggested format in which the participants talk about the assignment of the week, discuss the topics for the current session, view the video segments and discuss them, summarize the new material, receive an overview of the next week's lesson, view the video family enrichment activity, and plan the activities to do at home. In 1993 Michael Popkin produced a revised version, Active Parenting Today, for parents of 2–12 year olds. The kit contains a leader's guide, a parents' guide, and two videotapes.

No special leadership training is needed for an elementary counselor to offer this program to parents in his or her school. The program is available from Active Parenting, Inc., 4669 Roswell Road, Atlanta, GA 30342.

Responsive Parenting

The Responsive Parenting program was developed in 1984 by Saf Lerman as a substantially revised version of the 1978 Parent Awareness Program. The focus is on positive parenting approaches to help parents reach a basic goal of developing good relationships with their children. Responsive Parenting is designed to reach all parents regardless of background, lifestyle, or ethnic, economic, or educational backgrounds. The program has been used with abusive parents, parents in prison, and parents of children with special needs. The participants have included grandparents, single-parent families, stepfamilies, foster parents, and adoptive parents as well as nuclear families.

Responsive Parenting is intended to be used as a group learning experience, although the materials can be used with individual parents. The program's goal is to help parents to do the following:

- Acquire relevant child-rearing information and positive parenting techniques for a broad range of topics.
- Understand the various stages of their children's growth.
- Find solutions to current problems they are facing with their children.
- Find sources of information for answering children's troubling questions.
- Form more loving relationships with their children.
- Encourage children to explore and express their fears and feelings.
- Clarify and share their own needs and feelings as parents and as people.
- Focus on the good aspects of life with children.
- Appreciate each child as a unique and valuable person.
- Build a special closeness with each child.
- Approach parenting responsibly, creatively, and with love.
- Enjoy their parenting more. (Lerman, 1984, p. 6)

The parenting program starts with an orientation session followed by nine weekly sessions each lasting from two to three hours. The suggested size of the group is 10 parents, which allows each member of the group to share concerns, personal feelings, and experiences. The nine sessions can stand alone as single lessons; this is an appealing factor for parents that cannot make a commitment of six to nine weeks for the other parenting programs. The nine sessions can also be used to build on one another with no particular order, other than the suggestion that lessons 1 and 2 be used as a base for the rest. The sessions topics are as follows:

Orientation Session: Introduction to Responsive Parenting

Session 1: A Positive Look at Parenting

Session 2: Positive Methods of Discipline

Session 3: Positive Approaches to Sibling Relationships

Session 4: Our Own Childhoods and How They Influence Our Parenting

Session 5: Positive Ways to Foster Self-Esteem

Session 6: A Helpful Approach to Sharing Sex Information with Children and Teenagers

Session 7: Relationships and Feelings Within the Family

Session 8: Helping Children Handle Fear

Session 9: Difficult Issues for Each of Us as Parents

The nine topic sessions are contained in the nine parent booklets, one for each session. The program materials include a leader's manual, the nine participant's booklets, three audiocassettes for discussion, and 10 charts used in highlighting major points. The manual contains an annotated bibliography of about 100 books and other materials that can be used by the leader during the discussion and also as recommended resources for the participants.

There are 13 follow-up sessions for any participants desiring to continue meeting. During these sessions, parents explore additional parenting issues and are supported for the positive parenting skills they are using. The handbook contains some suggestions about leading a group, presenting the material, and conducting the sessions. The Responsive Parenting program is available through American Guidance Service, at the address previously given.

The Next STEP

The Next STEP program is designed for those that have completed the STEP program and desire a follow-up course. This course was developed by Don Dinkmeyer, Gary McKay, Don Dinkmeyer, Jr., James Dinkmeyer, and Joyce McKay in 1987. The Next STEP is intended to take the participants a step further in building their confidence and developing their parenting skills. This program includes the problem-solving group, in which the parents gain experience in working together to solve problems. The parents are each given the opportunity to present a specific problem that may be troubling them at home. There is a seven-step sequence that the group uses to help each other find solutions. The program is not a revision of STEP and is not intended to replace STEP.

The six sessions in the Next STEP program are as follows:

Session 1: Taking a Fresh Look at Your Parenting

Session 2: Building a Self-Esteem

Session 3: How Lifestyle Beliefs Affect Your Parenting

Session 4: Stress—Coping with Changes and Challenges

Session 5: Making Decisions as a Family

Session 6: Gentle Strength and Firm Love

The session materials are more than enough to cover a typical two- to two-and-one-half-hour class; the materials can be used for additional sessions, or the leader can choose the materials that will best meet the needs of the class.

The Next STEP kit includes a leader's guide, the Effective Parent handbook, three audiocassettes for discussion, and a problem-solving chart. A three-segment video is also available for purchase that reviews STEP skills, models a problem-solving group in action, and shows family meetings taking place. In addition to the section on group leadership skills in the leader's guide, there is also a section on how to deal with group members who create problems. No special training is necessary for an elementary counselor to lead a Next STEP program. This kit is also available from American Guidance Service.

Strengthening Stepfamilies

Strengthening Stepfamilies, written by Linda Albert and Elizabeth Einstein in 1986, is a group study program appropriate for use with stepfamilies. This program was designed to deal with the kinds of problems and issues that stepfamilies have in general, not specific problems in the families of the participants. One of the distinctive aspects of this program is the involvement of the entire family in the learning process through the use of the Encouragement Packet, which contains 30 at-home activities.

The leader's guide suggests that 10 to 15 people make the ideal study group, with the group meeting for two hours each week. Another suggestion is an intensive-weekend format with the 10 hours all on one weekend or split between two weekends of five hours or more each. The topics covered in the five sessions are as follows:

Session 1: Understanding the Pitfalls and Potential of Stepfamily Living

Session 2: Strengthening the Couple Relationship

Session 3: Creating Effective Roles and Relationships

Session 4: The Stepchild's Dilemmas

Session 5: The Stepfamily's Journey

The lessons are in the participant's handbook, Strengthening Your Stepfamily, and are used in conjunction with the at-home activities in the Encouragement Packet. The kit, in addition to the leader's handbook, also includes three audiocassettes, wall charts, and blackline masters for the reproduction of material. Strengthening Stepfamilies is also available through American Guidance Service. This program is an appropriate program for elementary counselors, requiring no additional training.

New Beginnings

New Beginnings, developed by Don Dinkmeyer, Gary McKay, and Joyce McKay in 1987, is written for single parents and stepfamilies. It is based on the parent education principles found in STEP. The course is designed to be completed in eight two-hour sessions, one for each of the chapters in the parent's manual. In addition to the leader's manual and parent's manual, there are four audiocassettes and discussion posters to be used during the sessions. The eight lesson guides are as follows:

Lesson Guide 1: Issues in Single Parenting and Stepfamily Parenting

Lesson Guide 2: Self-Esteem

Lesson Guide 3: Relationships and Behavior

Lesson Guide 4: Personality and Emotional Development

Lesson Guide 5: Communication Skills

Lesson Guide 6: Decision Making

Lesson Guide 7: Discipline

Lesson Guide 8: Personal and Family Challenges

The sessions in New Beginnings are arranged so that each session builds on the concepts and skills of the previous one. The New Beginnings kit is available from Research Press, 2612 North Mattis Avenue, Champaign, Illinois 61821.

Additional Helps

In addition to the parenting programs described above, there are other excellent materials for use with parents of elementary-age children. One of these, *The Do's and Don'ts of Parent Involvement* (McLaughlin, 1993), discusses how to build a positive school-home partnership. The book is divided into three sections:

Section One: Taking a Good Look at Parent Involvement

Section Two: Reaching Out!

Section Three: Parents Reach Out—to the School and each Other

The majority of the book contains sample surveys, letters, and bulletins, plus other tools to help insure parent involvement. The surveys and other tools are permitted to be reproduced in sufficient quantities to use in organizing and maintaining parent involvement. The book is written for administrators, teachers, counselors, parents and families, and community groups.

Another program, *Project Self-Esteem* (McDaniel & Bielen, 1990), is a parent-involvement program for improving self-esteem and preventing drug and alcohol abuse for children in grades K–6. Although it is not a parent education program, it uses teams of parents in the school setting; Project Self-Esteem is unique in that it is designed to be taught in the classroom by a team of four parents. The lessons cover a number of topics including attitude, compliments, rumors, goal setting, listening, stealing and teasing, assertive training, and alcohol and drug abuse. The kindergarten and first-grade programs have five 20-minute sessions, designed to be taught on alternate weeks; the second/third-grade program has twelve 40-minute sessions to be taught on alternate weeks; fourth- and fifth-grade classes have eleven 40-minute sessions, and the sixth-grade program has nine 40-minute sessions. The program is set up so that if parent volunteers are not available, the lessons can be taught by the teachers. The author strongly feels that parent involvement should be a requirement, with the elementary counselor helping the parents become comfortable with the lessons. Again, the Parent Advisory Council, discussed in Chapter 12, is an excellent resource for getting parents in the community involved in the school and in the vital education of their children.

Summary

The various programs discussed in this section have all been proven effective in the elementary school setting for use by counselors, teachers, and interested parents. The author has found that parents that have taken these courses often make effective coleaders, particularly a male parent as coleader with a female counselor in conducting a group for single parents, or a female parent as a coleader with a male counselor. These groups usually have far more single mothers than single fathers who often do not have a coparenting relationship or any communication with the children's father. This serves to bring in a male perspective, or female when single fathers are members of the group, which may be helpful to the mother. All of the kits described above have publicity packets containing information on setting up parent groups, how to advertise them, and how to put together a group.

One of the other resources available to parents, not in a program form, is the book *Safe at School* (Saunders, 1994). It is an action and awareness book for parents of K–12 children, discussing such topics as "Violence and Crime in Schools," "Discipline," "Supervision," "Disaster Preparation," and "Legal Issues." The book tells parents how to get involved in school safety, how to understand the school's point of view, funding for safer schools, and other of topics interest to parents.

This was not intended to be an exhaustive list of all available parenting programs and help for parents. In the author's experience in four states, these have been particularly effective in the elementary school. An elementary counselor that has not had the rewarding experience of conducting parent groups will find any of these easy to use.

The following suggestions have proved to be useful in setting up groups for elementary school parents. If the elementary counselor is willing to conduct groups in the evening, the fathers are more apt to attend. Another group that is usually successful is kindergarten parents if a group is offered to these parents during the school day while the children are in school, or in the evening. Parents of children this age are often anxious to get help with their child-raising concerns. Providing babysitting services for the parents at the school is another way to insure that the parents will attend. This is an excellent way for the Parent-Teacher Association to get involved by providing the monies for child care so that all parents can attend the sessions. Sometimes parents are hesitant to come to the school for a variety of reasons, particularly if they have had a negative school experience themselves. Conducting the parenting classes in a community building, a church, or a meeting room at an apartment complex might encourage parents to attend that otherwise would not.

The American School Counselor Association (ASCA) position paper called "The School Counselor and Family/Parenting Education" (see Appendix M for the complete statement) addresses the positive benefits of counselor-led parent education programs. The position of ASCA is this: "The school counselor, as part of the comprehensive school counseling program, takes an active role in providing family/parenting education in the schools."

Richard Riley, as Education Secretary, addressed the state of American education, launching a "family involvement campaign" that had as its aim encouraging adults to be involved with their children's lives: "America's adults and children are losing touch with one another, and parents and schools must move urgently to help bring them together" (Riley, 1994, p. A5). Conducting parent education classes to help parents cope with their frustrations and concerns would be a major step in this direction. If children and their parents aren't reached in elementary school, the children are often lost to the larger community. An elementary school counselor committed to conducting parenting classes throughout the school year would be hard-pressed to find a better use of his or her time.

Program Accountability and Evaluation

Introduction

School districts that have never had the benefit of an elementary counselor do not fully understand just how extensive their services are, how they are developmental in nature and preventive in their effect. A school superintendent, in a primarily middle-class school district, was highly concerned with the "sharp increase" in violent incidents among students in his district, including at the elementary school level; this district had just recently felt the influence of gangs. The superintendent noted that the district was responding with "aggressive" disciplinary measures but "lacks the resources to treat the roots of the violence by such steps as counseling for abused and neglected youngsters." He stated that "we know what the answer is. Every kindergarten teacher in the district can tell you by November which kids are likely candidates to be involved in serious problems" (Cadman, 1994, p. B1).

The superintendent obviously was not aware of the scope and function of a developmental elementary school counseling program, a program that does more than provide "counseling for abused and neglected youngsters." It is critical that all elementary school counselors assess and evaluate their programs, making sure that their constituencies are fully aware of the services they provide, including the benefits derived for the entire school. It is only when elementary counseling programs are well documented and highly visible that others, such as the superintendent quoted above, not only will become aware of what elementary counseling can do but will "find" the resources to establish an elementary school counseling program.

At a time when the public is increasingly in the mood to hold the schools accountable for their performance, the schools' counseling and guidance program should be equally accountable. The elementary school counseling and guidance program should be identifiable and measurable as an essential service in the school and in the community if it is going to survive when budget cuts are made.

This chapter will look at both the accountability of elementary school counseling programs and the evaluation of these programs. The words *accountability* and *evaluation* will be taken literally. *Accountability* means "the state of being accountable, responsible or liable, answerable" (Webster, 1983, p. 13). *Evaluation* means "to determine the worth of; to appraise; the process of being evaluated" (Webster, 1983, p. 632). Within this framework, accountability and evaluation will be viewed from a positive perspective—one in which the counselors themselves initiate the process in order to make sure they have a viable program that meets the needs of all of the children in their schools, forming a partnership with parents, teachers, and other school staff to accomplish this very important task.

Accountability

In order for the elementary school counseling program to be accountable, it must be systematically planned. A frequent criticism of school counseling programs is that they are often the result of one of two processes: (1) They occur by trying to be "all things to all people," or (2) they just occur in response to the demands of the school, with the counselor reacting to crises. Either way, the program will suffer and the elementary counselor will be responding to more demands than he or she can possibly fulfill.

Often counselors do not have a clear picture in their own minds of what their role should be in the school. Although in many ways elementary counselors have more alternatives and options today than they did when elementary counseling first became a reality, the demands of their job are increasing. They are being told what to do by legislators, school boards, superintendents, principals, teachers, parents, and counselor-educators; often entirely different things. Some say career guidance ought to be the major emphasis; others say to take care of all of those problem kids needing immediate attention; someone else says to concentrate on running groups; and still others say to work mostly as a consultant with teachers and administrators. On top of all this, we say it is the responsibility of the counselor to go into the school and devise a role and function that serves the school needs. The elementary school counselor is the most vulnerable person on the school staff, expected to be responsive to too many needs.

In 1990 Beverly O'Bryant, president of the ASCA at the time, wrote about some issues that we as professional members need to address nationwide. One issue came up as the result of her meetings with the CEOs of various businesses and corporations as she traveled around the country. This group told her that counselors don't really project an image that says they are accountable: "The corporate sector says they really don't know what we do other than listen to problems and schedule classes. The corporate sector does not yet recognize or understand a generic professional counseling model which is preventive, developmental and comprehensive that has significant product outcomes when implemented appropriately by trained professionals" (1990, p. 2). O'Bryant further stated that "school counselors must produce, provide and articulate accountability statutes nationwide. Every school counselor should be able to cogently describe to Person X *what* they do, *how* they do it, and the statistical effect of what they do" (p. 2). All elementary school counselors should pay particular attention to this challenge if our goal is to increase the availability of services for all of the children in our elementary schools, not just the children "in crisis." When the public sector has full awareness of the actual services performed by elementary school counselors, including their impact, the dissolution of these services will not occur.

Accountability has been the subject of many articles appearing in our professional counseling journals for the past 15 years or so. Gysbers and Henderson (1988) go back to the 1960s to trace the accountability movement in education. They noted the intensifying of the accountability movement in the 1970s through the emphasis on career guidance and career education. They saw the 1980s as the decade in which developmental guidance programs were stressed, leading to the 1986 College Entrance Examination Board's report, *Keeping the Options Open: Recommendations,* which recommended that all schools develop a K–12 comprehensive developmental guidance program. They emphasized guidance in the schools as a program with similar characteristics to other educational programs, including the following:

1. Student outcomes (student competencies);
2. Activities and processes to assist students in achieving these outcomes;
3. Professionally recognized personnel; and
4. Materials and resources. (Gysbers & Henderson, 1988, p. 30)

Accountability involves professional responsibility in these areas to the students, teachers, administrators, parents, school board, and the constituents in the community.

Baker (1992) recommends that accountability have both personal as well as collegial roots because school counselors, in a professional setting, are involved with other professionals—teachers, school psychologists, and administrators: "It seems logical that all individuals gainfully employed, including school counselors, would want information providing evidence of their effectiveness with suggestions for positive changes" (Baker, 1992, p. 191). He also notes the advantages of the counselor's initiating the evaluation process that is used to provide accountability data rather than waiting for others who aren't as knowledgeable about the counseling services to initiate the process. The significance of this cannot be overstated.

One way to establish accountability in an elementary school counseling program is through a research study that looks at the entire school counseling program. Most counselors decry their lack of time to accomplish the myriad of tasks they face each day without imagining taking the time necessary to devote to a research study. A simple research study can be built into an elementary counselor's existing schedule without involving an undue amount of extra time, particularly if the counselor is in a position to contact a university-level colleague, a former counseling department professor, or another counselor to collaborate with, to conduct a joint study.

As an example of a straightforward approach to a research study, the author joined forces with an elementary school counselor in an attempt to identify the counseling program's success in increasing children's self-esteem. It was the counselor's first year in a school that did not have counseling services prior to this time. The school district's teachers and staff had identified a real need for some counseling help for the children in the school, particularly at the intermediate grades. Based on this, the counselor had planned her initial interventions in fourth, fifth, and sixth grades. The counselor and the author met with the school staff, presenting the potential research study in order to look at the effects of counseling with these children. The principal and teachers were open to having the study carried out in their school and looked forward to the proposed plan. Each of these grades had two classrooms, so one classroom in each grade was designated as a control group and the other was designated as the experimental group. The author administered the Piers-Harris Children's Self-Concept Scale (Piers, 1985) to all six classrooms involved in the study before the counselor conducted any classroom guidance activities with these children. This was done to insure that the results would be consistent and would not be biased in any way by the students' response to someone in the school setting. The counselor conducted 30-minute classroom guidance sessions three times each week during the first semester in the three experimental classrooms using two different programs of self-esteem activities. The children in the control classrooms were seen by the counselor only if they were referred for counseling. The teachers in the control group classrooms were told that the counselor would spend an equal amount of time in their classrooms during the second semester.

At the end of the first semester, the author again administered the Piers-Harris Children's Self-Concept Scale as a posttest in each of the six classrooms. Because only six classrooms were involved, the scoring was done by hand: the total raw score was calculated first, followed by the raw scores for each of the six cluster scales covered in the test. The individual student scores were graphed on the profile form, available from the test publisher, with the pretest in red ink and the posttest in blue ink for easier comparison; these were made with a simple pretest/posttest comparison of the individual profile forms for each child. The profile showed corresponding T-scores and percentile scores for each of the six scales; the raw scores could also be converted to stanine scores if desired. The profiles provided a graphic illustration of the success of the counselor's efforts in conducting classroom guidance activities in building self-esteem. The teachers and principal were pleased with the results, and the teachers in the experimental classroom very verbal in their support of the new counseling program.

This was not a complicated or sophisticated research activity; it did not need to be. This study provided immediate accountability for the newly hired counselor in a school district that did not have previous counseling services. The author has since conducted another study in a district without an elementary counselor, using one elementary school as the control school, and placing an intern in another school designated as the experimental school. The Coopersmith Self-Esteem Inventories were used in this study because first-, third-, and fifth-grade classrooms were involved. The author is currently conducting a study in one school in another school district, with the counselor and two interns providing services. In this school third-, fourth-, and fifth-grade classrooms are involved, with the author administering Harter's Self-Perception Profile for Children in both the control and experimental classrooms. This is a low-income, high-ethnic-minority district with many children who are non-English proficient; it has been designated as a high-risk area with a spoken need of increased counseling services. The purpose of the research is to clearly identify the need to expand the current counseling services for the school board; the superintendent is already convinced. It seems to the author that those engaged in the training of school counselors would want to take the time necessary to teach the counselors-in-training some simple research methods, both by instruction and by example.

Jackie Allen, the 1993–94 ASCA president, suggested action-oriented research to promote school counselor advocacy and accountability, noting that school counselors have not effectively used research (1992). In response to counselors asking "Why do research?" she stated that "research when understood as a proactive professional activity becomes imperative for the advocacy, advancement, and accountability of school counseling" (Allen, 1992, p. 1). Because action-oriented research focuses on immediate application, the counselor is able to examine a specific counseling program or intervention. Allen also noted the use of research as a basis for proactive public relations, a real benefit to school counselors in a time of increasing demand for accountability in education.

It is interesting to note the difference in emphasis on research in the K–12 school setting and at the university level. From the university point of view, research is an integral part of the job, particularly when tenure and promotion are based on professional research and subsequent writing and publication. In the K–12 school setting, research is never an expected task or function of the school counselor, or anyone else on the staff for that matter. During the many years that the author has been involved in the field of counseling, at both the K–12 and university levels in several states, very few school counselors expressed an interest in or professed to be knowledgeable about research being done in the schools. It is hard to imagine a more fitting partnership in the field of school counseling than the elementary school counselor and the university professor—this would be a beneficial partnership for both, with the professor lending his or her expertise in research methods and data collection and the school counselor desiring to show accountability in the school counseling program involved in program evaluation.

Demands for accountability can be initiated either to prove a counseling program's effectiveness or to improve its effectiveness, according to Bleuer (1983). She identified an accountability system, summarized below, that clearly outlines the process involved for a program desiring to be accountable:

1. *Identify stakeholders.* The first step in designing an accountability system is to identify the audience—who will use the data?
2. *Clarify purposes.* Once all stakeholders have been identified, meet with representatives of each group to determine the types of data needed and how it will be used. This also sets the stage for collaborative teamwork.
3. *Specify program objectives.* Identify stakeholder consensus on the importance of specific program objectives. This can be done informally or it may require a needs assessment.
4. *Identify activities needed to achieve objectives.* The counselor may need to identify the counseling strategies that will be most effective in achieving program objectives.
5. *Identify resources needed to achieve objectives.* Stakeholders must understand what the program needs in the way of personnel, facilities, equipment, and supplies, in addition to public relations.
6. *Identify needed evidence.* Specify the sets of evidence that will demonstrate that (a) resources are available and used, (b) activities are conducted as planned, and (c) objectives are being achieved.

7. *Analyze costs.* It may be important to clarify with stakeholders what should be included in cost considerations so that something they consider important isn't overlooked.

8. *Prepare reports.* The text of the report should be as brief as possible, with graphic displays wherever appropriate. (Bleuer, 1983, p. 3)

Establishing an accountability study can be viewed with anticipation or dread, depending on the purpose of the study. This is usually dependent upon how the counselor views it—if he or she believes that the sole purpose of the accountability study is to evaluate his or her effectiveness as a counselor, the study will be feared. If, on the other hand, the counselor views an accountability study as a way to gain feedback on the program, whether or not it is meeting the needs of the students and staff, the study will be eagerly anticipated. If the counselor is proactive and asks his or her advisory council, a fellow counselor, or a university professor to help with the study, the counselor is establishing his or her desire to be accountable. The next section on evaluation will look at the process of evaluating the elementary school counselor and the counseling program from a positive perspective.

Evaluation

Educational accountability has been increasingly stressed, with taxpayers demanding evidence that the schools are giving them their money's worth. The way to supply this evidence is through appropriate evaluations of school programs; the emphasis in this section is on the elementary school counseling program.

The ASCA position statement called "The School Counselor and Their Evaluation," (see Appendix N for the complete statement) was adopted in 1978, reaffirmed in 1984, and revised in 1986. The position states that "an annual evaluation of each school counselor should take place. This evaluation must be based upon specific facts and comprehensive evaluation criteria recognizing the differences between evaluating counselors and classroom personnel and conforming to local and state regulations" (American School Counselor Association, 1986). The rationale of the position of the ASCA states the following:

> *Since the primary purpose of the evaluation process is to assure the continued professional growth of school counselors, the ASCA is committed to the continued improvement of the process. It is recommended that each counselor be evaluated with regard to the implementation of the district's written counseling program and school counselor job description. The plan and the school counselor need to be evaluated and reviewed annually. The plan needs to contain specific goals along with objectives which emphasize student outcomes. It should be a dynamic document, modified annually to reflect the changing needs of the students and the improved skills of the counseling staff. As the ASCA is committed to the improvement of school counseling programs, the Association welcomes the opportunity to aid local administrators, department heads, and others charged*

> *with the improvement or development of evaluation instruments and procedures.*
> *(American School Counselor Association, 1986)*

The ASCA position statement clearly takes evaluation out of the optional category for all elementary school counselors that are members of ASCA. It seems apparent that this statement has not been widely discussed or disseminated among practicing school counselors.

There are a variety of ways to evaluate a school counseling program. In the following section, four of the methods of establishing accountability through evaluation will be discussed, one in detail. These include (1) the Missouri Comprehensive Guidance Program Model, (2) ASCA's Professional Development Guidelines for Elementary School Counselors, (3) an Accountability Study for Developmental Guidance and Counseling, and (4) an "Action Plan."

The Missouri Comprehensive Guidance Program Model (MCGP)

The most extensive framework for evaluating comprehensive school guidance programs was developed in Missouri, based on work starting in the 1970s and 1980s (Gysbers, Hughey, Starr, & Lapan, 1992). The current program model was developed as a process to help districts throughout the state plan, develop, implement, and evaluate their K–12 comprehensive guidance programs. The MCGP model is a framework for the evaluation of the program, the personnel, and the program results. Gysbers and Henderson (1988) earlier identified five steps involved in assessing a current guidance program. These five steps are summarized below:

> *Step 1: Identify Current Resource Availability and Use.* Gathering concrete information about the available resources is essential to making any program decisions. The resources identified are human, financial, and political. They note that the most critical human resources data gathered are the recording of counselors' actual program-related behaviors, because the counselors are the basic program resource.
>
> *Step 2: Identify Current Guidance and Counseling Activities.* A major task in assessing the current program is identifying and recording the activities of the guidance staff. Recording these activities insures preciseness and also creates more visibility for the counselors.
>
> *Step 3: Determine Student Outcomes.* This task identifies the student outcomes for each activity that is undertaken. This is in response to questions such as "Why do we do this? How are students different as a result of this activity?" Another part of this assessment is gathering information about what students know, learn, and need.
>
> *Step 4: Identify Who Is Served.* In this step, the assessment defines who is actually being served by the guidance program, including the level of service they receive. The number and percentage of students achieving a particular outcome and how this outcome was achieved are identified for each activity or group of activities.
>
> *Step 5: Gather Perceptions.* The last step is to gather perceptions about the current program from students, teachers, counselors, administrators, parents, and community

members. The data gathered helps to identify supportive people who may be used as resources. (Gysbers & Henderson, 1988, pp. 91–112)

Once the data have been summarized and disseminated, the persons involved should analyze the results and establish program priorities. In this process a determination can be made in answer to the question, "How does what we are doing now compare and contrast with what is desired from our program?" (1988, p. 117). The establishment of priorities insures that the tasks identified as most critical will be addressed first.

ASCA's Professional Development Guidelines for Elementary School Counselors

The elementary school counselor guidelines were written to correspond to a previously developed secondary school self-audit in style and format. They are intended to be viewed as a description of an ideal program at the elementary school level, and are to be used as a self-evaluation rather than in a team or school approach. The manual is divided into five interrelated sections. The sections can be used individually or the manual can be used as a whole in the self-evaluation process. The five sections are outlined below:

Section I: Philosophy and Policies of the Counseling Program

Section II: Program Development and Implementation

Section III: Role and Function of the Elementary School Counselor

    A. General Role and Function
    B. Individual and Group Counseling
    C. Classroom Guidance
    D. Peer Facilitation
    E. Consultation
    F. Coordination
    G. Referrals
    H. Assessment

Section IV: Specialized Populations in Counseling

Section V: Professional Development (American School Counselor Association, 1990b, p. v)

There are basic principles in each section, and each of these principles has a series of questions. The questions have five response options, from "always" to "never." Each section also has space for the elementary school counselor to identify areas that need change and the plans for implementing these changes. An example of the questions listed under Section I, Philosophy, would be, "Does the philosophy clearly define the role of the guidance/counseling program in the school?" (p. 1). An example of a question listed under Section II, Program Development, is, "Do you survey students, teachers, and administrators on a regular basis to determine program needs?" (p. 5). The manual has a list of books, pamphlets, and agencies that can be used as resources for individual reference or for in-service workshops.

Accountability Study for Developmental Guidance and Counseling

Robert Myrick has long emphasized developmental guidance and counseling programs in the schools and, along with this emphasis, has viewed accountability as a matter of being responsible to oneself and to others (Myrick, 1993). Myrick noted three basic ways to look at accountability studies, all three in response to questions: (1) What are the needs to be met? (2) What is being done to meet these needs? (3) Is the counselor intervention making a difference? These three approaches to accountability studies are summarized below:

1. **What are the needs to be met?**
Questions that might be directed to students, teachers, parents, or administrators include "Who will receive guidance and counseling and what are their problems? What special interests and needs do they have?" A needs assessment, conducted either formally or informally as a survey, will provide valuable information that will enable the counselor and others to answer these questions.

A brief needs assessment, usually no more than one page, can be put together more quickly and tallied in less time than a lengthy instrument. Problem checklists administered in the classroom have been used effectively to define these needs.

2. **What is being done to meet those needs?**
Many counselors have trouble telling others what they do. Tallying the six basic interventions, suggested as counselor activities for a developmental guidance and counseling program, provides information for those desiring specific information on counselor interventions.

3. **Is the counselor intervention making a difference?**
Providing answers for only the first two questions will not help those that want to know whether counselors are making a positive difference. It is advisable to ask the students, parents, and teachers what they think. Although these data have certain limitations, if the recipients of the counseling services aren't satisfied, other conclusions about the guidance and counseling services are meaningless. (Myrick, 1993, pp. 323–328)

When these three questions are addressed and answered, an accountability study can be planned and carried out.

An "Action Plan"

A plan to evaluate guidance and counseling programs that the author has found successful for the past 20 years will be described in this section. The evaluation process consists of six steps, in logical order: (1) assessing needs, (2) setting priorities, (3) establishing goals, (4) developing objectives, (5) evaluation, and (6) analysis and follow-up. These six steps are expanded in the following section.

Step 1: Assessing Needs.   There are a variety of ways a needs assessment can be carried out; the following one was used successfully in 16 school districts in a southwestern state a number of years ago. It is just as appropriately used today. The state board of education was considering the funding of elementary school counseling programs at the same time as the state public school finance office was questioning the effectiveness of school counseling programs in general. The state director of guidance services formed a statewide advisory council to address this issue. The advisory council consisted of a state board of education member; a school district superintendent; an elementary, junior high, and high school principal; an elementary, junior high, and high school teacher; an elementary, junior high, and high school counselor; the president of the state counselor association; the chair of the University Counseling Department; and the director of guidance services. The group met together over a period of one year establishing the guidelines for carrying out the evaluation process. A major task was constructing questionnaires for the students and teachers that would be used as a basis for establishing the need for counseling at all three levels.

There were very few counselors at the elementary level in the smaller school districts, necessitating two different questionnaires for this level: one for elementary schools without a counselor (Figure 11–1) and one for elementary schools with a counselor (Figure 11–2).

The advisory council recommended using the elementary level questionnaires only in grades four through six, reading the questions to the children as they filled them out; this

FIGURE 11–1   Student Reaction in School without a Counselor

Student Reaction to Guidance/Counseling Program
ELEMENTARY LEVEL (NO COUNSELOR)

Please mark an "X" in the boxes that apply to you:

	YES	NO	NOT SURE	SOME-TIMES
1. Is there someone in your school that you can talk to if you have a problem?				
2. Can you talk to this person when you want to?				
3. Have you ever talked to this person about something that bothered you?				
4. Would you feel free to talk to this person if you had a personal problem?				
5. Would you like to have someone help you know more about yourself?				
6. Would you like to have someone help you find out how to take tests and explain to you how you did on the tests?				
7. Do you need someone to help you when you are scared, being teased, or are pushed around?				
8. Has your principal or teacher ever talked to your parents?				
9. Would you like to have someone come to your classroom and talk about making friends and understanding others?				
10. Would you like to know the different kinds of work people do to help you decide what you can be when you grow up?				

FIGURE 11–2   Student Reaction in School with a Counselor

Student Reaction to Guidance/Counseling Program
ELEMENTARY LEVEL

Please mark an "X" in the boxes that apply to you:

	YES	NO	NOT SURE	SOME-TIMES
1. Do you know who your counselor is?				
2. Do you know what the counselor does at school?				
3. Have you ever talked to the counselor?				
4. Can you see your counselor when you want to?				
5. Does the teacher send you or your classmates to see the counselor?				
6. Would you feel free to talk to the counselor if you had a personal problem?				
7. Would you like to have the counselor help you know more about yourself?				
8. Would you like to have the counselor help you find out how to take tests and explain to you how you did on the tests?				
9. Does the counselor and the teacher work together to try to help you?				
10. Do you have someone to help you when you are scared, being teased, or pushed around?				
11. Do you know that the counselor is there to help you at all times?				
12. Can you talk about your real feelings about things with your counselor?				
13. Has the counselor ever talked to your parents?				
14. Would you like to have the counselor come to your classroom and talk about making friends and understanding others?				
15. Would you like to know the different kinds of work people do to help you decide what you can be when you grow up?				

would eliminate the problem of some children not understanding the questions or having difficulty reading some of the words. The teacher inventory was given to all of the teachers to fill out at their convenience, and a box in the office in each school was designated for returning the questionnaires (Figure 11–3).

Step 2: Setting Priorities.   The needs identified by the students and teachers in the questionnaires are used to establish priorities. The data contained in the analysis of the questionnaires serve as descriptions of the existing counseling program, enabling the elementary school counselor and the school's advisory council to make comparisons. Comparing the desired program with the existing program highlights the changes to be made in the counseling services.

Step 3: Establishing Goals.   The next step is to establish the goals for the counseling program. The needs identified in the questionnaires are translated into specific, measurable goals. These goals provide the base from which outcome-stated objectives for the counseling program are developed. This allows those involved in the process to assess, at a later date, whether or not these goals were reached.

FIGURE 11–3   Teacher Inventory of Guidance/Counseling Services

We would like to obtain an indication of your awareness of the Guidance and Counseling Services in your school and the extent to which you believe they are adequate. This information should be useful in improving these services to students when indicated. Please be frank in your appraisal.

DIRECTIONS: To the right of each question mark an "X" to indicate whether or not the activity is carried out in your school.	Part of your school program?		
	YES	NO	NOT SURE
1. Is an organized program of guidance available to all students?			
2. Have guidance services been provided to orient new students to the school?			
3. Do you discuss with the students the career/vocational areas in the subjects you are studying?.............................			
4. Have you participated with the counselor and other teachers in case conferences concerning students?			
5. Does the staff plan cooperatively the evaluation of the achievement of students in relation to their potential?			
6. Does the counselor explain students' standardized ability and achievement test results to the teachers?			
7. Does the counselor help teachers to understand their students?			
8. Does the counselor help the teacher use and understand student records?...			
9. Do the students feel free to go to the counselor to discuss school and/or personal problems?.............................			
10. Does the student's behavior tend to improve as a result of counseling experiences?			
11. Has the counselor worked with you in classroom guidance activities?			
12. Would you like to have the counselor work with you in your classroom on developmental guidance experiences?			
13. Do you refer students to the counselor?.....................			
14. Do you seek help from the counselor in your study of and attempt to help your students?			

Step 4: Developing Objectives.   Objectives should be defined in behavioral terms with a description of how they will be achieved and in what time frame. A large district with over 100 elementary schools, each with a full-time counselor, used a writing team consisting of six elementary school counselors and a district office guidance and counseling coordinator to establish the model for the districts's K–6 guidance/counseling program. The program identified three areas of student development using the following terms: (1) educational domain, (2) social domain, and (3) life planning/career domain. The three domains were each addressed in four dimensions: (1) self and others, (2) feelings and emotions, (3) values and attitudes, and (4) coping strategies and behavior (Albuquerque Public Schools, 1982). Figure 11–4 illustrates one domain, the educational domain, with goals and their objectives addressed in each dimension for grades K–5, as an example of elementary counseling goals and objectives.

Step 5: Evaluation.   Evaluation is a critical step needed to measure whether or not the objectives were met, and to what extent. Evaluation of the program itself, including the progress of individual students, is obtained by assessment of the attainment of the goals

FIGURE 11–4   Goals and Objectives in the Educational Domain

Goal A **Self/Others**	*Goal B* **Feelings and Emotions**
Students will develop an accurate perception of themselves and others as learners in the educational setting.	Students will demonstrate a growing ability to understand the importance of their feelings in the educational experiences.

Objective 1: K–5
    Students will develop a functional awareness of ways people are alike and different.
Outcomes
K: Students will be able to describe themselves.
1st: Students will be able to describe other people and how they differ from themselves.
2nd: Students will be able to relate things they are accomplishing.
3rd: Students will be able to share things they can do now that they could not do before.
4th: Students will be able to describe important events that affect themselves and others in the learning process.
5th: Students will be able to identify those skills helpful in the learning process.
	Objective 1: K–5
	    Students will become aware of the positive feelings related to the process of learning.
	Outcomes
	K: Students will be able to describe things they learned at school.
	1st: Students will be able to tell how things they learned at school help them at home.
	2nd: Students will be able to tell why learning is important.
	3rd: Students will become aware of the feeling of being proud and relate things that make them feel proud.
	4th: Students will begin to describe things that will make them want to learn.
	5th: Students will begin to identify how feelings of accomplishment develop.

Goal C **Values and Attitudes**	*Goal D* **Coping Strategies and Behaviors**
Students will develop values and make decisions and plans that are consistent with their interests and abilities.	Students will develop and incorporate skills that lead to becoming effective learners.

Objective 1: K–5
    Students will become aware that others may have different ideas.
Outcomes
K: Students will be able to describe things they learn with their friends.
1st: Students will be able to relate things they would like to learn with friends.
2nd: Students will be able to recognize that a variety of learning environments can be productive.
3rd: Students will be able to describe the concept of disagreement and how it affects peer relationships.
4th: The student will begin to show the ability to listen to others' ideas without accepting or rejecting them.
5th: The student will begin to demonstrate the expression of independent views in an acceptable fashion.
	Objective 1: K–5
	    Students will be aware of appropriate behaviors in the educational setting.
	Outcomes
	K: Students will be able to relate directions they are asked to follow.
	1st: Students will begin to understand the importance of task completion.
	2nd: Students will begin to demonstrate a realization of the necessity for rules.
	3rd: Students will demonstrate the use of communication skills.
	4th: Students will realize that people obtain rewards for accomplishment.
	5th: Students recognize the relationship between their skills and goal achievement.

and objectives. Using an objectives-based assessment process enables the counseling program to be reviewed on an annual basis in order to ascertain the effectiveness of the program in meeting the needs of the children in the school.

Step 6: Analysis and Follow-Up   At this point the elementary counselor and the advisory council meet to discuss the results of the total evaluation process. The areas of need are identified as well as the areas where the effectiveness of the program has been established. Any concerns will be noted for follow-up activities and subsequent meetings. (Holmgren, 1976)

This evaluation process, like many others that have been used to evaluate school counseling programs, is a result of the input of a number of dedicated educational professionals. Fortunately, evaluation of school counseling programs is an area that has long been identified as a need—this has allowed for a proliferation of good instruments and methods of carrying out this process. An elementary school counselor truly desiring to establish accountability in his or her school counseling program will find a number of studies available for use.

Additional Accountability Programs

Another program that includes an evaluation self-study is *Walking the Talk,* a workbook designed to assist in the development of a local comprehensive school counseling program (Trotter, 1992). The evaluation aspect of the program is administered at the beginning of the program development to insure that it is responsive to the consumers of the counseling services. As a part of this, a time and task analysis is used to describe how the counselor's time is spent across the work week in 30-minute intervals. The appendices include a "Sample Program Evaluation Self-Study" form that incorporates (1) a description of the school, community, and counseling program; (2) the structural components: program philosophy and planning; (3) counseling curriculum; (4) individual student planning; (5) responsive services; (6) system support; and (7) summary of counseling program self-study (Trotter, 1992, pp. 88–95). Another area of interest in building or improving an elementary school counseling program is the list of competencies by grade level in three areas: (1) personal/social goals; (2) educational goals; and (3) career goals (pp. 96–102).

Fairchild (1993) indicated the need for courses, workshops, and self-study materials to be made available for school counselors to increase their accountability efforts; these could be offered through professional organizations and university training programs. His specific suggestions for providing this assistance included supplying information in the following areas:

- Methods for developing questionnaires for collecting accountability data
- Specific methods for obtaining information, especially for obtaining process and outcome information
- A comprehensive list of sample instruments and procedures
- Methods for analyzing the data, synthesizing the information, and reporting the findings in an understandable way to different consumer groups
- Comprehensive, time-efficient accountability systems and models
- Exemplary models that are currently being used in the field
- Computer-assisted accountability programs (Fairchild, 1993, p. 373)

In two national surveys of school counselors information was solicited regarding their accountability efforts. One of the most frequently identified barriers to collecting accountability information was the significant time involvement. Fairchild believed this barrier could be eliminated by providing counselors with an efficient model with numerous examples of forms and questionnaires, and a good computer software program for analyzing the results.

An integral part of being accountable is the responsibility of knowing the ethical and legal standards that govern the elementary school counselor and the school counseling program. The next section will address these issues from the perspective of the elementary school counseling program.

Ethical Standards and Counselors

Whenever elementary school counselors are involved in counseling relationships with students, they must be knowledgeable about the ethical guidelines and legal parameters that govern this relationship. The ASCA Ethical Standards for School Counselors were revised in 1992. The November 1992 issue of *The School Counselor* published the revised standards and also an excellent article by Wayne Huey discussing the revision and the reasoning behind the changes (Huey, 1992). This article should be required reading for all perspective and practicing counselors. Huey's discussion of the changes and how they came about places the ethical standards in a less intimidating form.

The new areas addressed by the revised ethical standards are computer technology, dual relationships, group counseling, peer programs, family changes, client differences, and the sharing of professional expertise.

The Ethical Standards for School Counselors document includes the following sections, summarized below:

Preamble

The preamble addresses the basic tenets of the counseling process and its corresponding responsibilities. The preamble also defines the purpose of the ethical standards. (See Appendix B for the complete standards.)

A. *Responsibilities to students.* Fifteen counselor responsibilities to students are identified, covering all areas of school counselor responsibility, such as the counselor's primary responsibility to the student, making appropriate referrals, and protecting the confidentiality of student records.

B. *Responsibilities to parents.* There are seven areas of responsibility to parents, such as respecting their inherent rights and responsibilities, confidentiality regarding parent information, and informing parent of the counselor's role.

C. *Responsibilities to colleagues and professional associates.* There are five areas of responsibility to colleagues, such as establishing and maintaining cooperative relationships with the professional staff, and treating colleagues with respect.

D. *Responsibilities to the school and community.* There are five areas of responsibility to the school and community, such as supporting the educational program, and appropriate reporting of inappropriate conduct.

E. *Responsibilities to self.* There are five areas of responsibility to self, such as staying within appropriate boundaries of professional competence, and keeping abreast of trends in the profession.

F. *Responsibilities to the profession.* There are six areas of responsibility to the profession, such as conducting self in a professional manner, and contributing to the development of the profession.

G. *Maintenance of standards.* Counselors are obligated to take appropriate action when colleagues are not demonstrating ethical behavior or when forced to work in a situation that does not uphold the ethical standards as indicated.

H. *Resources.* A list of professional documents that counselors should be aware of and act in accordance with is provided.

All elementary counselors should make it a priority to familiarize themselves with the complete ethical standards reprinted in the appendices. They are too extensive and too significant to attempt to summarize in this chapter; it is the responsibility of the counselor to know these standards and how they apply in their particular setting. Huey (1992) states this succinctly: "The 1992 *Ethical Standards for School Counselors* is designed to be a concise, practical document which is an outgrowth and reflection of changes in society and the profession of school counseling. It represents a good beginning point for the practice of ethical behavior" (p. 92).

An excellent text on the ethical and legal issues relative to school counseling, edited by Wayne Huey and Theodore Remley, Jr., was published by the ASCA in 1988. Both professionals were aware of school counselor concerns regarding ethical dilemmas: Huey had served as chair of the ASCA Ethics Committee and Remley as a practicing attorney. The primary intent of their book was to provide a resource for practicing school counselors, although it can be used in counselor education courses and by others involved in the schools needing information on ethical and legal issues in school counseling. The first chapter in the text, by Huey, has a section called "Ethical Standards for School Counselors: Test Your Knowledge." Twenty-five cases have been selected that refer to specific standards; the respondent is to put an *A* if he or she agrees with the resolution, or a *D* if he or she disagrees. At the end of each case, the specific ethical standard is indicated. Correct answers are given at the conclusion, with a score interpretation by number of correct answers. The author has used all of these at various times in counselor training classes when the Ethical Standards document is discussed. They provide an excellent vehicle for discussion, with a definite increase in student awareness of how the ethical standards apply. Counselors also need to be aware that their own personal values, beliefs, and attitudes greatly affect their interpretation of the standards (Huey, 1988).

Remley (1988) differentiated between *law* and *ethics,* enabling the reader to fully understand them. There are a number of ethical and legal issues that relate to elementary school counseling; three of these are analyzed in his article: (1) confidentiality and privileged communication, (2) the counselor as a witness in court proceedings, and (3) counselor malpractice. In discussing guidelines for confidentiality responsibilities to children, he suggested that counselors take the following steps:

1. Always inform the child before another person is consulted regarding the child's problem. The child's consent is desirable but not always necessary.

2. Try to involve the child in the decision-making process once adults are contacted. Avoid taking actions that may create for the child a feeling of betrayal by the counselor or other involved adults.

3. Keep the child informed of decisions as they are made. (Remley, 1988, p. 97)

Privileged communication exists between the elementary school counselor and the child as a client in a number of states, unless state statute dictates otherwise. It is important for the elementary counselor to find out what the ruling is in his or her state. The counselor that practices the professional ethics established by ASCA will have little difficulty or worry regarding liability.

Ferris and Linville (1988) address the changing roles of counselors in discussing the child's rights in counseling. As an example, the relationship of the ethical standards to the elementary counselor's current emphasis on consultation with teachers, parents, and administrators is questioned; their question is whether or not a client's right to their privacy and confidentiality is being compromised in a consulting relationship, according to the ethical standards. Some of the other ethical dilemmas that might be faced by a school counselor, according to Ferris and Linville, are in the areas of reporting child abuse, the reporting of test scores, and informal communications. They stress the need for counselors to develop the skills to help them appropriately analyze specific situations with ethical integrity. In conjunction with the ethical standards, the elementary counselor should also be knowledgeable regarding confidentiality. The American School Counselor Association position paper, "The School Counselor and Confidentiality," can be found in Appendix O.

Legal Issues in Counseling

A very readable book covering the laws governing schools, students, and teachers should be at the fingertips of every elementary counselor, particularly because the school's ability to control student behavior seems to be increasingly limited. One such book that interprets various issues in a highly understandable way discusses school attendance; a student's right to an education and procedural due process; freedom of speech and expression; search of students and seizure of their property; student discipline and the school standing in loco parentis; education of the handicapped; sex discrimination; student records, which includes their defamation and privacy; and student testing (Alexander & Alexander, 1984).

Another book on school law includes psychologists and social workers in addition to school counselors (Fischer & Sorenson, 1991). The book is intended for laypersons without prior knowledge of the law; because of this, the material is presented in a highly understandable way in order to make counselors aware of the legal processes in their work environment. Some of the topics discussed include confidentiality and the duty to warn, civil and criminal liability, student's right to privacy and education records, legal issues regarding the testing and grouping of students, students with special education needs, behavior control and student discipline, child abuse and neglect, and the rights of students. A variety of school counselor rights such as "May counselors be dismissed for belonging to controversial organizations?" and "May schools require pregnant counselors to take a specified leave of absence?" are discussed (Fischer & Sorenson, 1991, p. xvii). The relationship of the U.S. court systems to educational controversies is explained, and the state court system is identified as the place where most school cases are litigated.

Another area where elementary counselors might be involved in legal issues is being asked to give testimony as an expert witness. Remley notes that "unless counselors are very secure in their knowledge of these areas, they probably should decline requests to appear as expert witnesses" (Remley, 1988). He draws attention to the fact that a counselor's credentials may be questioned, including coursework that qualifies the counselor to be considered an "expert." The opposing attorney will often bring in a more qualified witness than the counselor, because there are many professionals with appropriate educational and professional expertise that could be called upon to testify.

An elementary school counselor is not expected to be knowledgeable about all of the relevant rules and regulations governing the schools and their students. What is expected is a working knowledge of the legal issues that are basic to their position as a counselor in an elementary school. In addition, the legal processes that govern and control the school and the rights of all of those involved in the school should be understood by the counselor. The laws and regulations are always subject to change making it necessary for the counselor to stay abreast of these changes by involvement in a professional association. The national American Counseling Association (ACA) convention usually has a presentation on law and ethics related to school counseling; this is invaluable as a means of keeping informed.

Summary

The rational evaluation of counseling programs should be of paramount concern to all elementary school counselors. Evaluation is an integral part of all elementary counseling programs that want to insure that the programs are meeting the needs identified in their schools. We are in the age of accountability—reasonable evidence is needed to prove that elementary school counseling is not a luxury but a necessity, meeting the needs of students, teachers, and parents. Being accountable includes knowing the ethical and legal standards applicable to the elementary school counseling program. All states have laws established for the protection of students; usually these laws also govern the activities of counselors in the state. Typically the certification or licensing laws provide the minimum standards by which the professional standards may be enforced. It is the responsibility of the elementary school counselor to be aware of the laws that directly govern school counselors in his or her state. Elementary school counselors who familiarize themselves with the ASCA Ethical Standards for School Counselors and the laws of their state regarding the legal status of children, confidentiality guidelines, and privileged communication will assure themselves of making informed decisions regarding the children in their care.

Chapter *12*

Where Do We Go from Here?

Introduction

The type of school counseling typically carried out by many "old-timers" is no longer effective, particularly at the secondary school level. We cannot try to solve the problems of today with the methods of counseling that were acceptable 15 or 20 years ago. There is often a complete mismatch between what is recommended for school counselors and the reality of the school counseling position. Because of this, many school districts are questioning the need for school counselors. Nowhere is this more evident than in California, where, since the mid-1980s, a significant number of school districts have eliminated or drastically cut back high school counseling services. This is a frightening occurrence in a state that in 1991 had approximately 12 percent of all the schoolchildren in the United States, involving a large number of counselors (G. Fulton, personal communication, July 1991). How did this happen? A variety of reasons have been given but the recurring theme reflects two areas of concern: (1) districts believed the needs of their constituents were not being met, and (2) there was a lack of awareness of what counselors actually do. Michael Kirst, a Stanford University professor of education, works with a large number of school superintendents. He discussed the decline in secondary school counseling, challenging California counselors and counselor educators alike: "You need a better state presence and organization and appeal to state legislators so that they have more awareness of what is going on. You need a better political and lobbying organization" (Kirst, conference speech, 1988).

A guest editorial by a New York high school counselor appeared in ACA's *Guidepost* in 1993, sounding a warning to school counselors in response to the American School Counseling Association (ASCA) advisory board's "Counseling 2000" initiatives. The counselor acknowledged the initiatives as praiseworthy but expressed doubt as to their impact at the school level. He asked two questions: "Are school counselors aware?" and

"How long will it take for them to understand that school counseling must change its focus and thrust? This is especially true at the secondary level, where change is needed, especially for secondary counselors" (Despres, 1993, p. 20). Depres faulted secondary school counselors for too easily accepting stereotypic roles of schedule changers, clerical quasi-administrators, and advisors for the college bound: "Many of us have become comfortable in these roles, giving up all creativity in our counseling and not reaching out to new opportunities" (p. 20).

A superintendent recently solicited help from the author for restructuring his school district's guidance and counseling program; the district does not have elementary school counselors in any of the elementary schools. He recognized that the need for elementary counseling services was urgent but at the same time stated that with the state's current budget crisis, he could not expand his counseling services at this time. He had held monthly meetings with his secondary school counselors throughout the previous year but could not convince them that their type of counseling, the type described by Despres in the previous paragraph, was no longer effective. He was soliciting the author's help and input to expand his counselors' current role to include the elementary school level, believing he could hire "much cheaper" help to handle schedule changes and other clerical-type tasks that occupied so much of his secondary school counselors' time. He was also concerned that his teachers were questioning the need for counseling at the secondary school level. The idea of adding elementary counseling services was excellent; the thought of "retraining" his current counselors to become proactive elementary school counselors able to handle the myriad demands and responsibilities of an elementary school counselor, as defined in this text, is not a good idea. Counselors so set in their ways that they have been unwilling to change, unwilling to become involved in state and national professional counseling organizations, and unwilling to take courses or attend workshops to update their skills, are not what the elementary counseling profession needs. Secondary school counselors frustrated with their current situation, desiring to get more involved with parents and teachers in a consultation role, counselors able to recognize the systems approach—that the school and the family and the community are all systems that interact with and impact each other—these counselors would be both a joy and a challenge to retrain as elementary counselors.

Elementary school counseling represents a significant opportunity and hope for our young people, the ultimate future of our society, as we move into the 21st century. We need to keep in mind the complacency of secondary school counseling programs of just a few years ago and make sure we have taken to heart the lessons to be learned from this in order to avoid making the same mistakes at the elementary level. A large number of today's youngsters entering our elementary schools come from homes that are barely coping, with parents leading such fragmented lives that they are unable to provide for their children's emotional and psychological needs. Children are simply not a priority in many homes, as parents are too busy searching for ways to meet their own needs and gain personal fulfillment. The problems and stressors that children bring with them to our elementary schools today were unheard of not too many years ago. The problems that were of paramount concern in the high schools a decade or two ago have surfaced in today's elementary schools.

In order to respond to the question, "Where do we go from here?" we need to look at several key areas: (1) enhancing the public image of the elementary school counselor, (2) establishing an effective advisory council, (3) selecting and training elementary counselors, (4) addressing future needs of an elementary school counseling program, and

(5) recommendations for "getting there from here." The remainder of the chapter will look at ways to address these issues and accomplish the tasks, creating a map to guide us in the process.

Enhancing the Public Image of the Elementary School Counselor

Rosalie Humphrey, as ASCA president-elect, challenged counselors to be advocates for school counseling: "It is 'the others,' the non-counselors, to whom we need to talk, to educate them of who we are, what we do, how we do it, where we do it and when we do it!" (1992, p. 15). She further challenged counselors with the following statement: "We can no longer afford to sit by and observe the system collapse onto itself, killing our profession, while we use our time and talents, our expertise and training to apply insufficient, inappropriate bandaid measures to the bleeding populace at our office doors" (p. 15). She challenged counselors to become leaders in the educational reform movement rather than be content with status quo.

The school reform and restructuring movement appears to be here to stay. The educational reform movement began to reemerge in the early 1990s in response to a national concern for changes in our schools. Out of frustration and impotence the public at large appears to hold the schools responsible for many of the shortcomings of children. Chapter 11 discussed the accountability of counseling programs, including ways to respond to criticism and establish accountability. The intent of this section is to describe avenues to market an elementary counseling program and to identify some ways of developing good public relations in the schools and community.

One of the states that addressed a court-ordered mandated educational reform was Kentucky. Although elementary school counseling was not mandated by the Kentucky Education Reform Act, it was left up to the local districts to choose what they wanted in order to insure their schools' success; this put the state in a position to market elementary school counseling programs (Holcomb & Niffenegger, 1992). In the process of the decision making, the burden fell on the local site-based management teams to define what *successful* meant for their schools. Holcomb and Niffenegger emphasized the need for marketing strategies in order to identify the tangible qualities of the program because counseling involves so many intangible elements. The Kentucky Education Reform Act outlined a number of reform goals that were to be accomplished; these demanded a child-centered approach that fit with a comprehensive developmental elementary counseling program. They tied the educational reform goals with the services that elementary counselors can provide to accomplish these goals and backed it all up with research references of effective elementary school counseling practices. This gave their proposal for elementary school counseling services for every school child in Kentucky a sense of direction and confidence as well as a means of accountability.

If the marketing plan of action that was successfully used in Kentucky is to be equally successful in any other locality, the plan must be able to accomplish the following tasks for maximum effectiveness:

   a. Know the specific school's unique needs,
   b. Link the unique needs of a school to what research says counselors can accomplish and tie this back into education reform goals,

   c. Know the target population networking and support systems,

   d. Devise a functional marketing campaign stressing the unique benefits of elementary counseling and the most effective media strategies,

   e. Make a commitment to work this plan aggressively, and

   f. Evaluate the effectiveness by the total number of schools whose site-based management team chooses the services of elementary counselors. (Holcomb & Niffenegger, 1992, p. 62)

School reform viewed from this perspective is reframed into a real opportunity to gain the services of elementary school counselors. Elementary school counselors should view this marketing plan of action as an opportunity to reevaluate their current programs as well as to develop new programs.

Mary Jo Hannaford, as ASCA public relations chairperson, encouraged us to look at just who our "publics" are in building public relations (1988). She viewed our publics as the parents, teachers, administrators, and the students, all reaching out for assistance. At the same time as they are looking for help, Hannaford noted that much of our public isn't aware of the training of school counselors and their focus on the developmental and preventive areas. She challenged counselors to be educators, educating legislators, school boards, private agencies, churches, and community organizations using the following strategies:

- Regular articles in school newspapers
- Special communication letters
- Presentations to club meetings and the community
- Special presentations at district or local meetings
- Write letters to local newspapers and magazines (Hannaford, 1988, p. 4)

This kind of public relations would put elementary counseling in the forefront of public education, helping others to know the valuable services performed by elementary school counselors on a daily basis.

Establishing an Effective Advisory Council

One of the best sources of good public relations is an advisory council; it functions in an advisory capacity and is invaluable as an advocate for the elementary school counseling program. The advisory council in an elementary school ideally has a membership that includes two or more teachers and parents, a student from fifth or sixth grade, a school board member, a member from the community, the school nurse, and the counselor. Whether or not to include the principal depends upon the principal and the group—sometimes parents and students will defer questions or responses to the principal, which could effectively hinder the process and intent of the advisory council. The advisory council should not consist of all "yes" people—sometimes an "agitator" is the best advocate of the program when he or she has a chance to be heard and be involved in the decision-making process. It is important to have at least one parent and one teacher that have some informal power with other teachers and parents in order to get the message out where it can be heard.

Advisory Council Strategies

Conducting a Needs Assessment   One of the most important tasks for the advisory council is to make plans to set up and carry out a counseling needs assessment. The unique needs of the particular school should be considered in developing the assessment instruments or revising one of the instruments discussed in Chapter 11. If, for example, there are a large number of single parents in the school, the counseling program may need to concentrate on providing these parents with some basic parenting skills and ways to handle their task as a single parent. The children may also need some help because of the added responsibilities in caring for a sibling or being alone for extended periods of time.

The advisory council needs to be responsive to the needs in their school, helping the counselor design the program around the identified needs. Jackie Allen, as ASCA president-elect, spoke of the challenges ahead for counselors: "making the paradigm shift in the role of school counselor in order to create effective counseling programs and services to meet student needs and to develop a viable professional role which will be perceived by school counselor publics as effective, an essential part of the school curriculum, and an invaluable element in the preparation of students for the 21st century" (Allen, 1993, p. 8).

Responding to Guidance Program Challenges   Another area where an advisory council will prove extremely valuable is in response to the recent movement to challenge developmental guidance materials and programs, particularly at the elementary school level. Since the early 1990s, challenges and attacks on school counselors' use of developmental guidance materials in their counseling programs have increased. Challenges are occurring all over the country, but "California, Oregon, Florida, and Texas lead the list" (McCullough, 1993. p. 1). McCullough wrote a three-part series, appearing in *Guidepost* in December 1993, January 1994, and February 1994 on the challenges to guidance programs and how to handle them or prevent them from occurring. An example of the extreme result of a counseling program being challenged was discussed in the first article of the series. A newly graduated K–8 counselor was hired in a small community in Montana. She made the development of self-esteem a primary goal of the counseling program in the school district where she was hired as a full-time counselor and teacher. She also conducted groups on peer relations and divorce. All the students were referred by their teachers, and the counselor sent letters to the parents informing them of the individual and small group work she was doing. The counselor used DUSO (published in 1971 and discussed in Chapter 9) and *100 Ways to Build Self Esteem in the Classroom* (published in 1976 and discussed in Chapter 4) as part of her structured materials. Parents began to voice some objections to the counseling program; although the counselor and principal met with parents and addressed their concerns, the objections to the use of these materials continued to escalate. It eventually culminated in the following action: "At a May 1991 school board meeting the new chairman of the board banned DUSO and *100 Ways to Build Self Esteem* and canceled the school counseling program" (McCullough, 1993, p. 12). These structured programs have been in use for a long time and, along with several others, have only recently come under attack. Citing these materials as a means of eliminating a school counseling program has some frightening ramifications. Elementary counselors need to be aware of the challenges and be prepared by being proactive rather than reactive.

Peterson and Poppen (1993) wrote an excellent monograph, *School Counselors and the First Freedom,* as a guide for responding to the challenges to developmental guidance materials and developmental counseling programs. They developed a 16-item checklist to help counselors and other school personnel make sure that the programs they are using have a sound educational basis. The monograph elaborates on the following checklist of actions to prevent problems:

1. Base developmental guidance programs on sound educational practices appropriate for the age and maturity level of students.
2. Relate developmental guidance goals and activities to district and state educational goals.
3. Obtain copies of district goals, state goals, state legislation, and district policy statements/actions relative to developmental guidance.
4. Obtain written parental consent for any practices for which federal law or district action requires permission.
5. Prepare a formal statement on policies for selecting print and non print guidance materials.
6. Ask the board of education to act formally on materials selection and materials reconsideration policies and procedures.
7. Ask Board of Education to act formally on "opting out" policies and procedures.
8. Obtain assurance from Board of Education that policies and procedures will be followed should a challenge occur.
9. Use advisory committees and other school and community groups to gain and maintain support for the guidance program.
10. Have in mind eight to ten individuals who can form a support team should a challenge occur.
11. Know the names, addresses, and telephone numbers of associations that will help should censorship issues and challenges arise.
12. Read "The School Counselor and Censorship," the position statement of the American School Counselor Association.
13. Stay informed about court cases that deal with challenges to school materials and programs.
14. Know the provisions of the Hatch Amendment and recognize that the Hatch Amendment applies only to federally funded programs.
15. Stay informed about the arguments, terminology, and tactics used by challengers.
16. Let people know about what is right with the guidance program. (Peterson & Poppen, 1993, p. 53)

The above referred Hatch Amendment was thoroughly spelled out and discussed in a two-part series in *The School Counselor* in the September 1987 and November 1987 issues (Kaplan & Geoffroy, 1987). Anyone desiring to familiarize themselves with the Hatch Amendment, also known as the Protection of Pupil Rights Amendment, should familiarize themselves with these articles. The complete ASCA position paper, "The School Counselor and Censorship," is in Appendix P.

An advisory council should be involved in reviewing all materials that the counselor intends to use in structured small group and classroom guidance activities. If the elementary counselor conducts several actual sessions for the advisory council, in advance of using these activities in the classrooms and in small groups, the council will be able to respond in an informed manner to school administrators, parents, and the school board when and if questions arise. The ideal plan would be to have a policy in place regarding the materials used in the counseling program rather than wait for challenges to occur. If the advisory council sends out a newsletter twice each semester to all of the parents describing the counseling and guidance program, listing the schedule of parent education groups, and informing them of various activities that will be going on with their children via a calendar of events, this will do a lot to allay some of the misunderstandings and concerns of parents regarding what is happening in the elementary school counseling program.

The guide developed by Peterson and Poppen is designed as a training guide to be used for training school counselors as well as for counselor presentations to school board members, administrators, and community groups. The guide contains the following materials:

Section I: The Right to Challenge and the Right to Respond

        Activity 1: Lecture

        Activity 2: Discussion Questions

Section II: The Challengers and the Challenged

        Activity 3: Lecture—Challenges to Guidance Materials and Programs

        Activity 4: Learning from Author and Publisher Responses

Section III: Professional Actions by Professional Counselors

        Activity 5: Lecture—Before a Challenge Occurs

        Activity 6: Lecture—After a Challenge Occurs

        Activity 7: Responsible Actions—Three Cases Identified and Described

Section IV: Resources on Challenges and Censorship

This section includes statements by the following professional associations:

        American Association of School Administrators

        American School Counselor Association

        American Library Association

        Association for Supervision and Curriculum Development

        The National PTA (Peterson & Poppen, 1993, pp. v–vi)

A number of pages in the guide are intended to be used as transparencies by the counselor who would like to present the information in a lecture format; they are professionally done and help those who are visual learners to instantly "hear" what is being said.

Selecting and Training Elementary School Counselors

The selection and training of elementary counselors are critical dimensions of a successful elementary school counseling program. Some modifications are needed in a number of our counselor education programs if we are to have an impact on the children of the 21st century. The modifications start with the selection of the students that will become the elementary school counselors of tomorrow. Seeking out sensitive, eager, energetic, and enthusiastic individuals who are not too timid to question the established educational processes within which we operate, individuals with the courage of their convictions, could do wonders for the school counselor image when they are well trained. Students that are bold, that are willing to take some risks, that are willing to be proactive, not reactive, students that are willing to challenge the phrase "We've never done that before" or "We always do it this way," could become a shot in the arm for the school counseling profession. As the person previously charged with interviewing and hiring a number of school counselors in two states, the author valued these qualities and sought them out in counselor applicants. For the past ten years, charged with interviewing and admitting students into the MA school counseling track, these same qualities are now sought in the program candidates.

Hackney (1990) addressed the preparation of counselors for future needs in a monograph reflecting the changes needed for counselor preparation in the 1990s. He challenged the readers to consider what we would say counselors should do if school counseling were just emerging today as a new concept. He asked how we would respond to the following questions: "How would their role complement the roles of teacher and administrator? What functions would counselors perform with children, families, educators, employers?" (Hackney, 1990, p. 78). Hackney correctly perceived that speaking of redefining the role and function of the counseling profession is a menacing threat to many in the profession. To the author, these are thought-provoking questions that would benefit all of us if we "brainstormed" them in counselor education programs, at elementary school faculty and staff meetings, at professional meetings with colleagues, and at advisory council meetings.

Hackney's plea is clear as he makes his recommendations for changes in counselor preparation to meet future needs: "We cannot miss the call for a developmental orientation" (Hackney, 1990, p. 91). The emphasis in our counselor education programs should be on a developmental approach to counseling and guidance in our elementary schools.

The developmental approach must include a systems approach, as discussed in Chapter 10. The systems approach helps to identify each of the systems that impact the child: the home, the school, the classroom, the peer group, the larger community—all exert their influence on the child. A crisis in any of these subsystems usually affects some, or all, of the other systems. We cannot afford to look at the child or the family in isolation; using a systems approach will influence the intervention strategies used by the elementary counselor. The counselor may intervene at various levels using this approach, depending upon how they interpret the particular behaviors of the referred child. Cause and effect are interactive from a systems viewpoint; the counselor is not bound into the *why* of the child's behavior but goes beyond to see whether or not the family or school system is breaking down in some way for that child. An elementary counselor working within the framework of the systems approach to counseling will realize that all members in the system influence the others in various ways.

The College Entrance Examination Board published a report in 1986, *Keeping the Options Open: Recommendations;* this was the final report of the Commission on Precollege Guidance and Counseling (CEEB, 1986). All but one of the eight recommendations made by the commission have relevance to the topics in this book; one of the eight is particularly relevant to this chapter. Recommendation 8 stated the following: "Revise the training of school counselors to include the specific skills and knowledge necessary to enable them to take a more central role in schools" (p. 28). As a part of this they stress the need for counselors to be knowledgeable about the schools as institutions—the way that schools operate and the counselor's role within this structure. They surveyed all counselor education programs across the country and produced some disturbing findings: "Overall, the number of courses focusing on the school-based aspects of counseling has decreased; instead courses and internships reinforce general counseling skills applicable to a variety of different settings, including many outside of schools" (p. 28). They noted the fact that many counselor education programs have a clinical focus, which is not truly effective in the school setting. It is hoped that when this report was made public that counselor education programs took note and made the necessary changes where applicable.

In addition to the expanded school role recommended above, counselors should look beyond to the community level. Children live and grow up in communities, not just in their homes. A study from the Center for Collaboration for Children, "Community Report Cards: Making Kids Count" (California State University, Fullerton, 1992), noted that "it is the local efforts in those communities that often determine whether national and state policies are working to help children and their families" (p. 1). The report included recommendations for assembling a broad-based coalition to assure the success of reaching kids and their families. "What is needed is an assembly of children-serving agencies, advocates, non-profit groups, funders, parents, and a broad spectrum of community leaders" (p. 5). The gathering together of a group of interested persons to discuss what the community wants for its children should be of significant interest to the elementary counselor who works, and often lives, in the community where the elementary school is located. A community effort such as the one described ends the "Blame Game" and makes all involved with children accountable. The counselor training program needs to help counselors-in-training become aware of the broader scope of their services. Often the counselor is not helped to see past the door of the school to the homes and community beyond.

Some of the concerns and challenges discussed in this section may necessitate changes in some of our counselor preparation programs to insure that the elementary school counselors prepared today will be equipped to face the problems of both today's and tomorrow's children. As a major part of this, we need to train our elementary school counselors to actively define their role, or it will be defined for them by someone who may not understand the objectives of a developmental elementary school counseling program. Sheeley (1990), in looking beyond the first 50 years of the Association of Counselor Educators and Supervisors (ACES), encouraged counselor educators and supervisors to embrace, not shun, the marketplace. This relates back to the first two sections of this chapter: enhancing the public image of the elementary school counselor through marketing and public relations, and establishing an effective advisory council. The following section will examine the counselor role of the future.

Addressing Future Needs of an Elementary School Counseling Program

In 1987 the American Association for Counseling and Development, now the American Counseling Association, along with ERIC/CAPS, sponsored a midyear conference with the topic of "Building Strong School Counseling Programs" (Walz, 1988). The intent was to capture the essence of the past 20 years of their mutual involvement and look at what the next 20 years would hold—it was referred to as the "20/20 conference." The emphasis of the conference was studying the past research on school counseling and deciding to what extent the findings would be useful in future programs. Walz (1988) suggested six different perspectives from the research conference that could affect the future of school counseling:

1. We must view information about counseling as essentially a body of friendly facts. Unless a positive attitude toward data exists, they will remain potentially useful, but practically useless.
2. Guidance research must be directed toward and contribute to major priorities and commitments.
3. Counselors need to practice copycat creativity—the acquisition and utilization of ideas and resources from disparate sources. One of our major goals should be to acquire those programs and practices that have worked well for others and to adopt and adapt them to our own circumstances. We can become copycats of others but creatively improve upon their efforts.
4. Marketing moxie will become an increasingly important factor in determining public acceptance and support of counseling programs and practices. There is increasing competition among service providers for the public dollars.
5. Change and improvements in counseling will occur only if we have gutsy guys and gals. Research can point the way to what needs to be done, but the impact of research depends upon whether counselors will work to implement research findings even without administrative support.
6. We have reached the point where we need to think about changing for the sake of changing. If we wait for clear, documented evidence that change is needed we will be too late. (Walz, 1988, pp. 205–206)

These six perspectives regarding research should be taken seriously by an elementary counselor planning on establishing and maintaining an effective elementary school counseling program. The counselor of the future needs to be research oriented in order to gain some fresh insights into the future needs of the profession. By establishing effective research practices, the elementary school counselor will also be able to respond quickly if the counseling services are ever questioned.

School Counseling 2000, discussed earlier in the chapter, is a packet developed by the American School Counselor Association (ASCA) to address the six National Education Goals, proposed by national leaders, designed to help insure success in our nations's schools. ASCA addressed these goals in Counseling 2000, summarized below:

Goal I: All children in America will start school ready to learn.

ASCA: The *counselor* works directly with *parents* and *teachers* to:

- help create a positive school climate in which children can learn
- assure a coordinated team effort to address needs of all students

Goal II: The high school graduation rate will increase to at least 90 percent.

ASCA: The *counselor* works directly with all *students, parents, community members,* and *employers* to:

- provide for the continual benefits of a comprehensive developmental school counseling program through life skills training
- ensure access to the services of other professionals including social workers, psychologists, and nurses

Goal III: . . . students will . . . demonstrate competency in challenging subject matter . . . ; and every school in America will ensure that all students learn to use their minds well, so that they may be prepared for responsible citizenship, further learning, and productive employment in our modern economy.

ASCA: The *counselor* works directly with *students* through developmental counseling curriculum to acquire *new basic skills* to:

- develop positive attitudes toward work
- develop transferable skills to facilitate changes throughout their lifetime

Goal IV: United States students will be first in the world in science and mathematics achievement.

ASCA: The *counselor* works directly with *students* to:

- emphasize the importance of math and science in the workplace
- identify the career opportunities for those who excel in math and science

Goal V: Every adult American will be literate and will possess the knowledge and skills necessary to compete in a global economy and exercise the rights and responsibilities of citizenship.

ASCA: The *counselor* works directly with *students* to:

- facilitate personal growth and development
- encourage life-long learning

Goal VI: Every school in America will be free of drugs and violence and will offer a disciplined environment conducive to learning.

ASCA: The *counselor* works directly with *students* to:

- provide education and information in conjunction with agencies about personal safety and prevention of abuse
- develop problem-solving and decision-making skills with a focus on self-assertion and conflict resolution (ASCA, 1993)

These goals, established by national leaders, are extremely ambitious and challenging goals to achieve in our schools as they exist today. School counselors at all levels must look at their part in helping their country achieve these goals, goals that every child in the United States is entitled to achieve.

Another packet from the National School Boards Association and the American School Counselor Association contains a program called "Caring Connections: Helping Young People from Troubled Homes" (Bell, 1994). This program was developed by a group of professionals representing the fields of family counseling, sexual abuse prevention and treatment, multicultural education, substance abuse prevention, and parental skills counseling. The 64-page handbook, directed to school counselors, outlines how to set up a caring program in the community and school in order to help young people from troubled homes. Elementary school counselors will find this program extremely helpful as they address the needs of at-risk children in their schools.

Recommendations for "Getting There from Here"

In order to achieve a well-balanced, effective, and valued elementary school counseling program, the elementary school counselor of tomorrow must have certain distinguishing characteristics, as discussed in this final section.

The Elementary School Counselor of the Future Will Be Visionary

Somewhere the statement "tiptoeing through life is a tragic waste" made enough of an impression on the author that it has permeated much of her training and supervision of elementary school counselors over the past years and, in turn, shaping some of the hopes and dreams for the future of elementary school counseling. There are others that share this belief; Crabbs noted that elementary school counselors in the 21st century will continue to believe that the school environment truly affects the development and behavior of a child. Knowing this, the counselor has the choice of making things happen or letting things happen—whatever route they take, they need to anticipate the future and make plans for the inevitable changes that will take place. He stated these implications for counselors: "Significant advances in elementary school guidance and counseling services will not occur until members of the profession share the same vision" (Crabbs, 1989, p. 165). An elementary school counselor with a clear vision of a comprehensive, developmental counseling program will greatly impact the future of countless children.

The Elementary School Counselor of the Future Will Collaborate on the Academic Achievements of Students

Gerler (1991) discussed the changing world of the elementary school counselor as both education and society move rapidly into a new century. There are a number of areas that he believed elementary counselors should be involved; one area of concern was the poor academic achievement of students: "If elementary school counselors are to fulfill their mission in schools, they must collaborate with teachers, parents, and school administrators in an effort to improve children's achievement" (Gerler, 1991b, p. 21). Elementary counselors can positively affect the achievement of students by implementing small group activities on study skills and classroom guidance activities on preparing for tests, developing good study habits, and so on. There is a wealth of material available for counselors to use as they help children achieve to a greater degree. If elementary counselors share in the academic concern, this will have a positive impact on both teachers and parents.

The Elementary School Counselor of the Future Will Adapt to New Role Demands

Another view of the future role of school counselors was provided by Welch and McCarroll (1993). Although they were looking at middle school counseling needs and counselor role, there are implications for the elementary school counselor. They provided a number of comparisons of counselor role in the past and present in various activities with an anticipated role in each of these areas for the future. For example, in the past and present role, "the counselor is a primary provider of direct services (supplier, furnisher, caterer, purveyor, provider)"; in the future role, "the counselor is a conduit between needs and resources (passage, passageway, channel)" (Welch & McCarroll, 1993, p. 49). An example of this is a peer counseling program in which the direct services are not provided by the counselor—this is already proving to be a successful program in many elementary schools. Here is another past and present counselor role: "The counselor is in a closed system;" and the future role, "The counselor is a community resource specialist" (p. 50). Counselors, for the most part, work with students, teachers, and administrators in the school; this needs to be expanded to include the community, with the problems it is facing with children and their families. This is the systems approach to working with the children in our elementary schools—becoming involved in the various systems where they are immersed.

The Elementary School Counselor of the Future Will Be Knowledgeable about New Education Reforms and Restructuring Concepts

An area not usually related to the role of the school counselor is the current emphasis by the Association for Supervision and Curriculum Development (ASCD) on the creation of quality schools based on the total quality management used by corporations. A 1993 "Program News" newsletter discussed how to create quality schools, with a portrait of a district-wide effort to use the quality philosophy in their restructuring endeavors. An educational consultant specializing in the quality philosophy was asked by a kindergarten teacher, "What does this have to do with me?" The consultant responded, "Teachers who are already burned out on reform ideas are right to be skeptical of another panacea. But the quality philosophy is not just another school improvement project. It's a complete paradigm shift in thinking. And teachers working in a school that is truly focused on the quality philosophy will gradually begin to see a new attitude amongst the students, the teachers, and the administrators" (Bonstingl, 1993, p. 3). Elementary school counselors should have an awareness of this approach because it is making its presence known to educators across the country. School administrators are always on the lookout for new ways to improve the educational efforts of their schools, particularly because the "old" ways of teaching and learning are not achieving the desired results. An elementary counselor knowledgeable about what is on the cutting edge of education will be better prepared to offer his or her services in significant ways. Hoyt, in discussing the "guidance versus counseling" controversy, stated that "it is essential that school counselors be viewed as educators by their colleagues in education—and this can best be done by emphasizing the guidance team approach" (Hoyt, 1993, p. 272). This fits with the idea of the elementary counselor working with the teachers and administrators in the inclusion of new approaches such as total quality management (TQM).

The Elementary School Counselor of the Future Will Be Apprised of the Educational Policy-Making in Their State and Will Recognize the Key Role of State Legislators in This Process

Chapter 1 discussed educational standards and policy making; the emphasis here is on the elementary counselor becoming politically astute. The National Conference of State Legislatures and the American Counseling Association (formerly the American Association for Counseling and Development) in 1990 published a monograph called *Children Achieving Potential: An Introduction to Elementary School Counseling and State-Level Policies* (Glosoff & Koprowicz, 1990). The document was prepared because school counselors have not been adequately involved in the school restructuring discussions or in formulating state policies. Glosoff and Koprowicz attributed this oversight to a lack of information by those involved: "The purpose of this document is twofold: to inform legislators, counselors, and other education professionals about elementary school counseling and the policies that have been formed in support of this profession; and to open the lines of communication between counseling professionals and state-level decision makers" (p. 1). The monograph has five chapters, the last two of which are of particular importance to this discussion: (1) Chapter 4 explored the roles of state legislators in developing policies, including legislative interest in elementary school counseling and state elementary counseling policies; (2) Chapter 5 listed recommendations for developing effective state elementary school counseling policy.

Looking first at the impact of state legislators and educational policy, they noted that "three ways they can affect policy are by allocating funds, creating mandates, and influencing public opinion" (Glosoff & Koprowicz, 1990, p. 19). The key to a state's mandating elementary school counseling is tied up in the previous statement—mandating elementary school counseling without providing the monies to fund the programs would be highly detrimental to elementary school counseling. Influencing public opinion would need to come before taxpayers' acceptance of the increase in taxes that would be required if their state were to mandate and fund elementary school counseling programs. In addition, counselor education programs need some "lead time" in order to recruit and train the number of elementary school counselors that would be required if every state immediately mandated elementary school counseling. Funding formulas would have to be decided at the state level, and at the same time the local education agency (LEA) would need to be involved in the process, because most states grant local districts a certain degree of autonomy.

As Glosoff and Koprowicz noted, in the area of education legislators are pulled in many directions trying to resolve the issues facing our children's education. Many of the solutions turn out to be short-term quick fixes that do not bring lasting improvement; elementary school counseling is a preventive measure that does result in long-term improvement. Legislators need to be knowledgeable about our elementary counseling programs. There is a need for states without the services of elementary counselors to look at other states that have successfully lobbied for elementary school counseling programs in order to present these results to their legislators. States whose successful efforts are described in the monograph are Florida, Arkansas, Virginia, Texas, and Washington.

Some of the recommendations for developing state policy are particularly important to this discussion:

- Legislators interested in expanding elementary school counseling programs should encourage the formation of a legislative study committee to determine the best ways to support elementary guidance and counseling statewide.
- Counseling professionals and educators who support such programs must become organized and active on the state level.
- Pilot projects are needed to serve as models for states and *must* include a thorough evaluation plan.
- Three- to five-year start-up periods are a sensible time frame to use when considering implementing a state mandate for elementary counseling. This provides time for the universities to prepare qualified elementary school counselors to fill new staffing needs; for policymakers on the state and local levels to develop needed financial support; and for counselors, educators, and parents to develop strong, effective comprehensive counseling programs.
- Realistic counselor/student ratios must be supported for counselors to be effective in helping students achieve academic, personal, and social success. A ratio of 1:300 is recommended. (Glosoff & Koprowicz, 1990, pp. 29–30)

The Elementary School Counselor of the Future Will Be Involved in Professional Development

Professional development activities are a vital part of the training and ongoing activities of elementary school counselors. Membership and active participation in local, state, and national organizations are necessary to insure the continuing growth of the elementary school counselor. Becoming a member of the American Counselor Association (ACA) and the American School Counselor Association (ASCA) entitles the counselor to receive valuable professional journals and the monthly newspaper; these alone are worth the membership dues. An additional benefit is the national convention, with 350 or more convention programs designed to provide practical and relevant information for the counselor's professional growth. An incredible number of ideas and activities are available each year for elementary school counselors at the national convention in the "Elementary Counselor Annual Share" session. In addition to the national association, the state counselor associations bring together professionals willing to learn from each other and share their own resources. Professional growth and development involves a give and take; collaborating with other counselors or with counselor educators to develop and present a program is essential for growth in the profession.

Summary

This chapter addressed ways to change and enhance the image of the elementary school counselor. Included in this process is the establishment of an effective advisory council to work in partnership with the counselor in the school. Another emphasis was the selection and training of elementary counselors as critical to the success of elementary school counseling programs. The chapter concluded with some recommendations for achieving the goals and objectives of a successful elementary counseling program.

In order to insure the success of his or her counseling program, every elementary school counselor should take responsibility for his or her own program and work to change the systems that are not effective for the students in the school. Fincher (1993) urged counselors to say, "I take responsibility for that," in all areas of counseling services. This takes courage and it may also require the counselor to become proactive, not reactive. Elementary school counseling is an exciting and challenging place to be in the 21st century. It requires a working knowledge of the contents discussed in this text to provide appropriate positive growth experiences for the youngsters in the schools. In addition to the knowledge, counselors must be able to articulate the vision of what elementary school counseling should be and become active spokespersons for elementary school counseling.

P a r t *IV*

Appendixes

The School Counselor and the Guidance and Counseling Program

American School Counselor Association
(Adopted 1974; reviewed and reaffirmed 1980; revised 1986)

Introduction

This position of the American School Counselor Association (ASCA) describes the elements of a comprehensive and developmental guidance and counseling program and the criteria upon which the quantity and responsibilities of qualified, differentiated staff members is based. The ASCA statements of counseling role and function for the elementary, middle/junior high, secondary and post secondary settings are an integral part of the design and implementation of guidance and counseling programs.

Philosophy

"Who am I?," "Who can I become as a person?" and "How can I best contribute to society?" are questions which guidance and counseling programs help all individuals to answer. In their design and operation, the guidance and counseling programs exist to improve the learning environment by involving students, staff, parents, community and others who influence the learning and development of the persons served by the program. Through individual and group contacts over a period of time, the counselor has a major role in helping all persons develop more adequate and realistic concepts of themselves, become aware of educational occupational opportunities and integrate their understanding of self and opportunities in making informed decisions.

Program Goals

A guidance and counseling program provides for direct involvement of a service to students, staff and community in order to facilitate achievement of the following program goals. Assist persons in developing:

1. A better understanding and acceptance of themselves; their strengths and limitations; aptitudes, needs, values, interests and worth as unique individuals.
2. Interpersonal relationships on the basis of mutual respect.
3. Problem-solving and decision-making.
4. Accepting increased responsibility for their educational, occupational and avocational development.

Standards

These standards are set forth in a manner which allows local school districts, institutions, agencies and others to design and implement guidance and counseling programs consistent with the unique needs found within each setting.

Program

1. There is a written guidance curriculum developed by counselors and with the involvement of appropriate others, specifying the overall guidance and counseling program as it involves and relates to the needs of the person in the school, institution, agency and community.
2. The basic program of guidance and counseling involves the process of consulting, providing information and coordinating services for all students. The program is comprehensive, developmental and is implemented through the guidance curriculum and through specialized approaches. Orientation, information, appraisal, placement, follow-up, follow-through, referral and research activities are included in the program.
3. There is evidence that all persons throughout the school, institution, agency and community have on-going opportunity to participate in the guidance and counseling program.
4. There is evidence that the guidance and counseling program is systematically planned, implemented and evaluated.
5. There is evidence that the guidance and counseling program may be continued on an extended basis during periods when classes are not in session as deemed appropriate for each school district, institution or agency. When each school district, institution or agency deems that these additional services are desired, counselors should be appropriately compensated.
6. The guidance and counseling program should be community oriented. If services are to be provided to preschoolers, dropouts, graduates and other community citizens, additional staffing needs to be provided.
7. Counselor taught or initiated units in decision-making, values clarification, career planning, test taking/study skills and/or similar units are offered.

8. The guidance and counseling program serves three to five year old children and their parents where pre-elementary school settings exist and there is an existing elementary guidance and counseling program.
9. The guidance and counseling program provides other innovative service(s) or activities which are designed to meet unique needs.

Staff

ASCA holds the position that appropriate numbers of staff shall be employed to implement a guidance and counseling program designed to meet the needs of the persons involved in the program. There is a direct correlation between the quantity and quality of guidance and counseling services and the number of counselees per certified counselor employed to provide that service.

1. The guidance and counseling staff is qualified and appropriately certified/licensed according to state agency standards.
2. The guidance and counseling staff is responsible for the design, implementation and evaluation of the services and activities prescribed in the program.
3. Professional, secretarial and/or para-professional staff are adequate in numbers to meet the objectives of the guidance and counseling program.
4. Provision is made for staff to attend or participate in intra- and inter-professional meetings and activities inside and outside the state.

Facilities

Appropriate and meaningful guidance and counseling activities with individuals and groups takes place in a wide variety of settings, the specific environment often being determined by circumstances. There are, however, continuing student, program and staff needs in which privacy and confidentiality of conversation and records require specific counseling facilities.

1. Each counselor is provided with pleasant, private quarters conducive to conferences of a confidential nature and adequate in size to accommodate three to five persons.
2. The counseling facilities are located in an area readily accessible to students and others.
3. Each counselor's quarters is equipped with adequate telephone service.
4. A conveniently located area adequate for group guidance and counseling activities is available.
5. Adequate provision is made for the storage and display of all records and materials used by the counselor(s) in carrying out the guidance and counseling program.
6. Career resource center(s) are established and appropriately staffed to facilitate use of career awareness, exploration, planning, preparation and progression of materials, equipment and supplies.

Materials and Equipment

There is adequate budget for purchasing, maintaining and developing the materials and equipment necessary to achieve the objectives of the guidance and counseling program.

Ethical Standards for School Counselors

American School Counselor Association (April 1992)

Preamble

The American School Counselor Association (ASCA) is a professional organization whose members have a unique and distinctive preparation, grounded in the behavioral sciences, with training in counseling skills adapted to the school setting. The school counselor assists in the growth and development of each individual and uses his/her specialized skills to ensure that the rights of the counselee are properly protected within the structure of the school program. School counselors subscribe to the following basic tenets of the counseling process from which professional responsibilities are derived:

1. Each person has the right to respect and dignity as a unique human being and to counseling services without prejudice as to person, character, belief or practice.
2. Each person has the right to self-direction and self development.
3. Each person has the right of choice and the responsibility for decisions reached.
4. Each person has the right to privacy and thereby the right to expect the counselor-client relationship to comply with all laws, policies, and ethical standards pertaining to confidentiality.

In this document, the American School Counselor Association has specified the principles of ethical behavior necessary to maintain and regulate the high standards of integrity and leadership among its members. The Association recognizes the basic commitment of its members to the *Ethical Standards* of its parent organization, the American Association for Counseling and Development (AACD), and nothing in this document shall be construed to supplant that code. *The Ethical Standards for School Counselors* was developed to complement the AACD standards by clarifying the nature of ethical responsibilities for present and future counselors in the school setting. The purposes of this document are to:

1. Serve as a guide for the ethical practices of all professional school counselors regardless of level, area, population served, or membership in this Association.
2. Provide benchmarks for both self-appraisal and peer evaluations regarding counselor responsibilities to students, parents, colleagues and professional associates, school and community, self, and the counseling profession.
3. Inform those served by the school counselor of acceptable counselor practices and expected professional deportment.

A. *Responsibilities to Students*

The school counselor:

1. Has a primary obligation and loyalty to the student who is to be treated with respect as a unique individual whether assisted individually or in a group setting.
2. Is concerned with the total needs of the student (educational, vocational, personal and social) and encourages the maximum growth and development of each counselee.
3. Informs the counselee of the purposes, goals, techniques and rules of procedure under which she/he may receive counseling assistance at or before the time when the counseling relationship is entered. Prior notice includes confidentiality issues such as the possible necessity for consulting with other professionals, privileged communication, and legal or authoritative restraints. The meaning and limits of confidentiality are clearly defined to counselees.
4. Refrains from consciously encouraging the counselee's acceptance of values, lifestyles, plans, decisions and beliefs that represent only the counselor's personal orientation.
5. Is responsible for keeping abreast of laws relating to students and strives to ensure that the rights of students are adequately provided for and protected.
6. Avoids dual relationships which might impair his/her objectivity and/or increase the risk of harm to the client (e.g., counseling one's family members, close friends or associates). If a dual relationship is unavoidable, the counselor is responsible for taking action to eliminate or reduce the potential for harm. Such safeguards might include informed consent, consultation, supervision and documentation.
7. Makes appropriate referrals when professional assistance can no longer be adequately provided to the counselee. Appropriate referral requires knowledge of available resources.

8. Protects the confidentiality of students records and releases personal data only according to prescribed laws and school policies. Student information maintained through electronic data storage methods is treated with the same care as traditional student records.

9. Protects the confidentiality of information received in the counseling relationship as specified by law and ethical standards. Such information is only to be revealed to others with the informed consent of the counselee and consistent with the obligations of the counselor as a professional person. In a group setting, the counselor sets a norm of confidentiality and stresses its importance, yet clearly states that confidentiality in group counseling cannot be guaranteed.

10. Informs the appropriate authorities when the counselee's condition indicates a clear and imminent danger to the counselee or others. This is to be done after careful deliberation and, where possible, after consultation with other professionals. The counselor informs the counselee of actions to be taken so as to minimize confusion and clarify expectations.

11. Screens prospective group members and maintains an awareness of participants' compatibility throughout the life of the group, especially when the group emphasis is on self disclosure and self-understanding. The counselor takes reasonable precautions to protect members from physical and/or psychological harm resulting from interaction within the group.

12. Provides explanations of the nature, purposes, and results of tests in language that is understandable to the clients.

13. Adheres to relevant standards regarding selection, administration, and interpretation of assessment techniques. The counselor recognizes that computer-based testing programs require specific training in administration, scoring and interpretation which may differ from that required in more traditional assessments.

14. Promotes the benefits of appropriate computer applications and clarifies the limitations of computer technology. The counselor ensures that (1) computer applications are appropriate for the individual needs of the counselee, (2) the counselee understands how to use the applications, and (3) follow up counseling assistance is provided. Members of underrepresented groups are assured of equal access to computer technologies and the absence of discriminatory information and values within computer applications.

15. Has unique ethical responsibilities in working with peer programs. In general, the school counselor is responsible for the welfare of students participating in peer programs under her/his direction. School counselors who function in training and supervisory capacities are referred to the preparation and supervision standards of professional counselor associations.

B. Responsibilities to Parents

The school counselor:

1. Respects the inherent rights and responsibilities of parents for their children and endeavors to establish a cooperative relationship with parents to facilitate the maximum development of the counselee.

2. Informs parents of the counselor's role, with emphasis on the confidential nature of the counseling relationship between the counselor and counselee.

3. Provides parents with accurate, comprehensive and relevant information in an objective and caring manner, as appropriate and consistent with ethical responsibilities to the counselee.

4. Treats information received from parents in a confidential and appropriate manner.

5. Shares information about a counselee only with those persons properly authorized to receive such information.

6. Adheres to laws and local guidelines when assisting parents experiencing family difficulties which interfere with the counselee's effectiveness and welfare.

7. Is sensitive to changes in the family and recognizes that all parents, custodial and noncustodial, are vested with certain rights and responsibilities for the welfare of their children by virtue of their position and according to law.

C. Responsibilities to Colleagues and Professional Associates

The school counselor:

1. Establishes and maintains a cooperative relationship with faculty, staff and administration to facilitate the provision of optimal guidance and counseling programs and services.

2. Promotes awareness and adherence to appropriate guidelines regarding confidentiality, the distinction between public and private information and staff consultation.

3. Treats colleagues with respect, courtesy, fairness and good faith. The qualifications, views and findings of colleagues are represented accurately and fairly to enhance the image of competent professionals.

4. Provides professional personnel with accurate, objective, concise and meaningful data necessary to adequately evaluate counsel and assist the counselee.

5. Is aware of and fully utilizes related professions and organizations to whom the counselee may be referred.

D. Responsibilities to the School and Community

The school counselor:

1. Supports and protects the educational program against any infringement not in the best interest of students.

2. Informs appropriate officials of conditions that may be potentially disruptive or damaging to the school's mission, personnel and property.

3. Delineates and promotes the counselor's role and function in meeting the needs of those served. The counselor will notify appropriate school officials of conditions which may limit or curtail their effectiveness in providing programs and services.

4. Assists in the development of: (1) curricular and environmental conditions appropriate for the school and community, (2) educational procedures and programs to meet student needs, and (3) a systematic evaluation process for guidance and

counseling programs, services and personnel. The counselor is guided by findings of the evaluation data in planning programs and services.

5. Actively cooperates and collaborates with agencies, organizations and individuals in the school and community in the best interest of counselees and without regard to personal regard or remuneration.

E. Responsibilities to Self

The school counselor:

1. Functions within the boundaries of individual professional competence and accepts responsibility for the consequences of his/her actions.
2. Is aware of the potential effects of her/his own personal characteristics on services to clients.
3. Monitors personal functioning and effectiveness and refrains from any activity likely to lead to inadequate professional services or harm to a client.
4. Recognizes that differences in clients relating to age, gender, race, religion, sexual orientation, socioeconomic and ethnic backgrounds may require specific training to ensure competent services.
5. Strives through personal initiative to maintain professional competence and keeps abreast of innovations and trends in the profession. Professional and personal growth is continuous and ongoing throughout the counselor's career.

F. Responsibilities to the Profession

The school counselor:

1. Conducts herself/himself in such a manner as to bring credit to self and the profession.
2. Conducts appropriate research and reports findings in a manner consistent with acceptable educational and psychological research practices. When using client data for research, statistical or program planning purposes, the counselor ensures protection of the identify of the individual client(s).
3. Actively participates in local, state and national associations which foster the development and improvement of school counseling.
4. Adheres to ethical standards of the profession, other official policy statements pertaining to counseling, and relevant statutes established by federal, state and local governments.
5. Clearly distinguishes between statements and actions made as a private individual and as a representative of the school counseling profession.
6. Contributes to the development of the profession through the sharing of skills, ideas and expertise with colleagues.

G. Maintenance of Standards

Ethical behavior among professional school counselors, association members and nonmembers, is expected at all times. When there exists serious doubt as to the ethical behavior of colleagues, or if counselors are forced to work in situations or abide by policies which do not reflect the standards as outlined in these *Ethical Standards for School Counselors* or the *ACA Ethical Standards,* the counselor is obligated to take appropriate action to rectify the condition. The following procedure may serve as a guide:

1. If feasible, the counselor should consult with a professional colleague to discuss confidentially the nature of the complaint to see if she/he views the situation as an ethical violation.

2. Whenever possible, the counselor should directly approach the colleague whose behavior is in question to discuss the complaint and seek resolution.

3. If resolution is not forthcoming at the personal level, the counselor shall utilize the channels established within the school and/or school district. This may include both informal and formal procedures.

4. If the matter still remains unresolved, referral for review and appropriate action should be made to the Ethics Committees in the following sequence:

   - local counselor association
   - state counselor association
   - national counselor association

5. The ASCA Ethics Committee functions in an educative and consultative capacity and does not adjudicate complaints of ethical misconduct. Therefore, at the national level, complaints should be submitted in writing to the ACA Ethics Committee for review and appropriate action. The procedure for submitting complaints may be obtained by writing the ACA Ethics Committee, c/o The Executive Director, American Counseling Association, 5999 Stevenson Avenue, Alexandria, VA 22304.

H. Resources

School counselors are responsible for being aware of, and acting in accord with, the standards and positions of the counseling profession as represented in official documents such as those listed below.

Code of Ethics (1989). National Board for Certified Counselors. Alexandria, VA.

Code of Ethics for Peer Helping Professionals (1989). National Peer Helpers Association. Glendale, CA.

Ethical Guidelines for Group Counselors (1989). Association for Specialists in Group Work. Alexandria, VA.

Ethical Standards (1988). American Association for Counseling and Development. Alexandria, VA.

Position Statement: The School Counselor and Confidentiality (1986). American School Counselor Association. Alexandria, VA.

Position Statement: The School Counselor and Peer Facilitation (1984). American School Counselor Association. Alexandria, VA.

Position Statement: The School Counselor and Student Rights (1982). American School Counselor Association. Alexandria, VA.

Ethical Standards for School Counselors was adopted by the ASCA Delegate Assembly, March 19, 1984. This revision was approved by the ASCA Delegate Assembly, March 27, 1992.

Appendix *C*

The School Counselor and Developmental Guidance

American School Counselor Association (Adopted 1978; reviewed and revised 1984)

During recent years a number of counselor educators and school counselors have advanced the proposition that counseling can and should become more proactive and preventative in its focus and more developmental in its content and process. Viewed in the context of an evolving societal emphasis upon personal growth and an expanding professional expertise, developmental guidance has resulted in a potentially dynamic and promising approach to the helping relationship of the school counselor. The concept of developmental guidance has been discussed under various rubrics, such as (deliberate) psychological education, human relations training, and preventative mental health. Developmental guidance is a reaffirmation and actualization of the belief that guidance is for all students and that its purpose is to maximally facilitate personal development.

Definition

Developmental guidance is that component of all guidance efforts which fosters planned intervention within educational and other human development services programs at all points in the human life cycle. It vigorously stimulates and actively facilitates the total development of individuals in all areas—personal, social, emotional, career, moral-ethical, cognitive, aesthetic—and to promote the integration of the several components into an individual life-style.

Endorsement

The American School Counselor Association (ASCA) formally endorses, supports, and encourages the incorporation of developmental guidance in the role and function of the school counselor.

Antecedents

In the past the role of the school counselor has suffered from the restrictions of historical precedent, philosophical tradition, financial support, administrative definition, and counselor selection and preparation. Counselor functions have often been limited to crises management, adjustment coordination, vocational guidance, and clerical and quasi-administrative tasks.

Catalysts

Prompted by cultural change, progressive philosophy, advancement of knowledge and methodological improvement in the behavioral sciences, a climate of open public discourse, pressures of educational accountability, institutional economics, and professional survival, the "traditional" work of the school counselor is in need of well-seasoned revision.

Direction

If counseling is viewed humanistically, holistically, and comprehensively—that is developmentally—then the rationale for developmental guidance is clearly defined: Counseling should be habilitative as well as rehabilitative, proactive as well as reactive, preventative as well as remedial, skill-additive as well as problem-reductive, and characterized by outreach as well as availability. Developmental guidance is the summative terminology which connotes this emphasis. Specifically, then, developmental guidance refers to the process and content of confluent human development as promoted by planned, purposeful, and sequential intervention.

Content

The content of developmental guidance will vary according to the developmental levels, stages and needs of participants; counselor competence and resources; and other factors. Examples of programs of contemporary interest include the following: human development (theories, stages, tasks, principles); career development (awareness, exploration, selection, employability skills); academic development (achievement motivation, study skills, test preparation, test wiseness); communication skills; interpersonal relations; decision making; values clarification; marriage and family planning; parent education; moral development; affective education; conflict resolution; leadership training; assertion training; relaxation training; human sexuality; drug education; death education; and situational adjustment and self-management (divorce adjustment, depression management, weight control, behavior modification). This list is not exhaustive.

Intervention

Many means and resources for developmental guidance intervention are available, and counselors should select from among these alternatives according to needs identified in his or her work situation. Examples of means of delivery include: mini-courses, academic release time from designated classes for developmental guidance activities, curricular scheduling of guidance activities, extended hours (after school and evening), and classroom guidance. Examples of techniques and resources include: resource centers and libraries; programmed texts and workbooks; co-facilitation and consultation with teachers, paraprofessionals, peer counselors, and others; counseling and educational kits; curricular aids, media, bibliotherapy, cinematherapy; contracting; and experiential education. Examples of strategies include: direct service delivery, consultation, team teaching, peer facilitating, and paraprofessional counseling.

Medium of Delivery

In terms of efficiency, as well as effectiveness, group approaches are the preferred medium of delivery for developmental guidance activities. By definition, "group" refers to a natural or created cluster of individuals, as small in number as two or of unlimited size. The clusters may be identified as families, classrooms and grades, employees, clients, or other composites of persons who come together as a result of shared need or purpose, common attributes, and/or other coincident characteristics.

Competencies

Essential preparation for developmental guidance intervention involves a thorough understanding of human development (descriptive and theoretical); knowledge of counseling theory and practice; competence in counseling techniques and group processes; skill in program development and management; assessment, appraisal, and diagnostic skills based on developmental concepts; practical competence in basic statistics, applied research, and program evaluation methods; and specific knowledge in the area of developmental emphasis. The counselor should be personally effective and comfortable in all areas in which developmental guidance intervention is offered.

Developmental guidance specialists must, at a minimum, be able to effectively deal with questions such as: What are the general characteristics, expectations, tasks, and behaviors of individuals at this state of development? What are this individual's characteristics, expectations, tasks, and behaviors? What can impede the process of development for this individual? What will facilitate the process of development for this individual?

Because the emphasis on developmental guidance is fairly new, counselor educators may need to modify the counselor education curriculum in order to prepare counseling students as proficient developmental interventionists. Because such an approach has often been taught as an ideal rather than as reality, as an attitude instead of a skill, counselor educators may be required to further develop their educative role.

Counseling students should seek to add the skills of developmental guidance intervention to their repertoire—if necessary, through adjuncts and alternatives to the usual counselor education curricula. Practicing counselors whose programs did not include developmental guidance components should seek to acquire the skills of developmental guidance intervention as part of their professional renewal efforts. The developmental guidance counselor should be involved in a continuing program of professional improvement in developmental guidance expertise and strategies.

Competencies may be acquired, maintained, and improved through a variety of means, for example, graduate study, workshops, institutes and seminars, meetings and programs of professional associations, self-study of journals, contemporary texts and instructional manuals, in-service education, continuing and extended education, internships, and consultation.

Implementation

Many administrators, teachers, other school personnel, students, and parents will be unaccustomed to the concept, intent, and outcome of developmental guidance; therefore, the counselor's competence must be visible; program development and planning thorough; rationale for programs convincing; conduct of procedures professional; and programs measured, evaluated and reported effectively, both formally and informally.

Implementation strategies for the initiation of developmental guidance will require both assertiveness and ingenuity. The entire guidance community, ASCA and its constituent organizations should strive to work in harmony to facilitate the implementation of developmental guidance programs.

The true impact of the developmental guidance concept loses meaning when discussed as a lofty goal, abstract concept or as an isolated piece of rhetoric. For the concept of a sequential and developmental guidance program to be truly meaningful to both the professional staff as well as parents and students, it must be part of a comprehensive K–12 guidance plan. A plan which states its aims in measurable outcomes for all students, specific activities and a built-in evaluation procedure with provisions for necessary annual revisions. There is a necessity for some form of needs assessment which addresses the legitimate needs of the entire school community. The counselor needs to be realistic in evaluating time and fiscal parameters. A curriculum for each grade level or special area is then developed, implemented, assessed and revised annually. In-service education needs to be considered when necessary.

School counselors need to develop their abilities to teach the attitudes necessary to enhance the academic success of their counselees, i.e., for a student to succeed in Geometry, the student needs more than the usual mathematical concepts. In addition, they need to deal with structure, boredom, intimidation and frustration. The plan should be presented to the appropriate educational agency for adoption. The effects of a written comprehensive K–12 guidance plan helps the consumer to realistically become aware of the goals, objectives and true roles of their local guidance department.

Guidelines

There are several general principles which should help insure quality and effectiveness in the implementation of developmental guidance:

1. The program should be systematic, sequential and comprehensive.
2. The program should be jointly founded upon developmental psychology, educational philosophy and counseling methodology.
3. Both process and product (of the program itself and the individuals in it) should be stressed.
4. All the personal domains—cognitive, affective, behavioral, experiential and environmental—should be emphasized.
5. Programs should emphasize preparation for the future and consolidation of the present.
6. Individualization and transfer of learning should be central to program procedure and method.
7. Evaluation and corrective feedback are essential.

Appendix **D**

Elementary School Counseling

American Counselor Association (November 1992)

Position Statement

The American Counseling Association (ACA) believes in the rights of each child and parent to adequate counseling services throughout the child's elementary education. To this end ACA supports educational, legislative, and advocacy efforts that (a) increase the competency of elementary school counselors to identify and meet the developmental needs of children, (b) establish specific comprehensive developmental guidance and counseling programs that foster the growth of each child, (c) promote activities that increase public awareness of the value of elementary school counseling programs, and (d) demonstrate the effectiveness of elementary counselors in helping all children meet their needs and adjust to the demands of a changing world.

The Problem

Young children are experiencing an increasing number of problems that inhibit their growth and development.

- It is estimated that 3.5 million elementary age students come from families with divorced parents and that 7.5 million live in single-parent homes.

- Currently, the number of counselors employed to serve children during these crucial elementary school years is less than half the number of counselors employed in secondary schools. The student:counselor ratio for pre-kindergarten through sixth grade is more than 1100:1.

Rationale

The elementary school counselor is certified or licensed as a professional who addresses the needs of students comprehensively through guidance instruction; group and individual counseling; consultation with parents, teachers, and other professionals and coordination of pupil personnel services and referrals. Counseling program activities must be continuous throughout the elementary grades, and the counselor:pupil ratio should not exceed 1:250.

The integration of comprehensive developmental counseling programs into all elementary schools will enhance the quality of personal, social, educational, and career development of all children and their families. The improved delivery of counseling services by full-time licensed counselors will empower them to make wise choices regarding their futures.

A p p e n d i x *E*

The School Counselor and Child Abuse/ Neglect Prevention

American School Counselor Association (Adopted 1981; revised 1985)

Introduction

The incidence of reported child abuse and child neglect has increased significantly, both nationally and statewide, during the past several years. Generally, state laws require people in the helping professions, who have reasonable cause to believe that a child is suffering serious physical or emotional injury, to report this situation to the appropriate authorities. School counselors are mandated reporters and need policies, referral procedures, and information. However, it is not simply a legal issue of reporting child abuse, but also a moral and ethical responsibility of school counselors to help children and adults cope with abusive behavior, facilitate behavioral changes, and prepare for parenting styles and positive interpersonal relationships. Counselors must commit themselves to providing strategies to help break the cycle of child abuse.

Rationale

There are societal beliefs and values that parents have the right to discipline their children as they choose. The consequence of such beliefs, to some individuals, is physical and/or emotional harm and lowered self esteem. The cycle of abuse seems to be self-perpetuating. Research shows that a large percentage of abusive parents were abused children.

Counselors having an understanding of the dynamics of child abuse can aid in early recognition and detection of families with the potential for child abuse. School counselors are often in a unique position to identify potential and actual cases of abuse/neglect of children. Responsible action by the counselor can be achieved through the recognition and understanding of the problem, knowing the reporting procedures, and participating in available child abuse information programs. The American School Counselor Association recognizes that it is the absolute responsibility of school counselors to report suspected cases of child abuse/neglect to the proper authorities. We also recognize that the abuse of children is not limited to the home and that corporal punishment by school authorities might well be considered child abuse. The American School Counselor Association supports any legislation which specifically bans the use of corporal punishment as a disciplinary tool within the schools.

Definitions

Abuse: The infliction by other than accidental means of physical harm upon the body of a child, continual psychological damage or denial of emotional needs.

Corporal Punishment: Any act of physical force upon a pupil for the purpose of punishing that pupil. This definition specifically excludes any reasonable force exercised by a school employee which is used in self-defense, in defense of other persons or property or to restrain or remove a pupil who is disrupting school functions and who refuses to comply with a request to stop.

Some examples of child abuse are:

1. Extensive bruises or patterns of bruises.
2. Burns or burn patterns.
3. Lacerations, welts or abrasions.
4. Injuries inconsistent with information offered.
5. Sexual abuse is any act or acts involving sexual molestation or exploitation, including but not limited to rape, carnal knowledge, sodomy, or unnatural sexual practices.
6. Emotional disturbance caused by continuous friction in the home, marital discord, or mentally ill parents.
7. Cruel treatment.

Neglect: The failure to provide necessary food, care, clothing, shelter, supervision, or medical attention for a child. Examples of child neglect are:

1. Malnourished, ill clad, dirty, without proper shelter or sleeping arrangements, lacking appropriate health care.
2. Unattended, lacking adequate supervision.
3. Ill and lacking essential medical attention.
4. Irregular/illegal absences from school.
5. Exploited, overworked.
6. Lacking essential psychological/emotional nurturance.
7. Abandonment.

Endorsements

The American School Counselor Association strongly endorses, supports and encourages incorporation into the counselor's role the following:

- The awareness that all state statutes make school counselors immune from both civil and criminal liability when reporting suspected cases of child abuse/neglect cases in good faith. Failure to report may result in legal penalties. Thorough knowledge of local child abuse policy and procedures is essential.
- It is not the responsibility of the school counselor to prove that the child has been abused/neglected, or to determine the cause of suspected abuse/neglect, or to determine whether the child is in need of protection.
- The protection of confidentiality and the child's right to privacy with discussion of the situation limited to school staff members who have a need to know or authorized personnel from appropriate agencies. Counselors should develop their position as a liaison between the school, child, and the appropriate agency.

Counselor Role

The American School Counselor Association encourages its members to participate in the implementation of the following guidance and counseling activities:

- Coordinate team efforts involving the principal, teacher, counselor, school nurse, protective services worker, and the child.
- Serve as a support to teachers, and other school personnel, especially if the child was abused as a result of a report sent home about the child from school.
- Emphasize the non-punitive role of protective services and allay fears that the child will be removed immediately from the home.
- Facilitate the contact between the child and the social worker. The issue of confidentiality and re-establishing the trust of the child after the report is made is critical to the child-counselor relationship.
- Provide on-going counseling services to the child and/or family after the crisis is over, or refer to an appropriate community agency.
- Provide programs designed to help prevent child abuse. Counselors can help children with coping skills and ways to prevent their own abuse by improving their self-concepts, being able to recognize stress in their parents, and being sensitive to cues that abuse may occur if their own behavior is not changed.
- Help teachers and administrators in understanding the dynamics of abuse and abusive parents, and in developing a non-judgmental attitude so they can react more appropriately in crisis situations.
- Provide developmental workshops and/or support groups for parents focusing upon alternative methods of discipline, handling anger and frustration, and enhancing parenting skills.

Summary

School counselors are key people in the child abuse prevention network. The school counselor must be able to guide and help, and provide all appropriate services during a crisis situation. Up-to-date information can sometimes mean a turning point in the life and behavior of an abusive family.

A p p e n d i x **F**

The School Counselor
and Sex Equity

American School Counselor Association (Adopted 1983)

Introduction

The members of the American School Counselor Association (ASCA) are committed to facilitating and promoting the fullest possible development of each individual. Part of the commitment involves reducing the barriers which limit that development, whether barriers of race, sex, ethnicity, age, or handicap. This position statement focuses primarily on equal opportunity and equal status for girls and boys, men and women. Many internal and external obstacles exist in school and society which inhibit students from developing their full potential. Not the least of these are sex-role stereotyping and socialization. Since the early 70s there has been a growing body of literature which clearly documents the existence of subtle and not-so-subtle attitudes and behaviors on the part of students, parents, teachers, counselors, and administrators which may prevent students from making certain choices and track them toward others which they are socialized to expect. To expand the range of options available to students, it is important that counselors become acutely aware of ways in which their own communications—verbal and nonverbal—and the communications of other adults in educational settings and professional associations may limit opportunities on the basis of sex.

Rationale

It is an assumption of the American School Counselor Association that if counselors are to understand how their attitudes and behaviors affect student options, they need to be aware of the conscious and often unconscious ways in which sex bias limits the development of girls and women; how sex stereotyping limits both women and men. One of the ways in which barriers are perpetuated is through language, our most personal form of communication. Another is through organizational activity, the way we structure our organizations and institutions, select leaders, and carry out plans.

During the 60s and 70s many federal and state laws were passed to protect individuals from sex and race discrimination in education and work. These included the Equal Pay Act of 1963, the Civil Rights Act of 1964, The Vocational Amendments of 1976, the Women's Educational Equity Act of 1974, Affirmative Action and Executive Orders, and Title IX. Although these have been important legal mandates to assure equal treatment under the law, we know that laws alone do not necessarily change attitudes and behavior, especially in an area so ingrained as sex roles.

ASCA believes that members in a field committed to human development need to be especially sensitive to the unconscious aspects of interpersonal communication in the schools which give students subtle messages about inequality of the sexes. The traditional invisibility of women in language and literature is one factor which has contributed to the negation of women as persons. ASCA also believes that the organization itself and its divisions should provide models of working toward equal status of women and men, not only for legal but for human development reasons.

The following guidelines, adapted from the Equity Guidelines approved by the American Association for Counseling and Development at the national convention in St. Louis, Missouri, in 1981, offer a departure point for examining our attitudes and behaviors as professionals and for facilitating our personal growth, particularly in the areas of inclusive/sex-fair language and organizational activity.

Assumptions

1. Issues of sex roles, equal opportunity, and bias continue to be a social concern of counseling professionals.
2. We are all products of our socialization and often unconsciously continue to exhibit stereotypic attitudes and behaviors about what girls and boys, men and women can and "ought" to do.
3. As counseling professionals, we are committed to principles of equal opportunity, facilitating human development, and promoting equity.
4. We are in accord with the professional associations, publishers, and journals which promote the use of sex-fair/inclusive language.
5. Both professional organizations and counselors as individuals need to become more conscious of the pervasive negative effects of sex-role stereotyping and socialization on ourselves, our clients, and our profession.

Guidelines

The American School Counselor Association encourages its officers, divisions, and members to study and implement the following Sex Equity Guidelines:

1. Interpersonal relations with students and colleagues, counselors try to use language which includes both sexes, male and female images or examples, and non-

sex-typed expectations regarding subjects, educational and vocational choices, and co-curricular activities.

2. Counselors become sensitive to ways in which their interpersonal attitudes and behaviors with secretaries, colleagues, and partners can have negative effects and provide negative models for students and other adults.

3. Recognizing that sex-role related attitudes and behaviors are socialized, counselors try to provide constructive feedback to those who may not yet have reached the point of awareness of the limiting and demeaning effects of sexist language.

4. In accord with principles of openness, trust, and positive regard, counselors encourage recipients of stereotypic attitudes and behaviors to let others know how they feel when such stereotyping occurs, e.g., "It really makes me feel bad when you say that," or, on the positive side, "Thank you for using inclusive language."

5. In oral and written language, ASCA members, officers, and speakers are encouraged to use inclusive and sex-fair language according to guidelines suggested by the American Counseling Association and the American Psychological Association.

6. In introducing speakers, conducting committee meetings, or in other interpersonal communications, ASCA members are urged to use equal phrasing to refer to or address women and men, e.g., "men and women," not "man and gals," or "Dr. Wright (male) and Dr. Nelson (female)," not "Dr. Wright and Helen."

7. In conducting meetings, giving speeches, or other leadership activities, avoid sexist humor that puts down or reflects negatively on either sex. Emphasize a person's competence and not appearance or marital status.

8. When planning elections or conferences, obtain as equal representation as possible of women and men, making sure that women have equal status, e.g., as speakers, not only as reactors, or panelists; women in key and visible management positions in the organization or conference.

9. Aim for equal participation for men and women in contributions to journals, special issues, newsletters, books, project leadership, grant proposals, conference summaries, and other oral and written communications and publications.

10. Include on ASCA and state division stationery a simple awareness statement, "The American School Counselor Association is committed to equal opportunity."

Appendix *G*

===============================

The School Counselor and the Education of the Handicapped Act

American School Counselor Association
(Adopted 1980, revised 1986)

The adoption of Public Law 94-142, and amended as P.L. 98-199, the education for all handicapped children act, by the federal government has provided the framework for more appropriate educational programming for exceptional students. Such components of the law as due process, individual educational programs and the least restrictive environment offer opportunities to utilize the counselor's skills for the benefit of this portion of their clientele. It is particularly important that the role of the counselor in these procedures is clearly defined and understood by all concerned.

The purpose of this position statement is to define those role functions that are and are not reasonably within the scope of P.L. 94-142. The American School Counselor Association (ASCA) believes school counselors might reasonably be expected to perform the following functions in the implementation of P.L. 94-142.

1. To assist in the identification of students with handicapping conditions, including securing informed parental consent for referral to the committee on the handicapped.
2. To serve as a member of the multi-disciplinary team for the purpose of defining the most appropriate educational planning and placement for children with handicapping conditions.

3. To prepare and present such portions of the student's individual educational programs at the meeting of the committee on the handicapped, as may relate to services to be performed or coordinated by the school counselor.

4. To provide input to the committee on the handicapped as to a student's present level of functioning, effective needs and the appropriateness of certain programs to meet those needs.

5. To provide supportive counseling for the parents of students with handicapping conditions as it relates to the educational objectives stated in the individual educational plan.

6. To provide guidance and counseling services to students with handicapping conditions consistent with those provided to students without handicapping conditions.

7. To provide educational counseling for students, as mandated by the committee on the handicapped, consistent with the objectives in the student's individual educational plan.

8. To consult with teachers, school psychologists, school social workers and other appropriate personnel on the educational and affective needs of exceptional students.

9. To assist in the development and implementation of professional development activities for staff working with exceptional students in self-contained or mainstreamed environments.

ASCA believes that there are certain responsibilities pertaining to the implementation of P.L. 94-142 that are NOT PRIMARILY those of the school counselor, although the counselor may be involved to varying degrees in these duties. It must be noted that while the school counselor has become increasingly involved in meeting the guidance and counseling needs of students with handicapping conditions, adequate staffing needs must be taken into consideration so as not to diminish the quality of guidance and counseling services provided to mainstream students. Practical consideration of local conditions and state regulations must limit the counselor's involvement in the following activities:

1. To serve as the local educational agency's one representative in formal due process procedures related to the placement of or programming for students with handicapping conditions.

2. To prepare individual educational programs for students with handicapping conditions other than those portions related to guidance and counseling services.

3. To act as the only source of information concerning the special educational programs of a district.

4. To make decisions concerning the placement or retention of exceptional students.

5. To serve in any supervisory capacity in relation to implementation of P.L. 94-142.

6. To serve as a member of the multi-disciplinary team reviewing placement referrals for students who are not normally a part of the counselor's caseload.

Appendix *H*

The School Counselor and Migrant Students

American School Counselor Association (Adopted 1984)

Migrant students have unique problems. School counselors should be encouraged to establish a network of support programs that meet the unique need of migrant students as well as be aware of existing programs which track the migrant students. The American School Counselor Association (ASCA) encourages the chief school officers of each state to be increasingly aware of these problems. Because there is a large portion of the population that is mobile, these students often have limited opportunities to meet differing state and local requirements for promotion and graduation.

There needs to be greater sensitivity to these needs. Migrant students should be allowed increased flexibility in the variation of course titles and content and competency measures which can be transferred from state to state. Migrant students' transcripts need to be individually evaluated.

ASCA further encourages each State Department of Education and/or local school agency to aid migrant students in credit accumulation and in the credit transfer process.

Appendix I

The School Counselor and Dropout Prevention/ Student At-Risk

American School Counselor Association
(Adopted 1989; revised 1993)

The Position of the American School Counselor Association (ASCA)

Counselors should work with other educators to provide early intervention for potential dropouts through a comprehensive, developmental, K–12 counseling program.

The Rationale

Any student may at any time be "at-risk" in respect to dropping out of school, becoming truant, performing below academic potential, contemplating suicide, or using drugs. The underlying reasons for these behaviors often deal with personal and social concerns such as poor self-esteem, family problems, neglect, or abuse. Students experiencing these concerns can be helped by professional school counselors.

The decision to drop out of school can carry with it devastating lifelong implications. The school counselor can identify potential dropouts and work closely with them to help them stay in school or find alternative means of completing their education.

The Counselor's Role

Professional school counselors at all levels make a significant, vital, and indispensable contribution toward the mental wellness of "at-risk" students. The role of the school counselor in working with these students is as follows: to provide consultation in identifying potential dropouts; to provide responsive programs to meet their needs, including individual, group, family and crisis counseling; to provide programs for individual planning, including academic, personal/social, educational and career counseling; to provide curriculum programs for all students within the comprehensive guidance program on decision-making/problem-solving skills, interpersonal skills; to provide support in-service presentations to school staff; to provide initiative for student referrals for additional specialized support services and to other community resources; to provide consultation with and support for parents/guardians of "at-risk" students.

The school counselor should work as a member of a team with other student service professionals to provide comprehensive and developmental programs for all students, including those identified as being potential dropouts.

Summary

Counselors should work with other educators and community resources to provide early identification and early intervention for potential dropouts through a comprehensive, developmental, K–12 counseling program. Counselors should also utilize specific interventions to work closely with those potential dropouts on their normal caseloads to help them stay in school or to find alternative means to complete their education.

Appendix *J*

Cross/Multicultural Counseling

American School Counselor Association (Adopted 1988)

The American School Counselor Association recognizes cultural diversities as important factors deserving increased awareness and understanding on the part of all school personnel, especially the school counselor.

A definition of cross/multicultural counseling is the facilitation of human development through the understanding and appreciation of cultural diversities with respect to language, values, ethics, morals, and racial variables.

The American School Counselor Association encourages school counselors to take action to assure students of culturally diverse backgrounds access to appropriate services and opportunities which promote maximum development. Counselors may utilize the following strategies to increase the sensitivity of students and parents to cultural diverse persons and enhance the total school and community environment.

1. Conduct self examinations of personal values, attitudes and beliefs toward cultural diversity.
2. Maintain awareness of concepts and techniques with a current library of cultural information.
3. Foster the interest of culturally diverse students in careers which have been traditionally closed.
4. Continue to upgrade materials utilized in the awareness and sensitivity groups.

5. Provide educational awareness workshops for teachers and cultural diverse parents at the local PTO/PTA meetings.
6. Develop a resource list of educational and community support services to meet the socioeconomic and cultural needs of culturally diverse students and their families.
7. Conduct student small groups to enhance self-esteem and cultural awareness.
8. Conduct classroom activities which develop acceptance and appreciation of cultural diversities.
9. Work within the larger community to identify cultural diversities and assist in the development of community-based programs which will propagate community acceptance of all culturally diverse populations in the larger population.

School counselors can encourage school districts to implement the following strategies to increase awareness of culturally diverse populations.

1. To include culturally diverse parents on curriculum development planning boards, committees, and other school projects.
2. Provide awareness workshops for faculty and staff on culturally diverse people.
3. Incorporate culturally diverse family resources into the educational process.
4. Develop workshops for culturally diverse parents to educate them on the school system's philosophy of education.
5. Promote schoolwide activities that focus on individual differences and contributions made by the cultural diverse persons.
6. Provide liaison services to facilitate communication between diverse populations in the school and community.
7. Adopt classroom materials that are free of culturally biased information and urge classroom teachers not to utilize any material of that caliber.

School counselors have the responsibility of insuring that the special needs of all students are met. Counselors have the skills necessary to consult with school personnel to identify alienating factors in attitudes and policies that impede the learning process. School counselors need to continue to be aware of and strive to insure that the rights of all students exist so as to maximize their potential in an environment that supports and encourages growth and development of the person.

The School Counselor and Group Counseling

American School Counselor Association
(Adopted 1989; revised 1993)

The Position of the American School Counselor Association (ASCA)

Every school district and every institution of higher learning should include and support the group counseling concept as an integral part of a comprehensive guidance and counseling program.

The Rationale

Group counseling, which involves a number of students working on shared tasks and developing supportive relationships in a group setting, is an efficient and effective way of dealing with developmental problems and situational concerns of students.

By allowing individuals to develop insights into themselves and others, group counseling makes it possible for more people to achieve a healthier personal adjustment, handle the stresses of a rapidly changing technological and complex environment, and learn to work and live with others.

The Counselor's Role

Within the parameters of a comprehensive school guidance program, many components are best delivered by means of group counseling. Group approaches are the preferred medium of delivery for developmental guidance activities, in terms of efficiency as well as effectiveness. School counselors will facilitate for many groups, as well as training others as group facilitators. Such groups might include the parent education group, the peer counselors group, or in-school support groups for students. The counselor will also be facilitating in the career guidance core committee, and may be involved in similar community outreach groups specific to a particular community/school district. The school counselor is involved in many clubs and parent programs in providing services to meet students' needs. Annual review of the work of each of these groups provides evaluation of its contribution to the overall program designed to meet the developmental needs of all of the students.

Summary

Group counseling has been found to be an efficient and effective medium of delivery in meeting the developmental needs and situational concerns of students. Groups, cooperative groups learning activities, and group counseling makes it possible for more people to achieve healthier personal adjustment in the face of rapid change and to learn to work and live with others. It is an integral part of a comprehensive guidance and counseling program and should be included and supported by every educational institution.

The School Counselor in Career Guidance: Expectations and Responsibilities

American School Counselor Association Role Statement
(Adopted 1984)

Introduction

Career Guidance has consistently been seen as a high priority needed by youth, their parents, school boards, the private sector, and the general public. Such expectations are at an all time high. As these expectations have risen, so, too, has the difficulty of the task facing the professional school counselor. The certain rapidity of occupational change, coupled with the uncertain nature of the emerging service/information oriented high technology society have combined to change career guidance practices in significant ways. This policy statement aims to recognize and react to some of these changes.

To do so demands that the professional school counselor recognize that the promise of high technology to increase both efficiency and effectiveness of operations applies to career guidance at least as much as to any other part of the formal education system. Thus, if the need for career guidance can be said to be greater than ever, so, too, is the potential for meeting this need. This potential can be recognized only if professional school counselors are willing to broaden their roles in ways that allow them to simultaneously take advantage of the promise and avoid the pitfalls implicit in a high technology approach to career guidance. The promises and pitfalls to be recognized include but are not limited to:

- The *promise* through computer assisted management (CAM) to relieve professional school counselors of the need to spend long hours in maintaining student records coupled with the potential *pitfall* of violating student confidentiality.
- The *promise* of greatly expanding the nature, scope, and accessibility of educational/occupational information systems through the use of videodiscs and telecommunication coupled with the potential *pitfalls* associated with assuring the validity and lack of bias found in such materials.
- The *promise* of making computerized career decision-making systems available to students coupled with the plentiful *pitfalls* of failing to use the counselor/student relationship to move towards comprehensive career planning.

Thus, while high technology holds obvious promise for increasing both the efficiency and the effectiveness of career guidance, it simultaneously calls for a broadening of counselor expertise and counselor activity. The challenge to counselors for broadening their role in career guidance is fully as great as is the need to make career guidance a high priority item.

To make career guidance a high priority item for professional school counselors several basic goals must be kept clearly in mind including:

- Delivering career guidance to persons in an equitable fashion that aims at excellence of delivery for each person.
- Taking advantage of the obvious opportunity of utilizing a wide variety of community resources in the delivery of effective career guidance.
- Protecting and enhancing individual freedom of career choices for every person served.
- Providing quality career guidance for all persons in the education system rather than limiting it to specific portions of the student population.
- Involving, to the greatest possible extent, all professional educators in the delivery of career guidance. In order to address this need to designate our role in career guidance as a high priority, ASCA has prepared this policy statement.

Career Guidance is a delivery system which systematically helps students reach the career development outcomes of self awareness and assessment, career awareness and exploration, career decision making, career planning and placement. The school counselor's role covers many areas within a school setting and career guidance is one of the counselor's most important contributions to a student's lifelong development. Career guidance can best be conceptualized by the following basic concepts:

- Career development is a lifelong process.
- Career guidance is deeply rooted in the theory and research of the career development process.
- Career guidance is developmental in nature (K–postsecondary) moving from self and career awareness—to career exploration—to career decision-making—to career planning—to implementation of decisions and plans. The entire developmental process can be repeated more than once during the life span.
- Career guidance recognizes and emphasizes education/work relationships at all levels of education.

- Career guidance views the work values of persons as part of their total system of personal values—and so views work as an integral part of a person's total lifestyle.
- Career guidance recognizes the importance of both paid and unpaid work. In doing so, it recognizes that the human need to work, for any given person, can be met by either, or both, paid and unpaid work. The School Counselor, as a Career Guidance professional, is the person to assume leadership in the implementation of career development outcomes. Furthermore, indirect services to parents, staff and the greater community, as they relate to the career development outcomes for students, are also the school counselor's responsibility. Indirect services include but are not limited to staff development, parent and school board presentation and the establishment of strong supportive linkages with business, industry and labor.

A Five Phased Approach to Career Guidance in an Education System

Career guidance professionals are most needed and can gain greatest recognition through participation in process-oriented approaches to educational change. Of the several kinds of process-oriented approaches to educational change, career education represents the most logical and certainly the most ready one available for consideration by the school counselor acting in their capacity as a career guidance professional.

Career Guidance calls for educational change beginning no later than kindergarten and extending through all of publicly supported education. Concepts must be delivered in an equitable manner to all students in order to bring a sense of meaningfulness and purposefulness to both the curriculum and the services of the educational system.

Career Guidance concepts have been influenced by the school counselor for many years but must now be broadened to invite support from faculty, staff, administration, students, parents and the very diverse segments of the broader community.

In order to broaden the support base, the person in authority must make clear to all school personnel that career guidance is everyone's responsibility. No one segment is in a position to deliver all of the concepts. However, one person must be appointed who will be held accountable and be given authority to develop, coordinate and monitor the total effort in order that a developmental delivery system is put in place and continues to function. The person responsible for this development and coordination should be a school counselor with management and organizational skills.

In order to implement a comprehensive career guidance program in an educational system the initial emphasis must be on an effective process-oriented effort aimed at educational change. The following are considerations which are necessary but not sufficient to meet the needs for the educational change.

- School counselors, administrators and faculty members must become sensitized to the concepts of career guidance.
- School counselors, administrators and faculty members must become familiar with the concept that career infusion need not result in the loss of teaching or counseling time.

- Faculty members must be able to make the same kinds of connections between the subject(s) taught and the world of work that the students will make between the subject(s) learned and the world of work.
- Professional development and activities related to implementation of this process shall take place during the school day with appropriate or usual compensation provided to participants.

Based on the philosophy and the practical outcomes listed above, the following five phased approach to career guidance will allow the school counselor to utilize his/her training and expertise in facilitating groups, coordinating activities and identifying and developing community contacts and resources.

Phase I

The Counselor as a Career Guidance Professional develops a broad base of understanding between the faculty members and the broader community. A series of inservice programs should be developed involving faculty members and significant members of both the private and public sectors of the community. The primary goals of these inservice programs include:

- Developing an understanding of career guidance.
- Developing a sensitivity to the concepts of race, sex and the exceptional student.
- Developing a "core committee" of persons representing all levels of the educational system with select representation from the private and public sectors.

Phase II

The Counselor as a Career Guidance Professional, with the "core committee" develops goals and objectives to form a skeleton around which sub-committees will add "flesh" in the form of faculty/counselor developed lessons and activities.

Phase III

The Counselor as a Career Guidance Professional facilitates the development of workshops conducted by core committee members for the purpose of developing sample activities which relate to each goal and objective at each level. Additional staff members from each level are invited to become resource persons for the committee. Emphasis is placed on the interaction of faculty from all levels of the system working together to develop clearly articulated and developmentally sequenced activities.

Phase IV

The Counselor as a Career Guidance Professional, utilizing the "core committee" coordinates the compilation of all of the goals, objectives and activities (the product of Phase III) and a resource appendix into one infusion document. This document, developed with and delivered to the teachers is to be used as a guide for infusion. The document is disseminated to all faculty and administration as well as to those community members participating in an advisory manner to the core committee.

Phase V

The Counselor as a Career Guidance Professional will call upon the "core committee" whenever needed for the purposes of revising, updating, disseminating and evaluating the career guidance program.

It should be noted that the role of the school counselor serving as a career guidance professional is one of coordinating and facilitating not the writing or implementing of the career infusion plan for the classroom teacher.

These five phases, if implemented effectively, insure infusion of career guidance into all curriculum areas starting early in the educational process. The school counselor as a career guidance professional can then concentrate on the delivery of a series of common, core experiences leading to career maturity through awareness, exploration, decision making and planning. These experiences should be developmental in nature and serve as the link that ties together all of the infusion efforts and focuses on the student in relation to his/her future work experience.

The common core experiences should provide the following for all students:

- Individual and group counseling to clarify work values and develop coping and planning skills.
- Formal and informal assessment of abilities, personality traits and interest.
- Occupational/career information through community linkages such as field trips, speakers, shadowing experiences, internships.
- A career information center providing job hunting skills, interviewing skills, educational and training opportunities and financial aid possibilities.
- Training, goal setting and decision making for the selection of tentative career paths based on the above.
- An opportunity for integration of academic and career planning leading to the selection of high school curriculum as it relates to the appropriate career clusters.
- An opportunity for continuous evaluation and revision of the goal setting process and action planning including an annual review of all students' plans of study.

This policy statement presents a philosophy, some explanations and a prepared plan of action concerning the role of the school counselor as a career guidance professional. This is only a beginning—much more work needs to be done to implement a pro-active stance for school counselors to meet the career development needs for all students. Parents, school boards and the public and private sector are applying pressure on the educational system to meet these needs—we can avoid becoming victims of structural educational reform by participating in it.

Appendix **M**

The School Counselor and Family/Parenting Education

***American School Counselor Association
(Adopted 1989; revised 1993)***

The Position of the American School Counselor Association (ASCA)

School counselors need to take an active role in the initiation, promotion, and leadership of providing family/parenting education in the schools.

The Rationale

Family/parenting education is specialized instruction on the practices of childrearing. Instruction and strategies are provided by trained group leaders, who provide guidance, resources and consultation on a regular basis.

Family/parenting education programs positively influence the attitudes of parents and cause behavioral changes in their children. Research findings indicate that school-sponsored parent education integrates home and school life. It provides families with a model of participation and control that provides benefits in other major life areas.

The Counselor's Role

Under a comprehensive school counseling program, grades K–12, the school counselor will include in its counselor-taught or initiated units community-oriented family/parenting education programs. The content of the developmental guidance will vary according to the developmental levels, stages and needs of the participants, but will be provided to students as part of the Family Life/Teen Parent component of the guidance program and to Parents as part of the Community Outreach component of the guidance program. Group approaches are the preferred means of delivery for developmental guidance activities in terms of efficiency and effectiveness. The goal of the parent education program is to improve parenting skills in interpersonal relationships on the basis of mutual respect, to improve problem-solving and decision-making skills, and to provide a "skill-bank" of alternative coping skills. The counselor also provides resources and educational materials for parents to continue their independent study of parenting skills.

Summary

Research findings indicate that school-sponsored parent education integrates home and school life, providing families with a model of participation and control that provides benefits in other major life areas. The school counselor, as part of the comprehensive school counseling program, takes an active role in providing family/parenting education in the schools.

Appendix *N*

The School Counselors and Their Evaluation

American School Counselor Association (Adopted 1978; reaffirmed 1984; revised 1986)

Since the primary purpose of the evaluation process is to assure the continued professional growth of school counselors, the American School Counselor Association (ASCA) is committed to the continued improvement of this process. It is this organization's position that evaluation must be based upon specific facts and comprehensive evaluation criteria which recognizes the differences between evaluating counselors and classroom personnel and which conform to local and state regulations. It is recommended that each counselor be evaluated with regard to the implementation of the district's guidance and counseling department's written plan. The plan, as well as the counselor, needs to be evaluated and reviewed annually. The plan needs to contain specific goals along with objectives which emphasize student outcomes. The plan needs to be a dynamic document which is modified annually to reflect the changing needs of the students and the improved skills of the counseling staff. As the American School Counselor Association is committed to the improvement of school counseling services, the Association welcomes the opportunity to aid local administrators, department heads and others charged with the improvement or development of evaluation instruments and procedures.

Appendix *O*

======================================

The School Counselor and Confidentiality

American School Counselor Association (Adopted 1974;
reviewed and reaffirmed 1980; revised 1986)

The members of the American School Counselor Association (ASCA) affirm their belief in the worth and dignity of the individual. It is the professional responsibility of school counselors to fully respect the right to privacy of those with whom they enter counseling relationships.

Confidentiality is an ethical term denoting a counseling practice relevant to privacy. *Privileged Communication* is a legal term denoting a requirement to protect the privacy between counselor and student.

Counselors must keep abreast of and adhere to all laws, policies and ethical standards pertaining to confidentiality. It is the responsibility of the counselor to provide prior notice to students regarding the possible necessity for consulting with others.

Where confidentiality is provided, ASCA recognizes that a counseling relationship requires an atmosphere of trust and confidence between the student and the counselor. A student has the right to privacy and to expect confidentiality. This confidentiality must not be abridged by the counselor except where there is a clear and present danger to the student and to other persons.

The counselor reserves the right to consult with other professionally competent persons when this is in the interest of the student. Confidentiality assures that disclosures made will not be divulged to others except when authorized by the student. Counseling information used in research and training of counselors should be fully guaranteed the anonymity of the counselee.

In the event of possible judicial proceedings the counselor should initially advise the school administration as well as the counselee if available, and if necessary, consult legal counsel. When reports are required to be produced, every effort should be made to limit demands for information to those matters essential for the purposes of the legal proceedings.

Guidelines

1. The main purpose of confidentiality is to offer counselees a relationship in which they will be able to deal with what concerns them without fear of disclosure. Furthermore, counselors have a similar responsibility in protecting the privileged information received through confidential relationships with teachers and parents.

2. In reality, it is the student who is privileged. It is the student's or student's parent or guardian in cases of minors who own information and the student or guardian has the right to say who shall have access to it and who shall not.

3. The counselor and student should be provided with adequate physical facilities that guarantee the confidentiality of the counseling relationship.

4. With the enactment of P.L. 93-380 which speaks to the rights and privacy of parents and students, great care should be taken with recorded information.

5. Counselors must be concerned about individuals who have access to confidential information. Counselors must adhere to P.L. 93-380.

6. All faculty and administrative personnel should receive in-service training concerning the privacy rights of students. Counselors should assume the primary responsibility for educating school personnel in this area.

7. It should be the policy of each school to guarantee secretaries adequate working space so that students and school personnel will not come into contact with confidential information, even inadvertently.

8. Counselors should undertake a periodic review of information requested of their students. Only relevant information should be retained.

9. Counselors will adhere to ethical standards and local policies in relating student information over the telephone.

10. Counselors should be aware that it is much more difficult to guarantee confidentiality in group counseling than in individual counseling.

11. Communications made in good faith concerning the student may be classified as privileged by the courts and the communicating parties will be protected by law against legal action seeking damages for libel or slander. Generally, it may be said that an occasion of this particular privilege arises when one acts in the bona fide discharge of a public or private duty. This privilege may be abused or lost by malice, improper and unjustified motive, bad faith or excessive publication.

12. When a counselor is in doubt about what to release in a judicial proceeding, the counselor should arrange a conference with the judge to explain the counselor's dilemma and get advice as to how to proceed.

13. Counselors have a responsibility to encourage school administrators to develop written policies concerning the ethical handling of all records in their school sys-

tem. The development of additional guidelines relevant to the local situation is encouraged.

14. Finally, it is strongly recommended that state and local counselor associations implement these principles and guidelines with appropriate legislation.

With the passage of the Family Educational Rights and Privacy Act, P.L. 93-380 (The Buckley Amendment), great care must be taken with recorded information. It is essential that counselors familiarize themselves with this Law which is a part of the omnibus Education Amendments of 1974 and support its intent to all their publics.

Provisions of this law on parent and student rights and privacy:

1. Deny federal funds to any educational institution that refuses a student's parents access to their child's school record. Parents also have the right to challenge the accuracy of any records.

2. Deny federal funds if records are released to outside groups without parent consent with exception of other school court orders and financial aid applications, with clearance procedures of parents even on the exceptions.

Ail counselors should have a copy of the complete law.

Appendix P

The School Counselor
and Censorship

American School Counselor Association (Adopted 1985)

Introduction

The membership of the American School Counselor Association (ASCA) is committed to facilitating and promoting the continuing development of each student through guidance and counseling programs within the schools. We recognize that an important aspect of this development involves teaching students the processes of information gathering and intellectual analysis, so that as adults they will be able to make informed decisions and exercise the rights and duties of citizenship in a democratic society. Such teaching requires that students be exposed to a diversity of viewpoints and ideas, a fundamental democratic right guaranteed in our Constitution's provision for free speech, free press and equal protection. Counselors must conscientiously support academic freedom in guidance and counseling and the protection of diversity in our pluralistic society. Counselors also safeguard the right of students to receive services appropriate to their needs as an integral part of the total school curriculum.

Rationale

It is the belief of ASCA that intellectual freedom, access to information and an affirmation of the right to independent thought are the essence of our democratic system. We recognize that within a pluralistic society, efforts to censor may exist, and that these challenges should be met with proper respect for the beliefs of the challengers. Recent reports of increased censorship activities imposed on schools, however, have created a climate that threaten the basic right of students to question, to deal with differences, and to learn to make rational decisions.

Definition

Censorship: The denial of a student's basic rights to receive any of the commonly recognized guidance and counseling services offered by school counselors.

ASCA encourages counselors to take the necessary actions to assure students free access to guidance and counseling information, to provide open exploration of alternative views, and to foster freedom of thought in accordance with our democratic society. Support for these activities is derived from the American School Counselor Association position statement on Developmental Guidance (reaffirmed 1984), which endorses counseling objectives of helping students to develop decision-making skills, to obtain information about themselves, to accept responsibility for their own actions, and to develop skills in interpersonal relationships. Under these guidelines, the school counselor will use unique professional skills to strengthen the entire process of learning in the schools.

The American School Counselor Association further encourages counselors to take necessary actions to assure students access to appropriate services which permit maximum development. The counselor has an obligation to respect each student as a unique individual and must be committed to making recommendations and providing services which best meet the student's needs.

Counselor Role

ASCA strongly endorses, supports, and encourages the incorporation of the following activities into the counselors role.

- The teaching of civic values in the schools including responsibility, accomplishment, respect and freedom as an effort to develop attitudes and behaviors necessary for effective citizenship.
- The providing of opportunities for students to develop critical thinking skills, self-insight and an understanding of diversity.
- The development of problem-solving skills essential to everyone in our society.
- The promotion of a climate of trust and positive interpersonal relationships that enhances academic achievement within the school.
- The advocacy of appropriate services to identify and meet student needs.

ASCA encourages its members to participate in the implementation of the following guidance and counseling activities:

- Provide guidance and counseling services and materials that will support the goals and objectives of the curriculum. This shall include the taking into consideration individual needs; the varied interests, abilities, socio-economic back-grounds and maturity level of the students served.

- Provide in schools a comprehensive collection of guidance and counseling mate-rials chosen in compliance with basic written selection criteria developed by the school district. Maximum accessibility to these materials should be provided to students, staff and parents.
- Provide guidance and counseling support for teachers and activities for students that will encourage growth and academic excellence.
- Provide guidance and counseling experience which recognizes diverse ideas and beliefs and their impact on American and world heritage and culture, thereby enabling students to develop intellectual integrity in forming judgments.
- Provide data to the school staff and community regarding goals, objectives and evaluation of the guidance and counseling program to insure implementation of changes when appropriate in accordance with state and local school board policies.

Prevention Strategies

- Be able to explain in everyday language your rationale for using various tech-niques, methods or approaches.
- Be able to demonstrate accountability with clear objectives, detailed methods and supportive data in everyday language.
- Keep parents informed through presentation at PTA meetings and parent study groups.
- Develop a brochure explaining the goals and processes of the guidance and coun-seling program.
- Launch an effective public relations campaign. Students are powerful public rela-tions agents when they have been taught how to tell others about the guidance and counseling program and the activities they are experiencing.
- Be aware of the issues and special interest groups in your community and gain an understanding of the issues that are upsetting to them.
- Develop a list of individuals or groups who can act as advocates.
- Establish a guidance and counseling advisory board.
- Identify the guidance and counseling program within the context of the overall school curriculum.
- Conduct student need assessments to establish the need and priority of services to be offered.
- Continue to review and test guidance and counseling materials and techniques in order to improve skills and service.
- Be aware of your school district's commitment to intellectual freedom and guid-ance and counseling.
- Review state and national legislation for bills which could restrict the counselor's role in developmental guidance.
- Lobby for legislation which would require each school district to provide a pre–K to 12 developmental guidance and counseling curriculum.
- Join groups which provide in service opportunities at the state and national level, such as ASCA and AACD.

Confrontation Strategies

- Be positive.
- Be an effective listener.
- Ask for specifics.
- Discuss rather than debate.
- Draw on program evaluation data to illustrate your examples.
- Defend principles of intellectual freedom, if necessary, rather than particular methods.
- Be open to the truth in any criticism offered.
- Relate guidance to learning.
- Meet again or refer.
- Identify potential human resources who would be willing to work with you.
- Be knowledgeable about the school district's formal complaint procedure.
- If an attack intensifies, consider going public or getting aid from professional organizations such as ASCA, NEA or AFT.

Summary

In order for students to develop in a healthy manner and obtain the skills necessary for citizenship, they need to exist in a climate which fosters the ability to make informed decisions based upon independent inquiry. School counselors have an obligation to support the basic tenets of democracy so as to help insure this healthy development of our counselees.

References

Adler, A. (1963). *The problem child.* New York: G. P. Putnam's Sons.

Albert, L., & Einstein, E. (1986). *Strengthening step-families leader's guide.* Circle Pines, MN: American Guidance Services.

Albuquerque Public Schools. (1978). *Guidance and counseling handbook.* Albuquerque: Author.

Albuquerque Public Schools. (1982). *K–12 Guidance/Counseling program.* Albuquerque: Author.

Alexander, K., & Alexander, M. (1984). *The law of schools, students, and teachers.* St. Paul: West.

Allen, J. (1992). *Action-oriented research: Promoting school counseling advocacy and accountability.* Ann Arbor: University of Michigan. (ERIC Counseling and Personnel Services Clearinghouse No. EDO-CG-92-6)

Allen, J. (1993, June). School counseling: Its presence, past, future. *The ASCA Counselor, 30* (5), 8–9.

Amatea, E. (1989). *Brief strategic intervention for school behavior problems.* San Francisco: Jossey-Bass.

Amatea, E., & Sherrard, P. (1991). When students cannot or will not change their behavior: Using brief strategic intervention in the school. *Journal of Counseling and Development, 69* (4), 341–344.

American Association of University Women. (1992). *The AAUW report: How schools shortchange girls.* Washington, DC: American Association for University Women Educational Foundation.

American Counseling Association (1993). Counseling and children's play [Special Issue]. *Elementary School Guidance and Counseling, 28* (1).

American Counseling Association. (1994). *Legislative update.* Alexandria, VA: Author.

American Psychiatric Association (1980). *Diagnostic and statistical manual of mental disorders* (3rd ed.). Washington, DC: Author.

American Psychiatric Association. (1994). *Diagnostic and statistical manual of mental disorders* (4th ed.). Washington, DC: Author.

American School Counselor Association. (1990a, December). ASCA defines the role of the school counselor. *The ASCA Counselor, 28* (2), 10.

American School Counselor Association. (1990b). *Professional development guidelines for elementary school counselors: A self-audit.* Alexandria, VA: Author.

American School Counselor Association. (1992, April). Ethical standards for school counselors. *The ASCA Counselor, 29* (5), 13–16.

American School Counselor Association (1993). *Children are our future—school counseling 2000.* Alexandria, VA: Author.

Ames, C., & Ames, R. (1984). Goal structures and motivation. *The Elementary School Journal, 85* (1), 39–52.

Anderson, B., & Vohs, J. (1992–93). Another look at section 504. *Coalition Quarterly, 10* (1). Boston: Federation for Children With Special Needs, 1–3.

Anderson, J. (1987). *PUMSY in pursuit of excellence.* Eugene, OR: Timberline Press.

Anderson, J. (1990). *Bright beginnings.* Eugene, OR: Timberline Press.

Anderson, L. (1990). A rationale for global education. In K. Tye, (Ed.), *Global education: From thought to action* (pp. 13–34). Alexandria, VA: Association for Supervision and Curriculum Development.

Ansbacher, H., & Ansbacher, R. (1956). *The individual psychology of Alfred Adler: A systematic presentation in selections from his writings.* New York: Harper & Row.

Arbuckle, D. (1970). *Counseling: Philosophy, theory, and practice.* Boston: Allyn & Bacon.

Arizona State Department of Education. (1976). *Creative Action Counseling and Useful Strategies (C.A.C.T.U.S.).* Phoenix: Author.

Asselin, C., Nelson, T., & Platt, J. (1975). *Teacher study group leader's manual.* Chicago: Alfred Adler Institute.

Atkinson, D., & Juntunen, C. (1994). School counselors and school psychologists as school-home-community liaisons in ethnically diverse schools. In P. Pedersen & J. Carey (Eds.), *Multicultural counseling in schools* (pp. 103–119). Boston: Allyn & Bacon.

Avasthi, S. (1990, July). Breaking through barriers to reach Hispanic immigrants. *Guidepost,* pp. 1, 4, 8.

Axline, V. (1947). *Play therapy.* Boston: Houghton Mifflin.

Axline, V. (1964). *Dibbs: In search of self.* Boston: Houghton Mifflin.

Backover, A. (1992, July). Attention deficit disorder—hard to detect, harder to treat. *Guidepost,* p. 8.

Bailey, W., Deery, N., Gehrke, M., Perry, N., & Whitledge, J. (1989). Issues in elementary school counseling: Discussion with American School Counselor Association leaders. *Elementary School Guidance and Counseling, 24* (1), 4–13.

Baker, S. (1992). *School counseling for the twenty-first century.* New York: Macmillan.

Ballard, J., Ramirez, B., & Zantal-Wiener, K. (1989). Public law 94-142, Section 504, and public law 99-457: Understanding what they are and are not. Reston, VA: The Council for Exceptional Children.

Balow, I., Farr, R., Hogan, T., & Prescott, G. (1984). *Metropolitan achievement tests: Sixth edition.* San Antonio: Psychological Corporation.

Banks, J. (1994). Transforming the mainstream curriculum. *Educational Leadership, 51* (8), 4–8.

Baruth, L., & Manning, M. (1992). Understanding and counseling Hispanic American children. *Elementary School Guidance and Counseling, 27* (2), 113–122.

Bedley, G. (1993). *Values in action!* Irvine, CA: People-Wise Publications.

Belkin, G. (1975). *Practical counseling in the schools.* Dubuque, IA: William C. Brown.

Bell, T., & Elmquist, D. (1994). *Caring Connections.* Ellisville, MO: SFM Direct Marketing, Inc/Fulfillment NOW! Division.

Bennett, W. (1986). *What works: Schools without drugs.* Washington, DC: U.S. Department of Education.

Benshoff, J., Poidevant, J., & Cashwell, C. (1994). School discipline programs: Issues and implications for school counselors. *Elementary School Guidance and Counseling, 28* (3), 163–169.

Berry, E. (1979). Guidance and counseling in the elementary school: Its theoretical base. *Personnel and Guidance Journal, 57,* 513–520.

Bibliotherapy for children and teens catalog. (1994). Washington, MO: Paperbacks for Educators.

Birk, J., & Blimline, C. (1984). Parents as career development facilitators: An untapped resource for the counselors. *The School Counselor, 31* (4), 310–317.

Bleuer, J. (1983). *Accountability in counseling.* Ann Arbor: University of Michigan. *Counselor quest.* ERIC Counseling and Personnel Services Clearinghouse.

Blocher, D. (1966). *Developmental counseling.* New York: The Ronald Press.

Blocher, D. (1980). Developmental counseling revisited. *Counseling and Human Development, 13* (4), 1–7.

Bonstingl, J. (1993, October). Why apply a business approach to schools? *ASCD Program News,* pp. 3–4.

Borba, M., & Borba, C. (1978). *Self-esteem: A classroom affair.* San Francisco: Harper & Row.

Bowen, M. (1978). *Family therapy in clinical practice.* New York: Jason Aronson.

Bowley, B., & Walther, E. (1992). Attention deficit disorders and the role of the elementary school counselor. *Elementary School Guidance and Counseling, 27* (1), 39–46.

Bowman, R., & Myrick, R. (1987). Effects of an elementary school peer facilitator program on children with behavior problems. *Elementary School Guidance and Counseling, 34* (5), 369–378.

Bradley, D. (1988). Alcohol and drug education in the elementary school. *Elementary School Guidance and Counseling, 23* (2), 99–105.

Brandt, R. (1993). What can we really do? *Curriculum Update, 5.*

Brandt, R. (1994). On educating for diversity: A conversation with James A. Banks. *Educational Leadership, 51* (8), 28–31.

Breckenridge, M., & Vincent, E.L. (1960). *Child development.* Philadelphia: W. B. Saunders.

Brown, D., Spano, D., & Schulte, A. (1988). Consultation training in the master's level counselor education programs. *Counselor Education and Supervision, 27* (4), 323–330.

Brown, L., Sherbenu, R., & Dollar, S. (1982). *Test of Nonverbal Intelligence* (TONI). Austin: Pro-Ed.

Bundy, M., & Boser, J. (1987). Helping latchkey children: A group guidance approach. *The School Counselor, 35* (1), 58–65.

Burdin, J., & McAulay, J. (1971). *Elementary school curriculum and instruction.* New York: The Ronald Press.

Burke, D., & Van de Streek, L. (1989). Children of divorce: An application of Hammond's group counseling for children. *Elementary School Guidance and Counseling, 24* (2), 112–118.

Cadman, C. (1994, February). In R. Rossman & G. Kovner, Petaluma youth violence growing. *The Press Democrat,* p. B1.

California State Department of Education. (1990). *Toward a state of esteem.* Sacramento: Office of State Printing.

California State University (1992). *Community report card: Making kids count.* Fullerton, CA: Center for Collaboration for Children.

California Test Bureau. (1978). *California Achievement Test (CAT).* Monterey, CA: CTB/McGraw Hill.

California Test Bureau. (1981). *Comprehensive test of basic skills* (CTBS). Monterey, CA: CTB/McGraw Hill.

Candoli, I., Hack, W., Ray, J., & Stollar, D. (1978). *School business administration: A planning approach.* Boston: Allyn & Bacon.

Canfield, J., & Siccone, F. (1993). *101 ways to develop student self-esteem and responsibility, vol. 1.* Boston: Allyn & Bacon.

Canfield, J., & Wells, H. (1976). *100 ways to enhance self-esteem in the classroom.* Englewood Cliffs, NJ: Prentice Hall.

Cano, M. (1994, February). What to tell children about prejudice. Presentation at the California Association for Counseling and Development Annual Convention, Los Angeles.

Carlson, J. (1980). Motivation: Building Students' feelings of confidence and self-worth. *Counseling and Human Development, 12* (6).

Casey, J. (1992). A conversation with Donald H. Blocher. *Journal of Counseling and Development, 70* (6), 659–665.

Child encouragement project (CEP). (1977). Title IV ESEA, Part C. Albuquerque: North Area Office.

Christian, B. (1983). A practical reinforcement hierarchy for classroom behavior modification. *Psychology in the Schools, 20,* 83–84.

Ciborowski, P. (1990). Group play therapy and children of divorce. *The ASCA Counselor, 28* (1), 4.

College Entrance Examination Board. (1986). *Keeping the options open: Recommendations.* New York: College Board Publications.

Commission on Teacher Credentialing. (1989). *Addition to Title 5 regulations, California code of regulations.* Sacramento: Author.

Community Board Program. (1987). *Conflict resolution resources.* San Francisco: Author.

Conners, C. (1990). *Conners' rating scales.* Los Angeles: Western Psychological Services.

Conoley, J., & Conoley, C. (1982). *School consultation: A guide to practice and training.* New York: Pergamon Press.

Coopersmith, S. (1981). *Coopersmith self-esteem inventories.* Palo Alto, CA: Consulting Psychologists Press.

Coopersmith, S. (1975a). *Developing motivation in young children.* San Francisco: Albion.

Coopersmith, S. (1975b). Building self-esteem in the classroom. In S. Coopersmith (Ed.), *Developing motivation in young children* (pp. 95–131). San Francisco: Albion.

Corey, G. (1977). *Theory and practice of counseling and psychotherapy.* Pacific Grove, CA: Brooks/Cole.

Corey, G. (1991). *Theory and practice of counseling and psychotherapy* (3rd ed.). Pacific Grove, CA: Brooks/Cole.

Corey, M., & Corey, G. (1987). *Groups: Process and practice* (3rd ed.). Monterey, CA: Brooks/Cole.

Cormier, L., Cormier, S., & Hackney, H. (1987). *The professional counselor: A process guide to helping.* Englewood Cliffs, NJ: Prentice Hall.

Corsini, R. (1959). The meaning of Adlerian family counseling. In R. Dreikurs, R. Corsini, R. Lowe, & M. Sonstegard (Eds.), *Adlerian family counseling* (pp. 1–6). Eugene, OR: The University Press.

Council for Accreditation of Counseling and Related Educational Programs. (1994). *1994 CACREP Accreditation Standards and Procedures Manual.* Alexandria, VA: American Counseling Association.

Council for Accreditation of Counseling and Related Educational Programs. (1988). *Accreditation procedures manual and application.* Alexandria, VA: American Counseling Association.

Cowan, D., Palomares, S., & Schilling, D. (1992). *Teaching the skills of conflict resolution.* Spring Valley, CA: Interchoice Publishing.

Crabbs, M. (1989). Future perfect: Planning for the next century. *Elementary School Guidance and Counseling, 24* (2), 160–166.

Cranston-Gingras, A., & Anderson, D. (1990). Reducing the migrant student dropout rate: The role of school counselors. *The School Counselor, 38* (2), 95–104.

Cunningham, L., & Peters, H. (1973). *Counseling theories: A selective examination for school counselors.* Columbus: Charles E. Merrill.

Curwin, R. (1993). The healing power of altruism. *Educational Leadership, 51* (3), 36–39.

Dade county mandates elementary counseling. (1985). *Guidepost, 28* (9), 2.

Darling-Hammond, L., & Wise, A. (1985). Beyond standardization: State standards and school improvement. *The Elementary School Journal, 85* (3), 315–336.

De Blassie, R. (1976). *Counseling with Mexican American youth.* Austin: Learning Concepts, Inc.

Despres, J. (1993, February). School reform and "workforce skills": A one-two knockout punch for school counseling? *Guidepost,* p. 20.

de Shazer, S. (1982). *Patterns of brief family therapy: An ecosystem approach.* New York: Guilford Press.

de Shazer, S. (1985). *Keys to solution in brief therapy.* New York: W. W. Norton.

de Shazer, S. (1988). *Clues: Investigative solutions in brief therapy.* New York: W. W. Norton.

de Shazer, S., Berg, I., Lipchik, E., Nunnally, E., Molnar, A., Gingerich, W., & Weiner-Davis, M. (1986). Brief therapy: Focused solution development. *Family Process, 25,* 208–221.

Dickenson, D., & Bradshaw, S. (1992). Multiplying effectiveness: Combining consultation with counseling. *The School Counselor, 40* (2), 118–124.

Dinkmeyer, D. (1968). Developmental counseling in the elementary school. In H. Peters and M. Bathory (Eds.), *School counseling: Perspectives and procedures* (pp. 105–111). Itasca, IL: F. E. Peacock.

Dinkmeyer, D. (1973). *Developing understanding of self and others (DUSO).* Circle Pines, MN: American Guidance Services.

Dinkmeyer, D., & Caldwell, E. (1977). In J. Muro & D. Dinkmeyer, *Counseling in the elementary and middle school.* Dubuque, IA: William C. Brown.

Dinkmeyer, D., & Dinkmeyer, D., Jr. (1982a). *DUSO-1* (Revised). Circle Pines, MN: American Guidance Services.

Dinkmeyer, D., & Dinkmeyer, D., Jr. (1982b). *DUSO-2* (Revised). Circle Pines, MN: American Guidance Services.

Dinkmeyer, D., & McKay, G. (1976). *Systematic training for effective parenting.* Circle Pines, MN: American Guidance Services.

Dinkmeyer, D., & McKay, G. (1989). *Systematic training for effective parenting* (2nd ed.). Circle Pines, MN: American Guidance Services.

Dinkmeyer, D., McKay, G., & Dinkmeyer, D., Jr. (1980). *Systematic training for effective teaching.* Circle Pines, MN: American Guidance Services.

Dinkmeyer, D., McKay, G., Dinkmeyer, D., Jr., Dinkmeyer, J., & Mckay, J. (1987). *The next STEP: Effective parenting through problem solving.* Circle Pines, MN: American Guidance Services.

Dinkmeyer, D., McKay, G., & McKay, J. (1987). *New beginnings.* Champaign, IL: Research Press.

Dougherty, A. M. (1992). School consultation in the 1990s. *Elementary School Guidance and Counseling, 26* (3), 163–164.

Dougherty, A., & Dougherty, L., & Purcell, D. (1991). The sources and management of resistance to consultation. *The School Counselor, 38* (3), 178–186.

Downing, J. (1988). Counseling interventions with depressed children. *Elementary School Guidance and Counseling, 22* (3), 231–240.

Downing, J., & Downing, S. (1991). Consultation with resistant parents. *Elementary School Guidance and Counseling, 25* (4), 296–301.

Dreikurs, R. (1959). Fundamental principles of child guidance. In R. Dreikurs, R. Corsini, R. Lowe, & M. Sonstegard (Eds.), *Adlerian family counseling* (pp. 17–21). Eugene, OR: University Press.

Dreikurs, R., & Grey, L. (1968). *A new approach to discipline: Logical consequences.* New York: Hawthorn Books.

Dreikurs, R., Grunwald, B., & Pepper, F. (1971). *Maintaining sanity in the classroom: Illustrated teaching techniques.* New York: Harper & Row.

Drum, D., & Figler, H. (1973). *Outreach in counseling.* New York: Intext Educational Publishers.

Drummond, R. (1992). *Appraisal procedures for counselors and helping professionals* (2nd ed.). New York: Merrill.

Dunn, L., & Dunn, L. (1981). *Peabody picture vocabulary test-Revised.* Circle Pines, MN: American Guidance Services.

Dupont, H., Gardner, O., & Brody, D. (1974). *Toward affective development.* Circle Pines, MN: American Guidance Services.

Duska, R., & Whelan, M. (1975). *Moral development: A guide to Piaget-Kohlberg.* New York: Paulist Press.

Edelman, M. (1994, May). A mother's day tribute. *Parade Magazine,* pp. 4–6.

Elkind, D. (1978). *A sympathetic understanding of the child: Birth to sixteen* (2nd ed.). Boston: Allyn & Bacon.

English, F. (1983). Goals and objectives. *Fundamental curriculum decisions.* Alexandria: Association for Supervision and Curriculum Development.

Ehrhart, J., & Sandler, B., (1987). Women shirk technical fields. *Guidepost, 29* (18), 16.

ERIC Clearinghouse on Elementary and Early Childhood Education (1990). Child sexual abuse: What it is and how to prevent it. *ERIC Digest.* Urbana, IL: Author.

Erk, R. (1995). A diagnosis of attention deficit disorder: What does it mean for school counselors? *The School Counselor, 42* (4), 292–299.

Esper, G. (1993, September 26). Center offers escape from life of hell. *The Press Democrat,* Santa Rosa, CA, pp. 10–11.

Evans, C. (1987). Teaching a global perspective in elementary classrooms. *The Elementary School Journal, 87* (5), 545–555.

Fairbanks, J. (1988). *Project L.I.N.C.: Linking an intervention network to children.* Long Beach, CA: Long Beach Unified School District.

Fairchild, T. (1993). Accountability practices of school counselors: 1990 national survey. *The School Counselor, 40* (5), 363–374.

Faller, K. C. (1993). *Child sexual abuse: Intervention and treatment issues.* Washington, D.C.: National Center on Child Abuse and Neglect.

Faust, V. (1968a). *The counselor–consultant in the elementary school.* Boston: Houghton Mifflin.

Faust, V. (1968b). *Establishing guidance programs in elementary schools.* Boston: Houghton Mifflin.

Ferris, P., & Linville, M. (1988). The child's rights: Whose responsibility? In W. Huey & T. Remley, Jr., *Ethical issues in school counseling* (pp. 20–30). Alexandria, VA: American School Counselor Association.

Fincher, T. (1993). Realizing our responsibilities. *American Counselor, 2* (4), 36.

Fine, M. (1992). A systems-ecological perspective on home-school intervention. In M. Fine, & C. Carlson (Eds.), *The handbook of family-school intervention* (pp. 1–17). Boston: Allyn & Bacon.

Fischer, L., & Sorenson, G. (1991). *School law for counselors, psychologists, and social workers.* New York: Longman.

Fleming, P., Martin, D., & Martin, M. (1986). Principals' opinions of elementary school counseling services. *Elementary School Guidance and Counseling, 21* (2), 167–168.

French, T. (1993, August). Parents are the real school dropouts. *The Press Democrat,* p. G1.

Frenza, M. (1984). Selected issues in elementary guidance. *Counselor quest.* University of Michigan: ERIC Counseling and Personnel Services Clearinghouse, 146.

Frymier, J. (1992). *Growing up is risky business and schools are not to blame,* Volumes I & II. Bloomington, IN: Phi Delta Kappa.

Garrison, R., Ivey, M., & Weinrach, S. (1991). Bullying in our schools. *1991 Annual Meeting of the American Association for Counseling and Development.* Reno, NV.

Gazda, G. (1986, Summer). Curriculum for training counselors. *ACES Newsletter,* pp. 30–31.

George, R., & Cristiani, T. *Counseling theory and practice* (2nd ed.). Englewood Cliffs, NJ: Prentice Hall.

Gerler, E. , Jr. (1982). *Counseling the young learner.* Englewood Cliffs, NJ: Prentice Hall.

Gerler, E., Jr. (1988). Recent research in child abuse: A brief review. *Elementary School Guidance and Counseling, 22* (4), 325–327.

Gerler, E., Jr. (1991a). Closing the 25th volume of *Elementary School Guidance and Counseling. Elementary School Guidance and Counseling, 25* (4), 242.

Gerler, E., Jr. (1991b). The changing world of the elementary school counselor. *Counselor quest.* Ann Arbor: ERIC Counseling and Personnel Services Clearinghouse, 21.

Gerler, R., Jr. (1992). What we know about school coun-seling: A reaction to Borders and Drury. *Journal of Counseling and Development, 70* (4), 499–501.

Gerler, E., Jr., & Anderson, R. (1986). The effects of classroom guidance on children's success in school. *Journal of Counseling and Development, 65,* 78–81.

Gibbs, N. (1990, October). Shameful bequests to the next generation. *Time,* pp. 42–46.

Gibson, R., Mitchell, M., & Higgins, R. (1983). *Development and management of counseling programs and guidance services.* New York: Macmillan.

Gilligan, C. (1982). *In a different voice.* Cambridge: Harvard University Press.

Glasser, W. (1961). *Mental health or mental illness.* New York: Harper & Row.

Glasser, W. (1965). *Reality therapy.* New York: Perennial Library.

Glasser, W. (1969). *Schools without failure.* New York: Harper & Row.

Glasser, W., & Zunin, L. (1973). Reality therapy. In R. Corsini (Ed.). *Current psychotherapies* (pp. 287–315). Itasca, IL: F. E. Peacock.

Glosoff, H., & Koprowicz, C. (1990). *Children achieving potential: An introduction to elementary school counseling and state level policies.* Washington, DC: National Conference of State Legislators; and Alexandria, VA: American Counseling Association.

Golden, L. (1988). Quick assessment of family functioning. *The School Counselor, 35* (3), 179–184.

Goldenberg, I., & Goldenberg, H. (1988). Family systems and the school counselor. In W. Walsh & N. Giblin (Eds.), *Family counseling in school settings* (pp. 26–38). Springfield, IL: Charles C. Thomas.

Gordon, I. (1979). The effects of parent involvement on schooling. In R. Brandt (Ed), *Partners: Parents and schools.* Alexandria, VA: Association of Supervision and Curriculum Development.

Gordon, T. (1975). *P.E.T.: Parent effectiveness training.* New York: New American Library.

Gowan, J., Coole, D., & McDonald, P. (1967). The impact of Piaget on guidance. *Elementary School Guidance, 1* (3), 208–217.

Gray, E. (1987). Latchkey children. *Counselor quest.* University of Michigan: ERIC Counseling and Personnel Services Clearinghouse, 96.

Greenberg, P. (1992, February). *Talking turns.* Presentated at the California Association for Counseling and Development, San Diego, CA.

Greer, J., & Wethered, C. (1987). Learned helplessness and the elementary student: Implications for counselors. *Elementary School Guidance and Counseling, 22* (2), 157–164.

Gresham, F., & Elliot, S. (1990). *Social skills rating system* (SSRS). Circle Pines, MN: American Guidance Services.

Guidance Projects Office. (1987). *STAGES.* Irvine, CA: Irvine Unified School District.

Guild, P. (1994). The culture/learning style connection. *Educational Leadership, 51* (8), 16–21.

Gum, M. (1969). *The elementary school guidance counselor: A developmental model.* St. Paul: Minnesota Department of Education.

Gumaer, J. (1980). Educators' study selection and evaluation of outcome in school consultation. *Personnel and Guidance Journal, 59* (2), 117–119.

Gysbers, N, & Henderson, P. (1988). *Developing and managing your school guidance program.* Alexandria, VA: American Association for Counseling and Development.

Gysbers, N., Hughey, K., Starr, M., & Lapan, R. (1992). Improving school guidance programs: A framework for program, personnel, and results evaluation. *Journal of Counseling and Development, 70* (5), 565–570.

Haack, M. (1994). Defining outcomes for guidance and counseling. *Educational Leadership, 51* (6), 33–35.

Hackney, H. (1990). Counselor preparation for future needs. In H. Hackney (Ed.)., *Changing contexts for counselor preparation in the 1990s* (pp. 77–93). Alexandria, VA: American Counseling Association.

Haley, J. (1987). *Problem solving therapy* (2nd ed.). San Francisco: Jossey-Bass.

Hammer, T., & Turner, P. (1990). *Parenting in contemporary society* (2nd ed.). Englewood Cliffs, NJ: Prentice Hall.

Hannaford, M. (1988, April). Public relations—are you serious? *The ASCA Counselor,* p. 4.

Hansen, J., Himes, B., & Meier, S. (1990). *Consultation concepts and practices.* Englewood Cliffs, NJ: Prentice Hall.

Hansen, J., Stevic, R., & Warner, R. (1986). *Counseling theory and process.* Boston: Allyn & Bacon.

Hart, S. (1991). Childhood depression: Implications and options for school counselors. *Elementary School Guidance and Counseling, 25* (4), 277–289.

Harter, S. (1985). *Manual for the self-perception profile for children.* Denver: University of Denver.

Havighurst, R. (1973) *Developmental tasks and education.* New York: David McKay.

Heathers, G. (1967). The role of innovation in education. In M. Hillson (Ed.), *Elementary education* (pp. 189–202). New York: The Free Press.

Helms, J. (1994). Racial identity in the school environment. In P. Pedersen & J. Carey (Eds.), *Multicultural counseling in schools* (pp. 19–37). Boston: Allyn & Bacon.

Henry, T. (1993, August 16). Drugs in school parents' top fear. *USA Today,* p. 1D.

Herr, E. (1985). *Why counseling?* Alexandria, VA: American Association for Counseling and Development.

Herr, E., & Cramer, S. (1992). *Career guidance and counseling through the life span.* New York: HarperCollins.

Herr, E., & Niles, S. (1994). Multicultural career guidance in the schools. In P. Pedersen & J. Carey (Eds.), *Multicultural counseling in schools* (pp. 177–194). Boston: Allyn & Bacon.

Herring, R. (1989). Counseling Native-American children: Implications for elementary school counselors. *Elementary School Guidance and Counseling, 23* (24), 272–281.

Herring, P. (1992). Biracial children: An increasing concern for elementary and middle school counselors. *Elementary School Guidance and Counseling, 27* (2), 123–130.

Hieronymus, A., Lindquist, E., & Hoover, H. (1978). *Iowa Test of Basic Skills* (ITBS). Chicago: Riverside.

Hinkle, J. (1992). Family counseling in the schools. *Counselor quest.* Ann Arbor, MI: University of Michigan, ERIC Clearinghouse on Counseling and Personnel Services.

Hinsvark, D. (1989–90). Cross-cultural counseling by Southeast Asian guidance aides. *California Association for Counseling and Development, 10,* 21–28.

Hirshey, G. (1988, August). What children wished their parents knew. *Family Circle,* 84–88.

Hoffman, L., & McDaniels, C. (1991). Career development in the elementary schools: A perspective for the 1990s. *Elementary School Guidance and Counseling, 25* (3), 163–171.

Holcomb, T., & Niffenegger, P. (1992). Elementary school counselors: A plan for marketing their services under the new education reform. *Elementary School Guidance and Counseling, 27* (1), 56–63.

Hollander, S. (1992). Making young children aware of sexual abuse. *Elementary School Guidance and Counseling, 26* (4), 305–317.

Holmgren, V. S. (1976). *Action plan for guidance and counseling.* Unpublished manuscript.

Holmgren, V. S. (1992). Who *really* defines the role of the elementary school counselor? Unpublished manuscript, Sonoma State University, Department of Counseling, Rohnert Park, CA.

Hood, A., & Johnson, R. (1991). *Assessment in counseling: A guide to the use of psychological assessment procedures.* Alexandria, VA: American Counseling Association.

Hoover,J., & Hazler, R. (1991). Bullies and victims. *Elementary School Guidance and Counseling, 25* (3), 212–219.

Horne, A. (1982). Counseling families—social learning family therapy. In A. Horne & M. Ohlsen (Eds.), *Family counseling and therapy* (pp. 360–388). Itasca, IL: F. E. Peacock.

Horne, A., & Ohlsen, M. (1982). *Family counseling and therapy.* Itasca, IL: F. E. Peacock.

Hosford, R. (1974). Behaviorism is humanism. In G. Farwell, N. Gamsky, & P. Mathieu-Coughlan (Eds.), *The counselor's handbook* (pp. 295–312). New York: Intext Educational Publishers.

Hosie, T., & Erk, R. (1993). Attention deficit disorder. *ACA Independent Reading.* Alexandria, VA: American Counseling Association.

Howard, M. (1993). Service learning: Character education applied. *Educational Leadership, 51* (3), 42–43.

Howell-Nigrelli, J. (1988). Shared responsibility for reporting child abuse cases: A reaction to Spiegel. *Elementary School Guidance and Counseling, 22* (4), 289–290.

Hoyt, K. (1993). Guidance is not a dirty word. *The School Counselor, 40* (4), 267–273.

Huey, W. (1988). Ethical standards for school counselors: Test your knowledge. In W. Huey & T. Remley, Jr., *Ethical and legal issues in school counseling* (pp. 3–9). Alexandria VA: American School Counselor Association.

Huey, W. (1992). The revised 1992 ethical standards for school counselors. *The School Counselor, 40* (2), 89–92.

Huggins, P. (1986). *Teaching cooperation skills.* Mercer Island, WA: ASSIST.

Humes, C., & Hohenshil, T. (1987). Elementary counselors, school psychologists, school social worker: Who does what? *Elementary School Guidance and Counseling, 22* (1), 37–45.

Humphrey, R. (1992, June). ASCA president elect reports to delegate assembly. *The ASCA Counselor, 29* (5), 14–16.

Humphrey, R. (1993, June). Presidential perspective. *The ASCA Counselor, 30* (5), 2–3.

Hunsicker, R. (1993, November). Who's really at risk? *Teachers in Focus.* Colorado Springs, CO: Focus on the Family.

Ivey, A., & Ivey, M. (1994). *The cultural identity group.* Amherst, MA: Authors.

Jackson, A., & Hayes, S. (1994, April). *Advanced multicultural counseling.* Presentation at the American Counseling Association Annual Convention in Minneapolis, MN.

Janzen, R. Melting pot or mosaic? (1994). *Educational Leadership, 51* (8), 9–11.

Jastak, S., & Wilkinson, G. (1984). *Wide-Range Achievement Test-Revised Administration Manual.* Wilmington, DE: Jastak Associates.

Jennings, C. (1993). From lone star to the big sky. *Technical Horizons in Education* (T.H.E.), *21* (1), 67–70.

Johns, K. (1992). Lowering beginning teacher anxiety about parent-teacher conferences through role-playing. *The School Counselor, 40* (2), 146–152.

Joint Study Group on National Education Goals (1992). *National education goals: America's school boards respond.* Washington, DC: U.S. Government Printing Office.

Jurensen, K. (1993, October 8). A report card for our schools. *USA Today,* p. 12A.

Kagan, S. (1989/1990). The structural approach to cooperative learning. *Educational Leadership, 47* (4), 12–15.

Kaplan, L., & Geoffroy, K. (1987a). The Hatch Amendment: A primer for counselors, part I. *The School Counselor, 35* (1), 9–16.

Kaplan, L., & Geoffroy, K. (1987b). The Hatch Amendment: A primer for counselors, part II. *The School Counselor, 35* (2), 88–95.

Kaufman, A., & Kaufman, N. (1983). *Kaufman assessment battery for children* (K-ABC). Circle Pines, MN: American Guidance Services.

Keat, D., II. (1990). Change in multimodal counseling. *Elementary School Guidance and Counseling, 24* (4), 248–262.

Kegan, R. (1982). *The evolving self.* Cambridge: Harvard University Press.

Kelly, G. (1990). The cultural family of origin: A description of a training strategy. *Counselor Education and Supervision, 30* (1), 77–84.

Kohlberg, L. (1978). The cognitive-developmental approach to moral education. In P. Scharf (Ed.), *Readings in moral education* (pp. 36–51). Minneapolis: Winston Press.

Kral, R. (1992). Solution focused brief therapy: Applications in the schools. In M. Fine & C. Carlson (Eds.), *The handbook of family-school intervention* (pp. 330–346). Boston: Allyn & Bacon.

Kral, R. (1988). *Strategies that work: Techniques for solutions in the schools.* Milwaukee: Brief Family Therapy Center.

Krathwohl, D. (1971). Stating objectives appropriately for programs, for curriculum, and for instructional materials development. In J. M. Palardy (Ed.), *Elementary school curriculum: An anthology of trends and challenges* (pp. 44–60). New York: Macmillan.

Krumboltz, J. (1968). Behavioral counseling: Rationale and research. In H. Peters & M. Bathory (Eds.), *School counseling: Perspectives and procedures* (pp. 118–125). Itasca, IL: F. E. Peacock.

Kyse, B. (1993, September). Where are your kids? We blame TV. We blame schools. Maybe it's time to mention parents. *The Press Democrat*, p. G1.

Ladson-Billings, G. (1994). What we can learn from multicultural education research. *Educational Leadership, 51* (8), 22–26.

Lambert, H. (1963). *Elementary education.* Washington, DC: The Center for Applied Research in Education.

Lamme, L., Krogh, S., & Yachmetz, K. (1992). *Literature-based moral education.* Phoenix: Oryx Press.

Lasko, C. (1986). Childhood depression: Questions and answers. *Elementary School Guidance and Counseling, 20* (4), 283–289.

Lavin, P. (1991). The counselor as consultant-coordinator for children with attention deficit hyperactivity disorder. *Elementary School Guidance and Counseling, 26* (2), 115–120.

Lee, R. (1993). Effects of classroom guidance on student achievement. *Elementary School Guidance and Counseling, 27* (3), 163–171.

Leiter, R. (1952). *Leiter International Performance Scale.* Chicago: Stoelting.

Leonard, P., & Gottsdanker-Willekens, A. (1987). The elementary school counselor as consultant for self-concept enhancement. *The School Counselor, 34* (4), 245–255.

Lerman, S. (1984). *Responsive parenting leader's manual.* Circle Pines, MN: American Guidance Services.

Lewis, B. (1991). *The kid's guide to social action.* Minneapolis, MN: Free Spirit.

Lickona, T. (1993). The return of character education. *Educational Leadership, 51* (3), 6–11.

Lindsay, N. (1993). *Dream catchers.* Indianapolis: JIST Works.

Locke, D. (1989). Fostering the self-esteem of African-American children. *Elementary School Guidance and Counseling, 23* (4), 254–259.

Locke, D., & Parker, L. (1994). Improving the multicultural competence of educators. In P. Pedersen & J. Carey (Eds.), *Multicultural counseling in schools* (pp. 39–58). Boston: Allyn & Bacon.

Lowe, R. (1982). Adlerian/Dreikursian family counseling. In A. Horne & M. Ohlsen (Eds.), *Family counseling and therapy* (pp. 329–359). Itasca, IL: F. E. Peacock.

Lunon, J. (1986). Migrant student record transfer system: What is it and who uses it? *Counselor quest.* University of Michigan: ERIC Counseling and Personnel Clearinghouse, 110.

Maes, W. (1978). Counseling for exceptional children. *Counseling and Human Development, 10* (8).

Manly, L. (1986). Goals of misbehavior inventory. *Elementary School Guidance and Counseling, 21* (2), 160–162.

Markwardt, F. (1989). *Peabody individual achievement test-Revised* (PIAT-R). Circle Pines, MN: American Guidance Services.

Mason, R. (1986). Counseling helps students adapt to relocation. *Guidepost, 29* (8), 8.

Mathias, C. (1992). Touching the lives of children: Consultative interventions that work. *Elementary School Guidance and Counseling, 26* (3), 190–201.

McCarney, S., & Bauer, A. (1989). *The parent's guide.* Columbia, MO: Hawthorne Educational Services.

McCullough, L. (1993, December). Guidance programs, outcome-based education face tough challenges. *Guidepost*, pp. 1, 12, 13.

McCullough, L. (1994, January). Do some school guidance programs contradict family and religious values? *Guidepost*, pp. 1, 12, 13.

McCullough, L. (1994, February). Challenges to guidance programs: How to prevent and handle them. *Guidepost*, pp. 1, 12, 13.

McDaniel, S., & Bielen, P. (1990). *Project self-esteem.* Newport Beach, CA: Enhancing Education.

McDaniels, C., & Puryear, A. (1991). The face of career development centers for the 1990s and beyond. *The School Counselor, 38* (5), 324–331.

McGoldrick, M., Pearce, J., & Giordano, J. (1982). *Ethnicity and family therapy.* New York: Guilford Press.

McGowan, S. (1992a). Why Jane can't read: The glass ceiling in America's schools. *Guidepost, 34* (11), 1, 8.

McGowan, S. (1992b). Making schools equitable: What counselors can do. *Guidepost, 34* (12), 1, 14.

McKay, J., Dinkmeyer, D., Jr., & Dinkmeyer, Sr. (1989). *Drug free.* Circle Pines, MN: American Guidance Services, Inc.

McLaughlin, C. (1993). *The do's and don'ts of parent involvement.* Spring Valley, CA: Interchoice.

McNamee, C. (1993). Herr encourages counselors to restore dignity. *Guidepost, 35* (12), 13.

McWhirter, J., McWhirter, B., McWhirter, A., & McWhirter, E. (1993). *At-risk youth: A comprehensive response.* Pacific Grove, CA: Brooks/Cole.

Meadows, N. (1993). The teacher's guidance handbook: An enhancement to consultation. *The School Counselor, 40* (3), 231–233.

Miller, G. (1986). State guidance consultants' views of elementary and middle school guidance and counseling. *Elementary School Guidance and Counseling, 21,* 166–167.

Miller, G. (1981). Psychological maturity: A new aim of school guidance. *Counseling and Human Development, 13* (10), 1–17.

Mitchum, N. (1989). Increasing self-esteem in Native-American children. *Elementary School Guidance and Counseling, 23* (4), 266–271.

Molnar, A., & de Shazer, S. (1987). Solution-focused therapy: Toward the identification of therapeutic tasks. *Journal of Marital and Family Therapy, 13* (4), 349–358.

Molnar, A., & Lindquist, B. (1989). *Changing problem behavior in schools.* San Francisco: Jossey-Bass.

Montoya, C. (1993, September). Elementary students learn to manage conflict. *Western Center News,* p. 1.

Moody, E., Jr. (1994). Current trends and issues in childhood sexual abuse prevention programs. *Elementary School Guidance and Counseling, 28* (4), 251–256.

Moore, H., & Strickler, C. (1980). The counseling profession's response to sex biased counseling: An update. *The Personnel and Guidance Journal, 59* (2), 84–87.

Moos, R., & Moos, B. (1981). *Children's Version of the Family Environment Scale* (CVFES). Palo Alto, CA: Consulting Psychologists Press.

Morrow, R. (1989). Southeast–Asian parental involvement: Can it be a reality? *Elementary School Guidance and Counseling, 23* (4), 289–297.

Mullis, F., & Berger, M. (1981). The utility of Bowen's theory of family therapy for school counselors. *The School Counselor, 28* (3), 195–201.

Muro, J., & Dinkmeyer, D. (1977). *Counseling in the elementary and middle schools: A pragmatic approach.* Dubuque, IA: William C. Brown.

Myrick, R. (1977). *Consultation as a counselor intervention.* Washington, DC: American School Counselor Association.

Myrick, R. (1989). Developmental Guidance: Practical considerations. *Elementary School Guidance and Counseling, 24* (1), 14–20.

Myrick, R. (1993). *Developmental guidance and counseling: A practical approach* (2nd ed.). Minneapolis: Educational Media Corporation.

Myrick, R., & Moni, L. (1972). Teacher in-service workshops: A developmental consultation approach. *Elementary School Guidance and Counseling, 7,* 156–161.

National Center for Prosecution of Child Abuse (1994). *Definitions for child abuse and child sexual abuse.* Alexandria, VA: American Prosecutors Research Institute.

National Occupational Information Coordinating Committee. (1989). *National career development guidelines—Local handbook for elementary schools.* Washington, DC: Author.

National Occupational Information Coordinating Committee. (1990). *NOICC pamphlet.* Washington, DC: Author.

National Training Consultants. (1990). Elementary Impact Training brochure. Ukiah, CA: Author.

Nelson, J. (1978). A reality therapy peer counseling program. *The Guidance Clinic.* West Nyack, NY: Parker.

Nelson, R. (1991). The counselor as reinforcer. *The School Counselor, 39* (2), 68–76.

Nelson, R., & Crawford, B. (1990). Suicide among elementary school-aged children. *Elementary School Guidance and Counseling, 25* (2), 123–128.

Neukrug, E., Barr, C., Hoffman, L., & Kaplan, S. (1993). Developmental counseling and guidance: A model for use in your school. *The School Counselor, 40* (5), 356–362.

Nichols, M. (1984). *Family therapy.* New York: Gardner Press.

Nicoll, W. (1992). A family counseling and consultation model for school counselors. *The School Counselor, 39* (5), 351–361.

Nugent, F. (1990). *An introduction to the profession of counseling.* Columbus, OH: Merrill.

O'Bryant, B. (1990). Poignant points for power based professionals. *The ASCA Counselor, 28* (2), 1–3, 17.

Oden, S. (1986). Developing social skills instruction for peer interaction and relationships. In G. Cartledge & J. Milburn (Eds.), *Teaching social skills to children* (pp. 246–269). New York: Pergamon Press.

Oliver, R., Oaks, I., and Hoover, J. (1994). Family issues and interventions in bully and victim relationships. *The School Counselor, 41* (3), 199–202.

Omizo, M., Hershberger, J., & Omizo, S. (1988). Teaching children to cope with anger. *Elementary School Guidance and Counseling, 22* (3), 241–245.

Omizo, M., Omizo, S., & D'Andrea, M. (1992). Promoting wellness among elementary school children. *Journal of Counseling and Development, 71* (2), 194–198.

O'Neil, J. (1994). Outcomes-based education comes under attack. *Curriculum Update, 36* (3), 1, 4–5.

Ostrower, E. (1987). A counseling approach to alcohol education in middle schools. *The School Counselor, 34* (3), 209–218.

Otis, A., & Lennon, R. (1982). *Otis-Lennon school ability test.* San Antonio: Psychological Corporation.

Pagliuso, S. (1976). *Understanding stages of moral development.* New York: Paulist Press.

Palomares, S., Schuster, S., & Watkins, C. (1992). *The sharing circle handbook.* Spring Valley, CA: Interchoice.

Palomares, U., & Ball, G. (1976). Methods in human development. In H. Bessell, *Theory manual.* San Diego: Human Development Training Institute.

Parman, M. (1989, September 17). Scary statistics about latchkey kids. *The Press Democrat,* p. B8.

Parnay, R. (1994, February 10). Teaching values in schools. *The Press Democrat,* p. B5.

Parr, G. (1991). Dilemmas in the workplace of elementary school counselors: Coping strategies. *Elementary School Guidance and Counseling, 25* (3), 220–226.

Parr, G., & Ostrovsky, M. (1991). The role of moral development in deciding how to counsel children and adolescents. *Elementary School Guidance and Counseling, 39* (1), 14–19.

Patros, P., & Shamoo, T. (1989). *Depression and suicide in children and adolescents.* Boston: Allyn & Bacon.

Patterson, C. H. (1986, Summer). Counselor training or counselor education. *ACES Newsletter,* 10–12.

Peck, R. (1992, February). *Group counseling for anger management.* Presented at California Association for Counseling and Development annual conference, San Diego, CA.

Pedersen, P. (1991a). Introduction to the special issue on multiculturalism as a fourth force in counseling. *Journal of Counseling and Development, 70* (1), 4.

Pedersen, P. (1991b). Multiculturalism as a generic approach to counseling. *Journal of Counseling and Development, 70* (1), 6–12.

Pedersen, P., & Carey, J. (1994). *Multicultural counseling in schools.* Boston: Allyn & Bacon.

Peeks, B. (1992, February). Parents-student-school: The problem-solving triad. *Communique,* pp. 27–28.

Peeks, B. (1993). Revolutions in counseling and education: A systems perspective in the schools. *Elementary School Guidance and Counseling, 27* (4), 245–251.

Peterson, M, & Poppen, W. (1993). *School counselors and their first freedom.* Ann Arbor: ERIC Counseling and Personnel Services Clearinghouse.

Piaget, J. (1932). *The moral judgement of the child.* London: Paul, Trench, Trubner & Co.

Piers, E., & Harris, P. (1984). *Piers-Harris children's self-concept scale.* Los Angeles: Western Psychological Services.

Popham, W. (1988). *Education evaluation* (2nd ed.). Englewood Cliffs, NJ: Prentice Hall.

Popkin, M. (1993). *Active parenting today for parents of 2–12 year olds.* Atlanta: Active Parenting.

Popkin, M., Garcia, E., & Woodward, H. (1986). *Active parenting learner's guide.* Atlanta: Active Parenting.

Public Law 93-247. (1974). National Child Abuse Prevention and Treatment Act. Washington, DC: U.S. Department of Health and Human Services.

Public Law 94-142. (1976, December). The Education for All Handicapped Children Act. *Federal Register.* Department of Health, Education, and Welfare, Office of Education. Washington, DC: U.S. Government Printing Office.

Purkey, W., & Schmidt, J. (1987). *The inviting relationship: An expanded perspective for professional counseling.* Englewood Cliffs, NJ: Prentice Hall.

Purkey, S., & Smith, M. (1985). School reform: The district policy implications of the effective schools literature. *Elementary School Journal, 85* (3), 353–389.

Radd, T. (1987). *The grow with guidance system.* Canton, OH: Grow with Guidance.

Ramsey, M. (1994). Student depression: General treatment dynamics and system specific interventions. *The School Counselor, 41* (4), 256–262.

Rathvon, N. (1990). The effects of encouragement on off-task behavior and academic productivity. *Elementary School Guidance and Counseling, 24* (3), 189–199.

Raven, J., Court, J., & Raven, J. (1983). *Manual for Raven's progressive matrices and vocabulary scales* (Section 3), Standard Progressive Matrices. London: Lewis.

Reasoner, R. (1982a). *Building self-esteem: Teacher's guide and classroom materials.* Palo Alto, CA: Consulting Psychologists Press.

Reasoner, R. (1982b). *Building self esteem: Parent's guide.* Palo Alto, CA: Consulting Psychologists Press.

Remley, T., Jr. (1988). The law and ethical practices in elementary and middle schools. In W. Huey & T. Remley, Jr., *Ethical and legal issues in school counseling* (pp. 95–105). Alexandria, VA: American School Counselor Association.

Remley, T., Jr., & Fry, L. (1988). Reporting suspected child abuse: Conflicting roles for the counselor. *Elementary School Guidance and Counseling, 22* (4), 253–259.

Rest, J. (1994, June). Moral judgement research . . . A personal history. *Guidepost,* p. 16.

Reynolds, S. (1993). Developmental School Counseling: An overview. *The ASCA Counselor, 30* (4), 12–13.

Reynolds, W. (1989a). *Reynolds child depression scale* (RCDS). Odessa, FL: Psychological Assessment Resources.

Reynolds, W. (1989b). *Reynolds child depression scale manual.* Odessa, FL: Psychological Assessment Resources.

Riles, W. (1982). *Guidelines for developing comprehensive programs in California public schools.* Sacramento: California State Department of Education.

Riley, R. (1994, March). Family ties to education. *The Press Democrat,* p. A5.

Rimm, S. (1986). *Underachievement syndrome.* Watertown, WI: Apple.

Robinson, T. (1992). Transforming at-risk educational practices by understanding and appreciating differences. *Elementary School Guidance and Counseling, 27* (2), 84–95.

Robinson, D., & Mopsik, W. (1992). An environmental-experiential model for counseling handicapped children. *Elementary School Guidance and Counseling, 27* (1), 73–78.

Rodgers, F. (1975). *Curriculum and instruction in the elementary school.* New York: Macmillan.

Rousseve, R. (1989). On minority identity and personal empowerment in contemporary America. *The School Counselor, 37* (2), 85–88.

Ruben, A. (1989). Preventing school dropouts through classroom guidance. *Elementary School Guidance and Counseling, 24* (1), 21–29.

Ruben, A. (1993). School children skeptical about girls' ability to become president. *Guidepost, 36* (1), 6.

Russell, T. (1993, February). *Family counseling skills for school counselors.* Presented at California Association for Counseling and Development annual convention in San Diego.

Salvia, J., & Ysseldyke, J. (1991). *Assessment* (5th ed.). Boston: Houghton Mifflin.

Samples, R. (1975). Serving intrinsic motivation in early education. In S. Coopersmith (Ed.), *Developing motivation in young children* (pp. 133–162). San Francisco: Albion.

Sandberg, D., Crabbs, S. & Crabbs, M. (1988). Legal issues in child abuse: Questions and answers for counselors. *Elementary School Guidance and Counseling, 22* (4), 268–274.

Saunders, C. (1994). *Safe at school.* Minneapolis: Free Spirit.

Schafer, C. (1990, May). Elementary School Counselors: Partners in child development. *Guidepost,* p. 1.

Schertzer, B., & Stone, S. (1980). *Fundamentals of counseling* (3rd ed.). Boston: Houghton Mifflin.

Schmidt, J. (1991). *A survival guide for the elementary/middle school counselor.* West Nyack, NY: The Center for Applied Research in Education.

Schwallie-Gidddis, P., Cowan, D., & Schilling, D. (1993). *Counselor in the classroom.* Spring Valley, CA: Interchoice.

Selekman, M. (1993). *Pathways to change.* New York: The Guilford Press.

Seligman, L., Weinstock, L., & Heflin, E. (1991). The career development of 10 year olds. *Elementary School Guidance and Counseling, 25* (3), 172–181.

Seligson, M., & Fink, D. (1988). Latchkey children and school-age child care. *Counselor quest.* University of Michigan: ERIC Counseling and Personnel Services Clearinghouse, 97.

Sheeley, V. (1990). ACES beyond fifty: Creating a future. *Counselor Education and Supervision, 29,* 251–157.

Simpson, R., & Fiedler, C. (1989). Parent participation in individualized education program (IEP) conferences: A case for individualization. In M. Fine (Ed.), *The second handbook on parent education* (pp. 145–171). San Diego: Academic Press.

Singleton, G. (1982). Bowen family systems theory. In A. Horne & M. Ohlsen (Eds.), *Family counseling and therapy* (pp. 75–111). Itasca, IL: F. E. Peacock.

Smey-Richman, B. (1989). *Teacher expectations and low achieving students.* Philadelphia: Research for Better Schools.

Smith, S. (1994). Parent-initiated contracts: An intervention for school-related behaviors. *Elementary School Guidance and Counseling, 28* (3), 182–187.

Sodowsky, G., & Johnson, P. (1994). World views: Culturally learned assumptions and values. In P. Pedersen & J. Carey (Eds.), *Multicultural counseling in the schools* (pp. 59–79). Boston: Allyn & Bacon.

Sonnenshein-Schneider, M., & Baird, K. (1980). Group counseling children of divorce in the elementary schools: Understanding process and technique. *The Personnel and Guidance Journal, 59* (2), 88–91.

Speight, S., Myers, L., Cox, C., & Highlen, P. (1991). A redefinition of multicultural counseling. *Journal of Counseling and Development, 70* (1), 29–36.

Squires, D., Huitt, W., & Segars, J. (1983). *Effective schools and classrooms: A research-based perspective.* Alexandria, VA: Association for Supervision and Curiculum Development.

Stanford, G. (1980). Improving group interaction with skill-building activities. *Counseling and Human Development, 13* (2).

Stefanowski-Harding, S. (1990). Suicide and the school counselor. *The School Counselor, 37* (5), 328–336.

Stephens, M. (1994, April). How we fail our kids, ourselves. *The Press Democrat,* pp. G1, G6.

Strazicich, M. (1983). *The school counselor and the migrant student.* Sacramento: California State Department of Education.

Strein, W., & French, J. (1984). Teacher consultation in the affective domain: A survey of expert opinion. *The School Counselor, 34* (4), 339–346.

Strother, J., & Jacobs, E. (1986). Parent consultation: A practical approach. *The School Counselor, 33,* 292–296.

Sue, D. (1992). The challenge of multiculturalism: The road less travelled. *American Counselor, 1* (1), 6–14.

Sue, D., Arrendondo, P., & Mc Davis, R. (1992). Multicultural counseling competencies and standards: A call to the profession. *Journal of Counseling and Development, 70* (4), 477–486.

Sykes, G. (1986). Introduction. *The Elementary School Journal, 86* (4), 365–367.

Tanner, L. (1978). *Classroom discipline for effective teaching and learning.* New York: Holt, Rinehart and Winston.

Tedder, S., Scherman, A., & Wantz, R. (1987). Effectiveness of a support group for children of divorce. *Elementary School Guidance and Counseling, 22* (2), 102–109.

The Educational Policies Commission (1967). *Federal financial relationships to education.* Washington, DC: The National Education Association.

Thiers, N. (1988). Bullying: Age-old problem pervasive in schools. *Guidepost, 30* (12), 1, 11.

Thomas, M. (1992). *An introduction to marital and family therapy.* New York: Merrili.

Thompson, C., & Rudolph, L. (1983). *Counseling children.* Pacific Grove: Brooks/Cole.

Thompson, C., & Rudolph, L. (1992). *Counseling children* (3rd. ed.). Pacific Grove: Brooks/Cole.

Thompson, R. (1987). Creating instructional and counseling partnerships to improve the academic performance of underachievers. *The School Counselor, 34* (4), 289–296.

Trice, A. (1991–1992). Effects of exposure to nontraditional models on third grade student's career aspirations and sex-typing. *CACD Journal, 19,* 25–30.

Trotter, T. (1992). *Walking the talk.* Alexandria, VA: American School Counselor Association.

Turnbull, B. (1985). Using governance and support systems to advance school improvement. *The Elementary School Journal, 85* (3), 337–351.

Tyler, R. (1971). Purposes for our schools. In J. M. Palardy (Ed.), *Elementary school curriculum: An anthology of trends and challenges,* (pp. 5–14). New York: Macmillan.

Van Hoose, W. (1968). *Counseling in the elementary school.* Itasca, Illinois: F. E. Peacock.

Waldfogel, S., Coolidge, J., & Hahn, P. (1972). The development, meaning and management of school phobia. In C. Lavatelli & F. Stendler (Eds.), *Readings in child behavior and development.* New York: Harcourt Brace Jovanovich.

Walz, G. (1988). Reflections and projections. In G. Walz (Ed.), *Building strong school counseling programs* (pp. 205–206). Alexandria, VA: American Association for Counseling and Development.

Watzlawick, P., Weakland, J., & Fisch, R. (1974). *Change: Principles of problem formation and problem resolution.* New York: W. W. Norton.

Webster, N. (1983). *Webster's new twentieth century unabridged dictionary* (2nd ed.). New York: Prentice Hall.

Wechsler, D. (1989). *Wechsler preschool and primary scale of intelligence—Revised* (WPPSI-R). San Antonio: Psychological Corporation.

Wechsler, D. (1991). *Wechsler Intelligence Scale for Children—III* (WISC-III). San Antonio: Psychological Corporation.

Welch, I., & McCarroll, L. (1993). The future of school counselors. *The School Counselor, 41* (1), 48–53.

West, J., & Idol, L. (1993). The counselor as consultant in the collaborative school. *Journal of Counseling and Development, 71* (6), 678–683.

Wickers, F. (1988). The misbehavior reaction checklist. *Elementary School Guidance and Counseling, 23* (1), 70–73.

Wielkiewicz, R. (1986). *Behavior management in the schools.* New York: Pergamon Press.

Wilder, P. (1991). A counselor's contribution to the child abuse referral network. *The School Counselor, 38* (3), 203–214.

Willis, S. (1993a, September). Challenges and choices. *Curriculum Update,* pp. 2, 3, 6, 8.

Willis, S. (1993b, November). Teaching young children. *Curriculum Update,* p .1.

Wittmer, J. (1992). *Valuing diversity in the schools: The counselor's role.* Ann Arbor, MI: University of Michigan. (ERIC Clearinghouse on Counseling and Personnel Services, EDO-CG-92-27).

Wolfgang, C., & Glickman, C. (1986). *Solving discipline problems.* Boston: Allyn & Bacon.

Wolverton, L. (1988). Classroom strategies for teaching migrant children about child abuse. *Counselor quest.* University of Michigan: ERIC Counseling and Personnel Services Clearinghouse.

Worden, M. (1981). Classroom behavior as a function of the family system. *The School Counselor, 28* (3), 178–188.

Worzbyt, J., & O'Rourke, K. (1989). *Elementary school counseling: A blueprint for today and tomorrow.* Muncie, IN: Accelerated Development.

Wubbolding, R. (1988). *Using reality therapy.* New York: Harper & Row.

Wynne, S., & Payne, C. (1980). Strategies for sex role counseling in secondary schools. *The Guidance Clinic.* West Nyack, NY: Parker.

Zinmeister, K. (1992). Growing up scared. In J. Frymier, *Growing up is risky business and schools are not to blame.* Bloomington, IN: Phi Delta Kappa.

Name Index

Subject Index

3 5282 00445 3422